Aly Elrefaei
Wellhausen and Kaufmann

Beihefte zur Zeitschrift für die alttestamentliche Wissenschaft

Edited by
John Barton, Reinhard G. Kratz and Markus Witte

Volume 490

Aly Elrefaei

Wellhausen and Kaufmann

—

Ancient Israel and Its Religious History in the Works
of Julius Wellhausen and Yehezkel Kaufmann

DE GRUYTER

G

ISBN 978-3-11-045212-9
e-ISBN (PDF) 978-3-11-045433-8
e-ISBN (EPUB) 978-3-11-045330-0
ISSN 0934-2575

Library of Congress Cataloging-in-Publication Data
A CIP catalog record for this book has been applied for at the Library of Congress.

Bibliographic information published by the Deutsche Nationalbibliothek
The Deutsche Nationalbibliothek lists this publication in the Deutsche Nationalbibliografie;
detailed bibliographic data are available in the Internet at http://dnb.dnb.de.

© 2016 Walter de Gruyter GmbH, Berlin/Boston
Printing and binding: CPI books GmbH, Leck
♾ Printed on acid-free paper
Printed in Germany

www.degruyter.com

MIX
Papier aus verantwor-
tungsvollen Quellen
FSC
www.fsc.org   FSC® C083411

Acknowledgments

This book is a slightly revised edition of a PhD thesis, entitled "The history of ancient Israel in the works of Julius Wellhausen (1844 – 1918) and Yehezkel Kaufmann (1889 – 1963)," which was accepted by the University of Göttingen in February, 2015. The study was conducted with the financial support of a German-Egyptian Research Long-Term Scholarship. Without its kind sponsorship, this work could not have been completed.

Throughout the writing of this work, Professor Reinhard G. Kratz has been an able guide. He has provided the necessary encouragement and academic environment needed to accomplish my work. His scholarly insights have enlightened and opened new perspectives. I have learned vastly from his incisive comments. I also wish to express my gratitude to Professor Rudolf Smend, who gave so generously of his knowledge. In addition, I have learned and benefited from discussions with Professor Hermann Spieckermann. Grateful acknowledgment is due to Professor Sebastian Günther and Professor Andreas Grünschloß for fruitful conversations.

I would also like to thank my colleagues Dr Peter Porzig and Dr Harald Samuel for their friendliness and endless support. I owe so much to my wife Shaimaa, and my children Omar and Oday; they have been a truly inspiring family. I am profoundly indebted to the publishing house de Gruyter as well as to the editors of BZAW for accepting my work for publication in the series. This work is dedicated to my parents who missed my love and care during my studies abroad.

Aly Elrefaei,
Göttingen 2015

Preface

Aly Elrefaei's study on Julius Wellhausen and Yehezkel Kaufmann is in many ways something unique. This is by all means true of its author and the selection of the topic. Aly Elrefaei is a native of Egypt and a Muslim who studied Semitic languages—particularly the different stages of Hebrew—as well as biblical studies at the University of Cairo. Already at his home university he engaged with the important philosopher of religion Yehezkel Kaufmann and his works—which are largely published in Hebrew—before coming to Göttingen in 2010 on a grant from the German Academic Exchange Service (DAAD) in order to write his dissertation. In Göttingen he learned German, not least in order to read the works of Julius Wellhausen, perhaps the most significant Christian biblical scholar and orientalist, in their original language. Alongside his dissertation research, Aly Elrefaei was involved as an associate member of the DFG-research training group (*Graduiertenkolleg*) entitled "Götterbilder – Gottesbilder – Weltbilder" up to its conclusion in December 2012 as well as in the international network "Old Testament Studies: Epistemologies and Methods" (OTSEM). The dissertation was completed in 2014 and was defended during the summer semester of 2015 in the field of Religious Studies at the Philosophical Faculty of the Georg-August-Universität Göttingen.

The topic of the dissertation itself is also unique. In current scholarship on the Hebrew Bible, neither Wellhausen nor Kaufmann—the two giants and antipodes of biblical studies during the transition from the 19th to the 20th century—play a major role, at least not explicitly. This is the case for several reasons. One reason is the language barrier, since today the discussion is largely conducted in English and few scholars in the field also have command of both German and Modern Hebrew. Another reason is that it is often thought that the questions and methodological approaches of the 19th and early 20th centuries, the period of historicism, have been outpaced and thus no longer need to be known. In fact, however, both Wellhausen and Kaufmann continue to exert a much stronger influence—even if in the background—than we are perhaps aware. These two figures represent two diametrically opposed perspectives for relating the biblical narrative to history, both of which have influenced the discussion up to the present. While some share the presupposition of the biblical narrative that Israel had a distinctive place in the world of the ancient Near East from the beginning and that everything happened—more or less—as the Bible recounts, others assume that Israel was a nation like any other and that the awareness of its distinctiveness only developed gradually under certain conditions and was a claim that stands closer to the end rather than the beginning of ancient Israel's history and the history of biblical literature.

The great merit of Aly Elrefaei's study is to have retraced and analyzed in detail the works of Wellhausen and Kaufmann with focused attention to the question of ancient Israel's earliest history, thus making their views on this question accessible to scholars today. Elrefaei precisely works out their methodological principles, their biographical, historical, and intellectual backgrounds, the setting of course in their argumentation, as well as their commonalities and differences. His treatment of Kaufmann makes accessible a body of work that is practically unknown in German- and English-language scholarship, and his treatment of Wellhausen and the comparison of the two scholars (re-)opens to English-language scholarship a means of accessing German intellectual history and historical research during the late 19th and early 20th centuries. The comparison of the two scholars reveals that the opposing positions of Wellhausen and Kaufmann are, of course, also influenced by personal factors and by their respective historical contexts. All the more striking is that both figures had more in common than they themselves perhaps were aware of or would have liked: source criticism, the figure of Moses as a starting point, the leading role of religion in Israel's early history, and a fixation with the question of the law. Their differences are not least based on their dating of "the law," namely, of the Priestly writing, which is debated once again today on linguistic grounds. In this respect, as Aly Elrefaei impressively demonstrates, the notion of "theocracy," its connection to prophecy, as well as the idea of monotheism play a decisive role. While Wellhausen saw a sort of "evolution" in the emergence of the law and of monotheism, Kaufmann—similarly, it should be mentioned, to Jan Assmann today—reckoned with a "revolution" that stood at the beginning of Israel's history.

It is with good reason that the author restricts himself to analysis and description and abstains from making a judgment for or against one of the two historical reconstructions. At the end of the study, he poses the question of which position stands up to criticism and answers this question in a balanced manner: "The question then arises as to which of the theories, Wellhausen's or Kaufmann's, stands up to criticism. I am afraid to say that answering this question in a direct way could do an injustice to the great contributions of Wellhausen and Kaufmann. It is true that the works of these two masters belong to their times and it would be unreasonable to see their thoughts only from today's perspective. Nevertheless, we should understand clearly that looking at the future we need to know where we are. With this borne in mind, the need to examine earlier and classic works is necessary. I am convinced that instead of a complete denial of Wellhausen and Kaufmann's reconstruction, we should look for what can be learned from the works of these two gifted scholars. For some of the thoughts of Wellhausen and Kaufmann in the history of ancient Israel and its religion still surprise us" (p. 274). With this modest statement, Aly Elrefaei indicates that his dissertation has laid the groundwork for further investigations. Such future studies would above all need to explain how the reconstructions of Wellhausen and Kaufmann relate to the methodological approaches and recent theories in the fields of History, Religious Studies, and in the Humanities more generally, in which certain ideas have been discovered anew that were already considered by Wellhausen and Kaufmann and only formulated differently.

Reinhard G. Kratz,
Göttingen, November 2015

Contents

Abbreviations

AJS	*Association for Jewish Studies*
AmSc	*American Scholar*
BA	*Biblical Archaeologist*
BiBe	*Biblische Beiträge*
BN	*Biblische Notizen*
BTZ	*Berliner Theologische Zeitschrift*
BWANT	*Beiträge zur Wissenschaft vom Alten und Neuen Testament*
BZAW	*Beihefte zur Zeitschrift für die alttestamentliche Wissenschaft*
CBQ	*Catholica Biblical Quarterly*
ExpTim	*Expository Times*
HAT	*Handbuch zum Alten Testament*
HeBAI	*Hebrew Bible and Ancient Israel*
HTR	*Harvard Theological Review*
HUCA	*Hebrew Union College Annual*
Int	*Interpretation*
JAAR	*Journal of the American Academy of Religion*
JAOT	*Journal of the American Oriental Society*
JBL	*Journal of Biblical Literature*
JBR	*Journal of Bible and Religion*
JETS	*Journal of the Evangelical Theological Society*
JISMOR	*Journal of the Interdisciplinary Study of Monotheistic Religions*
JJTP	*Journal of Jewish Thought and Philosophy*
JNES	*Journal of Near Eastern Studies*
JR	*Journal of Religion*
JQR	*Jewish Quarterly Review*
JSOT	*Journal for the Study of the Old Testament*
JSOTSup	*Journal for the Study of the Old Testament Supplement Series*
JTS	*Journal of Theological Studies*
MGWJ	*Monatsschrift für Geschichte und Wissenschaft des Judentums*
OBO	*Orbis biblicus et orientalis*
PAAJR	*Proceedings of the American Academy of Jewish Research*
PJB	*Palästina Jahrbuch*
ResQ	*Restoration Quarterly*
RGG	*Religion in Geschichte und Gegenwart*
SJOT	*Scandinavian Journal of the Old Testament*
ThLZ	*Theologische Literaturzeitung*
ThR	*Theologische Rundschau*

TRE	*Theologische Realenzyklopädie*
TynBul	*Tyndale Bulletin*
VT	*Vetus Testamentum*
WO	*Die Welt des Orients*
ZAW	*Zeitschrift für die alttestamentliche Wissenschaft*
ZDPV	*Zeitschrift des Deutschen Palästina- Vereins*
ZKG	*Zeitschrift für Kirchengeschichte*
ZRGG	*Zeitschrift für Religions- und Geistesgeschichte*
ZThK	*Zeitschrift für Theologie und Kirche*

Introduction

The subject matter of this study extends widely over time, moving from the events of thousands of years ago to the thinking on these events of two very learned scholars of quite different cultural, intellectual and religious backgrounds. What drew me to this topic? I have made Julius Wellhausen and Yehezkel Kaufmann the subject of my research for two reasons. The first was due to a chance encounter of personal significance and the second to knowledgeable advice from an expert on biblical studies. As for the first, when I was in Egypt in 2010, I had the good fortune to find the massive, eight-volume *Toledot* by Kaufmann written in Hebrew. Thus when I came to Germany, my hope was to study Jewish religious thought in the works of Kaufmann. However, on the advice of my supervisor, who recommended a comparison between Wellhausen and Kaufmann, I took courage and made my way through Wellhausen's works, finding indeed interesting grounds for comparison.

As becomes clear in a study of this field, there is no unanimity regarding the interpretation of Israel's history and its religion. In order to place the works of Julius Wellhausen and Yehezkel Kaufmann in the context of a broader scholarly debate, it is essential to mention the considerable size and scope of the key issue, that of "the history of ancient Israel". Questions regarding Israel's history and historical reconstruction are not new; they have been asked for a long time. Various attempts have been made to construct a picture of ancient Israelite history. Scholars widely differ in their approaches, ranging from source analysis to seeking insights through form and traditional criticism and the discoveries of archaeology. The result has been copious hypotheses, all of which has contributed considerably to understanding the history of ancient Israel and its religion.

Scholars of Israel's history not only vary in their methods of interpretation, but also diverge from each other in their point of departure. In this context, Herbert Donner refers to the two major sources for writing on the history of ancient Israel: the literary and the archaeological materials.[1] Donner asserts that both literary sources and archaeological data are important and should not be regarded as two contrasting approaches.[2] The respective works of Martin Noth and William Albright represent the main scholarly discussion in the second half of 20th century. Based on the study of ancient Israelite traditions, Noth identified differ-

---

1 Herbert Donner, *Geschichte des Volkes Israel und seiner Nachbarn in Grundzügen* I (ATD Ergänzungsreihe 4/1. Göttingen: Vandenhoeck & Ruprecht, 1995), 22.
2 Herbert Donner, *Geschichte des Volkes Israel* I, 22.

ent themes in the Pentateuch.[3] In Noth's thinking, "History can only be described on the basis of literary tradition, which records events and specifies persons and places."[4] Noth proposed that an amphictyonic league of different groups of people combined together and formed what has become known as Israel. However, Noth asserted, "The history of Israel, in the strict sense of the history of a more or less definable entity, only begins on the soil of Palestine."[5] Pressing archaeology into service, William Foxwell Albright and his followers paid more attention to extra-biblical data.[6] The basic assumption of Albright is that archaeology would confirm the reliability of biblical traditions. As he puts it, "Archaeological and inscriptional data have established the historicity of innumerable passages and statements of the Old Testament."[7] Moreover, the Albright school assumed that early Israelite traditions, particularly those related to patriarchal stories, rest on some foundation.[8] Thus, for example, John Bright maintains, "The Bible's picture of the patriarchs is deeply rooted in history. Abraham, Isaac and Jacob stand in the truest sense at the beginning of Israel's history and faith."[9]

If the question at the times of Martin Noth and William Albright was, "When does the history of Israel begin?" recent studies on the history of Israel tend to abandon much of the early Israelite tradition, arguing that they can no longer be regarded as a source for writing about ancient Israel's early history.[10] Alongside the non-consensus on reconstructing the history of Israel, there are some fallacies that have sharpened the divisions among scholars.[11] This gives us a strong

---

3 These themes are: Guidance out of Egypt, Guidance into the land of Canaan, Promise to the Patriarchs, Guidance in the Wilderness, and Revelation at Sinai. On this see Martin Noth, *Überlieferungsgeschichte des Pentateuch* (Stuttgart: Kohlhammer, 1948).
4 Martin Noth, *Geschichte Israels* (Göttingen: Vandenhoeck & Ruprecht, 1950). Quotation from English translation (The History of Israel, Rev. ed. New York: Harper & Row, 1960), 42.
5 Martin Noth, *The History of Israel*, 53.
6 W. F. Albright, "Archaeology Confronts Biblical Criticism," *AmSc* VII (1938): 176–88; idem, "The Ancient Near East and the Religion of Israel," *JBL* LIX (1940): 85–112. See further G. Ernest Wright, *Biblical Archaeology* (Philadelphia: Westminster Press, 1957).
7 Albright, "Archaeology Confronts Biblical Criticism," 181.
8 See, in particular, W. F. Albright, *The Biblical Period from Abraham to Ezra* (New York: Harper & Row, Publishers, 1949).
9 John Bright, *A History of Israel* (Philadelphia: Westminster Press, 1981[3]), 103.
10 For a discussion see, J. Maxwell Miller, "Is it Possible to Write a History of Israel without Relying on the Hebrew Bible?" In *The Fabric of History: Text, Artifact and Israel's Past* (ed. D.V. Edelmann; JSOTSup 127; Sheffield: JSOT Press, 1991), 93–102. Philip R. Davies, *In Search of 'Ancient Israel'* (Sheffield; Sheffield Acad. Press, 1992, repr., 1999). Thomas L. Thompson, *Early History of the Israelite People: From the Written and Archaeological Sources* (Leiden: Brill, 1992).
11 On these fallacies, see Walter C. Kaiser, *A History of Israel: From the Bronze Age Through the Jewish Wars* (Nashville, Tenn: Broadman & Holman, 1998).

indication of how complicated and complex the beginnings of Israel were.[12] The debate continues and scholars have been asking such provoking questions as, "Can a 'history of Israel' be written?"[13] Or "On choosing different models of interpretations,"[14] "what directions should we take?"[15] More recently, new questions have been raised by Reinhard Kratz:

> Die Geschichte Israels setzt die Existenz einer Größe mit Namen „Israel" voraus. Je nachdem, seit wann und wie lange diese Größe existierte, reicht die Geschichte Israels. Hinter dieser simplen Feststellung steckt ein großes Problem: Die Frage nach Anfang und Ende der Geschichte des antiken Israel im 1. Jahrtausend v. Chr.[16]

It should be mentioned that the foregoing debate addresses only one side of the problem. The controversy extends also to include the question, "Who has determined the course of writing the history of ancient Israel?" Almost one century has elapsed since the German historian and Jewish philosopher Franz Rosenzweig wrote, "Eine lebendige Einwirkung jüdischer Gelehrter auf die Anschauungen vom A.T. ist nicht mehr zu erwarten, weil die klassische Zeit der Konsolidierung dieser Ansichten abgeschlossen ist."[17] In the justification of Rudolf Smend, this was not only because the Jewish scholars – not without reason – claimed to have a more direct relationship to the Old Testament than the Christians, but more because the problems of Bible criticism in general were still relatively foreign to them.[18] Smend goes further to maintain that there was, with

---

12 Alexander Rofé, "Clan Sagas as a Source in Settlement Traditions," in "A Wise and Discerning Mind": Essays in Honor of Burke O. Long (ed. Saul M. Olyan and Robert C. Culley; Providence: Brown Judaic Studies, 2000), 191–203 (203).
13 Lester L. Grabbe ed., Can a 'History of Israel' Be Written? (JSOTSup 245; Sheffield: Sheffield Academic Press, 1997).
14 J. M. Sasson, "On Choosing Models for Recreating Israelite Pre-Monarchic History: to Michael C. Astour on His 65th Birthday," JSOT 21 (1981), 3–24.
15 Hans M. Barstad, "The History of Ancient Israel: What Directions Should We Take?" in Understanding the History of Ancient Israel (ed. Hugh Godfrey Maturin Williamson; Oxford: Oxford University Press, 2007), 25–48.
16 Reinhard G. Kratz, Historisches und biblisches Israel: Drei Überblicke zum Alten Testament (Tübingen: Mohr Siebeck, 2013), 1.
17 Franz Rosenzweig, Der Mensch und sein Werk: gesammelte Schriften, Bd 1: Briefe und Tagebücher (ed. Rachel Rosenzweig and Edith Rosenzweig-Scheinmann; The Hague: Nijhoff, 1979), 264.
18 Rudolf Smend, "Wellhausen und das Judentum," ZThK 79 (1982): 249–282.

only few exceptions, no Jewish Bible scholarship in the 19th century that would even halfway satisfy modern expectations.[19]

These controversial themes – the history of ancient Israel, historical reconstruction, Jewish and Christian scholarship – have prompted the subject of this study. It is mainly an analysis and a comparison of the works of two leading authorities on biblical studies: Julius Wellhausen (1844–1918) and Yehezkel Kaufmann (1889–1963). We know that Wellhausen's *Prolegomena* first appeared in 1878 with the title Geschichte Israels I, and that the first volume of Kaufmann's *Toledot* appeared in 1937. This is a very long time ago. One might rightly ask why I have made just these two scholars the subject of my research – and/or why it is necessary to study these rather outdated works in biblical interpretation?

To answer this question, I call to my aid the views of Albrecht Alt and Manfred Weippert. According to Alt, "Scholarship is made in periodicals. Books are already out of date when they finally appear. Today no one reads long books – a long book is a bad one."[20] If we concede Alt's claim, no one would read Kaufmann's *Toledot,* which comprises some 2700 pages. Thus I prefer to turn instead to Manfred Weippert who asserts that the histoy of ancient Israel is nothing more than (Gebäude von Hypothesen):

> ...jede zusammenfassende Darstellung einer Lokal- und Volksgeschichte wie die der Geschichte des alten Israel ist nichts anderes als ein Gebäude von Hypothesen, das vom methodischen Standard der Disziplin, der Quellenlage, dem Stand der Forschung, dem 'Zeitgeist' und nicht zuletzt von der in all das verstrickten und sich mit alledem auseinandersetzenden Individualität des jeweiligen Historikers determiniert ist. Da die Determinanten aber nicht eindeutig umschrieben sind, sondern Wahlmöglichkeiten und auch subjektive Faktoren enthalten, sind zwar nicht beliebig, aber doch unterschiedlich gestaltete Gebäude möglich.[21]

Several points should be considered. Although advances in knowledge in the field of biblical studies since Wellhausen and Kaufmann's day have challenged

---

19 Rudolf Smend, "Wellhausen und das Judentum," 275. In point of fact, there are some other reasons for the delay in acceptance of biblical criticism by Jews. For a discussion see Menahem Haran, *Biblical Research in Hebrew: A Discussion of its Character and Trends* (Jerusalem: Magnes Press, Hebrew University, 1970). See also Christian Wiese, *Challenging Colonial Discourse: Jewish Studies and Protestant Theology in Wilhelmine Germany* (Leiden: Brill, 2005). See further Edward Breuer and Chanan Gafni, "Jewish Biblical Scholarship between Tradition and Innovation," in *Hebrew Bible, Old Testament: The History of its Interpretation, vol. III/I, The Nineteenth Century* (ed. Magne Sæbø and Peter Machinist (Göttingen: Vandenhoeck & Ruprecht, 2013), 262–302.
20 On this see Rudolf Smend, "Albrecht Alt," in *From Astruc to Zimmerli: Old Testament Scholarship in three Centuries* (Tübingen: Mohr Siebeck, 2007), 132–156 (140).
21 Manfred Weippert, „Geschichte Israels am Scheideweg," *ThR* 58 (1993): 71–103 (72).

much of their thinking, scholarship today still builds on the foundations laid by them. In fact, many scholars since Wellhausen and Kaufmann's time have concerned themselves with their works and thoughts.[22] The consequences of their work are still felt today. This, of course, does not mean that biblical research has not moved beyond the propositions of these two scholars. Today, so far as I am aware of, no one would accept Wellhausen's reconstruction, or Kaufmann's interpretation without modification. The Hebrew Bible is no longer the single source for writing about ancient Israel. It has become known that "the Israel of literary tradition is not the Israel of history."[23] New discoveries along with a diversity of new disciplines have opened a whole new perspective on the issue. However, we should consider the voices of Wellhausen and Kaufmann in the context of their times rather than dismiss them because they fail to meet modern standards. This study illustrates the great impact of these two significant figures and shows that they are not irrelevant to current concerns.

The second point to be considered is that Wellhausen's work represents a synthesis of the religious development of ancient Israel, while Kaufmann's work emphasizes the singularity of the Israelite religion.[24] Another point relates to their religious traditions. Wellhausen's work is considered to be the most important point of contact between Jewish and Christian Bible scholars.[25] On the other hand, Kaufmann's arguments presuppose certain polemics against Christi-

---

22 No survey of the discipline would be complete without reference to the works of Wellhausen and Kaufmann. One could also say that there is no serious study of the history of Israel and the composition of Pentateuch that could overlook Wellhausen's relevant thesis. Anyone who is interested in these subjects will be inevitably led to Wellhausen. Although there was no 'Wellhausen's school,' his works founded a school. On this see Reinhard G. Kratz, "Wellhausen, Julius," *TRE* 35 (2003):527–536 (534). As for Kaufmann, his study on the origin of monotheism has been often been discussed and criticized in relation to the history of the Israelite religion. Further, Kaufmann's works became the starting point for many Jewish bible scholars such as H. L. Ginsberg (1903–1990) Menahem Haran (1924–), Moshe Weinfeld (1925–2009), Jacob Milgrom (1923–2010), and Moshe Greenberg (1928–2010). These scholars and others have worked out Kaufmann's hypothesis, emphasizing the antiquity of the Priestly Code. For the influence of Kaufmann's writings on North American scholars, see S. David Sperling, *Students of the Covenant: A History of Jewish Biblical Scholarship in North America* (Atlanta: Scholars Press, 1992), 77, 93, 104.
23 Reinhard G. Kratz, *The Composition of the Narrative Books of the Old Testament* (London: T & T Clark, 2005), 309. Translated by John Bowden from the German *Die Komposition der erzählenden Bücher des Alten Testaments* (Göttingen: Vandenhoeck & Ruprecht, 2000).
24 Recent study on the Israelite religion has classified Wellhausen and Kaufmann as representing two paradigms in biblical research. See Ziony Zevit, *The Religions of Ancient Israel: A Synthesis of Parallactic Approaches* (London: Continuum, 2001).
25 Magne Sæbø, *On the Way to Canon: Creative Tradition History in the Old Testament* (Sheffield: Sheffield Academic Press, 1998), 145.

an Bible scholars.[26] Considering this, we should ask whether both Wellhausen's and Kaufmann's own religious traditions determined the direction and themes of their exegetical work. This and other related questions make it important to find out the nature of the real clash between these two prominent and influential scholars.

It is true that Wellhausen and Kaufmann represent two different traditions of thought and intellectual settings. Any direct comparison would likely do injustice to each of them in some way. However, since the strongest refutation of Wellhausen's theory came from Kaufmann, it is meaningful to study Kaufmann together with Wellhausen.[27] Kaufmann was the first who dared to exploit the historical critical method to counter Wellhausen's hypothesis on the history of the Israelite religion, using it to build his imposing structure. As this study will show, the dispute between Wellhausen and Kaufmann revolves around basic issues regarding ancient Israel and its religious history. Both Wellhausen and Kaufmann have some points in common, but differ in their approach to writing history. They accepted and applied the historical-critical method, but were divided as to its results. Both agree that the Old Testament/Hebrew Bible is the primary source on which to base writing about the history of ancient Israel, but differ concerning the authority of its text. In the thinking of Wellhausen and Kaufmann, biblical religion is the key to understanding biblical history, but they diverge as to the substance and beginning of that religion.

This raises a question: If their methods were more or less the same how did they manage to reach such different conclusions? It should be made clear that if we wish to evaluate Wellhausen and Kaufmann's histories, we must go back to their own periods and milieus. Both represented the methodologies, presuppositions and the ideologies of their times. In his understanding of the historian's task, Wellhausen sought to write the history of Israel as one would write the history of any other nation. Kaufmann, on the other hand, was a child of his cultural background in his attempt to defend the religion of Israel and the antiquity of its foundation.

To continue on this point, Wellhausen's work is that of a Christian scholar, while that of Kaufmann represents the Jewish understanding of Scripture. This prompts us to raise another question: Can a Jewish scholar and/or a Christian

---

26 See, in particular, Yehezkel Kaufmann, *Christianity and Judaism: Two Covenants* (trans. by C. W. Efroymson. Jerusalem: Magnes Press, Hebrew University, 1988). Kaufmann's polemic against Christian scholars was continued in Jon D. Levenson's works. See S. David Sperling, *Students of the Covenant: A History of Jewish Biblical Scholarship in North America,* 128 – 129.

27 Stephen A. Geller, "Wellhausen and Kaufmann" *Midstream* 31, no. 10 (1985): 39 – 48 (39).

writer interpret the Bible without bias?[28] And, is it possible to get rid of preconceived notions? This is, of course, a long-standing issue and is really difficult to answer.[29] In my opinion, it is not advisable to limit the discussion to this narrow view. Here it is important to mention that although Wellhausen's and Kaufmann's interpretations represent an example of the divergence between Christian and Jewish Old Testament scholarship, their works are not entirely determined by personal belief and religious identity. The works of Wellhausen and Kaufmann show that they viewed Israel's history from the vantage point of its religious history. They shared the assumption that Israel's history could be apprehended in the context of its religion.

Going into more depth on the divide between Wellhausen and Kaufmann, we should mention their essential methodological differences. The central point of departure for Kaufmann's approach is the history of ideas. That is to say, Kaufmann articulates the essense of Israelite religion in terms of its concepts and ideas. He proposes that monotheism is Israel's religious idea and a new creation of the spirit of Israel generated by Moses. Kaufmann insists that monotheism developed with Israel's history from the very beginning. In Kaufmann's view, Israel's religion is non-mythological and therefore it becomes impossible to conceive of a gradual development from polytheism. By contrast, Wellhausen introduces the religion of Israel in the framework of its historical circumstances. He attempts to contextualize the religion of Israel. In Wellhausen's reading, the early beginning of Israel's faith is marked by its normal character, like other religions. In this way, Wellhausen's revolution theory becomes the antipode of Kaufmann's position.

The question then arises as to how I posit myself with regard to the theories of Wellhausen and Kaufmann? Coming from a perspective outside of the Jewish academic and the German Protestant frames of reference, it is my hope that this study of Wellhausen and Kaufmann may provide some basis for reaching a middle ground between these two poles. The study proceeds from analyzing their respective views on Israel's history and religion, to identifying and comparing the

---

28 Thus, for example, it has been claimed that "it is difficult to find a volume that would introduce biblical literature in an interesting way to readers who do not identify with Judaism or Christianity." On this see Martin J. Buss, "The Relevance of Hermann Gunkel's Broad Orientation," in Ute E. Eisen and Erhard S. Gerstenberger, eds., *Hermann Gunkel Revisited: Literatur- und Religionsgeschichtliche Studien* (Berlin: Lit, 2010), 71–80 (73).
29 For a discussion see Jon D. Levenson, *The Hebrew Bible, the Old Testament, and Historical Criticism: Jews and Christians in Biblical Studies* (Louisville: Westminster/John Knox Press, 1993).

thoughts of these two giants. Attention will be given to the intellectual and historical settings of Wellhausen and Kaufmann.

My understanding of Wellhausen is based on the assumption that he moved from a criticism of the sources, mapping out different stages of religious development in Israel, to a historical synthesis on the history of Israel and Judah. The three phases of Wellhausen's structure reflect his three major works: 1) *Die Composition des Hexateuchs und der historischen Bücher des Alten Testaments*[30]; 2) *Prolegomena zur Geschichte Israels*[31]; 3) *Israelitische und jüdische Geschichte.*[32] With regard to Kaufmann, I move from his literary analysis of the relationship of the Torah and Prophets and his dating of the Priestly Code, to his phenomenological interpretation of the history of Israelite religion. My analysis of Kaufmann is based on three points: 1) his arguments about the antiquity of the Torah literature; 2) his interpretation of the Israelite religion, particularly his view on monotheism; 3) his historical reconstruction of early Israelite traditions in Canaan. The first two issues are discussed in his multi-volume *Toledot ha-emunah ha-yisraelit*, especially the first volume (Books 1–3) from 1937–1938.[33] Kaufmann's thesis on the traditions of conquest and settlement is detailed in his two commentaries on Joshua (1959) and Judges (1962).

From what has thus far been said, it becomes evident why the works of Wellhausen and Kaufmann remain an impetus to further inquiry. In order to avoid putting Wellhausen or Kaufmann at a disadvantage, I have treated each of them separately and postponed a comparison to the end of my thesis. The structure of my work is thus divided into three parts. The first deals with Wellhausen's reconstruction of ancient Israel. In this section, I have chosen to proceed from literary criticism to religion to history. In other words, my investigation follows that of Wellhausen, who started with critical analyses of the sources, then moved on to examine the "place of law" with emphasis on the religious devel-

---

30 Third edition, Berlin 1899 (reprinted as 4th ed., Berlin, 1963); First appeared in *Jahrbuch für deutsche Theologie* 1876/77. Quotations in this study follow the 4th ed., Berlin, 1963.

31 The original German edition entitled *Geschichte Israels I*, 1878; 2nd ed. 1883 *Prolegomena zur Geschichte Israels*; 3rd ed. 1899, reprinted 1927, 1972, 1981, 2001. ET (of 2nd ed.) *Prolegomena to the History of Israel*, Edinburgh, 1885, reprinted 1957). Quotations are mainly from the English translation (*Prolegomena to the History of Israel: With a Reprint of the Article Israel from the Encyclopaedia Britannica* (Atlanta: Scholars Press, 1994).

32 Berlin 1894, 1895[2], 1897[3], 1901[4], 1904[5], 1907[6], 1914[7], 1921[8], 1958[9], 2004[10]. My analysis of Wellhausen's reconstruction of the history of Israel is based on his *Israelitische und jüdische Geschichte* (10th edition, Berlin: de Gruyter, 2004).

33 Yehezkel Kaufmann, *Toledot Ha-'emuna Ha-Isr'aelit Me-Yami Ḳedem 'ad Sof Bayit Sheni* (4 vols., Tel Aviv: Bialik Institute-Devir, 1937–1956). Quotations and translations in this study from the 10th ed., Jerusalem, 1975.

opment of ancient Israel. Wellhausen's work on the Old Testament was comple-mented by his writing of the historical synthesis *Israelitische und jüdische Ge-schichte*.

The second part of this study concentrates on Kaufmann. Generally, my anal-ysis of Kaufmann moves from his literary criticism (where Kaufmann distin-guishes the Torah from literary prophets) to phenomenology (basic character of Israelite religion, nature of popular religion, monotheism and polytheism as two different worldviews) and ends with sketching the early history of ancient Israel. At the end of this section, I have given a detailed description of Kauf-mann's historical setting and an overview of the sources of his exegetical ap-proach.

The third part of this work seeks to shed light on the fundamental disagree-ments between Wellhausen and Kaufmann, i.e. to clarify the real divide between them. In my understanding, there are three areas in which these differences can be distinguished: religious history, the authority of biblical texts, and in a con-structed model of pre-monarchic Israel. The religious history which involves the basic problems of interpretation is, in my view, the most important point of disparity. At the heart of this comparison lie their two different models of pre-monarchic Israel. These will be elucidated in some detail, based particularly on how they interpreted the notion of theocracy. At the end of this study, I will highlight some of the basic assumptions that underlie both Wellhausen's and Kaufmann's reconstructions. This will be followed by my summary and evalua-tion of their respective views.

Biographical aspects

1 Julius Wellhausen (1844 – 1918)

Much has been written on Julius Wellhausen.[34] In this context, Rudolf Smend pointed out, "Kein Alttestamentler ist mit so viel Bewunderung gelesen, keiner so erbittert bekämpft worden wie Wellhausen."[35] It can be said that Wellhausen gained a wide reputation because the course of his labours "shows a remarkable consistency of aim and methodology."[36] Judging from his pioneering works on the Old Testament, Islam, and the New Testament, it is fair to place Wellhausen among the great German historians.[37]

Wellhausen was born in Hameln in 1844. When he was eighteen, he went to Göttingen to study theology.[38] Having received his licentiate in 1870, Wellhausen acted for two years as a private tutor. His academic career started as professor of the Old Testament in Greifswald (1872 – 1882)[39], where most of his most controversial books were composed.[40] He taught in Halle (1882 – 1885) and accepted an appointment as professor for Semitic languages in Marburg (1885 – 1892). As the successor of Paul Anton de Lagarde, Wellhausen was given a professorship in Göttingen in 1892, where he lived until his death on January 7, 1918.

---

34 See, for example, Lothar Perlitt, *Vatke und Wellhausen: Geschichtsphilosophische Voraussetzungen und historiographische Motive für die Darstellung der Religion und Geschichte Israels durch Wilhelm Vatke und Julius Wellhausen*. (Berlin: A. Töpelmann, 1965). Also Hans-Joachim Kraus, *Geschichte der Historisch-Kritischen Erforschung des Alten Testaments* (Neukirchen-Vluyn: Neukirchener Verlag, 1982³). See further Douglas A. Knight, *Julius Wellhausen and his Prolegomena to the History of Israel* (Chico: Scholars Press, 1983). Rudolf Smend, *Julius Wellhausen: Ein Bahnbrecher in drei Disziplinen* ([erweiterte Fassung eines Vortrags, gehalten in der Carl-Friedrich-Von-Siemens-Stiftung Am 16. Dezember 2004]; München: Carl-Friedrich-von-Siemens-Stiftung, 2006).
35 Rudolf Smend, *Deutsche Alttestamentler in drei Jahrhunderten* (Göttingen: Vandenhoeck & Ruprecht, 1989), 99.
36 R. E. Clements, "The Study of the Old Testament," in *Nineteenth Century Religious Thought in the West III* (ed. Ninian Smart; Cambridge: Cambridge University Press, 1985), 129.
37 On this see Reinhard G. Kratz, "Wellhausen, Julius," *TRE* 35 (2003): 527 – 536.
38 See Rudolf Smend, "Wellhausen in Göttingen," in *Theologie in Göttingen* (ed. B. Moeller; Göttinger Universitätsschriften A 1, 1987), 306 – 324.
39 Alfred Jepsen, "Wellhausen in Greifswald: Ein Beitrag zur Biographie Julius Wellhausens," in *Der Herr ist Gott: Aufsätze zur Wissenschaft vom Alten Testament* (Berlin: Evangelische Verlagsanstalt, 1978), 254 – 270.
40 Rudolf Smend, "Julius Wellhausen: 1844 – 1918," in *From Astruc to Zimmerli: Old Testament Scholarship in Three Centuries* (Tübingen: Mohr Siebeck, 2007), 91 – 102 (95).

As is well known, Wellhausen's work on the Old Testament marked a turning point in the history of biblical scholarship.[41] He gave classic expression to the efforts of his forerunners, including Wilhelm Martin Leberecht de Wette (1780 – 1849) and Karl Heinrich Graf (1815 – 1869). Wellhausen prepared the ground for his later works by concerning himself with the historiographical tradition of ancient Israel. He approached this through philology and text criticism (*Der Text der Bücher Samuelis*, 1871), moving towards source and literary criticism (*Die Composition des Hexateuchs*, 1876/77). On the controversy over the sectarians of the Second Commonwealth, Wellhausen's book *Die Pharisäer und die Sadducäer* (1874), against the thesis of Abraham Geiger (1810 – 1874), put forward the idea that the Pharisees were a religious party, while the Sadducees were more political. In his magnum opus *Geschichte Israels 1* 1878 (*Prolegomena zur Geschichte Israel* 1883), Wellhausen outlined a new view of the history of Israelite religion, showing how it moved from a simple, spontaneous and natural religion to one of law and rituals. He questioned the historical dating of the Priestly Code, proposing that it fitted the conditions of the Second Temple period. Moreover, Wellhausen drew attention to the dominance of the prophetic and historical narrative, maintaining that the Law was not the starting point of Israel's history but a product of historical and religious development. As a result of his critical investigation, Wellhausen brought into focus the antithesis of Israel and Judaism, regarding them as two different worldviews. In 1894, Wellhausen presented a historical synthesis of the history of Israel and Judah. "In order to better understand ancient, pre-exilic Israel he applied himself increasingly to the study of Old Arabian and early Islamic history."[42] Wellhausen himself says that he moved from the study of the Old Testament to Arabic studies with the aim of acquiring knowledge about "den Wildling kennen zu lernen, auf den von Priestern und Propheten das Reis der Thora Jahves gepfropft ist."[43]

Wellhausen's work on the Old Testament was not the last phase of research. However, his brilliant presentation of the problem summed up more than a cen-

---

41 A full bibliography of Wellhausen's publications is found in *Beihefte zur Zeitschrift für die Alttestamentliche Wissenschaft* 27 (Studien zur semitischen Philologie und Religionsgeschichte: Julius Wellhausen zum 70. Geburtstag am 17. Mai 1914 gewidmet von Freunden und Schülern, ed. Karl Marti,1914), 351 – 368. For the recently updated autobiography of Wellhausen, see Rudolf Smend, *Briefe: Julius Wellhausen* (Tübingen : Mohr Siebeck, 2013).
42 Kurt Rudolph, "Wellhausen, Julius," *Encyclopedia of Religion* (ed. Lindsay Jones, 2nd ed., vol. 14 (Detroit: Macmillan Reference USA, 2005), 9714 – 9715 (9714).
43 Wellhausen, *Muhammed in Medina*, (Berlin: Reimer, 1882), 5.

tury of critical investigation,[44] and re-determined the course of the history of Israel.[45] Of the far-reaching contribution of Wellhausen's exegesis it has been said, "Die treffendste Charakterisierung jener Mitte, die zugleich ein Anfang gewesen sein könnte, verdankt die alttestamentliche Wissenschaft keinem geringeren als Julius Wellhausen."[46]

Wellhausen's interpretation of the history of ancient Israel caused agitation and many rejected his critical views.[47] My aim here is to show how an important scholar like Yehezkel Kaufmann, who came from a different tradition of thought, reacted and criticized Wellhausen's theories. While Wellhausen's work is considered to be the most important contribution to historical critical method, Yehezkel Kaufmann is the only Bible scholar to have combined in his research such a comprehensive interpretation of Israelite religion with a critique of Wellhausen. In his massive *Toledot*, Kaufmann sought to invalidate Wellhausen's position with regard to the order of the pentateuchal sources, and thereby to undermine his hypothesis on the emergence of monotheism in ancient Israel. Interestingly enough, although Kaufmann accepted the essentials of the historical-critical approach, his presentation is closer to tradition.[48] In what follows, I shall give a brief profile of Yehezkel Kaufmann's life and work.[49]

---

44 In describing the great impression that was made by Wellhausen's *Prolegomena*, Kuenen wrote, "Wellhausen's treatment of our theme, for which I must refer to his book itself, was so cogent, so original, and so brilliant, that its publication may be regarded as the 'crowning fight' in the long campaign." See A. Kuenen, *An Historico-Critical Inquiry into the Origin and Composition of the Hexateuch: Pentateuch and Book of Joshua* (London: Macmillan, 1886), xxxix. See further Herbert F. Hahn, *Old Testament in Modern Research* (London: SCM, 1956).
45 Henning Graf Reventlow, *Epochen der Bibelauslegung*, Bd. 4 (München: Beck, 2001), 302–316.
46 Ernst A Knauf, *Data and Debates: Essays in the History and Culture of Israel and its Neighbors in Antiquity, Daten und Debatten: Aufsätze zur Kulturgeschichte des antiken Israel und seiner Nachbarn.* (ed. Hermann Michael Niemann; Konrad Schmid; Silvia Schroer; Alter Orient und Altes Testament 407; Münster: Ugarit-Verlag, 2013), 445.
47 For a survey see Raymond F. Surburg, "Wellhausen Evaluated after a Century of Influence," *Concordia Theological Quarterly* 43, no. 2 (1979): 78–95.
48 Emanuel Green, S. David Sperling and Haim M. I. Gevaryahu, "Kaufmann, Yeḥezkel (1889–1963)," in *Encyclopaedia Judaica* (ed. Michael Berenbaum and Fred Skolnik, 2nd ed., vol. 12 (Detroit: Macmillan Reference USA, 2007), 33–35 (34).
49 A complete intellectual history of Kaufmann's life and work have been provided by Thomas M. Krapf, *Yehezkel Kaufmann: Ein Lebens und Erkenntnisweg zur Theologie der Hebräischen Bibel* (Berlin: Institut Kirche und Judentum, 1990).

2 Yehezkel Kaufmann (1889 – 1963)

2.1 Life

Yehezkel Kaufmann was a distinguished Jewish historian, biblical scholar, and nationalist.[50] His research combined philosophy, sociology and religious studies.[51] Kaufmann was often described with such words as, "Never married, a small, ascetic, retiring man, his life was wholly given over to thought, writing, and research."[52]

Kaufmann was born in 1889 in Dunajiwzi, in the province of Podolia, Ukraine. In 1907, he went to Odessa to study at the modern Yeshivah.[53] Following his stay in Odessa, Kaufmann continued his studies at the Academy of Oriental Studies in St. Petersburg. From 1914, Kaufmann pursued his studies at Bern University, earning his doctorate in Kantian philosophy in 1918.[54]

In 1920, Kaufmann moved to Berlin where he spent the eight years that preceded his emigration to Palestine in 1928. For about twenty years Kaufmann worked as a teacher in Beth Hasepher Hareali in Haifa. Moshe Greenberg mentions that Kaufmann's personal characteristics, along with his unorthodoxy and uncompromising self-assurance, combined to keep him out of the Hebrew University during the best twenty years of his creative life.[55] Kaufmann was appointed a professor of the Bible at the Hebrew University of Jerusalem in 1949 until 1957. In recognition of his achievements and their impact on biblical studies

---

50 For a more recent biography of Kaufmann, see Thomas Staubli, "Yehezkel Kaufmann: Die Berne Jahre eines Genies" in *Wie über Wolken: Jüdische Lebens- und Denkwelten in Stadt und Region Bern*, 1200 – 2000 (ed. René Bloch and Jacques Picard; Chronos, 2014), 241 – 252.
51 See, in particular, Menahem Haran, "On the Border of Faith," (in Hebrew) *Moznaim* 24 (1966), 53.
52 Moshe Greenberg, *Studies in the Bible and Jewish Thought* (Philadelphia: Jewish Publication Society, 1995), 175.
53 It has been said that "the Odessa of Kaufmann's youth was the center of the East European Jewish enlightenment and home of many of the thinkers who would later become the central figures of cultural Zionism." On this see Joseph Turner, "The Notion of Jewish Ethnicity in Yehezkel Kaufmann's Golah Venekhar," *Modern Judaism* 28, no. 3 (2008): 257 – 282 (257).
54 For the influence of philosophy on Kaufmann's writings, see Peter Slyomovics, "Y. Kaufmann's Critique of Wellhausen: A Philosophical-Historical Perspective," (in Hebrew) *Zion* 49 (1984): 61 – 92. See further Eliezer Schweid, "Biblical Critic or Philosophical Exegete? The Influence of Herman Cohen's The Religion of Reason on Yehezkel Kaufmann's History of Israelite Religion," (in Hebrew) in *Masuot: Mehkarim be-sifrut ha-Kabalah uve-mahashevet Yisrael mukdashim le-zikhro shel Prof. Efrayim Gottlieb* (ed. Efraim Gottlieb, Michal Kushnir-Oron, and Amos Goldreich; Jerusalem: Bialik Institute, 1994), 414 – 428.
55 Greenberg, *Studies in the Bible*, 176.

and Jewish life, Kaufmann was awarded the Bialik Prize in 1956, the Israel Prize in 1958, and the Bublik Prize in 1961. After a long illness, Kaufmann died in Jerusalem on October 9, 1963.

2.2 Main interest

Though Kaufmann studied and received his doctoral degree in philosophy[56], it is said that he made few contributions to philosophy.[57] Kaufmann's main interest was the riddle of Jewish existence. His early writings were devoted to inquiry into the problem of the Jewish Diaspora through the ages. Kaufmann's thoughts were shaped and sharpened quite early in his life. Ideologies such as socialism, Zionism, the Bund, Yiddish culture, assimilation and traditional Jewish religion formed his thinking. This appears in his first article in 1914, "The Judaism of Ahad ha-Am", in which Kaufmann takes issue with Ahad ha-Am's assumption that Judaism is a product of a collective will to survive. In breaking with the prevailing nationalist interpretations of his time, Kaufmann's view was that it was religion that ensured Jewish survival in exile. It is probably fair to say that Kaufmann was moved by the situation of the Jewish people in diaspora and that this led him to search for solutions to the problem of the Jewish fate. In other words, Kaufmann looked at the past with eyes open to the present. Joseph Turner explicates Kaufmann's position as follows:

> The immediate historical background of his discussions concerning the nature of Jewish existence includes the precarious status of Jewish society in central Europe following World War I, the disintegration of the East European Jewish community, mass emigration to the United States and the building of Zionist settlements in the Land of Israel. There are those in the literature on Kaufmann's thought who have pointed out its pedagogical character. That is to say, Kaufmann investigated Jewish history not only in order to understand and make sense of it, but also in order to formulate a program in regard to the type of activity necessary in order to deal with the problems of the present.[58]

---

56 Jesekiel Kaufmann, *Eine Abhandlung über den zureichenden Grund: Teil 1. Der logische Grund* (Berlin: E. Ebering, 1920). See further Thomas Staubli, "Yehezkel Kaufmann: Die Berne Jahre eines Genies," 246–248.
57 Greenberg, *Studies in the Bible.* 175. See further Job Y. Jindo, "Revisiting Kaufmann: Fundamental Problems in Modern Biblical Scholarship. From Yehezkel Kaufmann's Criticism of Wellhausen," *Journal of the Interdisciplinary Study of Monotheistic Religions* 3 (2007): 41–77(44).
58 Joseph Turner, "The Notion of Jewish Ethnicity in Yehezkel Kaufmann's Golah Venekhar," *Modern Judaism* 28, no. 3 (2008): 257–282 (257–258).

2.3 Major works

Kaufmann is considered to be the most influential Jewish Bible scholar of modern times. He is called the towering Jewish personality in biblical scholarship [59] Perhaps this was due to Kaufmann's scholarly erudition and abundant production.[60] It is true that Kaufmann touched upon all issues of biblical study and Jewish history. The results of his investigations were massive volumes written in Modern Hebrew.[61] When he was asked for his curriculum vitae, it is said that he replied, "I have no biography, only a bibliography."[62]

Kaufmann's first important work (*Golah ve-Nekhar*, "Exile and Alienhood" (4 vols. 1929 – 30) is a socio-historical study on the fate of the Jewish people from ancient times to the modern period. The book deals mainly with the post-biblical and diaspora ages. It is a systematic empirical interpretation in which Kaufmann examines the factors that have shaped Jewish history through the ages. Reading Kaufmann, one must conclude that the monotheistic idea was the decisive factor ensuring the nation's survival in exile.[63] In point of fact, Kaufmann's *Golah* is an attempt to discover the historical process that formed the experience of the Jewish people.[64] Highly important, Kaufmann's *Golah ve-Nekhar* made a profound impression within Jewish intellectual circles. On March 9, 1930, the Hebrew poet Haim Nahman Bialik wrote to Dr. J. L. Magnes, Chancellor of the Hebrew

---

59 Nahum Sarna, "From Wellhausen to Kaufmann," *Midstream* 7, no. 3 (1961): 64–74 (64).
60 For a complete bibliography of Kaufmann's writings, see the Hebrew section in *Yehezkel Kaufmann Jubilee Volume: Studies in Bible and Jewish Religion* (ed. Menahem Haran; Jerusalem: Magnes Press, 1960), א-· .
61 Menahem Haran points out that Kaufmann used a literary style that gives his writing clarity and makes him a great writer in his time. He further notes that Kaufmann, like Wellhausen, used a literary form that makes his arguments more convincing. On this see Menahem Haran, "On the Border of Faith," (in Hebrew) *Moznaim* 24 (1966), 53. Another observation was made by Joseph Turner who remarked, "Kaufmann wrote in Hebrew and as much as possible chose his terminology according to the usage prevalent in Hebrew sources – especially in the Bible. Nonetheless, he could not ignore the usage of terms prevalent in contemporary European discourse." See Joseph Turner, "The Notion of Jewish Ethnicity in Yehezkel Kaufmann's Golah Venekhar," 260.
62 According to Thomas Krapf, although Kaufmann's saying is shrouded in legend, it credibly conveys both an idiosyncrasy of Kaufmann and the existential tragedy of his life. On this see Thomas M. Krapf, "Some Observations on Yehezkel Kaufmann's Attitude to Wissenschaft des Judentums," in *Proceedings of the Eleventh World Congress of Jewish Studies*, vol. 2 (Jerusalem: World Union of Jewish Studies, 1994), 69–76 (70).
63 Laurence J. Silberstein, "Kaufmann, Yehezkel," in vol. 8 of *Encyclopedia of Religion* (ed. Lindsay Jones. 2nd ed., 15 vol. Detroit: Macmillan Reference USA, 2005): 5108–5109.
64 See, in particular, David Shahar, "The Historical – Cultural Heritage and its Educational Significance in Yehezkel Kaufmann's Outlook (in Hebrew) מעוף: מעשה, no.5 (1999):135 – 156.

University, "Mark well the name of the author: Yehezkel Kaufmann. I have a feeling that Jewish thought has found a redeemer."[65]

It should be mentioned that the subject of Kaufmann's *Golah ve-Nekhar* was not new. A number of Jewish thinkers (Pinsker, Ahad ha-Am, Dubnow) have also inquired into Jewish history and the fate of the Jewish people, suggesting different answers as to the causes of Jewish exile. What distinguishes Kaufmann from the others is that "he placed the fundamental character of Jewish existence as an object of systematic historical thought."[66] It was Kaufmann's *Golah* that provided a comprehensive exposition to Jewish history. For these reasons, it has been righty observed that:

> Anyone seeking to understand the relationship of religion and nationalism in Jewish life must read it for its brilliant delineation of the role of these forces in Jewish history. Anyone seeking to understand the history of Zionism must consider the treatment of nationalist thought and Kaufmann's own nationalist position as presented in Golah ve- Nekhar. And, finally, anyone seeking to understand the problems of alienation and exile which exist in our own time will find in these volumes insights as applicable to the present situation of Jews in the Diaspora as they were to that of European Jewry in the 1920 s.[67]

Furthermore, Kaufmann was convinced that an understanding of the perpetual Jewish exile may be attained only after getting to the root of the character of Jewish history. Hence, Kaufmann turned to the Bible, which he thought to be the foundation of Jewish history. Having found the centrality of religion in Jewish history, Kaufmann studied the Bible and biblical religion with the aim of discovering the originality of Israelite ideas.

The second major study of Kaufmann is *Toledot ha-emunah ha-yisraelit: Mi-yeme Ḳedem 'ad Sof Bayit Sheni*, "The History of Israelite Religion". The book provides a comprehensive history of the biblical period. Its subject is the history of

---

65 H. L. Ginsberg, "Yehezkel Kaufmann," *Reconstructionist* 29, no. 14 (1963): 27 – 29 (28). Laurence Silberstein pointed out, "It would be a mistake, therefore, to regard Gola v'Nekhar as essentially an academic undertaking. Like all of Kaufmann's previous writing it, too, was permeated by a profound concern for the pressing issues confronting the Jewish people." On this see Laurence J. Silberstein, "Exile and Alienation: Yehezkel Kaufmann on the Jewish Nation," in *Texts and Responses. Studies Presented to Nahum N. Glatzer on the Occasion of his seventieth Birthday by his Students* (ed. Michael A. Fishbane, Nahum Norbert Glatzer; Leiden: Brill, 1957), 239 – 256 (251).
66 Joseph Turner, "The Notion of Jewish Ethnicity," 258.
67 Janet Koffler O'Dea, "Israel With and Without Religion: An Appreciation of Kaufmann's Golah Ve-Nekhar," *Judaism* (Winter 1976): 85 – 97 (85).

Israelite religion from its beginning to the end of the Second Temple period.[68] Kaufmann's *Toledot* is an accumulation of the serious labour of twenty years. At its core, Kaufmann displays an extensive and grand history of Israelite religion up to the Babylonian exile.[69] Kaufmann's main thesis is that monotheism emerged in Israel as a new intuitive idea and not through gradual evolution. He makes a sharp distinction between Israelite religion and paganism. He further argues that the sources of the Torah in general and the Priestly Code in particular present a picture of pre-exilic Israel. In addition, Kaufmann proposes that the body of the Torah is ancient, not later than the early monarchy period. In the face of classical criticism, Kaufmann drew attention to the monotheistic character of popular religion,[70] making the point that the prophets based themselves on popular and priestly religion.

Seen from the Jewish perspective, Kaufmann's *Toledot* was an epoch-making contribution to the history of biblical exegesis.[71] Kaufmann's *Toledot* was described as "ein klassisches Werk das neuhebräischen Humanismus darstellt."[72] Although Kaufmann did not start his career as a bible scholar, his biblical studies represent a long-overdue Jewish approach to the Bible.[73] In this context, Menahem Haran has mentioned that Kaufmann's biblical research met the needs of his generation. As he puts it, "Bible research becomes the cornerstone in explaining the essence of Judaism and in solving the mystery of Jewish survival.

---

[68] Vol. I, 3 parts, pp. 763; Vol. II, 2 parts, pp. 764; Vol. III, 2 parts, pp. 687; Vol. IV, 546 pages. The first three volumes were abridged and translated into English by Moshe Greenberg under the title *The Religion of Israel* (Chicago: Chicago University Press, 1960). The beginning of volume 4 was translated into English by C.W. Efroymson under the title *The Babylonian Captivity and Deutero-Isaiah* (New York: Union of American Hebrew Congregations, 1970).

[69] The four parts of the Hebrew original trace the history of Israel's religion from earliest times down to the end of the Persian period (333 B.C.E.). The author's plan, as indicated in the Hebrew title, was to bring the story down to the end of the Second Commonwealth (70 CE.). But Kaufmann, instead of bringing this work to an end, turned to writing commentaries on Joshua and Judges. On this see H. L. Ginsberg, "Yehezkel Kaufmann," 28.

[70] See Kaufmann, *Toledot* III, 7. For a discussion of the character of popular religion in biblical scholarship, see J. Berlinerblau, "The 'Popular Religion' Paradigm in Old Testament Research: A Sociological Critique," *JSOT*, no. 60 (1993): 3–26.

[71] For its importance, Kaufmann's *Toledot* has been called "*Torat Eretz Yisrael*". On this see Nahum Sarna, "From Wellhausen to Kaufmann".

[72] Schalom Ben-Chorin, *Jüdischer Glaube: Strukturen einer Theologie des Judentums anhand des Maimonidischen Credo; Tübinger Vorlesungen* (Tübingen : Mohr, 1975), 201.

[73] See, for example, Benjamin Uffenheimer, "Some Reflections on Modern Jewish Biblical Research".

That is to say, it was precisely he that found in the Bible, 'the right key for solving all problems and difficulties'."[74]

These two major works of Kaufmann (*Golah* and *Toledot*), focus on two main issues: Jewish history and Israelite religion. As far as Kaufmann's view on Jewish history is concerned, we note that he places Judaism as religion at the centre of Jewish history and the main reason for Jewish survival through the centuries. With regard to Israelite religion, Kaufmann asserts the antiquity of Israelite monotheism, maintaining that it was a new and original idea that broke away from its environment.[75] Hence, Kaufmann's works are interrelated. They postulated the idea that Jewish history is based on ideas that are rooted in Israelite religion.

Kaufmann wrote other works that were intended to either reinforce earlier thoughts or discuss contemporary Jewish issues. These include commentaries on the Book of Joshua (1959) and the Book of Judges (1962). As it appears from the list of bibliography in Kaufmann's works, Kaufmann took issue with the school of Alt-Noth concerning the historicity of early Israelite tradition in Canaan. He argued that the conquest was accomplished by means of a massive destruction of the Canaanites. It is worth noting that these commentaries are important, as they show that Kaufmann's uncompromising position concerning the reliability of biblical tradition remained unchangeable. That is to say, there is no alteration in his assessment of central points like the origin of monotheism and historicity of biblical account. His analyses of Joshua and Judges were intended to attest the earliest phase of the religion of ancient Israel. In this way, Kaufmann credited the biblical story of conquest and settlement and appeared to dismiss the contribution of archaeology and extra-biblical materials.

Fortunately, not all of Kaufmann's work appeared in Hebrew. Earlier, in 1930 and in 1933, two articles in the *Zeitschrift für die alttestamentliche Wissenschaft* were published. They addressed two subjects: 1) the theocratic ideal of Judaism (ZAW 48/1931, 23–43) and 2) the relationship of the Torah and the Prophets (ZAW 51/ 1933, 35–47). In 1956, Kaufmann published his monograph *Ha-Sippur ha-Mikra'i al Kibbush ha-Arez*, of which an English version had been published previously (*The Biblical Account of the Conquest of Palestine*, 1953); His essay on "The Biblical Age" appeared in *Great Ages and Ideas of the Jewish People* (edited by L.W. Schwarz, 1956). In this essay, Kaufmann gave an overall description of the history of Israel from its genesis to the Hellenistic period. During the last part of his life, Kaufmann wrote several articles that summed up his main thesis as presented in *Toledot*. These articles were collected and published with the title

---

74 Menahem Haran, *Biblical Research in Hebrew*, 22.
75 *Toledot* I, 224.

Mi-Kivshonah shel ha-Yeẓ irah ha-Mikra'it "From the Secret of the Biblical World," in 1966.

The aforementioned intellectual biography serves two points. First, it delineates the route Kaufmann took from his interest in Jewish history to becoming a Bible scholar. Second, it puts Kaufmann and his work in proper perspective. For reasons that this study will undertake to highlight, Kaufmann's contribution was not widely known within scholarly circles.[76] Though Kaufmann's arguments contain valuable insights, they failed to persuade the general majority of biblical scholars. However, the outstanding importance of Kaufmann's work lies essentially in its great impact on Jewish Bible studies and on Jewish scholars. As for the first, it is said that Kaufmann's biblical research "closed the breach which Christian theology had made between biblical and post-biblical Judaism."[77] Regarding his influential writings on Jewish scholars, Jon Levenson points out, "The reverence in which Kaufmann continues to be held among most Jewish biblical scholars is owing not only to the magnitude of his intellectual achievement, but also to the endurance of that need to clear out a place for Jews in the field and to counter the anti-Jewish positions which had taken root early in its history and had never been completely dislodged."[78] Furthermore, it is still recognized today that Kaufmann is "the greatest and most influential Jewish biblical scholar of modern times."[79] These are only a few examples showing how Kaufmann's Bible research occupies such a prestigious position in Jewish history and biblical studies.[80]

---

76 As far as I know, only few works exist that discuss Kaufmann's ideas. Among these are: Emanuel Green, *Universalism and Nationalism as Reflected in the Writings of Yehezkel Kaufmann with Special Emphasis on the Biblical Period* (Ph.D. dissertation, New York University, 1968); Thomas M. Krapf, *Yehezkel Kaufmann: Ein Lebens- und Erkenntnisweg zur Theologie der Hebräischen Bibel* (Berlin: Institut Kirche und Judentum, 1990); Thomas M. Krapf , *Die Priesterschrift und die vorexilische Zeit: Yehezkel Kaufmanns vernachlässigter Beitrag zur Geschichte der biblischen Religion* (OBO 119; Freiburg,1992); Peter Slyomovics, *Yitzhak Julius Guttmann and Yehezkel Kaufmann: The Relationship of Thought and Research* (in Hebrew) (Jerusalem, The Hebrew University, 1980).
77 Menahem Haran, *Biblical Research in Hebrew*, 21.
78 Jon D. Levenson, "Why Jews are Not Interested in Biblical Theology," in *Judaic Perspectives on Ancient Israel* (ed. Jacob Neusner, Baruch A. Levine, and Ernest S. Fredrichs; Philadelphia: Fortress Press, 1987), 281 – 307 (291).
79 Benjamin Sommer, *The Bodies of God and the World of Ancient Israel* (New York: Cambridge University Press, 2009), 2.
80 Perhaps it would be sufficient here to refer to Baruch Schwartz who, in describing Kaufmann's position among Jewish biblical scholars, writes, "Constant reference to his work pervades all serious Pentateuchal scholarship produced by Jews, be it exegetical-philological or historical-phenomenological. Whether endorsed or challenged, he, not Wellhausen, is the starting point for academic Pentateuchal studies among Jewish biblical scholars." On this see Baruch J.

Writing a book on Wellhausen is an enterprise. This becomes more fraught with danger when attempting to compare Wellhausen's thoughts with those of any other biblical scholar, not to mention Yehezkel Kaufmann. Nevertheless, since Kaufmann devoted most of his life's work to disproving Wellhausen's hypotheses, a comparison between Yehezkel Kaufmann, who is regarded as the "towering figure in modern Jewish Bible scholarship,"[81] and Julius Wellhausen, whose work is described as "one of the literary achievements of German Science in the nineteenth century,"[82] is likely to shed much light on their insightful and useful works. A comparison of the two is therefore clearly to demonstrate that their works are indeed relevant to contemporary discussions in Israel's history.

Schwartz, "The Pentateuch as Scripture and the Challenge of Biblical Criticism: Responses among Modern Jewish Thinkers and Scholars," in *Jewish Concepts of Scripture* (ed. B. Sommer; New York: New York University Press, 2012), 203–229 (227).

81 On this see Moshe Greenberg in the preface to the reissue edition of Kaufmann, *The Biblical Account of the Conquest of Canaan*, 1985, 9. Kaufmann is also known as "Der erste jüdische, historisch-kritische Bibelwissenschaftler." On this see Thomas Staubli, *Wer knackt den Code? Meilensteine der Bibelforschung* (Düsseldorf: Patmos, 2009) 69–70.

82 Franz Rosenzweig described Wellhausen *Israelitische und jüdische Geschichte*: "Das Grundbuch der heutigen Wissenschaft ist noch immer Wellhausens israelitische und jüdische Geschichte, ein kurzes und prachtvoll zu lesendes Buch, eine der literarischen Leistungen der deutschen Wissenschaft des neunzehnten Jahrhunderts." Franz Rosenzweig, *Briefe und Tagebücher* Bd. II, 1170. See further Rudolf Smend, "Wellhausen und das Judentum," 277, n. 138. See also Daniel Weidner, "Geschichte gegen den Strich bürsten: Julius Wellhausen und die Jüdische, Gegengeschichte," *ZRGG* 54, no. 1 (2002): 32–61, n. 113.

Part I Julius Wellhausen's Reconstruction of the History of Israel

Chapter One:
From Source and Literary Criticism to
Historical Synthesis

1 Introduction

To start with, Wellhausen examines the biblical text with the aim of writing the history of ancient Israel. The beginning of Wellhausen's inquiry into the text of the Old Testament is a study on the Book of Samuel entitled *Der Text der Bücher Samuelis*, 1871. This was followed by a number of articles in 1866/1876 in *Jahrbuch für deutsche Theologie*. Wellhausen was mainly concerned with the problem of the composition of the Hexateuch. In 1878, he completed his analysis with a study of the Books of Judges and Kings. By the year 1889, Wellhausen's source and text analysis had been collected together in a book entitled *Die Composition des Hexateuchs und der historischen Bücher des Alten Testaments*.[83]

It is not without meaning that Wellhausen made the Book of Samuel his first point of departure. Although Wellhausen's study was basically an examination of the text of Samuel, his historical interest is obvious.[84] Moreover, it is said that Wellhausen, by studying the historical books of the Old Testament, was able to get insight into the character of Israelite historiography.[85] Having inquired into the literature of the Pentateuch and the historical books, Wellhausen turned to writing his masterpiece *Prolegomena zur Geschichte Israels*. Wellhausen's *Prolegomena* caused a stir and was an epoch-making piece of scholarship. It is mainly a criticism of the Pentateuch/Hexateuch sources. The results gained from literary and historical analysis of the sources were later used as basic information for Wellhausen's, *Israelitische und jüdische Geschichte*, in 1894.

---

83 Rudolf Smend has pointed out, "By no means all the conclusions were new, but he summed up earlier literary criticism and took it further, simplifying it and at the same time refining it." See Rudolf Smend, "Julius Wellhausen: 1844 – 1918," in *From Astruc to Zimmerli: Old Testament Scholarship in three Centuries* (Tübingen: Mohr Siebeck, 2007), 91 – 102 (95).
84 Friedemann Boschwitz, *Julius Wellhausen: Motive und Maßstäbe seiner Geschichtsschreibung* (2 ed. Darmstadt: Wiss. Buchges, 1968), 5. See further Reinhard G. Kratz, "Julius Wellhausen" *TRE* 35 (2003): 527 – 536.
85 Rudolf Smend "Julius Wellhausen (1844 – 1918)," in *Dictionary of Biblical Interpretation*, vol. 2 (ed. John H. Hayes; Nashville: Abingdon Press, 1999), 629 – 631 (630).

It should be made clear that Wellhausen was not the first to introduce the historical-critical method.[86] Nor did Wellhausen speak the last word on Old Testament exegesis.[87] However, the theories of Wellhausen obtained wide circulation. It was through his works that biblical criticism became the standard model for generations.[88] What was decidedly new and original about Wellhausen was that he placed critical analysis at the service of history. For Wellhausen, literary criticism and historical reconstruction went hand in hand.[89] In other words, he constructed both the history of Israel's literature and the history of Israel itself. The combination of these two facets, literature and history, safeguarded Wellhausen's hypothesis and gave it an enduring value. Moreover, Wellhausen's work did not only comprise collecting data and analysing its content. The process was difficult and complicated. Wellhausen himself admitted, "The literary and historical investigation on which we thus enter is both wide and difficult."[90]

In fact, Wellhausen attempted to reconstruct a historical synthesis on the basis of the literary sources.[91] He began his study on the history of Israel using source analysis of the documents to literary criticism and historical reconstruction. His primary focus was on the literary sources instead of pre-literary stages. By means of literary and tendency criticism, Wellhausen sought to find

---

86 Reinhard G. Kratz, "Eyes and Spectacles: Wellhausen's Method of Higher Criticism," *Journal of Theological Studies* 60 (2009): 381–402.

87 Herbert F. Hahn, *The Old Testament in Modern Research*, 17.

88 George Cooch pointed out, "With the publication of Wellhausen's 'Composition of the Hexateuch' in 1876 and his 'History of Israel 1' in 1878, the hypothesis which Vatke-Graf and Kuenen had expounded in their books, and Reuss and Lagarde in their lectures, ceased to be the possession of isolated scholars and become public property." On this see George Peabody Gooch, *History and Historians in the Nineteenth Century* (2. ed. London: Longmans, Green (1954), 482.

89 John H. Hayes, "Wellhausen as a Historian of Israel," in *Julius Wellhausen and his Prolegomena to the History of Israel*, Semeia 25 (ed. Douglas A. Knight; Chico: Scholars Press, 1983), 37–60 (42).

90 Wellhausen, *Prolegomena to the History of Israel*, 12–13. In his assessment of Wellhausen's method of interpretation, Reinhard Kratz points out, "The procedure is never mechanical but fits the subject, takes account of the unpredictable and refractory, and sometimes leaves things just as they are. Nor is the methodology ever one-sided; it always consists in the combination of divergent directions of questioning, as a rule a criticism which starts from philology and textual criticism of the literary sources with an interest in history and the history of religion. Where the sources fail, Wellhausen's imagination takes over: "Unfortunately, my imagination is far more lively than my understanding; the reasons are always unattractive to me." See Reinhard G. Kratz, "Eyes and Spectacles: Wellhausen's Method of Higher Criticism," 387–388.

91 See Otto Eissfeldt, "Wellhausen, Julius," RGG^3, vol. 6 (1962):1594–1595.

the motives that lay behind the compositional documents. In addition, Wellhausen endeavoured to reach back to the original and genuine tradition. In so doing, he proceeded from philology and textual criticism to source and literary criticism, with the aim of obtaining information for historical reconstruction. Perhaps it was Wellhausen's interest in history that gave his presentation clarity and insight. He wrote, "History, it is well known, has always to be reconstructed...the question is whether man constructs well or ill."[92] In what follows I shall demonstrate how Wellhausen started from source and literary criticism and came up with a new synthesis on the history of ancient Israel.

2 Principles of Wellhausen's historiographical approach

2.1 Literary sources and Tendenzkritik

Wellhausen was convinced that only pertinent literary sources could provide a reliable description of what really happened. To Wellhausen, historical reconstruction is based on literary sources. He therefore used the literature of the Old Testament as a master text for historical investigation. This means that Israel's early history could be reconstructed from the literary and written tradition.[93] It comes, then, as no surprise that Wellhausen refused to speculate about the pre-literary stage in ancient Israel. He felt that inquiry into pre-literary traditions could hardly deliver historical information. Kurt Rudolph has rightly mentioned that for Wellhausen, "Historiography was built upon historical literature; the study of the history of pre-literary traditions and comparative studies, whether in the realm of the history of religion or literature, seemed to him of secondary importance and of no historical consequence."[94] Wellhausen's position of relying on the written tradition of ancient Israel is in accordance with the historical writing and historiography of the 19th century.[95]

---

92 Wellhausen, *Prolegomena*, 367.
93 Carl Heinrich Becker, *Islamstudien: Vom Werden und Wesen der islamischen Welt*, Bd. 2 (Hildesheim: Olms, 1967; reprint of the Leipzig edition, 1932), 475–476.
94 Kurt Rudolph, "Wellhausen as an Arabist," in *Julius Wellhausen and his Prolegomena to the History of Israel*, 120.
95 Stephen Geller mentions that Wellhausen, like the 19th century higher critics, is literature-bound, deriving almost all his evidence from the written traditions of the Bible. Geller has also remarked that Wellhausen cannot deal with those aspects of biblical traditions which precede the stage of literary fixation and oral tradition. On this see Stephen Geller, "*Wellhausen and Kaufmann*," *Midstream* 31, no. 10 (1985): 39–48 (42).

Wellhausen drew a picture of ancient Israel's history based on literary sources. In his reconstruction of the beginning of early Israel, he realized that there is no direct Hebrew literature dating from that time. He recognized that we can have only an approximate idea of what happened. In the words of Wellhausen:

> Das Gesetz reicht nicht von ferne an die mosaische Zeit heran. Wenn dem so ist, so gibt es keine direkten literarischen Quellen, aus denen der Mosaismus auch nur so zu erkennen wäre wie etwa die Lehre Jesu aus den Evangelien. Will man nicht ganz darauf verzichten, den Anfang der israelitischen Geschichte darzustellen, so bleibt nur übrig, ihn aus der Fortsetzung zu erschließen, wodurch sich freilich nur ungefähre Ergebnisse gewinnen lassen. Ein Vorgreifen in die Folgezeit hinein läßt sich dabei nicht vermeiden.[96]

In order to understand Wellhausen's position, we might call to our aid Hermann Gunkel's traditio-historical approach.[97] The way by which both Wellhausen and Gunkel grasped the nature of Israelite tradition reveals quite opposite views. While Wellhausen worked with literary and written sources, Gunkel sought to go behind the written sources to discover the pre-literary stage in which the tradition had been transmitted orally. This methodological divergence becomes clear in Wellhausen's critique of Gunkel's approach. In his judgment of Gunkel's *Schöpfung und Chaos*, Wellhausen points out that Gunkel "hat vielleicht antiquarisches Interesse, ist aber nicht die Aufgabe des Theologen und des Exegeten."[98] The implication of Wellhausen's assessment of Gunkel is clear. Wellhausen saw the task of the biblical scholar as examining the tradition as handed down in literary documents, not speculating about its pre-literary stages. He called for scholars to concentrate on the text and its literary composition and not to be distracted with problems related to oral transmission. Kurt Rudolph sums up Wellhausen position, "Investigations of pre-literary traditions behind written works fail to comprehend the essence of such works and cannot be regarded as scientific or methodical."[99]

---

96 Wellhausen, *Israelitische und jüdische Geschichte* (2004[10]), 16.
97 On Gunkel's approach see Werner Klatt, *Hermann Gunkel: zu seiner Theologie der Religionsgeschichte und zur Entstehung der formgeschichtlichen Methode* (Göttingen: Vandenhoeck & Ruprecht, 1969). See also Ute E. Eisen and Erhard S. Gerstenberger, eds., *Hermann Gunkel Revisited: Literatur- und Religionsgeschichtliche Studien* (Berlin: Lit, 2010). For Gunkel's biography, see Konrad Hammann, *Hermann Gunkel: eine Biographie* (Tübingen : Mohr Siebeck, 2014).
98 Wellhausen, "Zur apokalyptischen Literatur," in *Skizzen und Vorarbeiten* VI (1899), 215 – 249.
99 Kurt Rudolph, "Wellhausen as an Arabist," 120. See further Diane Nunn Banks, *Writing the History of Israel* (Library of Hebrew Bible/ Old Testament Studies 438; London: Clark 2006), 69 – 70.

Consistent with his stand, Wellhausen's historical synthesis on the history of ancient Israel as it appears in his *Israelitische und jüdische Geschichte* is based on historical evidence gained from literary analysis of written sources.[100] He used the narrative of the Old Testament to construct his portrait of the course of Israelite history. Wellhausen moved from literary material to history. In other words, it is on the Old Testament text that Wellhausen based his far-reaching interpretation of Israel's history and religion. Peter Machinist pointed out that Wellhausen's *Israelitische und jüdische Geschichte*

> provid[es] the narrative history, especially political, of ancient Israel to virtually the end of the Second Temple period. What is immediately obvious about it is that for the period of ancient Israel it is a narrative written essentially out of the Old Testament, and follows therewith the internal dynamics of Israelite history…Once more, therefore, we are in the presence of the Old Testament as master text.[101]

We have seen that Wellhausen refused to speculate about the pre-literary stage of Israel's tradition. His method of interpretation is based on literary and written documents. Getting at the roots of the original content of the text, Wellhausen combined in his research both literary criticism and tendency criticism. He was not content to stop with an analysis of the text and the history of its literary composition. Once he identified his sources or documents, he turned to uncovering the motives of their authors, with the aim of learning what had not been explicitly mentioned in the text. In so doing, Wellhausen employed the method of tendency criticism initiated by Ferdinand Christian Baur.[102] This method examines the original shape of the text, the larger original content of literary units, and then the motive for the change from the original. In the words of Friedemann Boschwitz, "Diese Methode sucht im Einzelnen die ursprüngliche Gestalt des Texts und im größeren Ganzen den ursprünglichen Inhalt der Berichte

---

100 Not only in the field of Old Testament study did Wellhausen rely on written and literary sources, but also in his Arabic and New Testament investigation. On this see, in particular, Kurt Rudolph, "Wellhausen as an Arabist," 114.

101 Peter Machinist, "The Road Not Taken: Wellhausen and Assyriology," in *Homeland and Exile: Biblical and Ancient Near Eastern Studies in Honour of Bustenay Oded* (ed. Mark Gelier, Alan Millard and Gershon Galil; Supplements to Vetus Testamentum 130; Leiden: Brill, 2009), 469–531 (520).

102 Herbert F. Hahn, "Wellhausen's Interpretation of Israel's Religious History: A Reappraisal of his Ruling Ideas," in *Essays on Jewish Life and Thought: Presented in Honor of Salo Wittmayer Baron* (ed. Joseph L. Blau; New York: Columbia University Press, 1959), 299–308 (305–306).

und literarischen Einheiten, zugleich mit dem Motiv für die Änderung des Ursprünglichen."[103]

As a literary critic, Wellhausen recognized that the sources mirrored the time in which they were composed. With this in mind, he endeavoured by means of tendency criticism to enter into the context of the authors of the sources. Thus, for example, Wellhausen called for an inquiry into the "sources" of the Chronicles. He tells us that the Chronicles reflect the time of its origin. In the words of Wellhausen:

> It must be allowed that Chronicles owes its origin, not to the arbitrary caprice of an individual, but to a general tendency of its period. It is the inevitable product of the conviction that the Mosaic law is the starting-point of Israel's history, and that in it there is operative a play of sacred forces such as finds no other analogy; this conviction could not but lead to a complete transformation of the ancient tradition[104]

This implies that Wellhausen was convinced that the sources are a literary composition of the prevailing ideas of a particular time. By analyzing the data of a given document, the temper and the context in which it was shaped could be obtained. Herbert Hahn sums up Wellhausen's position:

> Wellhausen was not content [...] to treat the sources as ends in themselves; that is, he was not content merely to accept the surface data presented by the sources. It was his conviction that the documents were the products of a whole intellectual or spiritual culture, and that the historian must go below the surface to grasp this larger whole. He must endeavour to live and think again the life and thought of which the documents were written expressions.[105]

Wellhausen was then confident that the literary sources are a true representation of their time.[106] Bearing this in mind, Wellhausen not only rearranged the order

---

103 Friedemann Boschwitz, *Julius Wellhausen: Motive und Maßstäbe seiner Geschichtsschreibung*, 13.

104 *Prolegomena*, 224, 225.

105 Herbert F. Hahn, "Wellhausen's Interpretation of Israel's Religious History," 305.

106 Thomas L. Thompson has pointed out that "the dictum of Wellhausen that a biblical document reflects the historical context of its own formation rather than the social milieu of its explicit referents to a more distant past is one that has hardly been overcome by any of the attempts to synthesize traditio-historical and archaeological research during the past century." On this see Thomas L. Thompson, "Text, Context and Referent in Israelite Historiography," in *The Fabric of History: Text, Artifact and Israel's Past* (ed. D. V. Edelman; JSOTSup 127. Sheffield: JSOT Press, 1991), 65–92 (65).

of the documents but also read them with intention and method.[107] In his view, everything should be reconstructed from the very beginning. He started by asking about the tendency of the sources and their relation to each other with eyes open to the literary and historical process.[108]

2.2 Original and genuine tradition

Wellhausen was obsessed with the conception of the original form of the tradition. Perhaps there is nothing more telling about Wellhausen than his idea of the original form. In his assessment of the tradition, he assumed that it had been subjected to change through the course of history. This occurred, according to Wellhausen, more than one time and in different periods. Thus, Wellhausen tells us that the tradition had been reshaped according to the spirit of each age, "Under the influence of the spirit of each successive age, traditions originally derived from one source were very variously apprehended and shaped; one way in the ninth and eighth centuries, another way in the seventh and sixth, and yet another in the fifth and fourth."[109] Here he alluded to the development of Israelite tradition as manifested in the three literary strata of the Pentateuch: First the Jehovist about the 9th and 8th century, then Deuteronomy in the 7th and 6th centuries, and finally the Priestly Code around the 5th and 4th centuries. This implies that Wellhausen recognized different layers in the tradition and strove to reach the original form. In so doing, he tried to trace the growth of the ancient Israelite tradition. Moreover, Wellhausen was able to grasp that Israel's history is a product of the outgrowth of traditions of ancient Israel and Judah. As Uwe Becker explained:

> Er hat die Überlieferung selbst in ihren Wandlungen nachgezeichnet und auf diese Weise ein Bild der inneren Entwicklung gewonnen…So ist die *Israelitische und jüdische Geschichte* auch nicht einfach eine gewöhnliche Darstellung der Geschichte Israels, sondern im Kern eine *Geschichte der jüdischen Überlieferung*, die aus dem antiken Israel und Juda herausgewachsen ist und in vielfältiger Weise angereichert und fortgeschrieben wurde.[110]

---

107 Daniel Weidner, "Geschichte gegen den Strich bürsten: Julius Wellhausen und die jüdische Gegengeschichte," *ZRGG* 54 (2002): 32 – 61.

108 Carl Heinrich Becker, *Islamstudien*, 476. See further Reinhard G. Kratz, "Eyes and Spectacles," 387.

109 Wellhausen, *Prolegomena*, 171.

110 Uwe Becker, „Julius Wellhausens Sicht des Judentums," in *Biblische Theologie und historisches Denken: Wissenschaftsgeschichtliche Studien: Aus Anlass der 50. Wiederkehr der Basler Pro-*

According to Wellhausen, the original tradition of ancient Israel was enriched in the course of history. In his point of view, the new materials were added to the genuine tradition by "repainting" the original picture of Israel's early history. The best way to understand Wellhausen's assessment is to quote his words:

> What in the common view appears to be the specific character of Israelite history, and has chiefly led to its being called sacred history, rests for the most part on a later re-painting of the original picture. The discolouring influences begin early. I do not reckon among these the entrance of mythical elements, such as are not wanting even in the first beginnings to which we can trace the course of the tradition, nor the inevitable local colour, which is quite a different thing from tendency. I think only of that uniform stamp impressed on the tradition by men who regarded history exclusively from the point of view of their own principles.[111]

In addition, Wellhausen emphasized that in the original and genuine content of the tradition, "The presupposition disappears and in connection with this the whole historical process assumes an essentially different, not to say a more natural aspect."[112] Here Wellhausen is referring to deuteronomistic redaction of the historical books. For example, Wellhausen identified a deuteronomistic revision in the Book of Judges in chronology and the religious connection of the events. In his opinion, "All this is no part of the original contents of the tradition, but merely a uniform in which it is clothed."[113] Moreover, Wellhausen identified what he called "tendency in the development of the tradition". As he puts it, "It is possible to trace even in the original narratives themselves certain differences of religious attitude which indicate to us unobtrusively and yet clearly that tendency in the development of the tradition which reached its end in the revision and ornamentation."[114] In this context Wellhausen made a distinction between the original and reshaped tradition. In his view, the original form of tradition was a natural version, while the religious and oriented narrative is secondary and revised. In his *Composition des Hexateuchs* which is dedicated to source analysis, Wellhausen distinguished between a *natürliche* and *religiöse* version of the Gideon story in the Book of Judges. At the end of his analysis of these two versions, he concluded, "Ohne Zweifel ist die natürliche Version 8,

motion von Rudolf Smend (ed. Martin Kessler and Martin Wallraff; Basel: Schwabe, 2008), 279–309 (287–288).
111 Wellhausen, *Prolegomena*, 293.
112 Wellhausen, *Prolegomena*, 234.
113 Wellhausen, *Prolegomena*, 230, 231.
114 Wellhausen, *Prolegomena*, 240.

4—21 die primäre, und die religiöse 6, 1—8, 3 sekundär. Bei der letzteren hat sich übrigens der ursprüngliche Kern durch spätere Zusätze erweitert."[115]

Gifted with a sense of literary insight, Wellhausen was able to differentiate between the primary and secondary versions of biblical narrative. This helps Wellhausen to realize that the original and genuine tradition lacks the presuppositions of the later, re-editing forms of the tradition. For example, in his examination of the stories about Abraham and Isaac, Wellhausen observed:

> The stories about Isaac, however, are more original, as may be seen in a striking way on comparing Genesis xx. 2–16 with xxvi 6–12. The short and profane version, of which Isaac is the hero, is more lively and pointed; the long and edifying version in which Abraham replaces Isaac makes the danger not possible but actual, thus necessitating the intervention of the Deity and so bringing about a glorification of the patriarch, which he little deserved.[116]

As a rule, Wellhausen discarded the religious version and inclined to the short and profane, which is more lively and pointed. Wellhausen's observation accords well with his understanding of the history of Israel. He tried to free history from the dogmatic and religious interpretation that had been added to it. In Wellhausen opinion, early Israelite tradition assumes a very natural beginning without theological bias. The notions of a "sacred history" and "sacred community" are products of the Judaism of the exile, not of ancient Israel itself. As Wellhausen puts it, "The ancient Israelites did not build a church first of all: what they built first was a house to live in."[117] Herbert Hahn sums up Wellhausen's position:

> What Wellhausen's method amounted to, essentially, was an attempt to restore the original historical tradition, freed of interpretations which obscured or even distorted it, to its rightful place as the genuine history. He believed that the didactic theology of the biblical documents, which found a causal relationship between the misfortunes of the people and their sin in deserting the Law, was no part of the original tradition. It was not the "natural" history of the people but a theological interpretation of history springing from the dominant conceptions of the post-exilic age. Wellhausen was convinced that it presented a conception of Israelite antiquity which was unrelated to the actual experience of the early Israelites. He was certain that the "natural" history of their experience was primary and the "religious" version of their history secondary. Hence he wanted to translate the tradition back into its "profane" form.[118]

---

115 Wellhausen, *Die Composition des Hexateuchs*, 221.
116 Wellhausen, *Prolegomena*, 320, n.1.
117 Wellhausen, *Prolegomena*, 255.
118 Herbert F. Hahn, "Wellhausen's Interpretation of Israel's Religious History," 306.

However, it should be mentioned that Wellhausen's preference for the original and natural does not exclude Israel's religious history. As Perlitt pointed out, "Wellhausen writes the history of Israel as a "profane history" analogous to any other history and renounces any attempt to demonstrate special "revelations" in it with the tools of the historian. But for him this "profane" history does not exclude "religious" history, but on the contrary includes it."[119] That is to say Wellhausen appreciated the early beginnings of the religion of Israel, Christianity, and Islam in their pure form without institution and dogmatic presuppositions. As Reinhard Kratz puts it:

> If we survey the whole of Wellhausen's work, we come upon a pattern of interpretation which is there from the beginning and keeps recurring in all three spheres of Old Testament, Arabic, and New Testament studies. It is the development of, or more properly the opposition between, the original beginnings of a religion or culture which grew up naturally and are still completely earthy, and the later stage, in which things have assumed an institutionally established, artificial, and dogmatic state.[120]

3 Dating the sources

The question is how did Wellhausen come up with the idea of reconstructing history from sources? To put it differently, what historical weight did Wellhausen attach to the sources of the Pentateuch/Hexateuch? It is well known that the source critical approach had long been established before Wellhausen.[121] What was decidedly new in Wellhausen's work was that he attempted to use results gained from source criticism for historical purposes. He was convinced that such sources could be used for writing history. He thought that history could be reconstructed after analysing the pentateuchal source, after he had classified

---

119 Lothar Perlitt, *Vatke und Wellhausen*, 232. See further John Barton, *The Nature of Biblical Criticism* (Louisville: Westminster John Knox Press, 2007), 53.

120 Reinhard G. Kratz, "Eyes and Spectacles," 383.

121 Much has been written about the source critical approach and documentary hypothesis. It might be sufficient here to say that it was through Wellhausen's work on the Old Testament that the documentary hypothesis has become a standard model for understanding the composition of the Pentateuch. Moreover, it was in Wellhausen's work that the source critical approach was perfected. On this see E. Kautzsch, Rec. "Welhausen, J., 'Geschichte Israels," *ThLZ* 2 (1879): 25 – 30. See also J. Alberto Soggin, *Introduction to the Old Testament: From its Origins to the Closing of the Alexandrian Canon* (Philadelphia:Westminster Press, 1976). See further Raymond F. Surburg, "Wellhausen Evaluated after a Century of Influence."

them in chronological order, and studied their tendency.[122] In addition, Wellhausen was aware of the inner relationship that connected the sources and the importance of this for historical reconstruction. In referring to earlier critics who had regarded sources as "distinct and independent", Wellhausen declares that this way of considering the nature of the sources is "very improbable."[123] He believed that more conclusions could be drawn. Thus, Wellhausen emphasized:

> Criticism has not done its work when it has completed the mechanical distribution; it must aim further at bringing the different writings when thus arranged into relation with each other, must seek to render them intelligible as phases of a living process, and thus to make it possible to trace a graduated development of the tradition.[124]

Furthermore, Wellhausen realized that the stages of development in the sources are identical with those of history. As he puts it, "In the Pentateuch the elements follow upon one another and from one another precisely as the steps of the development demonstrably do in the history."[125] Moreover, Wellhausen connected the three strata of the Pentateuch with the development of Israel's history. That is to say, fixing the order of the pentateuchal sources was the same as reconstructing the different phases of Israel's history. Endowed with a sense of history and deep insight into the successive stages of the development process of the sources, Wellhausen wrote:

> It was not seen that most important historical questions were involved as well as questions merely literary, and that to assign the true order of the different strata of the Pentateuch was equivalent to a reconstruction of the history of Israel. As regards the narrative matter it was forgotten that, after the Jehovistic, Deuteronomic, and Priestly versions of the history had been felicitously disentangled from one another, it was necessary to examine the mutual relations of the three, to consider them as marking so many stages of an historical tradition, which had passed through its successive phases under the action of living causes, and the growth of which could and must be traced and historically explained.[126]

---

122 Douglas A. Knight, *Rediscovering the Traditions of Israel: The Development of the Traditio-Historical Research of the Old Testament, with Special Consideration of Scandinavian Contributions* (SBL9 Missoula: University of Montana, 1973), 66–67.
123 Wellhausen, *Prolegomena*, 295.
124 Wellhausen, *Prolegomena*, 295.
125 Wellhausen, *Prolegomena*, 13.
126 Wellhausen, "Pentateuch and Joshua," *Encyclopaedia Britannica* 18 (New York Hall, 9th ed., 1885), 505–514 (508).

Thus Wellhausen thought that by interrogating the sources and putting them in the correct historical order, he could write the history of ancient Israel. With regard to the Jehovist, for example, Wellhausen tells us:

> In language, horizon, and other features, it dates from the golden age of Hebrew literature, to which the finest parts of Judges, Samuel, and Kings, and the oldest extant prophetical writings also belong, – the period of the kings and prophets which preceded the dissolution of the two Israelite kingdoms by the Assyrians.[127]

Having dated the Jehovist, Wellhausen turned to reveal its character and tendency. He noted that the Jehovist "does not even pretend to being a Mosaic law of any kind; it aims at being a simple book of history."[128] Wellhausen went further to say, "The Jehovist is essentially of a narrative character and sets forth with full sympathy and enjoyment the materials handed down by tradition."[129]

The second source to which Wellhausen attached more importance is Deuteronomy.[130] To Wellhausen, Deuteronomy has to be dated in accordance with 2 Kings. 22.[131] He pointed out that Deuteronomy, when it was first discovered, was purely a law-book.[132] In addition, Wellhausen proposed, "Deuteronomy was composed in the same age as that in which it was discovered, and was made the rule of Josiah's reformation, which took place about a generation before the destruction of Jerusalem by the Chaldaeans."[133] Accordingly, Wellhausen

---

127 Wellhausen, *Prolegomena*, 9.

128 Wellhausen, *Prolegomena*, 9.

129 Wellhausen, *Prolegomena*, 7.

130 Konrad Schmid has mentioned that Wellhausen was far removed from 20th century pandeuteronomismus. In his opinion, "Der Deuteronomismus war für Wellhausen keine zentrale Deutekategorie, Wellhausen war noch weit vom Pandeuteronomismus des späten 20. Jh. entfernt. Man muss in den Prolegomena immerhin bis S.227 lesen, bis man bei der Beschreibung des Richterschemas aus Jdc 2 erstmals auf das Adjektiv 'deuteronomistisch' stößt." For more on this subject, see Konrad Schmid, "Hatte Wellhausen Recht? Das Problem der literarhistorischen Anfänge des Deuteronomismus in den Königebüchern" in *Die deuteronomistischen Geschichtswerke: Redaktions- und religionsgeschichtliche Perspektiven zur "Deuteronomismus"-Diskussion in Tora und Vorderen Propheten; internationales Symposium* (ed. Markus Witte; Berlin: de Gruyter, 2006), 19–43 (24).

131 Nevertheless, Wellhausen emphasizes that he did not, like Graf, "so use this position as to make it the fulcrum for my lever. Deuteronomy is the starting-point, not in the sense that without it it would be impossible to accomplish anything, but only because, when its position has been historically ascertained, we cannot decline to go on, but must demand that the position of the Priestly Code should also be fixed by reference to history." On this see Wellhausen, *Prolegomena*, 13.

132 Wellhausen, *Prolegomena*, 345.

133 Wellhausen, *Prolegomena*, 9.

suggested, "Deuteronomy allows the real situation (that of the period during which, Samaria having been destroyed, only the kingdom of Judah continued to subsist) to reveal itself very plainly through that which is assumed (xii.8, xix.8)."[134] More important is Wellhausen's depiction of Deuteronomy as the period of preparation and transition in the religious history of ancient Israel. As he puts it:

> Even Deuteronomy, which was written not long before the exile, regards the period before the monarchy as a time of preparation and transition, not to be counted complete in itself: Israel must first acquire fixed seats and a settled way of living, and then Jehovah also will choose a seat for Himself and make known His desires with regard to the cultus.[135]

The third source, for which *Prolegomena* was chiefly concerned to fix its date, is the Priestly Code. From the outset, Wellhausen acknowledged that opinions differ widely about the exact date of the Priestly Code. In his view the difficulty with accurate dating of the Priestly Code arises mainly because "it tries hard to imitate the costume of the Mosaic period, and, with whatever success, to disguise its own."[136] In addition, Wellhausen realized that the priestly source in the Pentateuch is characterized by its legislation laws. He even called the Priestly Code "the standard legislative element" in Pentateuch.[137] He further pointed out that the priestly source betrays the circumstances of the post-exile times, where the law was the dominant factor in the religious life: "All the distinctive peculiarities of the work are connected with the influence of the law: everywhere we hear the voice of theory, rule, and judgment."[138] Consequently, Wellhausen suggested that the Priestly Code was published and introduced in the year 444 B.C., a century after the exile.[139]

Now, if the Jehovist is characterized by affinity with Israelite tradition and Deuteronomy is depicted as the period of transition, what is the position of the priestly source with regard to ancient Israelite traditions? The answer from Wellhausen is, "By its taste for barren names and numbers and technical descriptions, the Priestly Code comes to stand on the same line with the Chronicles and the other literature of Judaism which labours at an artificial revival of the old tradition."[140] Moreover, Wellhausen noted that the Priestly Code in its portrait of

---

134 Wellhausen, *Prolegomena*, 9.
135 Wellhausen, Prolegomena, 253–254.
136 Wellhausen, *Prolegomena*, 9.
137 Wellhausen, *Prolegomena*, 405.
138 Wellhausen, *Prolegomena*, 361.
139 Wellhausen, *Prolegomena*, 405.
140 Wellhausen, *Prolegomena*, 350.

early Israel as a sacred community stands furthest from the origin of the tradition."[141] With this in mind, Wellhausen concluded that the priestly source was estranged from the heart of original tradition. To quote Wellhausen:

> In the eyes of the Priestly Code, Israel in point of fact is not a people, but a church; worldly affairs are far removed from it and are never touched by its laws; its life is spent in religious services. Here we are face to face with the church of the second temple, the Jewish hierocracy, in a form possible only under foreign domination.[142]

Furthermore, Wellhausen was concerned with the idea of the historical weight of each of his sources. In explaining about how he proceeded to examine the sources, Wellhausen said, "The procedure which, when applied to Deuteronomy, is called historic-critical method, is called, when applied to the Priestly Code, construction of history."[143] He started by comparing the tradition as given in the Jehovist and Priestly Code and concluded:

> It would not be impossible to trace inner development of the tradition in the intermediate stages between the two extremities. To do this we should have to make use of the more delicate results of the process of source-sifting, and to call to our aid the hints, not numerous indeed, but important, which are to be found in Deuteronomy and in the historical and prophetical books.[144]

This procedure enables Wellhausen to differentiate between the oldest and the latest phase of tradition as given, respectively, in the Jehovist and the Priestly Code. Pursuing this further, we might refer to the second part of Wellhausen's *Prolegomena,* which is devoted to examining the "history of tradition". In introducing his subject, Wellhausen used a motto from Hesiod, according to which "the half is more than the whole."[145] The implication is of great importance to understanding Wellhausen's assessment of the sources and their historical credibility. Wellhausen meant that the Israelite tradition in pre-exilic Israel is of more historical value than the Jewish tradition in post-exilic times. In addition, Well-

---

141 Wellhausen, *Prolegomena,* 359.
142 Wellhausen, *Prolegomena,* 150.
143 Wellhausen, *Prolegomena,* 367.
144 Wellhausen, *Prolegomena,* 360.
145 Smend has noted, " It was with 'the half' that his sympathy lay, which meant the patriarchs, kings and prophets, acting as living people according to the impulse of their nature and their circumstances, governed neither by the force of cultic institutions nor by the pattern of theological conceptuality." See Rudolf Smend, "Julius Wellhausen: 1844 – 1918," in *From Astruc to Zimmerli: Old Testament Scholarship in Three Centuries* (Tübingen: Mohr Siebeck, 2007), 91 – 102 (97).

hausen drew attention to considering the tradition before it was reshaped under the influence of deuteronomist and priestly legislators. He argued that the tradition in the historical books had been subjected to editing and redaction. As he puts it:

> The original sources of the Books of Judges, Samuel, and Kings stand on the same platform with the Jehovist; the editing they received in the exile presupposes Deuteronomy and the latest construction of the history as contained in Chronicles rests on the Priestly Code.[146]

Wellhausen's view, as it seems to me, suggests that only little could be known of the genuine tradition due to it having been remodelled during the exile. Based on source critical examination, Wellhausen refused to attach historical value to patriarchal stories in the Pentateuch. He writes:

> It is true, we attain to no historical knowledge of the patriarchs, but only of the time when the stories about them arose in the Israelite people; this later age is here unconsciously projected, in its inner and its outward features, into hoar antiquity, and is reflected there like a glorified mirage. The skeleton of the patriarchal history consists, it is well known, of ethnographic genealogy.[147]

Wellhausen preferred sources that reflect the period it deals with, not those that are merely a projection of the past. In his opinion, the Jehovist delivers more historical information than the priestly source does. This can be seen when considering the figure of Moses as depicted in the Jehovist and priestly sources of the Pentateuch. In the Jehovist, which Wellhausen regarded as representing the old phase of tradition, Moses appears as the deliverer of his people from the Egyptians. By contrast, Moses of the priestly source is a religious founder and legislator. Moses of the Jehovist is a man of God who is working in history, not in literature. The priestly sources, by making Moses the founder of the law, detached him from genuine tradition and from his age. With eyes open to differences between the tradition in its beginning as opposed to its latest phase, Wellhausen concluded that the Moses of the Jehovist appears more original than the Moses of the Priestly Code. Wellhausen tells us the following:

> As from the literary point of view, so also from the historical, the Moses of the Jehovist appears more original than the Moses of the Priestly Code...According to the Priestly Code, Moses is a religious founder and legislator...The whole significance of Moses consists in the office of messenger which he holds as mediator of the law; what else he does is of no importance. That the law is given once and for all is the great event of the time, not

---

146 Wellhausen, "Pentateuch and Joshua," 513.
147 Wellhausen, *Prolegomena*, 318–319.

that the people of Israel begin to appear on the stage of the world. The people are there for the sake of the law, not the law for the sake of the people. With the Jehovist, on the contrary, Moses' work consists in this, that he delivers his people from the Egyptians and cares for it in every way in the wilderness...The Torah is but a part of his activity...Here all is life and movement: as Jehovah Himself, so the man of God, is working in a medium which is alive; is working practically, by no means theoretically, in history, not in literature...In the Priestly Code the work of Moses lies before us clearly defined and rounded off...It is detached from its originator and from his age...This precipitate of history, appearing as law at the beginning of the history, stifles and kills the history itself.[148]

We may note that while basically declining the truth of the patriarchal stories, reckoning them as founded on no historical facts, Wellhausen was still inclined to regard the age of Moses as historical. This seems, one could say, somehow selective and puzzling. Wellhausen justified his approach in the following explanation:

It involves no contradiction that, in comparing the versions of the tradition, we should decline the historical standard in the case of the legend of the origins of mankind and of the legend of the patriarchs, while we employ it to a certain extent for the epic period of Moses and Joshua. The epic tradition certainly contains elements which cannot be explained on any other hypothesis than that there are historical facts underlying them; its source is in the period it deals with, while the patriarchal legend has no connection whatever with the times of the patriarchs.[149]

4 From literary criticism to historical synthesis: Summary

In the foregoing discussion, I have attempted to prove that Wellhausen built his reconstruction of early Israel on results derived from source and literary criticism. I have also shown that he employed the method of tendency criticism to reveal the origin and genuine tradition. In addition, we have noted that Wellhausen put source and literary analysis at the service of historical reconstruction. Now, it has become clear that Wellhausen sought to reconstruct the history of ancient Israel using its literary written tradition with the help of the historical critical method.

Wellhausen was interested in the text of the Old Testament and used his philological knowledge to analyze it.[150] His first study in this regard was an exami-

---

148 Wellhausen, *Prolegomena*, 345–347.
149 Wellhausen, *Prolegomena*, 360.
150 Johs. Pedersen, "Die Auffassung vom Alten Testament," *ZAW* 49 (1931): 161–181.

nation of the text of the Books of Samuel in 1871. This was followed, as mentioned above, by a number of articles that originally appeared in JDTH between 1866 and 1877 (later published in *Die Composition des Hexateuchs und der Historischen Bücher des Alten Testaments in 1899*). With an eye to history and historical reconstruction, Wellhausen recognized the importance of results gained from text and literary criticism. As he wrote, "Das gewonnene Resultat ist zugleich ein kritisches Prinzip von einschneidenden Konsequenzen."[151] In this context Kurt Rudolph pointed out:

> Wellhausen was a philologian at heart and as such also a historian; for in his day philology meant not only the study of languages but immersion in the history and culture associated with the language one studied...Yet Wellhausen was never willing to stop there but placed all his philological learning and ability at the service of history.[152]

Proceeding from the text and source critical approach, Wellhausen went further, to literary criticism and historical reconstruction. He said, "Ich bin von der Textkritik auf die literarische Kritik geführt worden, weil sich ergab, dass manchmal die Grenze nicht zu finden war, wo die Arbeit des Glossators aufhörte und die des Literators anfing."[153] Wellhausen's *Prolegomena* (first under the title *Geschichte Israel 1*, 1878) is the fitting sequel of his earlier labours.[154] In *Prolegomena*, Wellhausen gave a detailed description of the religious development of ancient Israel. His inquiry is divided into three parts. The first and largest part is devoted to the history of the worship in which Wellhausen identified the main stages in the history of the Israelite cult. The second part, according to Wellhausen, "Traces the influence of the successively prevailing ideas and tendencies upon the shaping of historical tradition, and follows the various phases in which that was conceived and set forth. It contains, so to speak, a history of tradition."[155] In this part Wellhausen compared the results gained from criticizing the pentateuchal sources with the tradition as given in the historical and prophetic books. Wellhausen used the results of his inquiry into the history of worship and history of tradition and drew a distinction between "Israel" and "Judaism." With the publication of his *Prolegomena*, many questions brought forth by

---

151 Wellhausen, *Die Composition des Hexateuchs*, 139.
152 Kurt Rudolph, "Wellhausen as an Arabist," 117–118.
153 Wellhausen, *Die Composition des Hexateuchs*, 314.
154 W. R. Smith, *Lectures & Essays of William Robertson Smith* (ed. Sutherland Black and George William Chrystal; London: Adam and Black, 1912), 601.
155 Wellhausen, *Prolegomena*, 13.

historical criticism were answered.[156] In a clear presentation, Wellhausen demonstrated that the Israelite religion had gone through different stages of development and undergone many changes in the course of its history. Moreover, he explained how the change in the literary tradition of the pentateuchal sources reflects the same change in the religious development of ancient Israel.

With the appearance of Wellhausen's *Israelitische und jüdische Geschichte* in 1894, his historical synthesis of Israel's history was founded. Without his earlier works, I would suggest, Wellhausen synthesis would not have emerged. It is evident from his historical presentation that it was based on critical works such as *Die Composition des Hexateuchs* and *Prolegomena zur Geschichte Israels*. From the outset, it appears that Wellhausen reconstructed the main phases of Israel's history without recourse to much of the tradition of the Old Testament. He only made use of material obtained through source and literary criticism.[157] Thus, for example, Wellhausen constructed a model of ancient Israel up to the monarchy that was characterized by its normal features and lacked any unique traits. He considered the stories of the patriarchs as a projection of the monarchic period with no historical reality. Moreover, Wellhausen said, "The religious starting-point of the history of Israel was remarkable, not for its novelty, but for its normal character."[158] In addition, we note that Wellhausen omitted many aspects of religious orientation associated with the events of Exodus. For example, he disregarded the account of giving the law at Sinai.

As it appears from Wellhausen's presentation that the three main phases in Israel's history as manifested in *Israelitische und jüdische Geschichte* are found under the headings, *"Gott, Welt und Leben im alten Israel," "Die prophetische Reformation,"* and *"Die Restauration".*[159] Under each of these rubrics, Wellhausen translated his critical studies on the Old Testament into narrative history. In

---

156 Walter Zimmerli, for example, mentioned that Wellhausen "set out a brilliant summary of the critical analysis of the Pentateuch which had been begun in the 18th century, and related this to the new presentation of the history of Israel". On this see Walter Zimmerli, *The Law and the Prophets: A Study of the Meaning of the Old Testament* (Oxford: Basil Blackwell, 1965), 23.
157 Hans-Joachim Kraus, *Geschichte der historisch-kritischen Erforschung des Alten Testaments* (Neukirchen-Vluyn: Neukirchener Verlag, 1982[3]), 270–272.
158 Wellhausen, "Israel," in *Prolegomena to the History of Israel*, 437.
159 Reinhard Kratz has pointed out that Wellhausen in these chapters presented a point of view which anticipated much of what we know today on the background of analogy with the ancient Near East and archaeology. Kratz sums up his view as follows, "Kurz gesagt handelt es sich um den Weg Israels und Judas vom altorientalischen Kleinstaat zum Volk JHWHs, religionsgeschichtlich ausgedrückt: vom hebräischen "Heidentum," das sich in nichts von seiner Umwelt unterscheidet, zur israelitisch-jüdischen Religion des Alten Testaments." See Reinhard G. Kratz, "Wellhausen, Julius (1844–1918)," *TRE* 35 (2003): 527–536 (530).

other words, he considered the Jehovistic tradition as most representing the early history of ancient Israel, but Deuteronomy as a product of prophetic reform, and the Priestly Code as a product of the Jewish tradition of restoration community that lived in the exile.

Thus source and literary criticism became for Wellhausen the means of reconstructing history. As Perlitt pointed out, Wellhausen took the road from literary criticism to historical reconstruction. He writes, "So kam Wellhausen auf methodisch sicherem Wege von der literarischen Analyse zur historischen Kritik...der Schritt von der Aussonderung der Quellen zur Einsicht in ihr geschichtliches Nacheinander verband sich aber in Wellhausen auf eine überaus glückliche Weise mit dem Willen zur historischen Darstellung."[160] Similarly, Rudolf Smend mentions that Wellhausen's critical investigation was directed mainly for the sake of historical synthesis.[161] He describes Wellhausen's methods as "Substruktion zu einem positiven Aufbaubetrieb."[162] Smend further emphasizes that Wellhausen's main interest was to provide a history of ancient Israel:

> Der Hauptgrund für sein Abseitsstehen war das aber noch nicht. Er lag darin, daß er die literarische Analyse nicht um ihrer selbst willen betrieb, als ‚Kegelspiel', wie er sagte, sondern als Mittel zum Zweck; und der Zweck war die historische Synthese, die Rekonstruktion der Geschichte des alten Israel.[163]

Thus, it appears that Wellhausen's interest in the critical approach was not an end in itself. Rather, as Ernest W. Nicholson remarked, "It was a means to solving a larger, and for him more urgent, problem – the history and development of Israelite religion from the pre-exilic period to the beginnings of Judaism in the post-exilic period."[154] It can also be said that Wellhausen built the groundwork

---

160 Perlitt, *Vatke und Wellhausen*, 168–169.

161 Rudolf Smend has mentioned that Wellhausen became less interested in literary analysis when his historical synthesis began to coalesce. He quotes Wellhausen's letter to Robertson Smith in 1882: "There are few people in Germany who understand that I really have more positive things in mind than Pentateuchal criticism." See Rudolf Smend, "The Work of Abraham Kuenen and Julius Wellhausen," in *Hebrew Bible, Old Testament: The History of its Interpretation III/I: From Modernism to Post-Modernism (the Nineteenth and Twentieth Centuries)* (ed. Magne Sæbø; Göttingen: Vandenhoeck & Ruprecht, 2013), 476.

162 Rudolf Smend, "Israelitische und jüdische Geschichte: Zur Entstehung von Juluis Wellhausens Buch," in *Geschichte, Tradition, Reflexion: Festschrift für Martin Hengel zum 70. Geburtstag* (Part 1, ed. Peter Schäfer; Tübingen: Mohr, 1996), 35–42 (36).

163 Rudolf Smend, *Julius Wellhausen: Ein Bahnbrecher in drei Disziplinen* (München: Carl Friedrich von Siemens Stiftung, 2006), 22.

164 Ernest W. Nicholson, *The Pentateuch in the Twentieth Century: The Legacy of Julius Wellhausen* (Oxford: Clarendon Press, 1998), 249.

for his historical synthesis, putting source and literary criticism at the service of history. With Wellhausen's work on the Old Testament, it became possible to put the sources in their historical order and at the same time to examine their historical credibility. His investigation was not merely a division of sources, but a clear presentation of their coring and tendency.[165] Wellhausen's great innovation, I would say, is that he made use of his critical analysis for the purpose of elucidating history. This enabled him to present his synthesis on the history of ancient Israel in a convincing way.

5 Julius Wellhausen: The historical setting

This part seeks to set Wellhausen's thinking in the intellectual context of his time.[166] To say that Wellhausen's view of ancient Israel's history and Israelite religion is predicated on the intellectual atmosphere of late 19th century is not the equivalent of denying his major contribution to biblical criticism.[167] But the fact is that Wellhausen did indeed build on his precursors, and was, of course, a child of his time. Wellhausen's thinking becomes clear when seen from the perspective of his own time.[168] However, two telling movements are often used to identify Wellhausen with the intellectual history of 19th century: romanticism and historicism. With respect to the first, there is a consensus that Wellhausen

---

165 Carl H. Becker described Wellhausen's peculiar way in dealing with the sources as follows: "Alle frühere Kritik war Einzelkritik gegenüber bestimmten Widersprüchen, erst Wellhausen übersah die Masse, gliederte sie und gewann neue Resultate durch Synopse und Kritik … Zunächst zog er die chronologischen Richtlinien, dann baute er die Quellenstellen ein, und schließlich zeichnete er mit genialem Strich die handelnden Personen." On this see Carl H. Becker, *Islamstudien*, 476.

166 On this issue see the brilliant contribution of John Barton, "Wellhausen's Prolegomena to the History of Israel: Influences and Effects," in *Text and Experience: Towards a Cultural Exegesis of the Bible* (ed. D. Smith-Christopher; Sheffield: Sheffield Academic Press, 1995), 316–29.

167 Smend has drawn attention to the fact that "from early on Wellhausen's opponents tried to discredit him by associating him with compromising movements of thought. Franz Delitzsch began it, by declaring Wellhausen's view to be "merely applications of Darwinisim to the sphere of theology and criticism." See Rudolf Smend, "The Work of Abraham Kuenen and Julius Wellhausen," 450.

168 Reinhard Kratz, however, warns not to overestimate this issue and – after having demonstrated the influence of his time on Wellhausen (the 'spectacles') – writes "….The fact that he was rooted in his time does not exclude the possibility that he can have seen some things correctly. At any rate Wellhausen's picture of Judaism, Christianity, and Islam cannot simply be bound up with the nineteenth century and its philosophies or ideologies." See Reinhard G. Kratz, "Eyes and Spectacles: Wellhausen's Method of Higher Criticism," 391.

in many ways owes much of his bias towards a natural and spontaneous beginning of religion to the romantic trend. As for the second, opinions vary widely. In
what follows I hope to demonstrate the impact on Wellhausen's thinking of the
intellectual environment of his time.

5.1 Wellhausen's bias towards romanticism

It was characteristic of the historical writing of the 19th century to revere the beginnings of human culture.[169] Therefore, it is assumed that Wellhausen's assessment of the religion of ancient Israel is indebted to the Romantic Movement.
Wellhausen saw the beginning of Israelite religion as the blossoming of life,
free impulses and spontaneous religion in intimate connection with the everyday
life of the people of Israel. The first and perhaps the most important supporter of
this view was Johann Gottfried Herder and his *Ideen zur Philosophie der Men-
schengeschichte* of 1784 – 1791. Herder saw human life as closely related to its setting in the natural world.[170]

To what extent was Wellhausen, in his depiction of ancient Israel, a follower
of Herder's philosophy? Biblical scholars, not few in number, tend to trace Wellhausen's understanding of the history of Israelite religion back to Herder's romantic view of history.[171] Herbert Hahn, for example, pointed out that Wellhausen's interpretation of ancient Israelite rituals as a natural expression of the
religious feelings and worship that grew out of life as a reflection of the human-
istic appreciation of religion was first expressed by Herder in the 18th century.[172]

---

169 As for the history of culture in Germany, see George W. Stocking, *Victorian Anthropology*
(New York: The Free Press, 1987), 20 – 25.
170 For romanticism and Herder, see R.G. Collingwood, *The Idea of History* (Oxford: Clarendon
Press, 1945). In this context, Blenkinsopp has suggested that, "It is an open question whether
Wellhausen's representation of ancient Israel as *Volk* which expressed itself in a religion of nature was directly indebted to the ideas of Romanticism. But his debt to the kind of romanticism
represented by Herder is unmistakably clear…" See Joseph Blenkinsopp, *Prophecy and Canon: A
Contribution to the Study of Jewish Origins* (University of Notre Dame Center for the Study of Judaism and Christianity in Antiquity 3; Notre Dame, 1977), 20.
171 Many scholars including (Kraus, Hahn, Perlitt and Rudolf Smend), support the idea that
Wellhausen is indebted to Herder. On this see R. J. Thompson, *Moses and the Law in a Century
of Criticism since Graf* (Supplements to Vetus Testamentum 19; Leiden: Brill, 1970), 46.
172 Herbert F. Hahn, *The Old Testament in Modern Research* (London: SCM Press, 1956), 13 –
14.

Similarly, Lothar Perlitt has mentioned that Wellhausen's dislike of anything artificial, schematic and constructed goes back to Herder.[173]

Furthermore, we note that Wellhausen emphasized the close relationship between religion and patriotism. This can be found in Wellhausen's famous quote, "Jehovah is the God of Israel, and Israel is the people of Jehovah."[174] Moreover, Wellhausen writes, "Jehovah and Israel, religion and patriotism...went hand in hand."[175] Ulrich Kusche has pointed to two important aspects that are peculiar to Wellhausen's historical interest and personal sympathies. There is first, "Das Werden des alten Israels." According to Kusche, Wellhausen was fascinated by the symbiosis of religion and patriotism which shows him the patriotic force of religion as an inspiring power of community self-assertion. The second factor is related to Wellhausen's presentation of the religion of ancient Israel and his emphasis upon religious individualism.[176]

In pursuing this further, it has been observed that individualism played a great role in Wellhausen's perception of ancient Israel. We read in *Prolegomena*, "Das göttliche Recht nicht bei der Institution, sondern bei dem Creator Spiritus, bei den Individuen."[177] However, Wellhausen asserted that Judaism left no place for the individual.[178] In Wellhausen's view, the idea of individuality appeared in Jeremiah's prophecy. He saw Jeremiah as the last prophet and felt that Israel's history basically ended with his prophecy.[179]

---

173 In addition, Perlitt said that Wellhausen's idyllic portrait of ancient Israel refers to Herder's preference for patriarchal times. See Lothar Perlitt, *Vatke und Wellhausen*, 211. Against this view, Weidner has argued that Wellhausen and Herder differ essentially in the way they describe Patriarchs. He notes that while Herder saw the Patriarchs "die vertraulichste, häuslichste, unschuldige wahrste Altväter- und Hirtengeschichte," Wellhausen, on the contrary characterized them as a warlike confederation." For more on this issue, see Daniel Weidner, "Geschichte gegen den Strich bürsten: Julius Wellhausen und die jüdische Gegengeschichte," 39.
174 Wellhausen, "Israel," 433.
175 Wellhausen, "Israel," 488.
176 Ulrich Kusche, *Die unterlegene Religion. Das Judentum im Urteil deutscher Alttestamentler: Zur Kritik theologischer Geschichtsschreibung* (Berlin: Institut Kirche und Judentum, 1991), 69–74.
177 Wellhausen, *Prolegomena zur Geschichte Israels* (1899⁵), 417. See also Rudolf Smend, *Das Mosebild von Heinrich Ewald bis Martin Noth* (Beiträge zur Geschichte der biblischen Exegese 3; Tübingen: Mohr (Siebeck), 1959), 33.
178 Wellhausen, *Prolegomena zur Geschichte Israels* (1899⁵), 417. Rudolf Smend has mentioned that Wellhausen in his bias towards individualism and dislike of the law was a child of the 19th century. See Rudolf Smend, *Julius Wellhausen: Ein Bahnbrecher in drei Disziplinen*, 53. See also Reinhard G. Kratz, "Eyes and Spectacles,".
179 Wellhausen, "Abriß der Geschichte Israels und Juda's," in *Skizzen und Vorarbeiten* I (Berlin, 1884), 74. See further Kusche, *Die unterlegene Religion*, 42.

In the light of what has been mentioned so far, it is easy to see Wellhausen's strong bias in favour of the free, individual, and natural elements of Israelite religion. At the same time, Wellhausen's dislike of religious institutions and fixed norms reflects the influence of the romantic tendency.[180] That Wellhausen was not in favour of dogmatic and formalized religion can be understood in his negative presentation of the post-exilic religion of Judaism.

5.2 Historicism[181]

Wellhausen was, without doubt, a historian.[182] In his undertaking to write the history of ancient Israel, he followed the German's principles of history writing laid down by Ranke and Mommsen.[183] It is also noted that the historical study of the source was a sound insight of German historiography.[184] Original sources were the main resource for writing history. Wellhausen's merit is that he attempted to write a history of Israel along modern historiographical lines.[185] Moreover,

---

180 Herbert Hahn drew the conclusion that Wellhausen's notion of the ideal society that had not yet become tangible in fixed, institutional form but was an association of free individuals guided by the unwritten laws of the natural order, was a Romantic notion akin to Herder's. On this see Herbert Hahn, "Wellhausen's Interpretation of Israel's Religious History," 304.

181 For the emergence of historicism in the 19th century and in biblical studies, see Gunter Scholtz, "The Phenomenon of 'Historicism' as a Backcloth of Biblical Scholarship," in *Hebrew Bible, Old Testament: The History of its Interpretation* III/1 (ed. Magne Sæbø; 2013), 64–89.

182 For a discussion see Horst Hoffmann, *Julius Wellhausen: Die Frage des absoluten Maßstabes seiner Geschichtsschreibung* (Marburg; University Dissertation, 1967). See further Lothar Perlitt, *Vatke und Wellhausen: Geschichtsphilosophische Voraussetzungen und historiographische Motive für die Darstellung der Religion und Geschichte Israels durch Wilhelm Vatke und Julius Wellhausen*. Also Friedemann Boschwitz, *Julius Wellhausen: Motive und Maßstäbe seiner Geschichtsschreibung*.

183 Clement pointed out, "Wellhausen was first and foremost a historian, well worthy of comparison with the giant figures of the Historismus movement in L. von Ranke, T. Mommsen and the earlier B. G. Niebuhr." See R. E. Clements, "The study of the Old Testament," in *Nineteenth Century Religious Thought in the West* III (ed. Ninian Smart; Cambridge: Cambridge University Press, 1985), 109–141 (128).

184 For a discussion see Perlitt, *Vatke und Wellhausen*. John Barton sums up Wellhausen's position, maintaining that Wellhausen followed the classical historians Niebuhr, Ranke, and Mommsen, precisely in their attempt to free historiography from its domination by any kind of philosophy. He quotes Perlitt who had pointed out that with Wellhausen we have a change of climate from philosophy to history, from systemization to the plain exegesis. On this see John Barton, *The Nature of Biblical Criticism*, 51.

185 In a letter to Abraham Kuenen (1828–1891), dated 5 August 1878, Wellhausen wrote: "Mein Ideal in allen Stücken ist Theodor Mommsen [1817–1903]" [My ideal in every detail

in perfecting the way for modern biblical studies, Wellhausen was not alone. He elaborated earlier efforts, including those of Graf *(Geschichtlichen Bücher des Alten Testaments, 1866)*, George *(Die älteren Jüdischen Feste, 1835)*, Vatke *(Die biblische Theologie, 1835)*, Keunen *(Godsdienst van Israel, 1869)*, Duhm *(Theologie der Propheten, 1875)*, and Kasier *(Das vorexilische Buch der Urgeschichte Israel, 1874)*.[186] In what follows I would like to highlight the efforts of those scholars who left their mark on Wellhausen's reconstruction of ancient Israel.

5.2.1 De Wette's Beiträge zur Einleitung in das Alte Testament
According to W. M. L. de Wette, the most important focus of attention for the scholar of Israelite history must be the history of religion. In the words of de Wette:

> Das wichtigste Augenmerk für den Forscher der israelitischen Geschichte muß die Geschichte der Religion und des Gottesdienstes seyn. Die Religion ist die Blüthe und Frucht der ganzen Israelitischen Geschichte, durch sie hat sich die unbedeutende Nation der Juden zum universalhistorischen Gang zu haben.[187]

It is well known that de Wette's *Beiträge zur Einleitung in das Alte Testament* laid the foundation for the historical reconstruction of ancient Israel.[188] This makes him the founder of modern biblical criticism.[189] Thomas Albert Howard sums up de Wette's position as follows:

> Although de Wette was not the first scholar to suggest that important developments in Judaism took place after Moses, his dissertation was later acclaimed because he was the first

---

is Theodor Mommsen]. See John H. Hayes, "Historiographical Approaches: Survey and Principles" in *Method Matters: Essays on the Interpretation of the Hebrew Bible in Honor of David L. Petersen* (ed. Joel M. LeMon and Kent Harold Richards; Resources for Biblical Study 56; Atlanta: Society of Biblical Literature, 2009), 195–212 (208).

186 See E. Kautzsch, Rec. "Wellhausen, J., 'Geschichte Israels".

187 W. M. L. de Wette, *Beiträge zur Einleitung in das Alte Testament: Erster und zweiter Band* (first published in Halle, 1806/1807, quotations in this study follow the reprinted edition of Hildsheim; Olms, 1971), 4.

188 For de Wette's works on the Old and New Testaments, see Rudolf Smend, *Wilhelm Martin Leberecht de Wettes Arbeit am Alten und am Neuen Testament* (Basel: Helbing & Lichtenhahn, 1958). See further Thomas Römer, "Higher Criticism: The Historical and Literary-Critical Approach – with Special Reference to the Pentateuch," in *Hebrew Bible, Old Testament: The History of its Interpretation* III/I (ed. Magne Sæbø; 2013), 393–423.

189 J. W. Rogerson, *W.M.L. de Wette, Founder of Modern Biblical Criticism: An Intellectual Biography* (JSOTSup126; Sheffield: Sheffield Academic Press, 1992).

to hint at a picture of Israel's history that differed markedly from that offered in the Old Testament itself. This innovation was the crucial idea behind his subsequent *Beiträge*, which laid the groundwork for Old Testament criticism in the nineteenth and twentieth centuries. It received classical formulation in the work of Julius Wellhausen.[190]

Wellhausen's understanding of Israel's history seems to have followed the lead of de Wette's *Beiträge.* Wellhausen himself acknowledged that many of his claims could be glimpsed in the works of de Wette.[191] In his assessment of de Wette's contribution, Wellhausen clearly stated that his work was an "epoch-making pioneer of historical criticism."[192] It was de Wette's pioneer work on the Old Testament that provided Wellhausen with the overall picture of Israel's history.[193] Furthermore, one cannot fail to notice that de Wette's hypothesis was taken on in Wellhausen's *Prolegomena zur Geschichte Israels.* This appears in Wellhausen's attempt to use historical criticism as the basis for writing the history of Israel. Kusche thus points out, "Von de Wette sieht Wellhausen die entscheidenden Anstöße für die Kritik der Quellen und ihre historische Zuordnung ausgehen."[194] In addition, de Wette was the first to relate biblical texts with historical events, that is, to date Deuteronomy to Josiah's time. Wellhausen, in reconstructing the history of worship in Israel, took de Wette's dating of Deuteronomy as his point of departure. Moreover, Wellhausen connected the centralization of worship with the Book of Deuteronomy. In essence, Wellhausen, in linking texts with institutions, was clearly a disciple of de Wette.[195]

5.2.2 Vatke's Biblische Theologie

In his introduction to *Prolegomena* Wellhausen writes, "My inquiry proceeds on a broader basis than that of Graf, and comes nearer to that of Vatke, from whom indeed I gratefully acknowledge myself to have learnt best and most."[196] It is worthwhile noting that Vatke's *Biblische Theologie* appeared in 1835, some

---

190 Thomas A. Howard, *Religion and the Rise of Historicism: W.M.L. de Wette, Jacob Burckhardt, and the Theological Origins of Nineteenth-Century Historical Consciousness* (Cambridge: Cambridge University Press 2000), 39.
191 Rudolf Smend, *Deutsche Alttestamentler in drei Jahrhunderten* (Göttingen: Vandenhoeck & Ruprecht, 1989), 38.
192 Wellhausen, *Prolegomena*, 4.
193 Kraus, *Geschichte der historisch-kritischen Erforschung des Alten Testaments*, 260.
194 Kusche, *Die unterlegene Religion: Das Judentum im Urteil deutscher Alttestamentler*, 62.
195 James. W. Watts, *Persia and Torah: The Theory of Imperial Authorization of the Pentateuch* (SBL symposium series 17; Atlanta: Society of Biblical Literature, 2001), 181.
196 Wellhausen, *Prolegomena*, 13.

forty years before Wellhausen's *Geschichte Israel*. Nevertheless, Wellhausen drew attention to the significance of Vatke's book and its contribution to understanding Israelite religion. In referring to Vatke's effort, Wellhausen tells us:

> The firemen never came near the spot where the conflagration raged; for it is only within the region of religious antiquities and dominant religious ideas, the region which Vatke in his *Biblische Theologie* had occupied in its full breadth, and where the real battle first kindled that the controversy can be brought to a definite issue.[197]

Moreover, Wellhausen praised Vatke's attempt to study the theocratic idea.[198] Wellhausen writes, "It is perhaps the principal merit of Vatke's *Biblical Theology* to have traced through the centuries the rise of the theocracy and the metamorphosis of the idea to an institution."[199] All of these outstanding insights of Vatke's *Biblische Theologie* paved the way for Wellhausen's great synthesis on the history of Israelite religion. Wellhausen described Vatke's *Biblische Theologie* as "the most important contribution ever made to the history of ancient Israel."[200]

It can be said that Vatke's major contribution to the history of Israelite religion is his study of the religious institutions in ancient Israel. He described the religious development in ancient Israel as having passed through different stages. In this regard, we note that Wellhausen's sketch of Israelite religion bases some of its claims on Vatke. However, Robertson Smith rightly remarked on the difference between Vatke's systematic presentation and Wellhausen's critical analysis. He wrote, "But Wellhausen's argument is much more telling than Vatke's because it rests on thorough critical analysis of the sources of the Pentateuch and historical books of the Old Testament."[201] Kusche sums up Vatke's position and its relation to Wellhausen as follows:

> Wellhausen folgt Vatke in der zeitlichen Ansetzung des Judentums nicht, er läßt es – wie de Wette – mit dem Exil beginnen. Andererseits hebt Wellhausen wie Vatke zahlreiche Elemente der exilisch – nachexilischen Zeit hervor, die bei Vatke gerade den religionsgeschichtlichen Fortschritt der alttestamentlich-kanonischen Religion belegen. Eine dialekti-

---

197 Wellhausen, *Prolegomena*, 12.
198 Nevertheless Weidner has pointed out that while Vatke regarded theocracy as an idea of monarchy, Wellhausen wrote in Prolegomena, "The Mosaic theocracy...is itself not a state at all, but an unpolitical artificial product...and foreign rule is its necessary counterpart." See Wellhausen, *Prolegomena*, 422. See also Daniel Weidner, "Geschichte gegen den Strich bürsten: Julius Wellhausen und die jüdische 'Gegengeschichte,'" 54.
199 Wellhausen, *Prolegomena*, 411.
200 W. R. Smith, *Lectures & Essays of William Robertson Smith*, 602.
201 W. R. Smith, *Lectures & Essays of William Robertson Smith*, 602.

sche Beziehung zwischen kanonischer und nachkanonischer Entwicklung, die für Vatke zentral ist, findet sich bei Wellhausen nicht.[202]

However, we cannot discuss the influence of Vatke on Wellhausen without mentioning the relation of both to Hegel's philosophy. The claim that Wellhausen's presentation of the history of Israel is built on Hegelian philosophy goes back to Martin Kegel who in 1923 wrote: "Hegel begat Vatke, Vatke begat Wellhausen."[203] In fact, much has been said on this subject and there is no need to become involved in such persistent controversy.[204] Perhaps we should quote Wellhausen's words in this discussion. In his letter of condolence to Vatke's son Theodor after the death of his father, Wellhausen wrote, "Hegelian or not: that is to me all the same, however your blessed father had a remarkably true feel for the individuality of matters."[205]

5.2.3 Graf's Die geschichtlichen Bücher des Alten Testaments

In his book *Die geschichtlichen Bücher des Alten Testaments* (1866), Graf arrived at the conclusion that the priestly cultic law in Leviticus and Numbers postdates Deuteronomy.[206] Graf's hypothesis was not merely a pivotal point in Wellhausen's reconstruction of the history of ancient Israel. Rather, it played a substan-

---

202 Kusche, *Die unterlegene Religion*, 65.

203 M. Kegel, *Los von Wellhausen!: Ein Beitrag zur Neuorientierung in der alttestamentlichen Wissenschaft* (Gütersloh: Bertelsmann, 1923), 10.

204 Herbert Hahn, for example, refuted the assertion that Wellhausen was influenced by Hegel's philosophy. He wrote: "Wellhausen's view of Israelite antiquity does not fit the Hegelian philosophy. Hegel described ultimate reality as in a continuous process of becoming…Wellhausen saw no progress toward complete realization in the history of Israel's religion." On this see Herbert Hahn, "Wellhausen's interpretation," 303. Perlitt, too, denied Hegelian influence on Wellhausen and connected Wellhausen with the tradition of German Historicism (Ranke, Mommsen). See Perlitt, *Vatke und Wellhausen*. Soggin made a good point when he remarked that "those who have rejected the documentary hypothesis as formulated by Wellhausen have sought its weak points in a possible Hegelian derivation, arguing that the system could be explained on the basis of this dependence. In other words, first Vatke and then Graf and Wellhausen would be said to have done no more than apply to the study of the Pentateuch a scheme drawn from Hegelian philosophy". See J. Alberto Soggin, *Introduction to the Old Testament*, 85.

205 Henning Graf Reventlow, *History of Biblical Interpretation*, vol. 4: *From the Enlightenment to the Twentieth Century* (Atlanta: Society of Biblical Literature, 2010), 323. See further Rudolf Smend, *Briefe: Julius Wellhausen* (Tübingen: Mohr Siebeck, 2013).

206 For a discussion of Graf's hypothesis and his work on the Old Testament, see Joachim Conrad, *Karl Heinrich Grafs Arbeit am Alten Testament: Studien zu einer wissenschaftlichen Biographie* (BZAW 425; Berlin De Gruyter, 2011).

tial role in shaping Wellhausen's experience and ideas. Wellhausen tells us how he came to know the Graf's hypothesis: "In the course of a casual visit in Göttingen in the summer of 1867, I learned through Ritschl that Karl Heinrich Graf placed the law later than the Prophets, and, almost without knowing his reasons for the hypothesis, I was prepared to accept it."[207]

It has been said that Wellhausen's picture of the history of Israelite religion owes too much to Graf's hypothesis.[208] Nevertheless, Wellhausen plainly stated that his procedure differed in some aspects from that of Graf. Thus, Wellhausen said, "I differ from Graf chiefly in this, that I always go back to the centralisation of the cultus, and deduce from it the particular divergences."[209] In addition, Wellhausen pointed out that he paid more attention than Graf did to "the change of ruling ideas which runs parallel with the change in the institutions and usages of worship."[210] In comparison to Graf's hypothesis, Wellhausen identified his position in the following manner:

> Not everything that I have brought forward in the history of the cultus and the tradition is a proof of the hypothesis; there is much that serves merely to explain phenomena at the basis of the hypothesis, and cannot be used as proving it...My procedure has intentionally differed from that of Graf in this respect. He brought forward his arguments somewhat unconnectedly, not seeking to change the general view which prevailed of the history of Israel.[211]

5.2.4 Ewald's Geschichte des Volkes Israel [212]

From the outset, it seems clear that Wellhausen wanted to be an historian. His interest in history, however, was kindled by Ewald.[213] Eduard Schwartz quotes

---

207 Wellhausen, *Prolegomena*, 3. Only a few would agree with Levenson in his contention that "it is fair to say that all his [Wellhausen] conceptual works on Israelite religion and Judaism are merely a footnote to that experience in the summer of 1867." On this see Jon D. Levenson, "The Hebrew Bible, the Old Testament, and Historical Criticism," in *The Future of Biblical Studies: The Hebrew Scriptures* (ed. Richard Elliott Friedman; Semeia studies 16; Atlanta: Scholars Press, 1987), 19–59 (32).
208 See, for example, Johs. Pedersen, " Die Auffassung vom Alten Testament," 171. Aslo Herbert Hahn, *Old Testament in Modern Research*, 12. See further Kusche, *Die unterlegene Religion*, 32. Joel S. Baden, *J, E, and the Redaction of the Pentateuch* (Forschungen zum Alten Testament 68; Tübingen: Mohr Siebeck, 2009), 32.
209 Wellhausen, *Prolegomena*, 368.
210 Wellhausen, *Prolegomena*, 368.
211 Wellhausen, *Prolegomena*, 368.
212 Heinrich Ewald, *Geschichte des Volkes Israel bis Christus* (Göttingen, 1843–1859).
213 Raymond F. Surburg remarked, "Ewald's presentation of the history of Israel fascinated Wellhausen, because the former was not a dry historian, but a lecturer who depicted historical relationships in glowing colors. In the estimation of Wellhausen, Ewald portrayed the religious

Wellhausen as saying, "Die theologischen Probleme verstand ich nicht. Mich interessierte Ewald und darum die Bibel, in der ich von Haus aus sehr gut Bescheid wusste."[214] As we have seen, Wellhausen derived the sense of literary criticism and connecting texts with institutions from de Wette. However, it was through Ewald that Wellhausen recognized the need for philology to understand the meaning of the Old Testament text. He came to know the Semitic languages through Ewald's teaching.[215]

Ewald was a pioneer in the field of Semitic languages. In his appraisal of Ewald, Wellhausen wrote, "Sein Talent für Beobachtung und Darstellung des Sprachlichen war groß, und auf dem Gebiete der Sprachwissenschaft liegen nicht nur seine ersten, sondern auch seine wichtigsten und originellsten Leistungen."[216] Moreover, Wellhausen affirmed that Ewald was a great teacher, "Ewald ist der Lehrer ohne Gleichen, von dessen Ideen die heutige semitische Philologie willig und widerwillig lebt."[217] All of this indicates that Wellhausen recognized the significance of Ewald's philological studies in understanding the text of the Old Testament. As O'Neill has noted, "Wellhausen learned from Ewald to work first by the closest examination of the detail of an ancient text and then to move from the smallest detail out towards a natural and balanced and simple picture of the complicated whole."[218] Nonetheless, Wellhausen recognized that his teacher had not followed the principles of methodological criticism as laid down by de Wette and Vatke. In Wellhausen's judgment, Ewald was 'der große Aufhalter' of critical research. Here is Wellhausen's assessment of Ewald:

---

content of the Old Testament as an entity that had developed and occurred in history. It was this procedure which sparked him to undertake the project of setting forth the history of the Old Testament as an historical process within which biblical religion had grown and ripened. Wellhausen's *Prolegomena to the History* of Israel endeavoured to do just that." See Raymond F. Surburg, "Wellhausen Evaluated after a Century of Influence," 79.

214 Eduard Schwartz, *Gesammelte Schriften I, Vergangene Gegenwærtigkeiten: Exoterica, Inter arma et post cladem, Dis manibus* (Berlin: Gruyter, 1938), 326–361.

215 Lothar Perlitt, *Allein mit dem Wort: Theologische Studien: Lothar Perlitt zum 65. Geburtstag* (ed. Hermann Spieckermann; Göttingen: Vandenhoeck & Ruprecht, 1995), 251.

216 See Wellhauseun's evalution of Ewlad in Wellhausen, *Grundrisse zum Alten Testament* (Theologische Bücherei 27, Altes Testament; München: Kaiser, 1965), 122.

217 See Wellhausen's contribution in F. Bleek, *Einleitung in das Alte Tetsament* (Berlin: Reimer, 1878), 644–656 (655).

218 John. C. O'Neill, *The Bible's Authority: A Portrait Gallery of Thinkers from Lessing to Bultmann* (Edinburgh: T & T Clark, 1991), 199.

> Er ist im Gegenteil der große Aufhalter gewesen der durch seinen autoritativen Einfluß bewirkt hat, daß die bereits vor ihm gewonnene richtige Einsicht in den Gang der israelitischen Geschichte lange Zeit nicht hat durchdringen können.[219]

In the preceding discussion, I have placed Wellhausen's thoughts in the historical context of the great critics of biblical studies. It would not be an exaggeration to say that Wellhausen succeeded in perfecting the historical critical method. His works on the Old Testament summed up more than a century of research in the critical study of the Old Testament. In addition, Wellhausen laid the foundation for subsequent biblical criticism by answering many questions raised by the historical criticism of the 19th century.

As we have seen, Wellhausen elaborated on the results of de Wette's literary and historical criticism. He benefited also from the works of Vatke and Graf concerning the religious development and the history of Israelite religion. In addition, Wellhausen learned how to solve problems related to philological issues, Ewald's legacy. With the help of all of these thinkers, Wellhausen developed a reconstructed picture of ancient Israelite history and religion based on results obtained from critical investigation. In a concise description of Wellhausen's historical setting and intellectual context, Reinhard Kratz writes:

> Everything seems to fit into the picture: the mixture of objectivity and subjectivity in the application of textual, literary, and tendency criticism and in the historiographical account, the sympathy for great personalities like the prophets and for the secular state with a monarchical constitution, the predilection for 'natural' origins, paganism, and the symbiosis of nation and religion, and the antipathy to any form of dogmatism and institution and the notion of a development from one to the other. Here Wellhausen seems to represent a way of thinking which combines elements of Romanticism, German Idealism, and Historicism and finds its fulfilment in the foundation of the German Reich under Bismarck.[220]

As we shall see, Wellhausen proceeded from critical analysis of the sources to a study of Israel's religious history and a historical reconstruction of ancient Israel. His works on the Old Testament is a summation of the criticism involving literary sources, religious history and historical reconstruction. Wellhausen was convinced that literary sources could be used for historical purposes. The history of ancient Israel is, in Wellhausen's view, the history of its religious development.

---

219 Wellhausen, *Grundrisse zum Alten Testament*, 131–132.
220 Reinhard G. Kratz, "Eyes and Spectacles," 391.

Chapter Two:
History of Israelite Religion

1 Introduction

This part aims to elucidate Wellhausen's interpretation of the history of Israelite religion. My investigation is guided by two assumptions. The first has to do with Wellhausen's reconstruction of ancient Israel, that is, his belief that the history of ancient Israel is the history of its religion. As for the second assumption, it is well known that Wellhausen identifies three phases of religious development in ancient Israel. These three phases reflect three different historical periods and can be recognized in the three literary strata of the Pentateuch. According to Wellhausen's structure, the first stage of religious development is manifested in the Jehovistic traditions referred to as (JE). Deuteronomy (D) refers to the second stage of religious development. The third phase of Israelite religion is to be found in the Priestly Code of the Pentateuch (P).

Building on results gained from literary analysis of the sources, Wellhausen saw the development of Israelite religion as moving from the naive and spontaneous Jehovistic tradition through to the centralization of the cult as found in Deuteronomy, to the formal and ritual Judaism of the Priestly Code. Considering these three stages of religious development in ancient Israel is, I would suggest, the key to understanding Wellhausen's hypothesis. Moreover, I have found that Wellhausen's view of Israelite religion, history, and literature is interrelated and forms an integrated whole. In what follows, I show that Wellhausen's historical reconstruction of the history of Israelite religion reflects his schematic three phases of the history of the pentateuchal sources. My discussion starts by giving an outline of Wellhausen's hypothesis on the place of law in the history of ancient Israel. I will then proceed to highlight Wellhausen's main phases of religious development.

2 The place of law in the history of Israel

It was one of the great contributions of Old Testament criticism that the "law" has become important for understanding the history of ancient Israel. This appears in Wellhausen's *Prolegomena to the History of Ancient Israel*, which is based on a study of law.[221] Wellhausen's interpretation of the history of Israelite religion was influenced by a reconstruction of the role of law in Israel's history.[222] Moreover, Wellhausen believed that with the introduction of the law, the history of ancient Israel came to an end and a new, artificial history was created.

Wellhausen was not the first to discover the importance of studying the laws as a key to understanding the ancient Israelite religion. The idea goes back to outstanding historians such as Theodor Mommsen and Fustel de Coulanges.[223] Wellhausen's interest in the place of law in Israel's history began early in his student days. He tells us of his personal experience as follows:

> In my early student days I was attracted by the stories of Saul and David, Ahab and Elijah; the discourses of Amos and Isaiah laid strong hold on me, and I read myself well into the prophetic and historical books of the Old Testament. Thanks to such aids as were accessible to me, I even considered that I understood them tolerably, but at the same time was troubled with a bad conscience, as if I were beginning with the roof instead of the foundation; for I had no thorough acquaintance with the Law, of which I was accustomed to be told that it was the basis and postulate of the whole literature. At last I took courage and made my way through Exodus, Leviticus, Numbers, and even through Knobel's Commentary to these books. But it was in vain that I looked for the light which was to be shed from this source on the historical and prophetical books. On the contrary, my enjoyment of the latter was marred by the Law; it did not bring them any nearer me, but intruded itself uneasily, like a ghost that makes a noise indeed, but is not visible and really affects nothing. Even where there were points of contact between it and them, differences also made themselves felt, and I found it impossible to give a candid decision in favour of the priority of the Law. Dimly I began to perceive that throughout there was between them all the difference that separates two wholly distinct worlds. Yet, so far from attaining clear conceptions, I only fell into deeper confusion, which was worse confounded by the explanations of Ewald in the second volume of history of Israel. At last, in the course of a casual visit in Gottingen in the summer of 1867, I learned through Ritschl that Karl Heinrich Graf placed the law later than the Prophets, and, almost without knowing his reasons for the hypothesis, I

---

221 For a discussion, see more recently Jeffrey Stackert, *A Prophet like Moses: Prophecy, Law, and Israelite Religion* (New York: Oxford University Press, 2014).

222 See John H. Hayes, "Wellhausen as a Historian of Israel," in *Julius Wellhausen and his Prolegomena to the History of Ancient Israel* (ed. Douglas A. Knight; Chico: Scholars Press, 1983), 37–60.

223 Baruch Halpern, *The First Historians: The Hebrew Bible and History* (University Park.: Pennsylvania State University Press, 1996), 22. Mommsen dedicated much time to Roman law and de Coulanges studied the cult and religion in Greek and Roman cultures. In addition, Jean Louis Ska has mentioned the influence of Edouard Reuss on Wellhausen in this regard. He notes that Wellhausen in his *Prolegomena* had quoted Reuss at length because of his insistence on the importance of law for the historian. See Jean Louis Ska, "The 'History of Israel': Its Emergence as an Independent Discipline," in *Hebrew Bible, Old Testament: The History of its Interpretation* III/I (ed. Magne Sæbø; 2013), 307–345 (339).

was prepared to accept it; I readily acknowledged to myself the possibility of understanding Hebrew antiquity without the book of the Torah.[224]

It was out of this experience that Wellhausen realized that the "law" is the key to understanding the history of ancient Israel. He undertook to study the law and determine its place in the history of Israel. The law thus turns into the subject of Wellhausen's *Prolegomena* in the history of Israel and it also becomes the focus of his inquiry into the history of Israelite religion. Although Wellhausen elaborated on the efforts of earlier thinkers, it was in his *Prolegomena* that the insights of Martin Leberecht de Wette, Eduard Reuss, Leopold George, Wilhelm Vatke, and Graf-Kuenen found clear explanation.

Not only did the law become the central idea in Wellhausen's investigation, but it also worked as the starting point of his inquiry into the history of Israel. In the introduction to his masterpiece *Prolegomena to the History of Ancient Israel*, Wellhausen says:

> In the following pages it is proposed to discuss the place in history of the "law of Moses"; more precisely, the question to be considered is whether that law is the starting-point for the history of ancient Israel, or not rather for that of Judaism, i.e., of the religious communion which survived the destruction of the nation by the Assyrians and Chaldaeans.[225]

Wellhausen goes on to explain what he means by law. In his words, "The Law, whose historical position we have to determine, is the so-called "main stack," which, both by its contents and by its origin, is entitled to be called the Priestly Code."[226] Wellhausen precisely clarifies his procedure concerning the place of law in the following manner:

> The point is not to prove that the Mosaic Law was not in force in the period before the exile. There are in the Pentateuch three strata of law and three strata of tradition, and the problem is to place them in their true historical order. So far as the Jehovist and Deuteronomy are concerned, the problem has found a solution which may be said to be accepted universally, and all that remains is to apply to the Priestly Code, also the procedure by which the succession and the date of these two works has been determined, that procedure consisting in the comparison of them with the ascertained facts of Israelite history.[227]

---

224 Wellhausen, *Prolegomena*, 10–11.
225 Wellhausen, *Prolegomena*, 1.
226 Wellhausen, *Prolegomena*, 8.
227 Wellhausen, *Prolegomena*, 366.

As it can be observed from Wellhausen's programmatic plan, there are three law codes in the Pentateuch and "the problem is to place them in their true historical order".[228] In so doing, Wellhausen followed the lead of de Wette, who had identified the book discovered in the temple in 621 BCE, during the time of King Josiah, with the book of Deuteronomy. According to the account in 2 kgs 22–23, Josiah launched a reformation of the cult based on the book found in the temple, that is, Deuteronomy. As a result of Josiah's reform, it is said that the cult was centralized in Jerusalem and prohibited elsewhere. Thus, the centralization of the cult became the central focus in Wellhausen's study of cultic and legal institutions in ancient Israel. By analyzing the major law codes in the Pentateuch, Wellhausen came to the conclusion that while the Book of Deuteronomy commanded the unity of the cultus, this is predicated on the Priestly Code.[229] This helps Wellhausen to arrange the laws in their chronological order and at the same time to determine their religious content. Thus, according to Wellhausen, the Jehovistic law corresponded to the 'older practice' of Israelite religion before centralization of the cult.[230] Then comes 'the original author of the centralization', the deuteronomic lawgiver.[231] "The centralisation of the cultus, the revolutionising influence of which is seen in the Priestly Code, is begun by Deuteronomy."[232] Accordingly, Wellhausen placed the laws of the Priestly Code in the second stage of legislation after Deuteronomy.[233]

Having arranged the chronological order of the three major codes in the Pentateuch, Wellhausen arrived at the idea that the laws of the Priestly Code were a post-exilic legislation. The law of the Priestly Code was made a law-book of Moses by Ezra and Nehemiah.[234] In Wellhausen's opinion, the Priestly Code is

---

228 Wellhausen, *Prolegomena*, 366.
229 Wellhausen, *Prolegomena*, 35.
230 Wellhausen, *Prolegomena*, 95.
231 Wellhausen, *Prolegomena*, 124.
232 Wellhausen, *Prolegomena*, 104.
233 Wellhausen, *Prolegomena*, 408. In addition to the centralization idea, Wellhausen depended on his inquiry into the place of law on studying the history of cultic practice and religious institution. Herbert Hahn has pointed out that Wellhausen "by combining Graf's method of arranging the ritual laws in logical sequence with Vatke's program for studying the religious institution of successive historical periods, [he] was able to show not only that there was an intimate connection between the succession of the law codes and the evolution of religious practice, but also that these parallel developments were intelligible only in the sequence which placed the P code and the P institution at the end." On this see Herbert F. Hahn, *The Old Testament in Modern Research*, 12.
234 Wellhausen, *Prolegomena*, 408.

"ein streng jüdisches Ritualgesetz."[235] Moreover, Wellhausen emphasized that
the law is not the starting point of Israel's history, but rather the product of Israel's intellectual development. "Das Gesetz ist das Produkt der geistigen Entwicklung Israels, nicht ihr Ausgangspunkt."[236] Wellhausen's conviction that
the law was not the starting point of Israel's history led him to place the law
after the prophets. As he puts it, "Nach den Propheten, hat das Gesetz (a potiori)
seine Stelle, und das ist es nicht mehr latent, sondern plötzlich sehr wirksam. Es
ist nicht israelitische, sondern jüdische."[237]

Thus, the place of law in the history of Israel was determined. It was the
product of the Jewish community who lived in the Babylonian exile. It did not
predate the prophets, but came afterwards. Rudolf Smend mentions that Wellhausen, before the appearance of his *Geschichte Israel 1* in 1878, wrote to Kuenen
on 28 August, 1874, telling him of his future plans, "If I can, in the next few years
I am going to write a book called something like "the Law and the Prophets."[238]
Two important things have to be observed: first, it was clear from the beginning
that Wellhausen planned to study the law. Second Wellhausen had in mind the
relationship of the law and the prophets. Later, Wellhausen undertook to determine this relationship.[239] He saw that the prophets and the law represented two
different worlds. Wellhausen's opinion that the law was later than the prophets
caused a stir. The late dating of the law changed the conventional picture of the
development of Israelite religion. To put it differently, it meant that the real
source of the people's religious spirit lay not with an ancient lawgiver, but
with the prophets.[240] In Wellhausen's judgment:

> Die Propheten reden nicht aus dem Gesetz, sondern aus dem Geist; Jahve spricht durch sie,
> nicht Moses. Ihre Thora ist ebensoviel wert als die Moses' und entspringt dem gleichen,
> perennierenden Quell. Das Wort Jahves ist das lebendige Wort in ihrem Munde, nichts ein für

---

235 Wellhausen, *Israelitische und jüdische Geschichte*, 175.
236 Wellhausen, *Israelitische und jüdische Geschichte*, 15.
237 Wellhausen, *Grundrisse zum Alten Testament*, 72.
238 Rudolf Smend, "The Work of Abraham Kuenen and Julius Wellhausen," 444.
239 Zimmerli pointed out that Wellhausen developed his great thesis under the key sentence:
"The law is later than the prophets." He explained Wellhausen's position concerning the relationship of law and Prophets as follows: "He saw them in a historical sequence. Prophecy
was a breaking through of truth, whereas in the law a particular hardening of this truth took
place. Moses, when dissociated from such a law encrusted in statutes, representing the beginning of a genuine simplicity which preceded both... Wellhausen never worked out a theological
concept of law. For him revelation took place in the course of history, and reached its climax in
the gospel. See Walter Zimmerli, *The Law and the Prophets*, 26.
240 Ronald E. Clements, *A Century of Old Testament Study* (Guildford, London: Lutterworth
Press, 1976), 11.

allemal Abgeschlossenes und Festgelegtes. Der Begriff einer schriftlichen Offenbarung ist ihnen fremd.[241]

Here Wellhausen emphasizes that the prophet knew only the living word of Yahweh not a written law. Moreover, Wellhausen demonstrated that the religion of Israel, under the impact of the law, lost its free impulse and the words of the prophets were overpowered. As Wellhausen wrote:

> The great pathologist of Judaism is quite right: in the Mosaic theocracy the cultus became a pedagogic instrument of discipline. It is estranged from the heart; its revival was due to old custom, it would never have blossomed again of itself. It no longer has its roots in childlike impulse, it is a dead work, in spite of all the importance attached to it, nay, just because of the anxious conscientiousness with which it was gone about. At the restoration of Judaism the old usages were patched together in a new system, which, however, only served as the form to preserve something that was nobler in its nature, but could not have been saved otherwise than in a narrow shell that stoutly resisted all foreign influences. That heathenism in Israel against which the prophets vainly protested was inwardly overcome by the law on its own ground; and the cultus, after nature had been killed in it, became the shield of supernaturalistic monotheism.[242]

The implication of Wellhausen's dating of the law was of far greater importance to his understanding of the history of Israel. He proposed that Israel's history came to an end with the introduction of the law. Thus, in *Abriss der Geschichte Israels und Juda's*, Wellhausen made it clear that the introduction of the law by Ezra marked the end of the history of Israel: "So bildet die Einführung des Gesetzes durch Ezra, das Endresultat der Geschichte Israels, auch äußerlich einen notgedrungenen Abschluss."[243] Furthermore, Wellhausen affirmed that the tradition had been systematically translated into the mode of view of the Law, as in Chronicles. Israel's past is remodelled on the basis of the law.[244] Wellhausen went further and explained the impact of the law of the Priestly Code on the writing of Israel's history in Chronicles:

> The fact that Chronicles represents the Israelite history in accordance with the Priestly Code has had the effect of causing its view of the history to be involuntarily taken as fundamental, but ought much rather to have caused it to be left altogether out of account where the object [was] to ascertain what was the real and genuine tradition.[245]

---

241 Wellhausen, *Grundrisse zum Alten Testament*, 75.
242 Wellhausen, *Prolegomena*, 425.
243 Wellhausen, "Abriß der Geschichte Israels und Juda's," 86.
244 Wellhausen, *Prolegomena*, 294.
245 Wellhausen, *Prolegomena*, 41.

Thus, Wellhausen noted that Israel's history as it appears in Chronicles is cut off from the past of the nation and lost its reality. As Wellhausen puts it:

> Es ist eine wahre Travestie der Geschichte, die geistliche moralisierende Tendenz vernichtet den ästhetischen Wahrheitssinn, stellt die Dinge nicht dar wie sie sind, sondern verwendet sie nur als Beispiele für ein paar dürftige Ideen und dichtet sie nötigenfalls mit großer Dreistigkeit danach um.[246]

In conclusion, Wellhausen saw that the introduction of the law in the post-exilic period not only cut the nation off from its past but also conveyed an unrealistic picture of its history. As Wellhausen puts it, "Das Gesetz verlieh der jüdischen Religion ihr eigentliches Gepräge...Die Juden führten kein geschichtliches Leben, sie malten sich die alte Zeit nach ihren Ideen aus und gestalteten die kommende nach ihren Wünschen."[247] Wellhausen goes into more depth on this direction, telling us that the reconstructed history of the Chronicle did not correspond to facts:

> It is not the case that the Jews had any profound respect for their ancient history ... It is well known that there have never been more audacious inventors of history than the rabbis. But Chronicles affords evidence that this evil propensity goes back to a very early time, its root the dominating influence of the Law, being the root of Judaism itself.[248]

3 The religion of ancient Israel

By the religion of "ancient Israel" Wellhausen meant the early phase of Israelite religion as depicted in the Jehovistic tradition of the Pentateuch which preceded the prophetic reformation. That is to say, Wellhausen distinguishes the Jehovistic traditions in the Pentateuch as reflecting the first stage of religious development in Israel. In Wellhausen's judgment, at this stage Israelite religion was in most intimate and manifold connection with ordinary life.[249] By inquiring into the history of worship and the history of tradition, Wellhausen came up with the idea that the religion of old Israel differed entirely from the religion of Judaism. He started by investigating the history of worship in Israel and distinguished three main stages: the stage prior to prophetic reform, the centralization of

---

246 Wellhausen, *Israelitische und jüdische Geschichte,* 187.
247 Wellhausen, "Abriß der Geschichte Israels und Juda's," 90.
248 Wellhausen, *Prolegomena,* 161.
249 Wellhausen, *Prolegomena,* 76.

cult, and the later stage which was marked by the dominating influence of the law.

To begin with, Wellhausen identified five aspects in the history of worship. These are: the place of worship, sacrifice, the sacred feasts, the Priests and the Levites, and the endowment of the Clergy. As for the first stage of religious development in Israel, Wellhausen points out, "Religious worship was a natural thing in Hebrew antiquity; it was the blossom of life, the heights and depths of which it was its business to transfigure and glorify."[250] He maintains that a multiplicity of altars existed in early Israel.[251] The restriction of worship to a specific or one legitimate place was unknown to the people of ancient Israel even as a pious desire.[252] The cultus is very old and goes back to pre-Mosaic usage. Sacrificial worship "rested upon customs inherited from the fathers."[253] Local shrines were the place where Israelites carried out their sacrifices in a very spontaneous way. Sacrifice was at first elementary and what was chiefly considered was the quantity and quality of the gifts.[254] Respecting the sacred feasts in ancient Israel, Wellhausen suggested that feasts were a purely natural occasions and had a joyous character. In addition, festivals rest upon agriculture because the fruitful soil was the "object of religion".[255]

In the Jehovistic portion of the Pentateuch, as Wellhausen observes, the high priest was left out in the cold, "for the really acting heads of the people are the Judges, people of an entirely different stamp, whose authority, resting on no official position, but on strength of personality and on the force of circumstances, seldom extends beyond the limits of their tribe."[256] In Wellhausen's view, "Until the cultus has become in some measure centralized the priests have no *locus standi*."[257] This inconspicuous position of the priest refers to the earliest period of the history of Israel.[258] On the same line, Wellhausen affirms that hereditary clergy did not exist from the very beginning of the history of Israel.[259] As for the endowment of the clergy, he makes it clear that in the earlier times, the priest was allowed to participate in a share of the offerings. "But he does not appear to

---

250 Wellhausen, *Prolegomena*, 77.
251 Wellhausen, *Prolegomena*, 29.
252 Wellhausen, *Prolegomena*, 22.
253 Wellhausen, *Prolegomena*, 61.
254 Wellhausen, *Prolegomena*, 61.
255 Wellhausen, *Prolegomena*, 91.
256 Wellhausen, *Prolegomena*, 127.
257 Wellhausen, *Prolegomena*, 128.
258 Wellhausen, *Prolegomena*, 128.
259 Wellhausen, *Prolegomena*, 143.

have had a legal claim to any definite dues of flesh."[260] In other words, Wellhausen asserts that there was no prescribed portion for the priests. "The priests received nothing more than the share which was generally customary. This is true in the first instance of the male firstlings of cattle."[261] This is, in short, the first stage of the history of worship and the history of Israelite religion as depicted in the Jehovistic stratum of the tradition. Religion was in intimate connection with the reality of the people. Multiplicity of altars existed as a matter of course and sacrifice was bound up with the very natural occasions of life. Festivals had no fixity in time. Priests shared with the people in the sacred banquets without having additional provisions.

In this way, Wellhausen shows us that the religion of old Israel is characterized by its connection with the life of the people of Israel. Its beginning was very ordinary in character. Wellhausen proposed that Yahweh was primarily Israel's God, and only afterwards (very long afterwards) did He come to be regarded as the God of the universe.[262] Yahweh was conceived of in ancient Israel as a 'helper' and this is what Israel looked for from Him, not salvation in the theological sense.[263] The implication of Wellhausen's reconstruction of the religion of old Israel reveals that he saw the history of Israelite religion at this stage as possessing no superior features. It cannot be distinguished from its surroundings. As Wellhausen saw it, the religion of Israel stands on the same platform as other religions. To quote Wellhausen:

> Das israelitische Altertum kann nicht mehr isoliert werden; man sieht zu deutlich, wie eng es auf allen Seiten mit der näheren und entfernteren Umgebung zusammenhängt. Auch über die historisch nachweisbare Berührung hinaus muß es unter die Analogie der allgemeinen Kulturentwicklung gestellt werden. Das israelitische Volkstum muß dem anderer Nationen vergleichen werden, und von dem Volkstum läßt sich die Religion nicht trennen.[264]

4 The prophetic reformation

According to Wellhausen, the second stage in the religious history of early Israel is marked by centralization of the cult. This idea first appeared in Deuteronomy, "which of all the books of the Pentateuch gives so imperious an expression to the

---

260 Wellhausen, *Prolegomena*, 153.
261 Wellhausen, *Prolegomena*, 155.
262 Wellhausen, "Israel," in *Prolegomena*, 429–542 (437).
263 Wellhausen, "Israel," 469.
264 Wellhausen, *Grundrisse zum Alten Testament*, 65.

restriction of the sacrificial worship to the one chosen place."[265] The consequences of centralization were of great importance in the history of worship in Israel. The cult severs its connection with local environment and human life. "In being transplanted from its natural soil it was deprived of its natural nourishment."[266] Sacrifice is removed from its original places. As a result, the older connection between life and faith broke down. In the words of Wellhausen, "A man lived in Hebron, but sacrificed in Jerusalem; life and worship fell apart."[267] The festivals, while still resting on agriculture, begin to be historicized.[268] "It is in Deuteronomy that one detects the first very perceptible traces of a historical dress being given to the religion and the worship."[269] As for the position of priests, Wellhausen notes that with the advance in centralization, priests become more prominent. "In Deuteronomy the priests, as compared with the judges and the prophets, take a very prominent position (xvi. 18–xviii. 22) and constitute a clerical order, hereditary in numerous families."[270] Moreover, it is in Deuteronomy that the regular use of the name 'Levites' for the priests begins for the first time.[271]

We have already mentioned that Wellhausen considered the Jehovistic tradition in the Pentateuch as representing the pre-prophetic period in the history of Israelite religion. The second stage of religious development is expressed in Deuteronomy, "as the Book of the Covenant, and the whole Jehovistic writing in general, reflects the first pre-prophetic period in the history of the cultus, so Deuteronomy is the legal expression of the second period of struggle and transition."[272] Moreover, Wellhausen proposed that Deuteronomy was the progeny of the prophetic spirit.[273] It crowned the work of the prophets.[274] As Wellhausen puts it, "Nowhere does the fundamental religious thought of prophecy find clearer expression than in Deuteronomy".[275]

In Wellhausen's view, the deuteronomic legislation was designed as reformation. The final result of the Deuteronomic Reformation was principally that the cultus of Jehovah was limited to Jerusalem and abolished everywhere else.[276]

---

265 Wellhausen, *Prolegomena*, 33.
266 Wellhausen, *Prolegomena*, 77.
267 Wellhausen, *Prolegomena*, 77.
268 Wellhausen, *Prolegomena*, 91.
269 Wellhausen, *Prolegomena*, 92.
270 Wellhausen, *Prolegomena*, 141.
271 Wellhausen, *Prolegomena*, 141.
272 Wellhausen, *Prolegomena*, 33.
273 Wellhausen, "Israel," 487.
274 Wellhausen, *Israelitische und jüdische Geschichte* (2004¹⁰), 129.
275 Wellhausen, "Israel," 487.
276 Wellhausen, "Israel," 488.

Wellhausen goes on to say, "Such was the popular and practical form of prophetic monotheism."[277] It should be mentioned that Wellhausen connected the centralization of the cult in Deuteronomy with the idea of monotheism. Where centralized worship is achieved, the idea of a single god can be found. To quote Wellhausen:

> It is only in Deuteronomy, moreover, that one sees to the root of the matter, and recognizes its connection with the anxiety for a strict monotheism and for the elimination from the worship of the popular heathenish elements, and thus with a deep and really worthy aim.[278]

According to Wellhausen, the second stage in the religious history of ancient Israel was marked by cultic reform. Wellhausen believed that the cult was the heathen element in the Israelite religion.[279] He declared that Josiah's reform, which was conducted in 621 BCE, was the first move towards centralizing the cult to one place. However, Josiah's effort was not completely successful and the multiplicity of altars remained until the nation lost its political independence. In the words of Wellhausen:

> Es gelang aber nicht alsbald; vor dem Exil blieben die lokalen Altäre noch immer bestehen, an die sich die heiligsten Erinnerungen von den Vätern her knüpften. Sie fielen erst, als durch die Losreißung der Nation aus ihrem Mutterboden die Tradition des Lebens, der Zusammenhang mit den ererbten Zuständen, gänzlich durchschnitten wurde.[280]

Though the prophets were unable to eradicate the heathen element in the cult of Yahweh, they nevertheless developed a different perception of God. The first step in this direction was initiated by Amos. He was the founder of a new phase of prophecy.[281] How was Yahweh conceived in Israel before the time of the prophet? Here is Wellhausen's answer:

> Nach dem populären Glauben war Jahve durch den Kultus an Israel gerufen worden weil er nur dort mit seinem Namen bekannt war, nur dort angerufen wurde, nur dort seine Wohnung und seine Altäre hatte. Dieses Band durchschneidet Amos. Jahve ist kein Gott, der der Opfer und Gaben bedarf, der sich durch sie bestechen läßt, der um des Kultus willen blindlings die

---

277 Wellhausen, "Israel," 488.
278 Wellhausen, *Prolegomena*, 36.
279 Wellhausen, *Prolegomena*, 422–423.
280 Wellhausen, *Israelitische und jüdische Geschichte*, 18.
281 Wellhausen, "Israel," 472.

> Partei seiner Verehrer und guten Bekannten ergreift. Was er von Israel verlangt, ist etwas Allgemeingültiges, nämlich die Gerechtigkeit; was er haßt, ist Unrecht und Frevel.[282]

It was the prophetic reformation that freed the conception of God from national barriers. In so doing the prophets were the spiritual destroyers of ancient Israel. As Wellhausen puts it, "The prophets had been the spiritual destroyers of the old Israel. In ancient times the nation had been the ideal of religion in actual realization. The prophets confronted the nation with an ideal to which it did not correspond."[283] Wellhausen further told us that the prophets added the ethical element to the religion of Yahweh:

> Until their time the nation had sprung up out of the conception of Jehovah; now the conception of Jehovah was casting the nation into the shade. The natural bond between the two was severed, and the relation was henceforward viewed as conditional. As God of the righteousness which is the law of the whole universe, Jehovah could be Israel's God only in so far as in Israel the right was recognized and followed. The ethical element destroyed the national character of the old religion.[284]

It comes then as no surprise that Wellhausen described the prophets as "the makers of new Israel".[285] The prophets broke with the older phase of the religion of Yahweh. Their emphasis on righteousness and justice brought about significant changes. In ancient Israel, the nation was the centre of religion, and its subject. In the thoughts of the prophets, religious individualism becomes the decisive factor. Thus, for example, the prophet Jeremiah asserted that, instead of the nation, the heart and individual conviction were to him the subject of religion.[286] In addition, Wellhausen pointed out that the prophets introduced a universalistic dimension to the religion of Yahweh.[287] In the words of Wellhausen:

> The first step towards universalism had been accomplished, towards at once the general diffusion and the individualisation of religion. Thus, although the prophets were far from

---

282 Wellhausen, *Grundrisse zum Alten Testament*, 91.
283 Wellhausen, "Israel," 491.
284 Wellhausen, "Israel," 473–474.
285 Wellhausen, "Israel," 464.
286 Wellhausen, "Israel," 491.
287 Wellhausen articulated the universalistic aspect of the relgion of the prophets in the following words: "Zu oberst ist er ihnen der Gott der Gerechtigkeit, Gott Israels nur insofern Israel seinen Ansprüchen genügt; sie kehren die hergebrachte Anordnung dieser beiden Fundamentalartikel des Glaubens um. Dadurch wird Jahve der Gefahr entzogen, mit der Welt zu kollidieren und an ihr zu scheitern, die Herrschaft des Rechts erstreckt sich gleichmäßig über Israel und Assur." See Wellhausen, *Israelitische und jüdische Geschichte*, 108.

originating a new conception of God, they none the less were the founders of what has been called "ethical monotheism.[288]

Wellhausen's view regarding the prophetic innovation in the religious history of ancient Israel requires consideration. Though Wellhausen confirmed the great part of the prophets in the religion of Yahweh, he nevertheless maintained, "The prophets did not form the tradition at first, but came after, shedding upon it their peculiar light. Their interest in history was not so great that they felt it necessary to write it down; they only infused their own spirit into it subsequently."[289] It should be also noted that Wellhausen's assessment of the prophetic contribution to the religion of Israel accords well with his declaration that the ethical monotheism of the prophets "was no product of the 'self-evolution of dogma', but a progressive step which had been called forth simply by the course of events."[290]

5 Israel and Judaism

We have seen that Wellhausen distinguished between the pre-prophetic religion of the Jehovistic tradition and the prophetic reformation as expressed in the centralization of the cult in Deuteronomy. These two stages in the history of Israelite religion were followed by a third one in which religion was radically changed under the impact of the Priestly Law. The free and spontaneous religion of ancient Israel was replaced by the formal and ritualistic Judaism of the Second Temple. In Wellhausen's thinking, introducing the law of the Priestly Code created two different religious worlds, that of Israel and that of Judaism.

The third phase in the history of religious development in Israel as it appeared in the Priestly Code of the Pentateuch has its historical place after Deuteronomy in the post-exilic period.[291] Thus, Wellhausen tells us that in comparison to Deuteronomy, which still stands in a close relation with the older period of worship, the Priestly Code "is hindered by no survival to present times of the older usage from projecting an image of antiquity such as it must have been; unhampered by visible relics of living tradition of an older state, it can idealise the past to its heart's content."[292]

---

288 Wellhausen, "Israel," 474.
289 Wellhausen, *Prolegomena*, 294.
290 Wellhausen, "Israel," 474.
291 Wellhausen, *Prolegomena*, 38.
292 Wellhausen, *Prolegomena*, 38.

In the history of worship the laws of the Priestly Code represent the third movement. With regard to the place of worship, Wellhausen points out that the Priestly Code presupposes the existence of one sanctuary from the very beginning. The idea of one legitimate sanctuary is so important to the Priestly Code that it "is unable to think of religion without one sanctuary, and cannot for a moment imagine Israel without it."[293] Wellhausen goes even further and maintains that the Priestly Code altered the ancient history by retro-imposing the idea of one legitimate sanctuary onto the very beginning of the nation. The Tabernacle of the Priestly Code is the copy, not the prototype, of the temple at Jerusalem.[294] In the same manner, sacrifice appears in the Priestly Code as Mosaic in origin. Its observance is based on the law given to Moses. Sacrifice becomes legal, the scrupulous fulfilment of the law.[295]

In describing the changes that altered the old performance of sacred feasts and festivals, Wellhausen observes two main movements that occurred in the Priestly Code: denaturalization and historisation. He points out, "The feasts entirely lose their peculiar characteristics, the occasions by which they are inspired and distinguished; by the monotonous sameness of the unvarying burnt-offering and sin-offering of the community as a whole. They are all put on the same even level, deprived of their natural spontaneity, and degraded into mere exercises of religion."[296] Wellhausen describes how the Priestly Code remodelled the old tradition concerning feasts as follows:

> The verification of the alleged denaturalisation of the feasts in the Priestly Code lies in this, that their historical interpretation, for which the way is already paved by the Jehovistic tradition, here attains its full development. For after they have lost their original contents and degenerated into mere prescribed religious forms, there is nothing to prevent the refilling of the empty bottles in any way accordant with the tastes of the period. Now, accordingly, the Feast of Tabernacles also becomes historical (Leviticus xxiii.), instituted to commemorate the booths under which the people had to shelter themselves during the forty years of wandering in the wilderness.[297]

In addition, the Priestly Code sets apart the priests' sons of Aaron from the rest of the priests. Instead of the deuteronomic formula 'the Priests the Levites', the Priestly Code has 'the priests and the Levites'.[298] Further, the Priestly Code as-

───────────

293 Wellhausen, *Prolegomena*, 36.
294 Wellhausen, *Prolegomena*, 36–37.
295 Wellhausen, *Prolegomena*, 61.
296 Wellhausen, *Prolegomena*, 100.
297 Wellhausen, *Prolegomena*, 102.
298 Wellhausen, *Prolegomena*, 147.

signed extra shares and dues to the priests. For example, Wellhausen notes that the tithe offering, which in its proper nature should apply only to products of definite measure such as corn and wine and oil (Deuteronomy xiv.23), was increased in the Priestly Code to include cattle.[299] All *kodashim* were apportioned to the priests.[300] What was originally left free and undermined becomes precisely measured and prescribed. In Wellhausen's opinion, "The enlargement of the amount assigned to the priests reflects the situation of the post-exilic community, where the priest was the head of theocracy. The immense augmentation in the income of the priests points to an increase of the hierocratic power."[301]

We have so far discussed Wellhausen's presentation of the history of Israelite religion in the three strata of the Pentateuch. According to Wellhausen, "The Jehovist might be regarded as the document which formed the starting-point of the religious history of Israel."[302] Perhaps it was Wellhausen's conviction that the Jehovist made no distinction between local and central that led him to regard the Jehovistic tradition as the first stage of Israel's religion. Centralization of worship to one single sanctuary marked the age of Deuteronomy and prophetic reform, the second stage in the history of Israel's religion.

By introducing the law of the Priestly Code, to which we now turn for discussion, the old religion of Israel disappeared and the religion of Judaism came to dominate. I shall start by examining what Wellhausen meant by 'law', and its relation to the prophets, and follow with an explanation of its impact on the Israelite religion. Finally, we will consider some differences between ancient Israel and Judaism.

It should be mentioned that Wellhausen did not deny the existence of law in ancient Israel. What Wellhausen refuted is the idea that systematic law existed from the very beginning. To put it differently, Wellhausen recognized that ancient Israel knew the law in the words of the prophets and in other forms such as priestly instructions.[303] However, the law which became the 'constitution of Judaism' in the post-exilic period had not existed in ancient Israel. According to Wellhausen's reconstruction, the law was introduced by the prophet Ezekiel, but was implemented and made the constitution of Judaism by Ezra.[304] Moreover, Wellhausen made clear the point that the law marked a crucial point in the history of Israel. "The introduction of the law, first Deuteronomy, and then the whole

---

299 Wellhausen, *Prolegomena*, 157.
300 Wellhausen, *Prolegomena*, 158.
301 Wellhausen, *Prolegomena*, 156.
302 Wellhausen, *Prolegomena*, 392.
303 See the introduction to *Prolegomena*, 5.
304 Wellhausen, *Israelitische und jüdische Geschichte*, 167; also, idem, "Israel," 497.

Pentateuch, was in fact the decisive step, by which the written took the place of the spoken word, and the people of the word became a 'people of the book'."[305]

An examination of the relationship between law and the prophets is of great importance in Wellhausen's reconstruction of the history of Israel. We have already mentioned that the prophetic reformation as expressed in Deuteronomy aimed at correcting the old popular worship and eradicating the heathen element of the cult. However, Wellhausen commented that the prophetic injunctions lost their vitality under the impact of the law: "But the result of the innovation did not correspond exactly to its prophetic origin. Prophecy died when its precepts attained to the force of laws; the prophetic ideas lost their purity when they became practical."[306] Wellhausen further explained how, under the force of laws dictating centralization of the cult, the prophetic doctrine as well as the old religion was brought to an end. As he puts it, "With the appearance of the law came to an end the old freedom, not only in the sphere of worship, now restricted to Jerusalem, but in the sphere of the religious spirit as well. There was now in existence an authority as objective as could be; and this was the death of prophecy."[307] In addition, Wellhausen illustrated how it came about that the prophetic reformation ended with strict and formal regulations. In his view, it was the hands of the priestly legislator that altered the old form of worship and replaced it with new, legitimate law. "The law of the legitimate cultus of Jerusalem, as it lies before us in the Priestly Code, reforms and destroys the old popular worship on the basis of Mosaic, i.e., prophetical ideas."[308]

Although Wellhausen asserted that the prophetic precepts had lost their purity under the impact of the law, he nevertheless remarked the close relationship between the prophets and the law. He deduced that "Propheten und Gesetz kein Gegensatz, sondern identisch sind, und im Verhältnis von Ursache und Wirkung stehen."[309] Wellhausen further maintained that the prophets paved the way for the law. In other words, Wellhausen saw the work of the prophets as a transition from ancient Israel to Judaism. To quote Wellhausen, "Die Prophetie kann vom Gesetz, von der jüdischen Frömmigkeit, und vom Christentum nicht getrennt werden; sie selber bildet schon den Übergang von der israelitischen zur jüdischen Geschichte."[310] More illuminating is what Wellhausen wrote in his *Abriß der Ge-*

---

305 Wellhausen, *Prolegomena*, 409.
306 Wellhausen, "Israel," 488.
307 Wellhausen, *Prolegomena*, 402.
308 Wellhausen, *Prolegomena*, 341.
309 Wellhausen, *Israelitische und jüdische Geschichte*, 130.
310 Wellhausen, *Israelitische und jüdische Geschichte* (1894), v.

schichte Israels, namely that the prophets were the founders of the religion of law
– "die Begründer der Religion des Gesetzes."[311]

One could rightly wonder how this close relation of the prophets and the law
accords with Wellhausen's view that the law is not the starting point of the prophetic message. As he puts it, "Die Propheten reden nicht aus dem Gesetz."[312]
Here Wellhausen points out that the transition from pre-exilic Israel to post-exilic Judaism was effected not by Deuteronomy but by Ezekiel the priest in prophet's mantle.[313] Wellhausen tells us how Ezekiel was the connecting link between
the prophets and the law:

> Ezekiel first pointed out the way which was suited for the time. He is the connecting link
> between the prophets and the law. He claims to be a prophet, and starts from prophetic
> ideas: but they are not his own ideas, they are those of his predecessors which he turns
> into dogmas. He is by nature a priest, and his peculiar merit is that he enclosed the soul
> of prophecy in the body of a community which was not political, but founded on the temple
> and the cultus.[314]

It goes without saying that Wellhausen's entire case is predicated on his position
towards the law. He would go for the idea that "there is no doubt that the law of
Ezra was the whole Pentateuch".[315] Wellhausen frequently demonstrated the impact of law in the history of Israel's religion. In Wellhausen's view, it was the law
that distinguished old Israel from Judaism. He described how, with the appearance of the law, religious practice was cut off from its natural impulse and acquired 'an abstract religious character'.[316] Before the law, religious worship in
old Israel was a natural thing; it was the blossom of life. The law severed this
connection between life and religion. In the words of Wellhausen, "Worship
no longer springs from an inner impulse, it has come to be an exercise of reli-
giosity. It has no natural significance; its significance is transcendental, incom-
parable, not to be defined; the chief effect of it, which is always produced with
certainty, is atonement."[317]

---

311 Wellhausen, "Abriß der Geschichte Israels und Juda's," 52.
312 Wellhausen, *Grundrisse zum Alten Testament*, 75.
313 Wellhausen, *Prolegomena*, 59.
314 Wellhausen, *Prolegomena*, 421.
315 Wellhausen, *Prolegomena*, 408.
316 Wellhausen, *Prolegomena*, 81.
317 Wellhausen, *Prolegomena*, 424.

Summing up his conclusions, Wellhausen dedicated the last part of his *Prolegomena* to differentiating between ancient Israel and Judaism.[318] We noted that Wellhausen drew attention to the differences between the Israel of ancient times as known to us through Kings and Prophets and Judaism of the Second Temple. What sets ancient Israel apart from Judaism is the idea of theocracy.[319] Thus Wellhausen explained how in ancient Israel, there was no theocratic influence. He wrote, "Old Israel had not shrunk to a religious congregation, public life was not quite absorbed in the service of the sanctuary; the high priest and the dwelling of Jehovah were not the centre round which all revolved."[320] Further, Wellhausen emphasized that theocracy in the form of a constitution did not exist in ancient Israel. Nor did a 'sacred organization' exist from the time of Judges and Kings.[321] However, theocracy can be recognized in the laws of the Priestly Code as addressed to the congregation of the Second Temple. As Wellhausen formulated it, "It is not from the atmosphere of the old kingdom, but from that of the church of the Second Temple, that the Priestly Code draws its breath."[322] Moreover, Wellhausen opined that theocracy appeared under the domination of foreign rule, "under the Persian domination the Jews built up an unpolitical community on the basis of religion."[323] In the same line, he wrote, "War and the administration of justice were regarded as matters of religion before they became matters of obligation and civil order; this is all that is really meant when a theocracy is spoken of."[324] Wellhausen then concluded that theocracy "war nicht der Ausgangspunkt der israelitischen Geschichte; wenigstens nicht in dem Sinne, wie sie im Pentateuch gefaßt wird, als eine Verfassung, die auf dem Kultus beruht und deutlicher Hierokratie zu benennen wäre."[325]

---

318 Reinhard Kratz points out that Wellhausen delineated Judaism in the Old Testament. In his point of view, Wellhausen, by means of literary and historical analysis of Old Testament literature, was able to draw the line of early Judaism as an independent entity which was far from being merely the antithesis of ancient Israel. On this see Reinhard G. Kratz, "Julius Wellhausen" *TRE* 35 (2003): 527–536 (532). See further Uwe Becker, "Julius Wellhausens Sicht des Judentums," in *Biblische Theologie und historisches Denken: Wissenschaftsgeschichtliche Studien: Aus Anlass der 50. Wiederkehr der Basler Promotion von Rudolf Smend* (ed. Martin Kessler und Martin Wallraff; Basel: Schwabe, 2008), 279–309.
319 For a detailed discussion of Wellhausen's view of theocracy and the opposite perspective of Kaufmann, see part 3 Chapter 9 of this study.
320 Wellhausen, *Prolegomena*, 422.
321 Wellhausen, *Prolegomena*, 411, 412.
322 Wellhausen, *Prolegomena*, 82.
323 Wellhausen, "Israel," 512.
324 Wellhausen, "Israel," 436.
325 Wellhausen, *Israelitische und jüdische Geschichte*, 18.

Based on the idea of the sacred institution, Wellhausen's distinction between Israel and Judaism is continued. He judged, "Of the sacred organization supposed to have existed from the earliest times, there is no trace in the time of the Judges and the Kings."[326] Wellhausen believed it to be difficult to imagine the existence of such organization in ancient Israel because it would have been inconsistent with the temper of the time and attitude of the people. In Wellhausen's view, "The history of the ancient Israelites shows us nothing so distinctly as the uncommon freshness and naturalness of their impulses."[327]

On the other hand, Wellhausen emphasized that the Priestly Code of the Second Temple "brought about a complete metamorphosis of the old tradition."[328] Although it knew the past of the people, it created new stories of its own and lived out of history:

> Judaism...lives on the stores of the past, but is not simply the total of what had been previously acquired; it is full of new impulses, and has an entirely different physiognomy from that of Hebrew antiquity, so much so that it is hard even to catch a likeness. Judaism is everywhere historically comprehensible, and yet it is a mass of antinomies.[329]

Thus, in Wellhausen's estimation, the old phase of the religion of Israel can be recognized in the Books of Samuel, Judges, and Kings. He proposed that the religion of ancient Israel came to an end with the fall of Samaria: "When Samaria fell, Israel shrivelled up to the narrow dimensions of Judah, which alone survived as the people of Jehovah."[330]

It might be safely concluded that Wellhausen saw the splendid time of Israelite religion as harking back to the time of Judges and Kings rather than during exile. Wellhausen's sympathy towards the early phase of Israelite religion is plainly evident from his writings. He appreciated simple and naive forms of religion more than ritual and dogmas. Wellhausen constructed a picture for the course of Israelite religion based on insights gained from his literary and historical reconstruction of the sources of the Pentateuch. In his resulting interpretation, Wellhausen dates the time of the prophets before that of the law. As explained in the introduction to *Prolegomena*, Wellhausen tells how he arrived at the conviction that the law should be placed after the prophets, maintaining

---

326 Wellhausen, *Prolegomena*, 412.
327 Wellhausen, *Prolegomena*, 412.
328 Wellhausen, *Prolegomena*, 361.
329 Wellhausen, "Israel," 508–509.
330 Wellhausen, *Prolegomena*, 24.

that there was between them, law and prophets, all the difference that separates two wholly distinct worlds.[331]

Having examined Wellhausen's thoughts on the different phases of religious development in ancient Israel, I proceed to go into more detail about Wellhausen's picture of early history. No fresh presentation of Wellhausen's reconstruction will be considered, but we intend to confirm our understanding of Wellhausen's move from literary criticism to religious history and historical synthesis.

331 Wellhausen, *Prolegomena*, 2–3.

Chapter Three:
Early History of Israel

1 Introduction

Israel's early history is considered the most debated question among historians of ancient Israel.[332] The structure of Wellhausen's hypothesis on the history of Israel shows that he moved from literature to religion to history. Therefore, I have chosen to proceed from Wellhausen's interpretation of the religious history of ancient Israel to his historical presentation of early Israel. By examining Wellhausen's reconstruction of the history of Israel to the pre-monarchic period, I intend to show that he used materials obtained from critical investigation of the pentateuchal sources to provide a historical picture of ancient Israel.

From the outset, it appears that Wellhausen attached importance to the pentateuchal documents as sources for reconstructing the history of Israel. As we have seen, in his study *Die Composition des Hexateuchs*, Wellhausen analysed the sources, criticized their content and put them in chronological order. This was followed by an inquiry into the role and status of law in the history of Israel. In *Prolegomena*, Wellhausen mapped out the religious history of ancient Israel as it appeared in the three strata of the Pentateuch; Jehovist, Deuteronomy and the Priestly Code. In the course of his investigation, Wellhausen determined that the early Israelites were similar to other tribes and peoples of the time. There was no theocracy in the beginning, no covenant theology, the unity of the Israelite tribes was a late construction, and Joshua's account of conquest contradicts historical facts. Wellhausen's *Israelitische und jüdische Geschichte* crowned his work and summed up earlier labour. His critical and literary analysis served as the basis for his work on the history of ancient Israel. In what follows I shall confine myself to Wellhausen's reconstruction of ancient Israel up to the pre-monarchic period. As will be shown, Wellhausen disregarded many of the pentateuchal materials, especially the legislative ones, and refused to make use of them as a basis for writing the history. We will also see how Wellhausen's thinking was influenced by his denial of the account of the law given at Sinai. More important is Wellhausen's assessment of the period of conquest and settlement. He argued that the Israelites were absorbed into the indigenous population of Canaan. My discussion starts with an outline of Wellhausen's reconstruction of the begin-

---

332 For a discussion see Lester L. Grabbe ed., *Can a 'History of Israel' Be Written?* (JSOTSup 245; Sheffield: Sheffield Academic Press, 1997).

ning of the people of Israel, followed by a description of Moses and his role in the history of ancient Israel, and at the end I shall look at Wellhausen's picture of the period of conquest and settlement in Canaan.

2 The beginning of Israel

In a very short and somehow modest description, Wellhausen tells us of the appearance of the Israelites on the stage of history. He describes how the people of Israel belonged to a Hebrew group which afterwards developed into Israel. This group of Hebrews included – along with the people of Israel – those of Edom, Moab, and Ammon. In Wellhausen's view, these four petty population groups must at one time have formed some sort of a unity and have passed through a common history which resulted in their settlement in southeastern Palestine. As for the origin of the people of Israel, Wellhausen maintained that:

> Some fifteen centuries before our era a section of the Hebrew group left its ancient seat in the extreme south of Palestine to occupy the not distant pasture lands of Egypt (Goshen), where they carried on their old calling, that of shepherds and goatherds. Although settled within the territory of the Pharaohs, and recognizing their authority, they continued to retain all their old characteristics – their language, their patriarchal institutions, their nomad habits of life.[333]

It is not surprising that Wellhausen's *Israelitische und jüdische Geschichte* contains no title or even subtitle with the terms 'patriarch', 'patriarchal age' or 'patriarchal religion'.[334] This is, of course, due to the fact that Wellhausen disregarded much of the tradition associated with the patriarchs in the Pentateuch. He believed that the patriarchal stories reflected the monarchic period and were intended to justify Israel's possession of Palestine and to legitimate cultic sites of non-Hebrew origin by linking them with the patriarchs.[335] In addition, Wellhausen rejected the idea that the patriarchs were historical personalities. Thus, for example, he said about Abraham, "He is certainly not the name of a people like Isaac and Lot: he is somewhat difficult to interpret. That is not to say that in such a connection as this we may regard him as a historical person; he

---

333 Wellhausen, "Israel," 429.
334 See Helmut Weidmann, *Die Patriarchen und ihre Religion im Licht der Forschung seit Julius Wellhausen* (Forschungen zur Religion und Literatur des Alten und Neuen Testaments 94; Göttingen: Vandenhoeck & Ruprecht, 1968), 13.
335 John H. Hayes and J. M. Miller, *Israelite and Judaean History* (Philadelphia: Westminster Press, 1977), 124.

might with more likelihood be regarded as a free creation of unconscious art."[336] Certainly, Wellhausen refused to speculate about the very beginning of the people of Israel. He found it difficult to accept the Genesis account about the patriarchal early history. In Wellhausen words:

> Die Geschichte eines Volkes läßt sich nicht über das Volk selber hinausführen, in eine Zeit, wo dasselbe noch gar nicht vorhanden war. Die Erzählungen über die Erzväter in der Genesis gehen von ethnologischen Verhältnissen und von Kultuseinrichtungen der Königszeit aus und leiten deren Ursprünge aus einer idealen Vorzeit her, auf die sie in Wahrheit nicht abgespiegelt werden.[337]

Wellhausen's assessment of the patriarchal stories fits well with results obtained from criticism and dating of the sources. In Wellhausen's opinion, the literary period of Israel could hardly have started before the ninth century B.C.[338] Thus, Wellhausen asserts:

> With reference to any period earlier than the century 850–750 B.C., we can hardly be said to possess any statistics. For, while the facts of history admit of being handed down with tolerable accuracy through a considerable time, a contemporary literature is indispensable for the description of standing conditions.[339]

Furthermore, Wellhausen deduced from his source criticism that the patriarchal stories were given in two different versions; by comparing the history of the patriarchs in the Jehovist version and that of the Priestly Code, he came to a far-reaching conclusion. Regarding the Jehovist, Wellhausen pointed out:

> In the Jehovist this skeleton of ethnographic genealogy is found covered throughout with flesh and blood. The patriarchs, Abraham, Isaac, and Jacob, are not mere names, but living forms, ideal prototypes of the true Israelite. They are all peace-loving shepherds, inclined to live quietly beside their tents, anxious to steer clear of strife and clamour, in no circumstances prepared to meet force with force and oppose injustice with the sword.[340]

---

336 Wellhausen, *Prolegomena*, 320.

337 Wellhausen, *Israelitische und jüdische Geschichte*, 10.

338 Wellhausen's general view of Hebrew literature is that the period before the late ninth century B.C. may largely be characterized as a nonliterary age, albeit that some literature (include prose history) existed prior to that time. See Lain William Provan, V. Philips Longman, *A Biblical History of Israel* (Louisville: Westminster John Knox Press, 2003), 27.

339 Wellhausen, "Israel," 464.

340 Wellhausen, *Prolegomena*, 320–321. In his description of the history of the patriarchs, "Wellhausen may be more radical and rigorous than Ewald, but he still looks for historical elements in the patriarchal narratives. For instance, he speaks of the patriarchs as "prototypes"

By contrast, Wellhausen noted that while in the Jehovist the patriarchs appeared in "living form," the Priestly Code removed the legends of the patriarchs from their historical setting. Therefore, Wellhausen found that the patriarchal history that appears in the Priestly Code to be:

> Dry ethnographic and geographical facts...all we learn of the patriarchs is their marriages and births and how they separated to the various dwelling-places of their descendants. The Priestly Code, moreover, strips the legends of the patriarchs of their local as well as their historical color.[341]

This is, in short, the major difference between the Jehovist and the Priestly Code with regard to portraying the history of the patriarchs.[342] What concerns us here is Wellhausen's ability to interrogate the sources and obtain information for historical purposes. He tended to accept the Jehovistic version of the history of the patriarchs and to disregard that of the Priestly Code. In Wellhausen's reasoning, "The Jehovist still lives in the spirit of the legend, but the Priestly Code is strange to that spirit, and does violence to the legend, by treating it from its own point of view, which is quite different from the old one."[343] Another explanation might be found in the following quotation, where Wellhausen shows how the Priestly Code reconstructed the patriarchal history:

> The patriarchs, having no tabernacle, have no worship at all; according to the Priestly Code they build no altars, bring no offerings, and scrupulously abstain from everything by which they might in any way encroach on the privilege of the one true sanctuary. This manner of shaping the patriarchal history is only the extreme consequence of the effort to carry out with uniformity in history the *semper ubique et ab omnibus* of the legal unity of worship.[344]

In addition, Wellhausen was wary of the 'legend' elements in the history of ancient Israel and called for only the general principle of that history to be considered:

> Die bestimmten und farbenreichen Einzelheiten, welche die Sage über die wunderbare Morgendämmerung der Geschichte Israels berichtet, können allerdings nicht als glaubwürdig gelten. Nur die großen Grundzüge der Vorgeschichte, die allgemeinsten Vorausset-

---

(*Vorbilder*) of the Israelites, using a word dear to Ewald." On this see Jean Louis Ska, "The 'History of Israel': Its Emergence as an Independent Discipline," 341.

341 Wellhausen, *Prolegomena*, 334.

342 For more on this issue, see Wellhausen, *Prolegomena*, 318–342.

343 Wellhausen, *Prolegomena*, 336–337.

344 Wellhausen, *Prolegomena*, 38.

zungen aller einzelnen Erzählungen über dieselbe, lassen sich nicht als erdichtet begreifen.[345]

3 Moses

Wellhausen saw the time of Moses as the formative period in the early history of Israel. That is to say, Wellhausen believed that Israel's history began with Moses. Therefore, it is important to understand how he assessed the events associated with Moses, such as the Exodus and Sinai tradition. According to Wellhausen, a section of the Hebrew group had left its original seat in southeastern Palestine in search of pasture. They migrated to Egypt, where they lived in the land of Goshan. In the course of time, their lives become impossible under the forced labor imposed upon them "for the construction of new public works in Goshen, an exaction which was felt to be an assault upon their freedom and honor, and which in point of fact was fitted to take away all that was distinctive of their Nationality."[346] It was not until the coming of Moses that deliverance became possible. Moses taught the people of Israel to regard self-assertion against the Egyptians as an article of religion.[347] "At a time when Egypt was scourged by a grievous plague, the Hebrews broke up their settlement in Goshen...and directed their steps towards their old home again."[348]

In such few details, Wellhausen gives us an account of the events preceding the Exodus from Egypt. Our conclusion remains the same, i.e. that Wellhausen did not rely on much of the pentateuchal traditions. This becomes even more evident in his treatment of the tradition associated with the events of the Exodus and Sinai. Although Wellhausen did not deny that the Exodus took place, he nevertheless described it in a very slight manner.[349] As in the case of the patriarchal history, Wellhausen found two different versions of the Exodus in the Jehovist and in the Priestly Code. In Wellhausen's view, the Jehovistic account of the Exodus is "more complicated", and that of the Priestly Code is "much simpler, but poorer in incidental features."[350] Moreover, Wellhausen observed that

---

345 Wellhausen, *Israelitische und jüdische Geschichte*, 10.
346 Wellhausen, "Israel," 429.
347 Wellhausen, "Israel," 430.
348 Wellhausen, "Israel," 430.
349 Wellhausen, for example, mentioned that the prophets are silent about the most important events of the Exodus. See Wellhausen, *Israelitische und jüdische Geschichte*, 11.
350 Wellhausen, *Prolegomena*, 352.

much of the Exodus tradition fits in with the ideology and style of the Priestly Code:

> The Exodus from Egypt is everywhere regarded as the commencement of Israelite history. In the Priestly Code it is made the epoch of an era (Exodus xii. 2), which is afterwards dated from, not only in years but even in months and days. It is unquestionable that this precise style of dating only came into use among the Hebrews at a very late period.[351]

Wellhausen detected another difference between the two versions of the Exodus in the Jehovist and the Priestly Code: "In the Jehovist the ostensible occasion of the Exodus is a festival which the children of Israel desire to hold in honor of their God in the wilderness. In the Priestly Code this occasion disappears; there can be no pre-Mosaic festivals."[352] Moreover, Wellhausen isolated the tradition of giving the law at Sinai from the Exodus. In his reading, "The Israelites arrived at Kadesh, the original object of their wanderings, not after the digression to Sinai but immediately after the Exodus, and they spent there the forty years of their residence in the wilderness. Kadesh is also the original scene of the legislation."[353] Wellhausen went further and maintained, "It was a further step to make Sinai the scene of the solemn inauguration of the historical relation between Jehovah and Israel. This was done under the poetic impulse to represent the constituting of the people of Jehovah as a dramatic act on an exalted stage."[354] The question then arises, what can be inferred from Wellhausen's reconstruction?

In point of fact, there are many decisive conclusions. It becomes clear that Kadesh and not Sinai is the true scene of Moses' activities. Kadesh is the place back to which the old tradition can be traced. Here is Wellhausen's conclusion:

> It was here and now that the people went to school with Moses; here, at the sanctuary of the camp, he declared law and judgment; and here, according to the view of the oldest tradition, the foundations of the view of the oldest tradition, the foundations of the Torah were laid (Exod. xviii.). The region of Kadesh was also the scene of almost all the miracles and other circumstances we read about Moses. Here he showed himself to be at once the father and mother of the people, their judge, priest and seer.[355]

---

351 Wellhausen, *Prolegomena*, 351.
352 Wellhausen, *Prolegomena*, 351–352.
353 Wellhausen, *Prolegomena*, 343.
354 Wellhausen, *Prolegomena*, 344.
355 Wellhausen, "Moses," *Encyclopaedia Britannica* 16 (1883): 860–861.

Another important understanding obtained from Wellhausen's reconstruction of Sinai tradition was that the Sinai pericope (Exod. 19–Num. 10) is quite independent of legislation and of law giving. In Wellhausen's thinking, the old tradition was suppressed in favor of the Sinai narrative. This was done under the influence of the Priestly Law. To illustrate, I quote Wellhausen:

> From Sinai the old tradition takes us by this and that station, mentioned by name, without delay to Kadesh. Here the chief part of the forty years' sojourn in the wilderness is spent; this...is the true scene of all the stories that are told about Moses. The Priestly Code takes us in this period, as in the legend of the patriarchs, not to definite places, but up and down in the wilderness of Sinai, in the wilderness of Paran, in the wilderness of Sin. Kadesh is with evident intention thrust as far as possible into the background – no doubt on account of the high sanctity the place originally had as the encampment for many years of the Israelites under Moses.[356]

Thus, Wellhausen concluded that the Exodus and Sinai tradition were two independent traditions. The picture of this period becomes clear when considering Wellhausen's depiction of Moses. We have already demonstrated that he made a distinction between the Moses of the Jehovist and the Moses of the Priestly Code. As a matter of fact, Wellhausen accepted the Jehovist portrait of Moses and rejected that of the Priestly Code. Furthermore, by discrediting the account of law giving on Sinai, Wellhausen minimized the significance of the legislation given in the Pentateuch as a source for the historical reconstruction of Moses. Consequently, Wellhausen saw Moses as the founder of the nation of Israel, not its law. The great work of Moses was that he saved his people and brought them together under his leadership in the region of Kadesh. In Wellhausen's view, the life that the Israelites had lived together under Moses "had been the first thing to awaken a feeling of solidarity among the tribes which afterwards constituted the nation; whether they had previously been a unity in any sense of the word is doubtful."[357] It comes then with no surprise that Wellhausen regarded the beginning of Israel's history as the coming of Moses. As he puts it:

> The time of Moses is invariably regarded as the properly creative period in Israel's history, and on that account also as giving the pattern and norm for the ages which followed. In point of fact the history of Israel must be held to have begun then, and the foundations of a new epoch to have been laid.[358]

---

356 Wellhausen, *Prolegomena*, 353.
357 Wellhausen, "Israel," 432.
358 Wellhausen, "Israel," 432.

According to Wellhausen, Moses was by no means a founder of theocracy as depicted in the Priestly Code. He did not bring a new religion to his people. "For Moses to have given to the Israelites an 'enlightened conception of God' would have been to have given them a stone instead of bread."[359] Wellhausen further maintained that Moses was far from originating new law. "In Wahrheit ist Moses etwa in dem gleichen Sinn der Urheber der ‚mosaischen Verfassung', wie Petrus der Stifter der Römischen Hierarchie."[360]

There can be no doubt that Wellhausen's presentation of Moses is based on materials obtained from criticism of the sources. Moses in the interpretation of Wellhausen lost much of what had been given to him in the tradition. Although Wellhausen did not deny the historicity of Moses, he questioned the biblical picture of Moses. Wellhausen tended to minimize the historical worth of the tradition associated with Moses, especially those characteristics found in the legislative portion of the Hexateuch. He suggested that it was important to look at the historical traditions about Moses and separate them from the legislative materials. In the words of Wellhausen: "Within the Pentateuch itself also the historical tradition about Moses (which admits of being distinguished, and must carefully be separated, from the legislative, although the latter often clothes itself in narrative form) is in its main features manifestly trustworthy, and can only be explained as resting on actual facts."[361] Thus Wellhausen sought to draw a picture of Moses based on what he thought to be the original and genuine tradition. In a telling quotation, Wellhausen summed up his view of Moses as follows:

> From the historical tradition, then, it is certain that Moses was the founder of the Torah. But the legislative tradition cannot tell us what were the positive contents of *his* Torah. In fact it can be shown that throughout the whole of the older period the Torah was no finished legislative code, but consisted entirely of the oral decisions and instructions of the priests, as a whole it was potential only; what actually existed were the individual sentences given by the priesthood as they were asked for. Thus Moses was not regarded as the promulgator once for all of a national constitution, but rather as the first to call into activity the actual sense for law and justice, and to begin the series of oral decisions which were continued after him by the priests. He was the founder of the nation out of which the Torah and prophecy came as later growths. He laid the basis of Israel's subsequent peculiar individ-

---

359 Wellhausen, "Israel," 437.
360 Wellhausen, *Prolegomena Zur Geschichte Israels* (1981[6]), 410. In this context, Wellhausen was accused of delivering a confusing picture about Moses. On this see Eva Osswald, *Das Bild des Mose in der kritischen alttestamentlichen Wissenschaft seit Julius Wellhausen* (Theologische Arbeiten 18; Berlin: Evangelische Verlagsanstalt, 1962), 53–54. See also Ernst M. Dörrfuss, *Mose in den Chronikbüchern: Garant theokratischer Zukunftserwartung* (BZAW 219 Berlin: De Gruyter, 1994).
361 Wellhausen, "Israel," 436.

uality, not by any one formal act, but in virtue of his having throughout the whole of his long life been the people's leader, judge, and centre of union.[362]

4 Conquest and settlement tradition

We note that Wellhausen, in reconstructing the events of conquest and settlement in Palestine, made use only of what he thought to be the genuine and historical tradition.[363] He deduced from the sources what could be used for writing the history of early Israel.[364] Wellhausen's analysis of the narrative of the Hexateuch enabled him to distinguish between different versions of the tradition related to the conquest and settlement. However, in the course of Wellhausen's investigation one cannot fail to notice that he credited the Jehovistic account of the conquest, which in this case represents the genuine tradition. In contrast, Wellhausen rejected the priestly account of the tradition because it draws a picture irrelevant to the reality of old Israel. Thus, Wellhausen maintains:

> The independent main stock of the Priestly Code, the Book of the Four Covenants, or the Book of Origins (Q), more and more gives way to later additions, and ceases altogether, it appears, at the death of Moses. It is at least nowhere to be traced in the first half of the Book of Joshua. and so we cannot reckon as part of it those extensive sections of the second half, belonging to the Priestly Code, which treat of the division of the land. Without a preceding history of the conquest these sections are quite in the air; they cannot be taken as telling a continuous story of their own, but presuppose the Jehovistic-Deuteronomic work.[365]

Wellhausen's analysis of the sources was followed by an inquiry into the narrative of the Hexateuch. He came to know the common points and major differences between the sources in their depiction of the traditions of conquest and settlement. Wellhausen then observed:

> The Priestly Code, agreeing in this with the Deuteronomistic revision, represents the whole of Canaan as having been made a *tabula rasa*, and then, masterless and denuded of population, submitted to the lot. First the tribe of Judah receives its lot, then Manasseh and Ephraim, then the two tribes which attached themselves to Ephraim and Judah, Benjamin and Simeon, and lastly the five northern tribes, Zebulon, Issachar, Asher, Naphtali, Dan.[366]

---

362 Wellhausen, "Israel," 438–439.
363 See Wellhausen, *Die Composition des Hexateuchs*, 208–210.
364 See Wellhausen, *Prolegomena*, Chapter 8 "The Narrative of the Hexateuch."
365 Wellhausen, *Prolegomena*, 357–358.
366 Wellhausen, *Prolegomena*, 358–359.

Conversely, Wellhausen mentioned that the Jehovist represents the tradition in a different way:

> According to the Jehovist, Judah and Joseph appear to have had their territory allocated to them in Gilgal (14:6) and not by lot, and to have entered into occupation of it from there. A good while afterwards the land remaining over is divided by lot among the seven small tribes still unprovided for, from Shiloh, or perhaps originally from Shechem (xviii. 2–10). Joshua alone casts the lot and gives instructions; Eleazar the priest does not act with him. Even here the general principle of the Priestly Code, which knows no differences among the tribes, is somewhat limited; but it is much more decidedly contradicted by the important chapter, Judges 1.[367]

Furthermore, Wellhausen distinguished between the Jehovist and the priestly accounts concerning the tradition related to the migration of the Israelite tribes to the land east of Jordan. According to the Jehovist, "The neighboring tribes place obstacles in their way, and the land in which they desire to settle has to be conquered with the sword."[368] The Priestly Code, on the other hand:

> Tells us as little of all this as in an earlier instance of the war with Amalek; from all it says we should imagine that the Israelites went straight to their mark and met with no difficulty in the region in question; the land is ownerless, and the possession of it is granted by Moses and Eleazar to the two tribes Reuben and Gad (Numbers xxxii.).[369]

It appears therefore that Wellhausen made a distinction between the Jehovist and the priestly accounts of the traditions related to the conquest and settlement. In fact, he found two different versions of the conquest in Joshua and Judges 1. In his view, the tradition of conquest as given in Joshua cannot be taken as a reliable description, while that of Judges 1 reflects the historical tradition. Wellhausen believed that Judges 1 belongs to the Jehovist and parallels the account of conquest as given in the Book of Joshua. Wellhausen writes, "This chapter, as well as the main stem of the Book of Judges, corresponds to

---

367 Wellhausen, *Prolegomena*, 358–359.
368 Wellhausen, *Prolegomena*, 355–356.
369 Wellhausen, *Prolegomena*, 355–356. According to Wellhausen, without the contact with other tribes, the Israelites would not have been able to keep marching on their way. In addition, Wellhausen pointed out that the enmity between the Israelites and other tribes inhabiting this area did not reflect Moses' time. He proposed that this hostility had appeared as a result of David's wars. On this see Wellhausen, *Die Composition des Hexateuch*s, 346.

the Jehovistic stratum of the tradition, to which also passages in Joshua, of an identical or similar import, may be added without hesitation."[370]

Wellhausen proposed that Judges 1 "tells the story of the conquest, and that in a manner somewhat differing from other sources."[371] Moreover, he observed that Judges 1 is "vastly nearer to the facts than that which prevails in the book of Joshua."[372] Wellhausen, to be sure, did not accept the priestly account of the conquest as given in the Book of Joshua. In his thinking, the priestly version "must be the narrative most remote from the origin of the Hebrew tradition."[373] Wellhausen summed up his view about Judges 1 and its contrast with the Book of Joshua as follows:

> Judges 1 presents certain anachronisms, and is partly made up of anecdotes, but these should not prevent us from acknowledging that the general view given in this chapter of the process of the conquest, is, when judged by what we know of the subsequent period of Israel, incomparably more historical than that in the Book of Joshua, where the whole thing is done at once with systematic thoroughness, the whole land being first denuded of its inhabitants, and then divided by lot among the different tribes.[374]

Guided by insights obtained mostly from source criticism and historical reconstruction Wellhausen sought to construct a historical sketch of early Israel in the pre-monarchic period. He made use only of what seemed to him to represent the historical tradition. This appears in his portrait of the conquest and settlement of Palestine. According to Wellhausen, there were two movements across the Jordan to take possession of the land of Canaan. The first attempt was made by Judah in conjunction with Simon and Levi, but it was far from prosperous. The second was led by the tribe of Joseph to which others attached themselves, only Reuben and Gad remaining behind on the old settlement.[375] As a re-

---

370 In Wellhausen's view, the difference which exists between Judges 1 and the Jehovistic main version in the Book of Joshua "is to be explained for the most part by the fact that the latter is of Ephraimite origin, and in consequence ascribes the conquest of the whole land to the hero of Ephraim or of Joseph, while Judges 1 leans more to the tribe of Judah." See Wellhausen, *Prolegomena*, 358–359. Furthermore, Wellhausen wrote: "Es scheint, dass in der gegenwärtigen Gestalt des B. Josua eine ältere Version restweise erhalten ist, die mit der von Jud. 1 näher verwandt war. Vgl. Jos. 9, 4—7. 12—14, wo statt Josua vielmehr der israelitische Mann handelt." See Wellhausen, *Die Composition des Hexateuchs*, 209.
371 Wellhausen, *Prolegomena*, 358.
372 Wellhausen, "Pentateuch and Joshua," 513.
373 Wellhausen, "Pentateuch and Joshua," 513.
374 Wellhausen, *Prolegomena*, 359.
375 Wellhausen noted that the narrative provides information only concerning the two tribes of Judah and Joseph. In Wellhausen's words "it is only of the movements of these two tribes that we

sult of the tribal movement across the Jordan, Wellhausen remarked a major change in the history of the tribes:

> A new division of the nation into Israel and Judah took the place of that which had previously subsisted between the families of Leah and Rachel; under Israel were included all the tribes except Simeon, Levi, and Judah, which three are no longer mentioned in Judges v., where all the others are carefully and exhaustively enumerated.[376]

Wellhausen assumed, "The army that went out against the Amorites from Kadesh was certainly not exclusively composed of men who, or whose fathers, had accomplished the passage of the Red Sea."[377] Wellhausen's assumption implies that not all the twelve tribes existed side by side in Kadesh.[378] Although he proposed that the unity of the tribes was established before the conquest of Palestine, he nevertheless suggested that the family of Leah had never been in Egypt. As Wellhausen puts it, "In Wirklichkeit sind vielleicht die Leastämme nie in Ägypten gewesen, sondern haben von ihren östlich angrenzenden Sitzen den stammverwandten Söhnen Raheis in Gosen, zur Zeit des Auszuges, die Hand geboten und sich erst damals zu einem Volke mit ihnen vereinigt."[379] Again, the implication is clear: Wellhausen regarded early Israel as consisting of the six Leah tribes with the addition of Joseph. The unity of the tribes was achieved by Moses, who introduced them the religion of Yahweh. Wellhausen theorized, "Perhaps the combination of Rachel and Leah in a national unity was only accomplished by Moses. Moses came from the peninsula of Sinai (Leah) to lead the Israelites there from Goshen (Joseph)."[380]

In this way, Wellhausen continued to map out the course of conquest and settlement in Palestine. He mentioned that the last achievement of Joshua was his victory against Jabin, King of Hazor and the allied princes of Galilee. Wellhausen pointed out that Joshua's defeat of Jabin and his allies enabled him to open up the north for Israelite settlers. One thing should be noted here. Although Wellhausen conceded that the conquest was conducted through military campaign,

---

have a regular narrative, and for Joseph this is limited to the first beginnings of his conquests. There is no mention of Joshua; a commander-in-chief of all Israel would indeed be out of place in this record of the conquest, but Joshua might have appeared in it as commander of his own tribe." See Wellhausen, "Pentateuch and Joshua," 513.

376 Wellhausen, "Israel," 441.
377 Wellhausen, "Israel," 431.
378 Wellhausen, *Prolegomena*, 432.
379 Wellhausen, *Die Composition des Hexateuchs*, 345.
380 Wellhausen, *Prolegomena*, 323.

he recognized the incompleteness of the conquest.[381] In Wellhausen's view, the preliminary work of the conquest took place under a united tribal effort but the rest was undertaken by individual tribes. As he put it, "The business of effecting permanent settlement was just a continuation of the former struggle, only on a diminished scale; every tribe and every family now fought for its own hand."[382]

Thus so far is Wellhausen's presentation of conquest and settlement tradition. As we have seen, it is characteristic of Wellhausen that he started by analyzing the sources and examining their historical credibility for historical purpose. As far as the tradition of conquest and settlement is concerned, Wellhausen based his analysis on three factors. He began by applying "historical criticism to the several versions of the way in which the tribes of Israel got possession of the land of Canaan."[383] As for the second step, he realized that he had to remove what he called 'alluvial deposits', by which he likely meant the religious presupposition of the author and the editing process implemented in the text.[384] The criterion Wellhausen then applied was, "Only it may stand as a general principle that the nearer history is to its origin, the more profane it is."[385] The chief purpose of Wellhausen was to identify the older phase of tradition in its genuine and historical origin. Towards this end, he suggested that the Jehovist provides a true picture of the tradition concerning the conquest. In contrast, Wellhausen pointed out that the Priestly Code presents a different account for the conquest, one that is far away from the Hebrew traditions.

5 The people of Israel in the land of Canaan

As usual, Wellhausen based his interpretation on information obtained from criticism of the sources. His presentation of the period preceding the monarchy shows that he distinguished between the historical sources and deuteronomic re-

---

381 In *Prolegomena* Wellhausen tells us that "the incompleteness of the conquest is acknowledged unreservedly; the Canaanites lived on quietly in the cities of the plain, and not till the period of the monarchy, when Israel had grown strong, were they subdued and made tributary". See Wellhausen, *Prolegomena*, 358. Wellhausen also emphasized "von einer vollständigen Eroberung des Landes war keine Rede." See Wellhausen, *Israelitische und jüdische Geschichte*, 35.
382 Wellhausen, "Israel," 444: see further Wellhausen, *Israelitische und jüdische Geschichte*, 35.
383 Wellhausen, "Pentateuch and Joshua," 512.
384 Wellhausen, *Prolegomena*, 228.
385 Wellhausen, *Prolegomena*, 245.

daction.[386] Thus, for example, he held that the Books of Judges, Samuel and Kings had been subjected to deuteronomistic revision. In Wellhausen's view, the original content of these books lacks the continuous chronology and religious connection of the events that were created by the historical work of a deuteronomic redactor.[387]

In order to reach the tradition in its original form, Wellhausen saw the need for a 'source-sifting' process.[388] In addition, he set up new rules for historical reconstruction. Among them is his requirement that "history has to take account principally, if not exclusively, of the natural version, which is dry in tone and lets things speak for themselves, not overlaying the simple story with the significance of its consequences."[389] In referring to the pre-deuteronomic version of tradition, Wellhausen tells us "in the pre-deuteronomic narratives, the difference is to be recognized less in the *kind* of piety than in the *degree* of it."[390]

It turns out that Wellhausen was aware of additions and supplements implemented in the original text. This appears, for example, in the analysis of the Book of Judges which Wellhausen reduced its original content. Thus, Wellhausen suggested that the chronological accounting of events and the religious pragmatism were not part of the original account.[391] In addition, Wellhausen disregarded Judges 19–21 as source of historical information. The reason is that these chapters belong to the Priestly Code and thus reflect the attitudes of the post-exilic situation. Wellhausen further observed that Israel is depicted as a "Sakrale Gemeinde." In his estimation, "Nicht bloß unter den Königen sind diese Zustände nicht zu finden, sondern erst recht nicht unter den Richtern, überhaupt nicht im alten Israel, sondern erst bei den nachexilischen Juden, wo es kein Volk, sondern nur noch eine Kirche gab."[392]

With this in mind, Wellhausen turned to reconstructing the main features of the period of Judges, without much recourse to deuteronomistic revision or priestly writings. Thus Wellhausen asserted that Canaan was not occupied at once and that the Israelite settlement was restricted to "the mountainous land, particularly the southern hill country of Mount Ephraim."[393] This means

---

386 See Hans-Joachim Kraus, *Geschichte der Historisch-Kritischen Erforschung des Alten Testaments*, 266–267.
387 Wellhausen, *Prolegomena*, 229.
388 Wellhausen, *Prolegomena*, 360.
389 Wellhausen, *Prolegomena*, 244–245.
390 Wellhausen, *Prolegomena*, 245.
391 Wellhausen, *Die Composition des Hexateuchs*, 211.
392 Wellhausen, *Die Composition des Hexateuchs*, 320.
393 Wellhausen, "Israel," 444.

that Wellhausen rejected the account of the whole destruction of Canaan as in the deuteronomistic version and the Priestly Code. He pointed out that the individual tribes during the period of Judges had a hard fight to maintain their position among the Canaanites. In Wellhausen's words, "Die Kanaaniten wurden nicht mit einem Schlage vertilgt, sondern allmählich aufgesogen."[394]

The implication of Wellhausen's understanding of the process of conquest and settlement in Canaan is worth noting. It means that the settlement was accomplished in two phases: the first was a military battle conducted by a number of tribes, succeeded by the occupation of a small territory in Canaan. This was followed by a long process of peaceful settlement. The reality, as Wellhausen saw it was that the Canaanites remained for centuries before the Israelites were able to subjugate them. This is what Wellhausen wrote in this regard:

> An eine Ausrottung der sämtlichen Ureinwohner zu denken, verbietet schon die Art und Weise der Eroberung. Von größeren Städten, welche unbezwungen blieben, ist uns ein ziemliches Verzeichnis erhalten, welches gleichwohl ganz lückenhaft ist und sogar aus unserer doch so ärmlichen Kunde sich vervollständigen läßt. Erst im Laufe von zwei drei Jahrhunderten wurden diese Städte eine nach der anderen unterworfen; unter den ersten Königen waren immer noch etliche übrig.[395]

Furthermore, Wellhausen observed that not all the tribes, but only some of them, had to fight against the Canaanites. This appears in the war waged by Barak against the allied kings of Canaan under the leadership of Sisera. To quote Wellhausen:

> It is only the individual tribes that come into the action; the Judges are tribal heroes, Ehud of Benjamin, Barak and Deborah of Issachar, Gideon of Joseph, Jephthah of Gilead, Samson of Dan. It was only for the struggle against Sisera that a number of tribes were united, receiving on that account extraordinary praise in the song of Deborah.[396]

Pursuing this further, Wellhausen made the point clear that the period of Judges is presented as the introduction of the monarchy. Thus Wellhausen asserted, "The period of the Judges presents itself to us as a confused chaos."[397] Moreover,

---

394 Wellhausen, *Grundrisse zum Alten Testament*, 82.
395 Wellhausen, *Israelitische und jüdische Geschichte*, 44.
396 Wellhausen, *Prolegomena*, 233–234. As for the song of Debora and its importance, Wellhausen said "Es wirft einen hellen Schein auch über die allgemeine politische und geistige Beschaffenheit des damaligen Israels." On this see Wellhausen, *Israelitische und jüdische Geschichte*, 37.
397 Wellhausen, *Prolegomena*, 5.

he noted, "It is nowhere said at the time when the Judges ruled," but "at the time when there was yet no king over Israel, and every man did what was right in his own eyes."[398] Based on this, Wellhausen concluded that during the period of Judges "Israel ist kein Organismus...Israel ist nur eine Idee."[399]

According to Wellhausen, the most important change that occurred in the period of the Judges was the growing number of the people of Israel in Canaan. He said that the reason for this rapid increase was absorption of the local population. In the words of Wellhausen, "The old population of the country, which, according to Deuteronomy, was to have been exterminated, slowly became amalgamated with the new. In this way the Israelites received a very important accession to their numbers."[400] Along the same lines, Wellhausen mentioned, "Die Israeliten der Königszeit hatten eine sehr starke Beimischung kanaanitischen Blutes, sie waren keineswegs reine Abkömmlinge derer, die einst aus Ägypten gezogen und in der Wüste gewandert waren."[401]

The most important change that marked the period of Judges is that the Israelite nomads became farmers in Canaan. Wellhausen proposed that the Hebrew tribes learned agriculture from the Canaanites, in whose land they settled. The transition from the life of the nomad to a sedentary life occurred during the period of Judges. As Wellhausen puts it, "Durch die Eroberung Palästinas wurden sie ansässig, binnen kurzem finden wir sie völlig zu Bauern geworden."[402]

In addition, Wellhausen made it clear that the historical development of Israel was due to its acceptance of the new civilization offered to them in Canaan. Without this merging with the culture of Canaan, Israel would have remained like its other neighbours. In Wellhausen's words:

> Had the Israelites remained in the wilderness and in barbarism, the historical development they subsequently reached would hardly have been possible; their career would have been like that of Amalek, or, at best, like those of Edom, Moab, and Ammon. Their acceptance of civilization was undoubtedly a step in the forward direction.[403]

It seems quite clear that Wellhausen regarded the period of Judges not as decline of the nation of Israel but of its rise. "Es war eine kritische Übergangsperiode, chaotisch, aber doch auch schöpferisch. Das Ende war nicht der Niedergang,

398 Wellhausen, *Prolegomena*, 233.
399 Wellhausen, *Israelitische und jüdische Geschichte*, 37.
400 Wellhausen, "Israel," 446.
401 Wellhausen, *Israelitische und jüdische Geschichte*, 44.
402 Wellhausen, *Israelitische und jüdische Geschichte*, 46.
403 Wellhausen, "Israel," 447; idem, *Israelitische und jüdische Geschichte*, 48.

sondern der Aufschwung der Nation."[404] Moreover, Wellhausen pointed out that it was during the period of Judges that the first attempt to establish kingship was made. He observed that Gideon's victory over the Midianites "transmitted to his sons an authority, which was not limited to Abiezer and Manasseh alone, but, however slightly and indirectly, extended over Ephraim."[405] In this manner, Wellhausen closed his reconstruction of the period of Judges by referring to Abimelech's attempt to establish himself as king over Israel, that is, over Ephraim and Manasseh.[406]

Moreover, it is evident that Wellhausen saw the rise of the Israelite monarchy as a necessity brought forth by the circumstances of the period of Judges. He writes, "At the end of the period of the Judges, Israel is not at the summit of power and prosperity, but in a state of the deepest humiliation and the means of saving the people from this state is seen in the monarchy alone."[407] In this context, we must note that Wellhausen's depiction of the period of Judges accords well with his overall outline of the history of ancient Israel. In Wellhausen's opinion, Israel as a nation began with Moses, but its real political history started with David.[408] It can be said that Wellhausen did not find anything unique or particular in premonarchic period. The reality was that the people of Israel were people just like any other. Neither the early history of Israel, nor Israel's religious history show distinct features. Wellhausen then concluded, "Israel ist nur eine Idee."[409] And Israel as an idea is equivalent to Jehovah.[410] In a word, Wellhausen would go for the idea that what set the Israelites apart from their neighbours was not a divine covenant, but acceptance of Canaanite culture.

404 Wellhausen, *Grundrisse zum Alten Testament*, 84.
405 Wellhausen, "Israel," 445–446.
406 Wellhausen, "Israel," 446.
407 Wellhausen, *Prolegomena*, 252.
408 Wellhausen, *Prolegomena*, 19–20, n.1.
409 Wellhausen, *Israelitische und jüdische Geschichte*, 37
410 Wellhausen, *Israelitische und jüdische Geschichte*, 37.

Part II **From Religion to History:**
Yehezkel Kaufmann's Interpretation
of Ancient Israel

Chapter Four:
History of Israelite Religion: Literary Analysis

1 Introduction

I have chosen to start with the literary analysis of Yehezkel Kaufmann for two reasons. First, Kaufmann's entire theory is based on the assumption that the Torah is the main source of Israelite religion.[411] Second, it has been said that Kaufmann's literary criticism of the Pentateuch and the literature of classical prophecy is intimately bound up with the history of religion.[412] This means that the origin of Israelite religion and the beginning of monotheism in Israel were of primary concern to Kaufmann. He begins his investigation by examining the relationship between the Torah and Prophecy and dating the Priestly Code with the aim of finding ancient material in the Torah literature. Kaufmann's endeavour, it will be shown, was to prove that the main source of the Pentateuch, the Priestly Code, reflects the early stages of Israelite religion. In so doing. Kaufmann argued that Priestly Laws preceded those of Deuteronomy and owed nothing to their essential features. Moreover, Kaufmann reconsidered the relationship between the Torah and the Prophets with the aim of demonstrating that the former lacked the main aspects of the latter. In Kaufmann's view, therefore, the Torah reflected a stage of religious development predating the Prophets. In what follows I shall highlight the main points of Kaufmann's view in this regard.

2 The Torah and prophecy

By examining the relationship between the Torah and prophecy, Kaufmann was trying to answer the following question: to what extent can the Torah be regarded as a source for the earliest stages of Israelite religion; is its monotheism pre-prophetic?[413] In order to provide a convincing answer to this question, Kaufmann divided the biblical books into larger units based on what he called "the idea-constants that appear in various books, bringing them into connection with one another and distinguishing them from books of other groupings."[414] Accord-

---

411 Kaufmann, *Toledot* 1, 46.
412 On this see Moshe Greenberg's preface to Kaufmann, *The Religion of Israel* (Chicago: The University of Chicago Press, 1960).
413 Kaufmann, *The Religion of Israel*, 157.
414 Kaufmann, *The Religion of Israel*, 157.

ing to Kaufmann's analysis, there are two literary groups: the Torah group, including the historical books (Former Prophets), and the Prophets. In Kaufmann's thinking, "The ideas of each group are so different as to preclude the possibility that the former was inspired by the doctrines of the latter."[415]

Kaufmann refused to see the distinction between Torah and prophecy as being merely a difference between priestly cultic and prophetic ethics. Instead, he maintained that they diverged in basic view.[416] Thus, for instance, Kaufmann contended that the religious perspective of the circle which produced the Torah was not formed under the influence of literary prophecy.[417] In addition, Kaufmann pointed out that the Torah and prophecy were two different and independent manifestations of the Israelite religion.[418] Kaufmann drew attention to the fact that the literary prophets have had little impact on the people of Israel and their influence was very limited.[419] The historical books, said Kaufmann, did not hint at any of the literary prophets. The Book of Kings, for instance, mentions only Isaiah, not as a preacher, but as a foreteller and wonder-worker.[420] Therefore, Kaufmann concluded that the prophetic books became known to the people only later on. He suggested that the literary prophets were in the eyes of their contemporaries 'prophets' like any other and only few people realized the new ideas contained in the teachings of literary prophets. Accordingly, Kaufmann deduced that literary prophecy was not at the centre of the religious life of the people of Israel.[421] More illuminating is Kaufmann's indication that the Book of Kings did not consider literary prophecy. This means that the religious horizon of the Book of Kings and historical books were not shaped in the school (בית מדרש) of literary prophecy.[422] In order to support his arguments, Kaufmann listed many differences separating the Torah group from the literary prophets. These included a view of Israel's history, cults and morality, and the doctrine of centralized worship, reform movement, as well as eschatology. In what follows I shall provide a precise overview of Kaufmann's arguments.

With regard to Israel's history, Kaufmann pointed out that the historical perspective of the Torah differed from that of the prophets. He noted that the prophets reproved the people of Israel for two types of sin, religious and moral, but

---

415 Kaufmann, *The Religion of Israel*, 157.
416 Kaufmann, *Commentary on Joshua*, 17–18.
417 Kaufmann, *Toledot* I, 24.
418 Kaufmann, *Toledot* I, 24–25.
419 Kaufmann, *Toledot* I, 25.
420 Kaufmann, *Toledot* I, 25.
421 Kaufmann, *Toledot* I, 26.
422 Kaufmann, *Toledot* I, 26.

that they particularly condemned moral sin. On the other hand, Kaufmann maintained that the historical books spoke only about religious sin with no mention of moral corruption. Furthermore, the prophetic denunciation of social corruption, injustice, oppression and suppression by the rich were absent from the historical books.[423] That is to say, while the prophets denounced social decay, the historical books made no mention of it. In addition, as Kaufmann demonstrated, in the Torah and historical books, Israel's sin was the worship of foreign gods and the adoption of heathen customs. The prophets, by contrast, condemned the people for moral corruption. This is how Kaufmann argued for the difference in historical view between the Torah and the literary prophets. The point he strove to make was that the Torah group differed strongly from the literary prophets in its understanding of the type of sin that affected Israel's history.[424]

Kaufmann's second reason for distinguishing the Torah's world from that of the literary prophets is related to cult and morality. The prophets emphasised the moral aspects of religion more than cult and rituals. This is not the case as far as the books of the Torah group are concerned. In the Torah group, according to Kaufmann, both religious ritual and moral aspects were given equal emphasis, and were indiscriminately juxtaposed.[425] He further maintained that the idea of morality was not overlooked in the Torah in favour of ceremonial or cultic matters. The absence of this idea was a sign not of a later stage than prophecy but of a stage that predated it. It was but a step from the moral outlook of the Torah to the doctrine of primacy of morality (cf. Deut.10:17 ff); but this step was never taken before the advent of prophecy.[426]

Respecting the idea of centralized worship, Kaufmann remarked that whereas the idea of a chosen place for worship dominated the Torah group and was the prevailing theme in Israelite thought from the end of the monarchy, it received no mention by the pre-deuteronomic prophets. Moreover, Kaufmann pointed out that no prophet asserted that God had to be worshiped at a specific site.[427] In the words of Kaufmann:

> It is decisive that neither Amos, Hosea, Isaiah, nor Micah reproach the north for not sacrificing at Jerusalem. For the manner of their worship, both Judah and Israel alike come in for denunciation. Worship at the high places was tainted with idolatrous rites that the prophets attacked, but so too was the worship of the Jerusalem temple. The sole conclusion that could be drawn from prophetic rebukes was that the worship at the high places (as at

---

423 Kaufmann, *Toledot* I, 27 – 31.
424 Kaufmann, *Toledot* I, 27 – 31; idem, *The Religion of Israel*, 158 – 160.
425 Kaufmann, *The Religion of Israel*, 160.
426 Kaufmann, *The Religion of Israel*, 160 – 161.
427 Kaufmann, *The Religion of Israel*, 161.

the Jerusalem temple) must be purged of its heathen elements, but not that the high places must be destroyed.[428]

Kaufmann concluded:

> The ban on high places in Deuteronomy and related literature is derived from the monotheistic idea. But this is a specifically priestly version of the monotheistic idea without roots in prophetic teaching. The prophets never drew this conclusion from their own doctrines; post-deuteronomic prophets accept the idea, but it is not their creation.[429]

What is remarkable, however, is Kaufmann's attempt to minimize the prophetic influence on Israelite religion. Thus, for example, he asserted that the social reform of the prophets had no place in Josianic reform. The prophets were mainly concerned with righteousness and matters of justice. Josiah, according to Kaufmann, was dismayed by the Torah's warnings of disaster for religious sin.[430] Moreover, the Book of Kings does not mention any prophet among the initiators of Josiah's reform. On the other hand, Kaufmann drew attention to the role of the priests as promoters of the reform movement. He argued that the reform was purely cultic. Based on this understanding, Kaufmann concluded that the priests were the standard-bearers of Josianic reform. Not a prophetic message but the book of the Torah found in the temple gave the initial impetus.[431]

At the end of his discussion on the differences between the Torah group and the literary prophets, Kaufmann explored the divergence in eschatology.[432] According to Kaufmann, prophetic eschatology reached its climax in the vision of the universal kingship of YHWH.[433] This vision was not yet present in the books of the Torah group. In Kaufmann's opinion, the outlook of the Torah literature could best be described as cosmic-national monotheism.[434] He further maintained:

---

428 Kaufmann, *The Religion of Israel*, 162.
429 Kaufmann, *The Religion of Israel*, 162. For more discussion, see Kaufmann, *Toledot* I, 34–37.
430 Kaufmann, *The Religion of Israel*, 163.
431 Kaufmann, *The Religion of Israel*, 163. According to Kaufmann, "That pre-exilic monotheism was fostered by priestly and popular circles, whose thought is reflected in the Torah rather than by the literary prophets, is manifested clearly in the accounts of the reforms of Hezekiah and Josiah." See Kaufmann, *The Religion of Israel*, 162.
432 Compare Kaufmann, *Toledot* I, 39–44.
433 Kaufmann, *The Religion of Israel*, 163.
434 Kaufmann, *The Religion of Israel*, 163.

The eschatological visions of the Torah lack the motif of a universal religious conversion; even in the golden age of the future the distinction between Israel and the idolatrous nations remains. The eschatological vision of the Torah is of an age in which Israel will dominate its enemies, or the heathen nations (Lev. 26: 7–13; Deut. 28: 7–14; 30: 7; 32: 34–43).[435]

These are the main points, as far as Kaufmann's view on the relationship between the Torah and the prophets is concerned. In contrast to the common view which overstated the role of the prophetic ideas in the history of Israelite religion, Kaufmann instead argued that the Torah had to be seen as the primary source of Israel's religion.[436] His view was that the Torah belonged to the earliest stage of religious development, which was prior to and independent of literary prophecy.[437] Much evidence attested to the antiquity of the Torah.[438] Thus Kaufmann wrote:

> The literature of the Torah group and the literary prophets must be regarded as distinct domains. The Torah cannot be understood as a later outgrowth of prophetic faith. Literary prophecy cannot, then, be considered the fountainhead or 'ideal source' of Israelite monotheism.[439]

As will be shown, Kaufmann tried to prove that monotheism did not grow out of prophetic doctrine.[440] The origin of Israelite monotheism was rooted in popular religion as reflected in the Torah literature.[441] Kaufmann saw the prophets as merely the ethical interpreters of traditions. Their message did not eradicate the inherited faith of the people. The main contribution of the prophets was to be seen as emphasising the moral dimension. They did not bring a new religion but built upon the existing Israelite religion. On account of this, Kaufmann concluded that the Torah was the literary product of the earliest stage of Israelite religion.[442] Its religious view was developed independently from prophetic influence.

435 Kaufmann, *The Religion of Israel*, 164.
436 Kaufmann, *Toledot* I, 23.
437 Kaufmann, *Toledot* I, 185.
438 Kaufmann gave a detailed exposition of this point in *Toledot* I, 185–201.
439 Kaufmann, *The Religion of Israel*, 165.
440 Kaufmann, *Toledot* III, 6–7.
441 Kaufmann, *Toledot* I, 221–254.
442 Kaufmann, *The Religion of Israel*, 166; See further, idem, *Toledot* I, 220.

3 Antiquity of the Priestly Code

3.1 The law corpora

Kaufmann believed that the Legal Corpora were the heart and essence of the Torah. Therefore, before proceeding to show the main arguments supporting Kaufmann's assumption that the Priestly Code predated Deuteronomy, it would not be out of place here to highlight his view of the law corpora of the Pentateuch, their characteristics and relationships. Equally important, as it will be shown, was Kaufmann's analysis of Deuteronomy.

Kaufmann considered the criticism of the pentateuchal laws to be the most significant part of Biblical Criticism.[443] He identified three law codes: the JE code of Exodus, the Priestly Code (P), chiefly in Exodus, Leviticus and Numbers; and thirdly the Laws of Deuteronomy (D).[444] According to Kaufmann, these three codes were distinct in terms of terminology and style. The larger Covenant Code, containing most of the JE laws, is composed in a terse and precise juristic style, whereas the Priestly Code is distinguished by its developed cultic terminology. The deuteronomic Code had much of the didactic and hortatory style of a sermon[445]. In addition, Kaufmann pointed out that the law codes were ideologically distinct from one another. He wrote:

> The command to love God is found some ten times in D; P lacks this idea, but commands, in its stead, to fear God. Profanation of God's name by man is an idea found only in P. No code other than P makes the alien and the Israelite equal under the law. D is alone in ascribing a deterrent function to punishment. Stoning is the sole capital punishment known to D; P speaks also of burning and stabbing (Num. 25:8). Stripes are mentioned only in D; 'excision' only in P.[446]

However, Kaufmann had a reservation regarding the relationship of the three law codes. He agreed that they had a large fund of laws and ideas in common. He also said that there were literary contacts between them, especially between the Covenant Code and Deuteronomy. Nevertheless, he remarked, "The differences – especially the incidental, trivial ones for which no intent can be assigned – are sufficiently marked to cast serious doubt on the conventional theory of their

---

443 For complete understanding of Kaufmann's view in this regard, see Kaufmann, *Toledot* I, 47–80.

444 Kaufmann, *Toledot* I, 48; also, idem, *The Religion of Israel*, 166.

445 Kaufmann, *The Religion of Israel*, 166.

446 Kaufmann, *The Religion of Israel*, 167. For a discussion see Kaufmann, *Toledot* I, 49–53.

evolution one from another."[447] Thus, for example, Kaufmann denied the assumption of classical criticism that Deuteronomy revised and developed, in its more generous spirit, the ancient laws of the Covenant Code.[448] He argued that Deuteronomy and the Covenant Code were independent crystallizations of Israel's legal-moral literature: "The common content and stylistic affinities are due to a common source. They cannot, however, be regarded as indicative of a literary-historical relationship."[449] Likewise, Kaufmann compared the laws of JE and P to determine whether or not the JE code served as the source of P.[450] Though he noted that most of the JE laws were to be found in P, he nevertheless refuted the assumption that P incorporated the laws of JE. In his view, "when both P and D were being composed, the laws of JE had not yet attained canonical status."[451]

Respecting the relationship between the D and P laws, Kaufmann rebutted the theory that placed D at an earlier stage of development, prior to P. That P displayed no knowledge of the D law of centralized worship was, in Kaufmann's view, enough to negate this assumption.[452] Kaufmann maintained that the laws of P were entirely different from those of D. For example, "P's priestly gifts do not supplement, but differ completely from, those of D. To be sure, P's gifts are more numerous, but the crucial point, so far as literary history is concerned, is that they do not include those of D."[453] Kaufmann continued:

> Parallel laws in P and D exhibit divergences that cannot be ascribed to differences in viewpoint. Numbers 33: 52 parallels Deuteronomy 7: 1–5, 25 f. (cf. 12: 2 f.), without enjoining the burning of idols or banning their silver and gold ornaments. Treating of prohibited foods, D enumerates the clean animals (Deut. 14: 4 f.), P the unclean only (Lev. 11). P knows the law of the Sabbath of the soil, but is silent regarding the release of debts in that year. P's enumeration of idolatrous practices in Leviticus 19: 26, 31; 20: 1–6 leaves out sorcery and charming, which are listed in Deuteronomy 18: 10 ff. Another divergence which can only be ascribed to distinct styles is P's stock phrase 'the stranger and the poor', as against D's 'stranger, orphan, and widow' (the latter two are never mentioned in P).[454]

Having examined the relationship of the three codes, Kaufmann reached a conclusion according to which "each of the three codes of the Torah is to be regard-

---

447 Kaufmann, *The Religion of Israel*, 167.
448 Kaufmann, *Toledot* I, 54–58; idem, *The Religion of Israel*, 168.
449 Kaufmann, *The Religion of Israel*, 168.
450 Kaufmann *Toledot* I, 58–61.
451 Kaufmann, *The Religion of Israel*, 169.
452 Kaufmann, *The Religion of Israel*, 169.
453 Kaufmann, *The Religion of Israel*, 169.
454 Kaufmann, *The Religion of Israel*, 170.

ed as an independent crystallization of Israel's ancient juristic-moral literature."[455] "What is of crucial historical importance," as Kaufmann demonstrated, "is the fact that each of the codes has its own characteristic style and that no cross-influences are in evidence."[456] Kaufmann further argued, "No traces of a priestly redaction can be detected in the laws of D or JE. More important, nothing characteristic of D's style can be seen in P. Nor was there warrant for the view that JE had undergone a deuteronomic editing."[457] In Kaufmann's view, this pointed to an independent literary history for each of the law codes.[458] At the end of his discussion on the fixation of the law codes, Kaufmann wrote:

> The codes were fixed and closed by the time the various Pentateuchal sources were being collected into one book. They were incorporated into the Torah book as finished entities and neither edited, revised, nor stylized. The narrative sources were blended, but the legal corpora – the heart and essence of the Torah – were preserved intact by the compilers. They were fitted into the narrative, but each corpus was incorporated as received.[459]

3.2 Deuteronomy

Kaufmann argued that while Deuteronomy contained ancient material, it was not of great import for the history of Israelite religion. Though Kaufmann accepted the classic view that Deuteronomy was promulgated in the region of Josiah, he nevertheless differentiated between an 'early' and 'late' Deuteronomy. In his view, 'early D' comprising chapters (1–11; 27–36) was pre-Josianic, while 'late D' in chapters (12–26) dated from Josiah's time in the 7th century BCE.[460] Moreover, in his analysis of the Priestly Code, Kaufmann argued that P predated any cult centralization as envisioned in Deuteronomy. Taking the unification of the cult as the point of departure, Kaufmann affirmed, "The historical philosophy of the book of Deuteronomy had no original connection with unification of the cult and is older than it."[461] Furthermore, "The idea of centralization is the touchstone by which we can distinguish the two major strata, Genesis-Numbers (JEP), and Deuteronomy-Kings (the deuteronomic stratum). Only in D and

---

455 Kaufmann, *The Religion of Israel*, 170; idem, *Toledot* I, 65.
456 Kaufmann, *The Religion of Israel*, 171.
457 Kaufmann, *The Religion of Israel*, 171.
458 Kaufmann, *The Religion of Israel*, 172; idem *Toledot* I, 79.
459 Kaufmann, *The Religion of Israel*, 172; idem, *Toledot* I, 79–80.
460 Kaufmann, "The Biblical Age," 4–7. For detailed analysis of Deuteronomy and Josiah's reform, see Kaufmann, *Toledot* I, 87–104.
461 Kaufmann, *Commentary on the Book of Joshua*, 5–7.

related literature is there a clear and unmistakable influence of the centralization idea."[462] More precisely, Kaufmann correlated the centralization of the
cult with a specific historical factor. In the words of Kaufmann:

> Since the idea of centralization in its deuteronomic form does not appear in the prophetic
> literature or the realities of the pre-Hezekiah age, it must be assumed to have arisen later.
> The stratum of D concerning the centralization of worship must be considered a product of
> the age in which it first appears as a historical factor, the age of Hezekiah and Josiah.[463]

Kaufmann, then, comes to the conclusion that:

> The novelty of the deuteronomic law is not the conception of a great central sanctuary of
> unique importance and holiness. From earliest times, the great sanctuaries of Shechem, Be-
> thel, Dan, Gibeon, and Jerusalem overshadowed the smaller local altars. To these great tem-
> ples, it was the custom to make pilgrimages three times a year (I Sam. 1; I Kings 8). The new
> feature of Deuteronomy is its emphatic interdiction of all sacrifice outside the one chosen
> site (Deut. 12:13 f., 17, 26 f.).[464]

As for the problem of D's composition, Kaufmann wrote:

> While the composition of D is a problem in itself, it is not of crucial import to the history of
> Israelite religion. Certain it is that D contains ancient materials, although their precise dat-
> ing cannot be fixed. But, except for its final chapters, D's style and character are its own.
> None of its peculiarities is to be found in the four preceding books of the Torah, and noth-
> ing of them has insinuated itself into D. No part of D requires a post-exilic dating, not even
> those passages that speak of exile and restoration.[465]

We have seen that Kaufmann related cult centralization, as manifested in Deuteronomy, with the reform of Josiah.[466] Kaufmann saw Josiah as the only king
who made a covenant on the basis of the book of Torah.[467] This evidence was

---

462 Kaufmann, *The Religion of Israel*, 205.

463 Kaufmann, *The Religion of Israel*, 174.

464 Kaufmann, *The Religion of Israel*, 173.

465 Kaufmann, *The Religion of Israel*, 174; idem, *Toledot* I, 104–108.

466 Kaufmann, "The Biblical Age," 71.

467 Kaufmann, "The Biblical Age," 71. Perhaps we should refer to Kaufmann's view concerning
the relationship of Josiah's reform and the book of Deuteronomy. In Kaufmann's view, "To what
extent a moral-religious book like Deuteronomy could have become a political constitution is
difficult to say; the experiment was made too near the collapse of Judah to tell. What can be
said is that in the Josianic reform, the priestly idea of a book of Torah as the basis of national
life took its first great step toward realization. This is its lasting historical significance." See Kaufmann, *The Religion of Israel*, 290.

taken by Kaufmann to support his view regarding the earlier date of the Torah and its importance as a basic book of national life. He writes, "Two purposes are manifest in Josiah's activity, the desire to centralize worship and the desire to establish a book of YHWH's Torah as the basis of national life. This latter, no less than the former, is a distinctive feature of the deuteronomic reform. The idea of a book of Torah as a popular book and the idea of the study of the Torah are given unique stress in Deuteronomy."[468] Moreover, Deuteronomy was "the first stage in the development of the Torah as a book in which the word of God is fixed and becomes binding upon the people."[469] In this way, Kaufmann considered the book of Deuteronomy to be the first canonized book. With Deuteronomy, "the period of Torah literature came to an end, and the formation of the Torah book began."[470]

4 Pre-deuteronomic characteristics of the Priestly Code

Kaufmann's dating of "P" to pre-exilic time strove to prove that the monotheistic idea was a product of the earliest stage of Israelite religion.[471] It is perhaps for this reason that Kaufmann undertook to study the priestly law as a literary product of ancient Israel. P, according to Kaufmann, contained ancient materials and reflected the earliest stage in religious history. As he put it, "The literary product of the ancient Israelite priesthood is the priestly stratum of the Torah (most of which is found from Exodus 25 to Numbers 36). Its laws and prescriptions give us an excellent idea of the part the priesthood played in the formation of Israelite monotheism."[472] As has been shown, Kaufmann ascribed the religious development of the Torah to a stage prior to classic prophecy. He also presupposed that P knew nothing of the peculiar ideas of D, especially the centralization of the cult.[473] Moreover, Kaufmann built a solid ground for his contention that P "fails completely to prohibit the cult at the high places."[474] In his commentary on the Book of Joshua, he stated that there was no opposition toward *bamoth*

---

468 Kaufmann, *The Religion of Israel*, 174.
469 Kaufmann, *The Religion of Israel*, 175.
470 Kaufmann, *The Religion of Israel*, 175; idem, *Toledot* I, 111–112.
471 For Kaufmann's contribution in this regard, see Thomas M. Krapf, *Die Priesterschrift und die vorexilische Zeit: Yehezkel Kaufmanns vernachlässigter Beitrag zur Geschichte der biblischen Religion* (OBO 119; Freiburg, 1992).
472 Kaufmann, "The Biblical Age," 26.
473 Kaufmann, *Toledot* I, 113.
474 Kaufmann, *The Religion of Israel*, 176.

in the priestly source, but against idolatry and impurity.[475] The most provocative argument in Kaufmann's reconstruction of the relationship between P and D was his statement that "none of the concepts that are peculiar to Deuteronomy are present in P."[476] The following are the main points in Kaufmann's discussion.

4.1 The chosen city and the camp

According to Kaufmann the idea of the 'chosen city,' which is peculiar to Deuteronomy, is missing from the P document. He noted that "the deuteronomic concept of centralization is not merely the abstract idea of an exclusive cult place, but the idea of an exclusive cult place at one chosen site. D's concept involves both a chosen temple and a chosen city."[477] The idea of a specific place of worship at one chosen site is, in Kaufmann's view, absent in P's law. He went so far as to maintain that "P [did] not even mention the law of appearing before YHWH on the three major festivals, let alone the requirement that this be done at a chosen site."[478] Moreover, Kaufmann pointed out that "in all the detailed laws of P prescribing the nature, the manner, and the times of sacrifice there [was] no reference to the place where the sacrificial meal [was] to be eaten."[479] This, in turn, means that P "fails to take notice of a basic consequence of the centralization law."[480] Furthermore, P's idea of 'camp' as a pure place does not parallel the sanctity of the deuteronomic 'chosen city'.[481] In attempting to validate his view, Kaufmann referred to the laws of Leviticus 14 as evidence of P's idea of the camp. He says, "P's camp represents at once a temple site as well as any city; D's separation of the two concepts is unknown to it."[482] The im-

---

475 Kaufmann, *Commentary on Joshua*, 240. Criticizing Kaufmann's assessment of the Priestly Code, Menahem Haran pointed out that Kaufmann "tries, to define P as the "law code for worship at the high places" and to claim that P does not actually demand cult centralization, on the ground that for P this idea has only conceptual and symbolic significance without practical implications – an interpretation which can by no means be adopted." See Menahem Haran, *Temples and Temple Service*, 7.
476 Kaufmann, *The Religion of Israel*, 176.
477 Kaufmann, *The Religion of Israel*, 176.
478 Kaufmann, *The Religion of Israel*, 177.
479 Kaufmann, *The Religion of Israel*, 177.
480 Kaufmann, *The Religion of Israel*, 177.
481 Kaufmann, *The Religion of Israel*, 177.
482 Kaufmann, *The Religion of Israel*, 178.

plication of all of this, in Kaufmann's view, is that D's characteristics of the one chosen place are absent from P's document.[483]

4.2 The festivals

In his analysis of the sacral feasts, Kaufmann was concerned to show that fixity in times and absence of natural spontaneity were common features in the festivals of ancient Babylonia, Egypt and other ancient civilizations, and hence could not be taken as evidence for the lateness of the Priestly Code.[484] According to Kaufmann, P's picture of Israelite festivals could more clearly be seen in Leviticus 23, which "not only recognizes a natural as well as ceremonial side to festivals, it provides the Israelite calendar with an agricultural festival missing from both JE and D – the celebration of the first sheaf."[485] Moreover, Kaufmann refused to see the Day of Atonement as a mournful memorial of historical sin. In his view, the Day of Atonement was "an annual purification of people and sanctuary, principally from ritual impurity. It had nothing to do with the sense of historic guilt that overwhelmed the Jews in the Babylonian exile."[486] Kaufmann found further evidence that P's festival laws were pre-deuteronomic, as seen, for example, in the custom of celebrating the feast of ingathering in booths which arose before centralization. In Kaufmann's opinion, D preserved only the name Tabernacle in this festival, but said nothing about dwelling in booths. The seven festival days were to be spent at the chosen site in the presence of YHWH. P, on the other hand, said nothing about appearing before YHWH, but still spoke of celebration in booths.[487]

4.3 Tent of meeting

Kaufmann constantly emphasized that "P" was unaware of the deuteronomic idea of centralization. The assumption that P's tent presupposed the centralization of the cult and therefore mirrored the conditions of the Second Temple was,

---

483 Kaufmann, *Toledot* I, 119.
484 See Moshe Weinfeld, *Getting at the Roots of Wellhausen's Understanding of the Law of Israel: On the 100th Anniversary of the Prolegomena* (The Institute for Advanced Studies, The Hebrew University, Jerusalem, 1979).
485 Kaufmann, *The Religion of Israel*, 178.
486 Kaufmann, *The Religion of Israel*, 178.
487 Kaufmann, *The Religion of Israel*, 179.

in Kaufmann's view, groundless.[488] Unlike D's 'place', P's tent was not a fixed and chosen site. P's tent was 'a portable sanctuary' in accord with the needs of the wandering tribes.[489] Thus, Kaufmann asserted:

> P knows of but one legitimate sanctuary, the 'tent of meeting'. But P's tent is not represented as a law, but as a historical fact...It was the only legitimate cult place. There is no intention, however, to exclude the legitimacy of many temple sites in the land after the conquest. That is why P is silent about the sin of the high places; it recognizes no such sin.[490]

However, there are hints that the local unity of worship that P depicts for the time of Moses was not a concept peculiar to priestly writing. Thus, for example, Kaufmann contended that JE also knew of only one camp and one tent. In the case of P, a priestly touch had been added with the insistence that only a sanctified precinct – and in the desert there was only one such precinct – was qualified for sacrifices.[491] All of these features are peculiar to P's tent of meeting and have nothing to do with the situation of the Second Temple.[492] Based on his perception of the nature of the tent of meeting, Kaufmann defined P's tent as "a priestly-prophetic vehicle, with the prophetic, the oracular, predominating."[493] He continued, "The lustrations performed in the tent are designed to make it fit for the divine revelation, for lawgiving, for judgment, for guiding the people through the desert, for the Urim and Thummim."[494]

4.4 The High Priest and the congregation

One aspect that was taken as strong evidence for connecting the Priestly Code with the time of the Second Temple time is the exalted role of the High Priest. This view holds that the High Priest of P stands at the head of the congregation

---

488 On this see Kaufmann, *Toledot* I, 126–127.
489 Kaufmann, *Toledot* I, 126; idem, *The Religion of Israel*, 176, 180.
490 Kaufmann, *The Religion of Israel*, 182.
491 Kaufmann, *The Religion of Israel*, 183.
492 Compare Kaufmann, *Toledot* I, 136–137.
493 Kaufmann, *The Religion of Israel*, 184.
494 Kaufmann, *The Religion of Israel*, 184. Jacob Milgrom remarked that "Kaufmann is misled by his theory that P legislated realistically for the period of the conquest, and that in particular P's Tent of Meeting is the prototype of the local bamah. This is a misreading of P, which predicates a single sanctuary in the land." See Jacob Milgrom, "Priestly Terminology and the Political and Social Structure of Pre-Monarchic Israel," *The Jewish Quarterly Review* 69, no. 2 (1978): 65–81 (71).

and is considered its leader. This situation was established under the domination of foreign rule in which the congregation was but a theocratic church.[495] Kaufmann challenged this view by arguing that there was "no connection between the priestly ideal of P and the position of priests in the age of the Second Temple."[496] He first started by clarifying that P's attitude toward the monarchy was favourable.[497] As Kaufmann put it:

> That the Israelites have no king in the desert is not a peculiarity of P's account; neither in JE are there stories or laws concerning kings. P's representation of the monarchy as a divine blessing and promise for the future is enough to show that its desert camp is not intended to depict the ideal form of Israelite society.[498]

Kaufmann further argued that P's depiction of the Mosaic age did not reflect the condition of the Second Temple period. P's camp was not a church, but an armed camp of the host of Israel. The purpose of the armed camp was not cultic exercise under the protection of foreign rulers, but the conquest of Canaan.[499] More important, according to Kaufmann, was the fact that at the head of this camp stood not the priest, but Moses. The importance of Aaron was restricted to the realm of the cult.[500] Therefore, Kaufmann justified the exalted role of the High Priest as being due to his supreme cultic position.[501] In Kaufmann's thinking, the High Priest did not stand in the place of Moses, but beside him.[502] Consequently P's portrayal of the High Priest fit well with the condition of the armed camp, where the role of the High Priest was chiefly restricted to oracles and sacrifices.[503]

---

495 See Kaufmann, *Toledot* I, 137.
496 Kaufmann, *The Religion of Israel*, 187.
497 The Talmudic scholar Ephraim Urbach, who agreed with Kaufmann that "P" does not know the theocracy of the Second Temple, rejected Kaufmann's claim that P shows a positive attitude towards monarchy. See Efraim Urbach, "Neue Wege der Bibelwissenschaft," *MGWJ* 82 (1938): 1–22 (12).
498 Kaufmann, *The Religion of Israel*, 185.
499 Kaufmann, *The Religion of Israel*, 185.
500 Kaufmann, *The Religion of Israel*, 185.
501 Kaufmann, *The Religion of Israel*, 186.
502 Kaufmann, *The Religion of Israel*, 186.
503 On this see Kaufmann, *Toledot* I, 141, 142.

4.5 The endowment of the clergy

Biblical critics judged that the provisions for the endowment of the clergy laid down in Deuteronomy predated those of the Priestly Code.[504] In addition, it was said that P transformed the sacral meal into an outright gift to the clergy, which fits well with the hierocracy of the post-exilic period. Kaufmann, an advocate for the greater antiquity of P, refused to see the dues for the clergy in P as a sign of its later appearance. From his point of view, "Being a collection of priestly toroth, P naturally gives more room to priestly and temple matters."[505] He claimed that a comparison of D and P law in this regard showed that P's dues could not be regarded as an expansion of those of D. Kaufmann contended that the laws of P did not include D's dues. Furthermore, P ignored the second tithe, the sacrificial portions that D assigns to the priests and the first shearings.[506] More important, in Kaufmann's view, "A comparison of what is common to the three legal codes reveals that P is closer to JE than to D."[507] Kaufmann further argues that the Levitical tithe could not have been established during the Second Temple, for he believed that during the Second Temple period no law demanded that any tithe be given to the sanctuary or to the priests and this despite the fact that priests, not Levites, were the dominant sacerdotal group.[508] The Levitical tithe, said Kaufmann, belonged to a time when the Levites were still numerous and served a significant function.[509] Annual Levitical tithes of the Second Temple era were remote from reality and a product of midrashic exegesis.[510] Kaufmann maintained that this annual tithe, which was to be brought to and eaten in the chosen city, first appears in D and was "invented by the author of the law of centralization to link the people with the chosen city."[511] He summed up by saying, "The annual Levitical tithe of Second Temple times is thus not

504 See Kaufmann's discussion of this point in *Toledot* I, 143–144.
505 Kaufmann, *The Religion of Israel*, 187.
506 Kaufmann, *The Religion of Israel*, 187–188.
507 Kaufmann, *The Religion of Israel*, 188; idem, *Toledot* I, 145.
508 Zion Zevit pointed out that the few sources upon which Kaufmann basds his conclusion were traditions associated with the famous Rabbi of the first-second centuries C.E., Eleazar ben Azariah. According to Zevit, Eleazar ben Azaiah declared that the Levitical tithe was given over to priests. See Ziony Zevit, "Converging Lines of Evidence Bearing on the Date of P," *ZAW* 94, no. 4 (1982): 481–511 (488).
509 Kaufmann, *Toledot* I, 147–159. Kaufmann compared the tithe laws in Deuteronomy with those of the Priestly Code.
510 Kaufmann, *The Religion of Israel*, 192.
511 Kaufmann, *The Religion of Israel*, 192.

found in the Torah at all. It was an impracticable result of the pious effort to har-
monize the divergent laws 'found written' in the ancient scrolls."[512]

4.6 Priests and Levites

While D regards the whole tribe of Levi as consecrated to the holy service
(Deut. 18: 6–8), a distinction is made in P between priests and Levites. This distinction, it is said, was caused by the Josianic reform through which the Levites
as descendants of the priests of the high places were disqualified from priesthood. This evidence was taken as an indication of the later date of P's law, in
which a difference is made between the priestly sons of Aaron and the rest of
the Levites. Such a situation could have only arisen in the circumstances of
the Second Temple.[513] Kaufmann rejected this and endeavoured to prove its fal-
lacy. He first showed that "neither D (especially Deut 18:6–8) nor the account of
the reform in II Kings 23:9 indicates in any way that the rural priests were demot-
ed. II Kings 23:9 speaks of a personal penalty that applied only to those who actually served at the high places."[514] In addition, Kaufmann noted, "The disqual-
ification and unfrocking of priests goes unnoticed in the Priestly Code."[515] To
support his standpoint, Kaufmann studied the history of the priests and Levites.[516] He assumed that the Levites were of pre-Josianic origin,[517] and suggested
that "the Aaronides [were] the ancient pagan priesthood of Israel. Presumably
they were swayed by the message of Moses, supported him, and influenced
the people to follow him."[518] Kaufman concluded that there was a fundamental
distinction between the priestly family (Aaronides) and the tribe, the Aaronides
being the ancient pagan priesthood of Israel.[519] This implies that Kaufmann inclined to accept P's description of Aaron and his followers.[520]

---

512 Kaufmann, *The Religion of Israel*, 193.
513 For more discussion on this point, see Kaufmann, *Toledot* I, 161–184.
514 Kaufmann, *The Religion of Israel*, 194.
515 Kaufmann, *The Religion of Israel*, 194.
516 Kaufmann, *Toledot* I, 169–184.
517 Kaufmann, *The Religion of Israel*, 196.
518 Kaufmann, *The Religion of Israel*, 197–198.
519 See Moshe Weinfeld, *The Place of Law in the Religion of Ancient Israel* (Leiden: Brill, 2004),
31.
520 See Kaufmann, *Commentary on Joshua*, 16–17. Also Moshe Greenberg, "A New Approach
to the History of the Israelite Priesthood," *Journal of the American Oriental Society* 70, no. 1
(1950): 41–47. Furthermore, Blenkinsopp pointed out that Kaufmann "did not deal with the
problem of why, if the Aaronites were in place from the beginning of Israel's existence, they

The above-mentioned discussion is intended to bring out Kaufmann's arguments concerning the antiquity of the Priestly Code and its pre-deuteronomic
features.[521] His point of departure was that the centralization of the cult,
which is peculiar to D, is completely absent from P. In addition, Kaufmann
drew attention to the fact that P's tent of meeting did not reflect the reality of
the Exile. It is "a portable sanctuary unconnected with any sacred site."[522] Moreover, Kaufmann mentioned that Ezekiel had no idea about the tent of meeting.
His priests were sons of Sadok, the contemporaries of David.[523] According to
Kaufmann's understanding, Ezekiel's laws were later than those of P. As for
the relationship between Ezekiel and P, Kaufmann wrote:

> [Ezekiel] is influenced by Deuteronomy, but more by the Priestly Code. The contacts with
> the Priestly Code – the whole of it, not merely the Holiness Code, which alone is allowed
> by critical dogma – are numerous and pervasive. That Ezekiel is the borrower is clear, for
> the matter in common has a natural context and fits into a larger framework in P, while in
> Ezekiel's context it is artificial or fragmentary, obviously adapted for a new purpose.[524]

Kaufmann, in effect, wanted to push the dating of the Priestly Code back towards
pre-exilic times.[525] Kaufmann's thesis was that the antiquity of particular forms is
evidence of the antiquity of the written documents that describe them.[526] Summing up his reconstruction of the Priestly Code, Kaufmann concluded:

---

and their eponym are so poorly attested in non-P writings to which a pre-exilic date can safely be
attached." See Joseph Blenkinsopp, "An Assessment of the Alleged Pre-Exilic Date of the Priestly
Material in the Pentateuch," *ZAW* 108, no. 4 (1996): 495 – 518 (501). Against Blenkinsopp's critique of Kaufmann, see Jacob Milgrom, "The Antiquity of the Priestly Source: A Reply to Joseph
Blenkinsopp," *ZAW* 111, no. 1 (1999): 10 – 22.

521 On this see, in particular, Kaufmann, "Probleme der israelitisch-jüdischen Religionsgeschichte," *ZAW* 48, no. 1 (1930): 23 – 43.

522 Kaufmann, *The Religion of Israel*, 289.

523 Kaufmann, *Commentary on Joshua*, 17.

524 Kaufmann, *The Religion of Israel*, 433.

525 Kaufmann placed the date of "P" before Hezekiah. He built his view on the assumption that
"there is no trace whatever of D's centralization idea in P; P must, therefore, have been composed before the age of Hezekiah." See Kaufmann, *The Religion of Israel*, 205. Menahem
Haran, who attempted to reach a middle ground between Wellhausen's and Kaufmann's position, criticized Kaufmann's concerning the dating of the Priestly Code. He felt that Kaufmann's
contention that P preceded D was unconvincing. Thus Haran remarked that although Kaufmann
admitted P's general antiquity, he did not attempt to fix the limits of the period to which it could
belong. See Menahem Haran, *Temples and Temple Service*, 7.

526 Against Kaufmann's proposition, George E. Mendenhall pointed out, "With literary documents as with archaeological strata, the document is dated by the latest content, not the earli-

In every detail, P betrays its antiquity. Its narrative preserves bold anthropomorphisms; its cult presupposes the existence of local altars. . . Its tithes are ancient; its thousands of Levites are a reflex of a distant past; its view of the prophets as the civil and military leaders of the people is archaic.[527]

5 The antiquity of Torah literature: Torah as a history source

As demonstrated, Kaufmann's basic tenet was that the Torah contained ancient material, going back to Israel's earliest period. He strove to prove the antiquity of the Torah literature.[528] From his point of view:

The Torah is the literary product of the earliest stage of Israelite religion, the stage prior to literary prophecy. Although its compilation and canonization took place later, its sources are demonstrably ancient – not in part, not in their general content, but in their entirety, even to their language and formulation.[529]

Moreover, Kaufmann was convinced that "the historical background of the Torah is authentic. Although its history is legendary, it is grounded on a tradition that has a sound basis."[530] As for the date of its crystallization, he suggested, "The ideas, the religious and political symbols of the Torah were fully formed by the time of the early monarchy. The literature continued, of course, to develop and pass through successive formulations; but, the symbols and ideals of early times remained intact."[531]

Kaufmann distinguished two stages in the development of the Torah: the period of the composition of the Torah literature and the age of the formation of the Torah book. The boundary between the two periods, in Kaufmann's view, was the reform of Josiah.[532] What was decidedly important to Kaufmann was that the legal materials were composed and fixed before the formation of the Torah book. The Torah was formed before the prophetic literature and therefore it reflected the first stage of Israelite religion. As he put it:

---

est." See George E. Mendenhall, *The Tenth Generation: The Origins of the Biblical Tradition* (Baltimore: Johns Hopkins University Press, 1973), 9, n. 36.
527 Kaufmann, *The Religion of Israel*, 206.
528 For Kaufmann's arguments see his *Toledot* I, 185 – 220.
529 Kaufmann, *The Religion of Israel*, 2.
530 Kaufmann, *The Religion of Israel*, 200.
531 Kaufmann, *The Religion of Israel*, 204.
532 Kaufmann, *The Religion of Israel*, 172.

> The Torah book was formed out of the desire of a penitent community to know and keep
> the law of God. Israel fastened naturally upon its early literary traditions, which contained
> the history and laws of its ancient covenant. The literature of Torah became the first stra-
> tum of the Bible, sealed and canonized at a time when prophetic literature was still unor-
> dered and still without decisive influence on the life of the people. The entire book is a tes-
> timony to the first age of Israelite religion, the age prior to literary prophecy.[533]

With this literary inquiry into the Torah literature, Kaufmann hoped to confirm
that the main source of the Torah, the Priestly Code, predated Deuteronomy
and therefore had to be placed in the context of the First Temple period.[534] In
his view, the differences that existed between the legal corpora indicate "an independent literary history for each of them."[535] Moreover, Kaufmann saw the
Torah literature as an entity different from that of prophetic literature.[536] His intention was to prove that the religious perspective of the Torah's literature, with
its monotheistic idea, had been developed independently from prophetic influence. The implications of all this for the history of Israelite religion is of great
importance. Kaufmann, to be sure, strove to make the Torah the primary source
for historical reconstruction. Nahum Sarna rightly remarked:

> The Torah becomes, once again, the starting point for historical inquiry. The sources do fur-
> nish us with genuine traditions about the times with which they purport to deal. Monothe-
> ism appears as a popular national phenomenon pervading the earliest traditions and
> moulding the earliest institutions of Israel.[537]

Perhaps it would be unfair to judge or even evaluate Kaufmann's view regarding
the antiquity of the Priestly Code and the Torah literature before getting to know
the whole structure of his thesis. Kaufmann's literary inquiry was only one pillar
upon which he based his construction. His investigation of the Torah literature
was followed by a comparative-phenomenological study of the religion of Israel.
Kaufmann's main concern was to highlight the basic ideas of Israelite religion
and to clarify the essential characteristics that set it apart from paganism.[538]

---

533 Kaufmann, *The Religion of Israel*, 211.
534 Kaufmann devoted about 220 pages of his *Toledot* to investigating the problem of the sources of the Pentateuch and their relevance to the history of the Israelite religion. See Kaufmann,
Toledot I.
535 Kaufmann, *The Religion of Israel*, 172.
536 On this see, in particular, Kaufmann, "Probleme der israelitisch-jüdischen Religionsgeschichte II," *ZAW* 51, no. 1 (1933): 35–47.
537 Nahum Sarna, "From Wellhausen to Kaufmann," 68.
538 Kaufmann, *Toledot* I, 1.

To get at the roots of Kaufmann's structure, the next chapter will examine the main arguments of Kaufmann concerning the character of Israelite religion.

Chapter Five:
Israelite Religion:
Phenomenological Interpretation

1 Introduction

Kaufmann, as the title of his *Toledot* implies, was fascinated with the phenomenology of biblical religion. It is therefore not surprising that he devoted most of his attention to the study of Israelite religion. With a rich analysis of the basic character of the Israelite and pagan religions, Kaufmann's phenomenological approach focused primarily on analysing the similarities and differences between the two.[539] In Kaufmann's view, the essence of Israel's religion was the absence of a mythological conception of the deity; it was a non-mythological religion. Kaufmann went even further, maintaining that monotheism was a product of the primal intuition of the people of Israel and the gap separating it from polytheism was not bridgeable. With a wealth of detail, Kaufmann undertook to describe how the Israelite religion, with its monotheist idea, parted ways from all other religious forms known in the ancient world.

Kaufmann thus sought to build a solid foundation for his theory about the history of Israelite religion. Moshe Greenberg rightly observed that "the distinctive character which [Kaufmann] ascribes to Israel's religion is the central pillar of his thought and underlies much of the later discussion."[540] My primary concern here is to show how Kaufmann, by means of comparative-morphological study of Israelite religion and paganism, was able to achieve far-reaching results. By arguing that Israel's religion was monotheistic from the very beginning, Kaufmann felt he could present 'a new position' in place of the classic interpretation, which had comprehended Israelite religion in terms of evolution. Did Kaufmann succeed in constructing a fundament on which where he could erect his ideas? This chapter will consider Kaufmann's understanding of Israelite religion. It aims to delineate the second pillar in Kaufmann's construction of the history of Israel.

---

539 The second part of volume I of Kaufmann's *Toledot* was dedicated to this subject. See Kaufmann, *Toledot* I, 221–416.
540 See Moshe Greenberg in the preface to Kaufmann's *The Religion of Israel*.

2 Israelite religion and paganism

No analysis of Kaufmann's view on the history of Israelite religion would be complete without considering his understanding of paganism. According to Kaufmann, "The Bible's ignorance of the meaning of paganism is at once the basic problem and the most important clue to the understanding of biblical religion."[541] It should be made clear that Kaufmann made a sharp distinction between 'pagan religion' and 'Israelite religion'. In his opinion, "The heart of the pagan idea is the conception of a primordial, supradivine realm which is the womb of all being."[542] By contrast, "The Israelite religion does not subject the Deity to a primeval realm."[543] Kaufmann went so far in his estimation as to say "the Bible is unaware of the nature and meaning of pagan religion."[544] He conceded that Israelite religion and paganism were historically related and that "Israel was always in contact with its pagan neighbours."[545] Nevertheless, he insisted that the Israelites were not familiar with paganism. Decisive for Kaufmann is the evidence that "the biblical age no longer knew pagan mythology."[546] Furthermore, Kaufmann contended, "There is no evidence that the gods and their myths were ever a central issue in the religion of YHWH. And yet this religion is non-mythological."[547] My discussion starts by examining the nature of pagan religion followed by a description of the basic character of Israelite religion as viewed by Kaufmann.

2.1 The nature of the pagan religion

In his massive *Toledot* Kaufmann provided us with an elaborate description of paganism and all its religious manifestations.[548] However, we shall limit the discussion of Kaufmann's view in this regard to what he called 'the fundamental idea' of pagan religion.[549] Kaufmann defined as pagan, "all the religions of mankind from the beginnings of recorded history to the present, excepting Israelite

541 Kaufmann, *The Religion of Israel*, 20.
542 Kaufmann, "The Biblical Age," 10.
543 Kaufmann, "The Biblical Age," 10.
544 Kaufmann, *The Religion of Israel*, 7.
545 Kaufmann, *The Religion of Israel*, 7, 20.
546 Kaufmann, *The Religion of Israel*, 11.
547 Kaufmann, *The Religion of Israel*, 20.
548 For more discussion see Kaufmann, *Toledot* I, 286–416.
549 See Kaufmann, *Toledot* I, 297–350.

religion and its derivatives, Christianity and Islam."[550] In his classification, Kaufmann relied on one idea that he considered to be "the distinguishing mark of pagan thought".[551] This was, "The idea that there exists a realm of being prior to the gods and above them, upon which the gods depend, and whose decrees they must obey. Deity belongs to, and is derived from, a primordial realm."[552] The great symbol of the essence of paganism, according to Kaufmann, is that "the gods are not ultimately sovereign; they emerge out of a pre-existent realm and are subject to a transcendent order."[553] From Kaufmann's perspective this definition implies that the basic premise of pagan religion is that gods are dependent on and influenced by a metadivine realm. As a result, a radical dichotomy between the gods and the pre-existent come into being, out of which in Kaufmann's opinion, both mythology and magic came forth.[554]

As we might observe, Kaufmann identified paganism with mythology. He defined myth as "the tale of the life of the gods".[555] Kaufmann further maintained, "In myth the gods appears not only as actors, but as acted upon."[556] "At the heart of myth is the tension between the gods and other forces that shape their destinies."[557] Kaufmann, then, deduced that paganism based its fundamental idea in myth, that is, "the existence of a realm of power to which the gods themselves are subject."[558]

What has been said about myth can be repeated with regard to the relationship of paganism and magic. In the words of Kaufmann, "Just as the fundamental idea of paganism found poetic expression in myth, so it found practical expression in magic."[559] "Magic," according to Kaufmann, "is an art whose purpose is to move occult powers to act in a desired manner."[560] Moreover, "The power of magic transcends the gods: they themselves employ it, for they too are in need of this almighty instrument which is independent of them and their will."[561] The way by which both myth and magic conceived of the deity led Kaufmann to connect paganism with myth and magic. He wrote, "Because

---

550 Kaufmann, *The Religion of Israel*, 21.
551 Kaufmann, *The Religion of Israel*, 21.
552 Kaufmann, *The Religion of Israel*, 21.
553 Kaufmann, "The Biblical Age," 9.
554 Kaufmann, *The Religion of Israel*, 22.
555 Kaufmann, *The Religion of Israel*, 22.
556 Kaufmann, *The Religion of Israel*, 22.
557 Kaufmann, *The Religion of Israel*, 22.
558 Kaufmann, *The Religion of Israel*, 22.
559 Kaufmann, *The Religion of Israel*, 23.
560 Kaufmann, "The Biblical Age," 9.
561 Kaufmann, "The Biblical Age," 9.

of the mythological nature of its gods, because of their subjection to a primordial realm, paganism was necessarily and essentially magical as well."[562] At the end of his discussion of the essential character of paganism and its association with myth and magic, Kaufmann emphasized that only by appreciation of the 'fundamental idea' of paganism could we be prepared to "understand the peculiar position of the Israelite religion in the history of culture."[563]

2.2 Basic character of Israelite religion

It is worth noting that Kaufmann's entire case presupposed his interpretation of Israelite religion and the unique character that set it apart from all other religions.[564] As mentioned, he distinguished sharply between the Israelite and pagan religions. Each had a distinct conception of 'deity' which put the two religions in quite direct opposition. In Kaufmann's view, "The basic idea of Israelite religion is that God is supreme over all. There is no realm above or beside him to limit his absolute sovereignty. He is utterly distinct from, and other than, the world; he is subject to no laws, no compulsions, powers that transcend him. He is, in short, non-mythological."[565] Kaufmann's emphasis upon the non-mythological character of god in Israelite religion is clear. He said that the basic character of Israelite religion reflected a level beyond, not before, mythology.[566]

We observe that Kaufmann put much more emphasis on the absence of myth in Israelite religion.[567] To quote him:

> The store of biblical legends lacks the fundamental myth of paganism: the theogony. All theogonic motifs are similarly absent. Israel's god has no pedigree, fathers no generations; he neither inherits nor bequeaths his authority. He does not die and is not resurrected. He

---

562 Kaufmann, *The Religion of Israel*, 24.
563 Kaufmann, *The Religion of Israel*, 24.
564 For Kaufmann's comprehensive analysis of this subject, see Kaufmann, *Toledot* I, 221–254, 417–588.
565 Kaufmann, *The Religion of Israel*, 60.
566 Kaufmann, *The Religion of Israel*, 61.
567 Against Kaufmann's assumption, Isac Leo Seeligmann pointed out "Andererseits kann man nicht a limine (wie es beispielsweise Kaufmann tat) die Existenz jeglicher mythischer Elemente im Glauben Israels abstreiten. Wir dürfen nicht das, was in der hebräischen Bibel erhalten ist, mit dem gleichsetzen, was in Israel verbreitet war – schließlich fehlt es nicht einmal in der Bibel an Überresten des Mythos." See Isac L. Seeligmann, *Gesammelte Studies zur Hebräischen Bibel* (Forschungen zum Alten Testament 41; Tubingen: Moher Siebeck, 2004), 164, no. 7.

has no sexual qualities or desires and shows no need of or dependence upon powers outside himself.[568]

Taking this further, Kaufmann supported his argument by saying that:

> The peculiar and unique character of Israel's non-mythologism stands out with particular clarity when the biblical stories of YHWH's battles are considered. Here we find that not only YHWH, but his entourage and even his "enemies" are non-mythologically conceived. YHWH has no companions and his antagonists are lifeless idols.[569]

In addition, Kaufmann demonstrated that there was no polemic against the fundamental question of the mythological conception of 'deity'.[570] In Kaufmann's view, "What mythical vestiges are found in the Bible (e.g. the defeat of Rahap and the dragon) are part of the belief of the biblical authors."[571] As far the Israelite religion is concerned, "No room remains for any divine antagonist of the one God. Even the demonic has become de-mythologized."[572] Moreover, Kaufmann believed that Israelite religion "did not proclaim a new chief god, a god who ruled among or over his fellows. It conceived, for the first time, a God independent of a primordial realm, who was the source of all, the demonic included."[573] Thus, Kaufmann came to conclude that by studying all religious phenomena of Israelite religion including magic, divination, oracles, dreams and cultic observances, it would appear that "the Bible showed absolutely no apprehension of the real character of mythological religion."[574]

Having elucidated the basic character of Israelite religion, Kaufmann summarised his case in the following manner:

> The biblical religious idea, visible in the earliest strata, permeating even the 'magical' legends, is of a supernal God, above every cosmic law, fate, and compulsion; unborn, unbegetting. knowing no desire, independent of matter and its forces; a God who does not fight other divinities or powers or impurity; who does not sacrifice, divine, prophesy, or practice sorcery; who does not sin and needs no expiation; a God who does not celebrate festivals of his life. An unfettered divine will transcending all being [575]

---

568 Kaufmann, *The Religion of Israel*, 60–61.
569 *The Religion of Israel*, 61–62.
570 Compare Kaufmann, *Toledot* I, 10; idem, "The Biblical Age," 13.
571 Kaufmann, *The Religion of Israel*, 122.
572 Kaufmann, *The Religion of Israel*, 65.
573 Kaufmann, *The Religion of Israel*, 66.
574 On this see Kaufmann, "The Bible and Mythological Polytheism," *JBL* 70, no. 3 (1951): 179–197; idem, *The Religion of Israel*, 66–121.
575 Kaufmann, *The Religion of Israel*, 121.

It seems that Kaufmann aimed to reveal the non-pagan characteristics of Israelite religion. In his thinking, "Israelite religion does not subject the Deity to a primeval realm. Its primary category, differing fundamentally from that of paganism, is the absolute freedom of the Godhead."[576] Moreover, Israel's conception of God is free from any magic allusions.[577] More important, as Kaufmann pointed out, was that the cult of Israelite religion differed from that of paganism. "The Israelite cult is not conceived of as charged with mysterious, transcendental power upon which the life and strength of the deity are dependent."[578] In this way, the Israelite religion liberated the deity from mythological-magical subjection, and developed a new conception of the universal rule of God.[579]

Before going ahead to discuss how Kaufmann conceived of popular religion and the nature of Israelite idolatry, a few remarks should be made. Kaufmann's definition of paganism and its identification with myth raises many problematic issues. To start with, we note that Kaufmann defined mythology in the narrow sense of stories about the gods, their activities and relationships.[580] Jon Levenson agrees with Kaufmann that instead of polemicizing against myth, Israel polemicized against the gods themselves. The war on myth and the war on the gods were entirely separate. Nevertheless, Levenson points out that although Kaufmann's observation was largely correct, his conclusion was not.[581] As for Kaufmann's examination of paganism, it has been said that "in dealing with paganism, Kaufmann does not offer the sort of catalogue of deities which scholars have frequently prepared, but attempts to locate a fundamental, underlying idea."[582] Moreover, Kaufmann's conception of "all forms of paganism" is criticized by Hillers, who says, "It is radically deficient, because he is not interested in Canaanite paganism or any concrete pagan community, but in all paganism, everywhere in the world... Such a cosmic view shows that Kaufmann's work was really more philosophical or theological than historical."[583] The strongest and at the same

576 Kaufmann, "The Biblical Age," 10.
577 Kaufmann, "The Biblical Age," 11.
578 Kaufmann, "The Biblical Age," 11.
579 Kaufmann, "The Biblical Age," 12.
580 In his review of Kaufmann's book *The Religion of Israel*, Hyatt remarked that Kaufmann did not use a wider definition of myth as employed by Bultmann. See J.P. Hyatt, "Yehezkel Kaufmann's View of the Religion of Israel," *Journal of Bible and Religion*, 29 (1961): 52–57.
581 Jon D. Levenson, *Sinai and Zion: An Entry into the Jewish Bible* (Minneapolis: Winston Press, 1985), 67.
582 Delbert R. Hillers, "Analyzing the Abominable: Our Understanding of Canaanite Religion," *Jewish Quarterly Review* 75, no. 3 (1985): 253–269 (262).
583 Hillers, "Analyzing the Abominable: Our Understanding of Canaanite Religion," 262.

time most comprehensive criticism of Kaufmann's interpretation of myth comes from Ehud Luz who wrote:

> Kaufmann's approach to myth is paradoxical: on the one hand he concurs with the nineteenth-century philosophers (esp. Hermann Cohen) who identify myth with paganism and deny its existence in the religion of Israel. On the other hand, he realizes that monotheism's historical potency lay in its symbolic expression. To solve this paradox, Kaufmann arbitrarily minimizes the significance of myth, and instead of talking about 'mythic' expression, he talks about 'legendary-symbolic expression'- a term that is most difficult to distinguish from myth! In this way he avoids the problem of mythic thought in the Bible. As Buber and Rosenzweig demonstrated, however, Judaism and myth are not necessarily contradictory. In fact, myth is an integral element in the religion of Israel.[584]

Although the above-mentioned critique of Kaufmann's interpretation of myth contains remarkable points, it ignores Kaufmann's main intention. In point of fact, Kaufmann avoided talking about any pagan allusions in the Hebrew Bible. To make this point more clear, I refer to Kaufmann himself, who affirmed, "No pagan Israelite sources have come down to us; hence we cannot make a sweeping categorical judgment".[585] As Moshe Greenberg rightly observed, "Kaufmann never again mentions 'pagan-Israelite sources'; indeed, he endeavours to minimize their presence to the vanishing point. What interested him was the mainstream of Israel's culture, and that, he was convinced, was to be found in the biblical record."[586]

3 Popular religion

Another point that deserves consideration is Kaufmann's characterization of Israelite religion as popular religion.[587] He drew attention to the monotheistic popular faith of the people of Israel. Furthermore, he rejected the assumption that the religion of Israel developed out of polytheism, arguing instead that Israelite religion was rooted in the popular beliefs of the people of Israel.[588] Seeking support for his view, Kaufmann studied the nature of Israelite idolatry, arriving at

---

584 Ehud Luz, "Jewish Nationalism in the Thought of Yehezkel Kaufmann," in *Binah: Studies in Jewish History, Thought, and Culture*, vol. 2 (ed. Joseph Dan; New York, 1989), 177–190 (182–183).
585 Kaufmann, *Toledot* I, 283.
586 Greenberg, *Studies in the Bible*, 186.
587 See Patrick D. Miller, *Israelite Religion and Biblical Theology: Collected Essays* (Sheffield: Sheffield Acad. Press, 2000), 159.
588 Kaufmann, *Toledot* I, 589.

the conclusion that Israelite idolatry differed from paganism. He showed that Israelite idolatry was fetishism, the worship of wood and stone. In addition, he questioned prophetic denunciation against the people of Israel and saw it as an invalid argument for syncretism in pre-exilic Israel. In the following, we shall examine Kaufmann's position concerning popular religion and the nature of Israelite idolatry.

3.1 The non-pagan character of Israel's popular religion

In his discussion of the popular religion of ancient Israel and its characteristics, Kaufmann asserted that there was no evidence of mythological or pagan beliefs implanted in the popular culture. For him, the question was whether the popular religion conceived of YHWH in pagan terms.[589] Kaufmann attempted to show that there was no struggle in Israel against popular notions regarding the mythological conception of 'deity'. In his opinion, "The biblical battle with Israel's idolatry restricts itself entirely to matters of practice, to rites and cults."[590] He went on to maintain that popular religion in Israel was not a syncretistic religion.[591] He also contended that the alleged relationship between Yahweh and Baal did not exist.[592] He argued against the view that Hosea strongly referred to the syncretistic worship of YHWH-Baal. Kaufmann wrote:

> This syncretism is a product of scholarly romancing. Such a fusion could have arisen only on the basis of a belief in the mythological Baal. The Bible, however, never refers to the mythological Baal, no polemic is waged against such a conception of him, nor is there a word of polemic against the worship of a syncretistic YHWH-Baal. First Hosea (Hos.1–3) reproves the people for following *baalim*, for thinking them to be 'lovers' who supply the prosperity which really YHWH has given them. Israel has "made over to Baal" the silver and gold that YHWH conferred upon her. In other words, YHWH and the *baalim* are absolutely distinct.[593]

---

589 Kaufmann, *The Religion of Israel*, 122.
590 Kaufmann, *The Religion of Israel*, 122.
591 Kaufmann, *Toledot* I, 590–593.
592 Kaufmann rejected syncretism and all signs of Baalization in the religion of Israel. However, there are many references indicating Yahweh- Baal worship after the settlement in Palestine. On this see, for example, Manfred Weippert, *Jahwe und die anderen Götter: Studien zur Religions-geschichte des antiken Israel in ihrem syrisch-palästinischen Kontext* (Tübingen : Mohr Siebeck, 1997).
593 Kaufmann, "The Bible and Mythological polytheism," 190.

Moreover, Kaufmann pointed out that although the names of the sons of Saul (Eshbaal), Jonathan (Meribbaal), and David (Beeliada) contain the epithet Baal, this was not enough evidence that Yahweh and Baal were merged into one. He explained, "The only syncretism here is titular. *Ba'al* means 'lord'...Crucial is the utter lack of evidence that YHWH was given any of the mythological attributes of Baal."[594] On the other hand, Kaufmann insisted on the non-pagan character of Israelite folk culture.[595] He presupposed that Israel's popular religion lacked the mythological practices of paganism. For example, Kaufmann remarked that the people of Israel did not practice magic in the name of YHWH. There was no belief in ecstatic prophecy. There was no polemic against the popular cult.[596] Kaufmann went so far as to say that popular religion in Israel was a monotheistic religion.[597]

In support of his argument about the nature of popular religion, Kaufmann drew attention to the fact that biblical faith was based on popular legends. In his view, biblical faith drew on popular legends even when it battled the backslidings of people into idolatry. "The popular legends and the beliefs they imply are the common property of the folk and the authors of the Bible."[598] Kaufmann found further evidence from the prophets. He said, "The God of the prophets is essentially the same as the God of the popular legends...Their God is the God of the popular religion; their faith rears itself upon the popular religion and is organically linked with it."[599] At this point Kaufmann arrived at his most significant conclusion concerning the nature of Israelite religion: "Biblical religion is therefore not an esoteric religion of a spiritual elite like the higher pagan religions, but is a growth that is rooted in and nourished by the popular religion of Israel."[600]

---

594 Kaufmann, *The Religion of Israel*, 123.
595 Kaufmann, *The Religion of Israel*, 39.
596 *The Religion of Israel*, 124–127.
597 Kaufmann, "The Biblical Age," 59. Kaufmann justified his view by working out a new explanation of "religious universalism". According to Kaufmann, "The national-territorial limitation of the religion of YHWH involved only his favor, his self-revelation, and his cult; it does not affect the extent of his rule." See Kaufmann, *The Religion of Israel*, 127.
598 Kaufmann, *The Religion of Israel*, 132.
599 Kaufmann, *The Religion of Israel*, 132–133.
600 Kaufmann, *The Religion of Israel*, 133.

4 Nature of Israelite idolatry

One point that Kaufmann strove to make was that pre-exilic Israel was a mono-theistic people.[601] He believed that idolatry was a mere vulgar phenomenon in Israel and never attained the level of a cultural force.[602] According to Kaufmann's understanding, "Israel was distinct from other nations of antiquity not by its idea of monotheism alone; it was equally distinct in its idolatry."[603] Because of its importance for understanding Israelite religion, Kaufmann constantly called for proper assessment of the nature of Israelite idolatry.[604] The following discussion seeks to clarify Kaufmann's position with the aim of learning how it illustrates his reconstruction of the history of Israelite religion.

According to Kaufmann, Israelite religion could not be described as idola-trous just because it at times deviated from the Mosaic Law, as dogmatic tradi-tion would have it. Likewise, it was inappropriate to explain Israelite religion as idolatrous because of any unawareness of Mosaic Law – as modern criticism often assumes.[605] Rejecting these two approaches, Kaufmann sought a different way to interpret the nature of Israelite idolatry. He called for consideration of the following questions: Whether YHWH was ever worshiped in Israel as one of many gods? Whether he was associated with a mythological pantheon? Whether Israelite idolatry was genuinely syncretistic?[606] In fact, by posing such questions Kaufmann intended to carve out a definition of idolatry that matched his inter-pretation of mythology, paganism, and popular religion. That is to say, he aimed to detach Israelite idolatry from mythology. Further, he wanted to show that Is-raelite idolatry was not authentic paganism. More important was to demonstrate that idolatry did not reach a level of popular creativity.

Kaufmann's first step was to prove that mythology and Israelite idolatry be-longed to two separate spheres.[607] He relied on three basic observations. First, there is no mythological story or fragment in the Bible in which a heathen god or hero is featured. Second, no myth is characterized as false or idolatrous.

---

601 For more details see Kaufmann, *Toledot* I, 659–685.
602 Kaufmann, "Israelite Religion," (in Hebrew) in *Encyclopaedia Biblica*, vol. 2 (ed. Eleazar L. Sukenik; Jerusalem, 1954), 747–750; idem, *Toledot* I, 678–679.
603 Kaufmann, "The Bible and Mythological Polytheism," 193.
604 Kaufmann, "The Biblical Age," 32.
605 Kaufmann, *The Religion of Israel*, 136.
606 Kaufmann, *The Religion of Israel*, 138.
607 Kaufmann, "The Bible and Mythological Polytheism," 182. For further discussion on this subject, see Moshe Halbertal and Avishai Margalit, *Idolatry*. Translated from Hebrew by Naomi Goldblum (Cambridge: Harvard University Press, 1992).

Third, no mythological matter is adduced with derogatory or polemical intent.[608] Also, Kaufmann noted that the struggle with idolatry was not a struggle against idolatrous myth.[609] He found no allusion to Israelite idolatry possessing any myth. In his judgment, all of this proved that Israelite religion was in essence non-mythological.[610] He said, "The biblical battle with idolatry does not involve a battle with myth. YHWH is the only god who has 'myths' – the popular legends, the idols and 'foreign gods' are mythless cult objects."[611] Moreover, Kaufmann contended that myth was eradicated early from Israel – since Moses's time. As he put it:

> If the struggle with idolatry does not involve a campaign against myth, it necessarily follows that the elimination of myth must have preceded this struggle. The advent of the new religion among the Israelite tribes of Moses' day shattered their early mythological beliefs, and the fragments which became embedded in the Bible were no longer felt to be 'idolatrous' and non-Israelite.[612]

If myth was uprooted in Israel from early times, what was then the nature of Israelite idolatry? The answer that comes from Kaufmann's side was, "The Bible embodies its conception of Israelite idolatry as fetishism."[613] He suggested that idolatry was conceived in Israel as fetishism, that is, the worship of wood and stone. Moreover, he insisted on a stop to the misunderstanding of paganism as fetishism. In the words of Kaufmann:

> Before we can appreciate the significance of Israelite religion we must free ourselves of the idea, prevalent throughout Biblical and post-Biblical Jewish literature and in Christian and Islamic thought as well, that paganism – the religion of all the nations of antiquity – was the 'worship of wood and stone', the worship of material objects and 'dumb idols'. We must, in short, cease to mistake paganism for fetishism.[614]

Having defined Israelite idolatry as fetishism, Kaufmann continued, "The worship of material objects is liable to degenerate into fetishism, but fetishism is not an essential element of polytheism."[615] In support of his view, Kaufmann em-

---

608 See Kaufmann, "The Bible and Mythological Polytheism," 181–182.
609 Kaufmann, "The Bible and Mythological Polytheism," 182.
610 Kaufmann also distinguished between positive and negative mythology, see Kaufmann, "The Bible and Mythological Polytheism,"181–182.
611 Kaufmann, *The Religion of Israel*, 146.
612 Kaufmann, "The Bible and Mythological Polytheism," 182.
613 Kaufmann, *The Religion of Israel*, 13.
614 Kaufmann, "The Biblical Age," 8.
615 Kaufmann, "The Bible and Mythological Polytheism," 180.

phasized that biblical literature agreed in its understanding of Israelite idolatry as fetishism. As for the stance of biblical narratives, Kaufmann pointed out, "In no Biblical story do any of the heathen gods appear as actor or acted upon, as conscious or perceptive, as speaking, moving, eating, etc."[616] Kaufmann gave several examples (the account of the golden calf in Exod 32; 2 Kgs 18:17–19:19; Dan 2–6) in which idolatry was depicted as fetishism.[617] Pursuing this further, Kaufmann contended, "In the majority of the stories about idolatry the narrator distinguishes two religious spheres: the sphere of the one living and acting god, the god of Israel, and the sphere of *elilim*, heathen fetishes unrelated to living gods."[618] At the same time, Kaufmann asserted that all pentateuchal sources agreed with regard to the conception of idolatry.[619] That is to say, "The fetishistic conception dominates all of Biblical legislation on idolatry."[620] In the same way, Kaufmann maintained that the prophets describe idolatry as fetishistic worship of wood and stone. He found hints in Amos, Hosea, Isaiah, Micah, Jeremiah, and Ezekiel that idolatry was nothing more than the worship of the work of hands.[621] More illustrative is Kaufmann's description of the prophetic understanding of the nature of Israelite idolatry. He wrote:

> Chapter upon chapter records denunciations hurled at apostate Israel for their straying after the gods of the nations. If ever there were a struggle with pagan myths and mythological conceptions of deity, we should expect to find its traces here. But we search in vain: not one word have the prophets for mythological beliefs, not only do they repudiate them. Not only do they fail to brand the pagan gods as demons or satyrs, they fail even clearly to deny their existence. In short, the prophets ignore what we know to be authentic paganism. Their whole condemnation revolves round the taunt of fetishism.[622]

In exploring the nature of Israelite idolatry, Kaufmann surveyed the history of idolatry in Israel.[623] He distinguished four phases in the history of Israelite religion. First, he defined the period from Moses to Joshua as non-idolatrous. Second, he saw the period of Judges as the first period of continuous national idola-

---

616 Kaufmann, "The Bible and Mythological Polytheism," 183; idem, *The Religion of Israel*, 13–17.
617 Kaufmann, "The Bible and Mythological Polytheism," 183–187.
618 Kaufmann, "The Bible and Mythological Polytheism," 183.
619 See Kaufmann, *The Religion of Israel*, 17–18.
620 Kaufmann, "The Bible and Mythological Polytheism," 189.
621 See Kaufmann, *The Religion of Israel*, 14–17, 142–144.
622 Kaufmann, *The Religion of Israel*, 14.
623 A detailed analysis of Kaufmann's view is found in *Toledot* I, 286–416.

try.[624] As for the third phase, Kaufmann characterized the days of Saul, David, and the young Solomon as the period of loyalty to Yahweh. An interval period extended from Solomon's last days till the exile introduced the second idolatrous time and the fourth phase in the history of Israelite religion.[625] Moreover, Kaufmann asserted that the biblical literature from 1 Sam 8 to 1 Kgs 10 never mentioned that Israel worshiped other gods.[626]

Furthermore, Kaufmann showed that "the popular idolatry that the prophetic books depict is [...] a magical, fetishistic, non-mythological worship of images."[627] He concluded that idolatry was not a fundamental idea. Rather, it was a superficial phenomenon with no roots in the beliefs of the people. In Kaufmann's opinion this suggested that "popular idolatry was not authentic polytheism, with mythology, temples, and priesthoods. It was vestigial idolatry, a vulgar superstition."[628]

As we have seen, Kaufmann's estimation of popular idolatry accorded well with the perception of the nature of Israelite idolatry. Neither popular idolatry nor Israelite idolatry contained any hints of myth. Of course, idolatry was found in Israel, but it was not authentic paganism, as Kaufmann demonstrated. He defined Israelite idolatry as fetishism, the worship of lifeless objects.[629] In Kaufmann's judgment, "Israelite idolatry was a vulgar phenomenon; it was magical, fetishistic and ritualistic and never attained the level of a cultural force."[630]

At the end of this discussion it might be useful to evaluate Kaufmann's view about Israelite idolatry. We have seen that he built his theory on the assumption that idolatry in Israel was conceived as fetishism. Scholars have disputed Kaufmann's conclusions on the nature and history of idolatry in Israel, especially his definition of idolatry as fetishism, perhaps because Kaufmann employed the term 'fetishism' with bewildering ambiguity.[631] José Faur, for instance, pointed out that "although Kaufmann used the term [fetishism] about one hundred

---

624 Nevertheless, Kaufmann mentioned that the evaluation of this period as idolatrous is part of the historiosophic idealism of the Bible, according to which every national sin is the result of apostasy. On this see Kaufmann, *The Religion of Israel*, 260.

625 Kaufmann, *The Religion of Israel*, 260.

626 Kaufmann, *From the Secret of the Biblical World* (in Hebrew) (Tel Aviv: Devir, 1966), 97.

627 *The Religion of Israel*, 144.

628 *The Religion of Israel*, 142.

629 Kaufmann, "The Bible and Mythological Polytheism," 193.

630 Kaufmann, *The Religion of Israel*, 147.

631 For different connotations of the term fetishism, see Sir Edmund Leach, "The Anthropology of Religion," in *Nineteenth Century Religious Thought in the West* III, 232–233.

times to contrast the biblical view of idolatry with 'authentic paganism', in no place did he define it."[632] He went on to argue:

> Fetishism is not a scientific category universally accepted. Rather, it expresses different concepts and ideas to different scholars. According to some, it is the worship of the spirit of the dead dwelling in the fetish. To others, it is the worship of everything except the sun and the stars. Some use it in the sense of the deification of nature, or the worship of spirits that dwell, influence, and speak by means of material bodies.[633]

Moshe Greenberg, although he accepted most of Kaufmann's assumptions, posed sound questions. He remarked:

> It is true that the polemic against idolatry consistently misrepresents pagan worship as fetishism – an argument that could not convince a theologically informed pagan. But what do we know of the level of belief in the pagan, let alone the Israelites, masses? How much of a mythological basis had the vulgar religion?[634]

Another aspect in Kaufmann's interpretation which deserves attention is related to his view concerning prophetic denunciation of Israelite idolatry. Kaufmann postulated the idea that prophets ignored authentic paganism and their criticism was mainly against rites. His analysis of the prophetic literature in this context is highly problematic. The two books that most clearly contradict Kaufmann's popular idolatry are Hosea and Ezekiel. Kaufmann dealt with the former by dividing Hosea into First Hosea and Second Hosea. As for the description of Israelite idolatry in the book of Ezekiel, Kaufmann asserted that Ezekiel was given to fantasy.[635]

In addition, Kaufmann's assumption about 'authentic paganism' was the object of criticism. As Faur pointed out:

> Kaufmann's notion of 'authentic paganism' is not based on any systematic analysis of the sources. Kaufmann did not see any need to substantiate his notion of 'authentic paganism'.

---

632 José Faur, "The Biblical Idea of Idolatry," *The Jewish Quarterly Review* 69, no. 1 (1978): 1 – 15 (5). For the etymology and definition of fetishism, see Alfred C. Haddon, Magic and Fetishism (London: Constable, 1910). Also, Günter Lanczkowski, "Fetishismus," in *TRE* 11 (1993): 143 – 44. See further Josef F. Thiel, "Fetishismus," in *RGG*⁴, vol. 3 (2000): 101 – 2.
633 In criticizing Kaufmann's view, Faur concluded, "Since Kaufmann never defined his understanding of this term, it is rather difficult to determine with any degree of certainty the sense of his repeated statement that pagan idolatry was not fetishism." See José Faur, "The Biblical Idea of Idolatry," 5.
634 Greenberg, *Studies in the Bible*, 186 – 187.
635 Compare, J. P. Hyatt, "Yehezkel Kaufmann's View of the Religion of Israel," 55. Hyatt also noted that Kaufmann believed in First and Second Isaiah, and First and Second Zechariah.

Accordingly, he did not examine the ancient texts bearing on our topic. What Kaufmann designates as 'authentic paganism' does not correspond to the religion of the Near East – it rather reflects Kaufmann's own particular convictions on this matter.[636]

As it appears, Kaufmann's examination of the nature of idolatry in Israel is somehow puzzling. In this regard Zeitlin observed that Kaufmann worked out a different understanding of the nature of Israelite idolatry which was neither a polytheistic nor a syncretic phenomenon. Zeitlin articulated Kaufmann's position in the following manner:

> For Kaufmann it would be permissible to speak of Israelite paganism only if it could be proved that there prevailed in Israel a mythological conception of Yahweh accompanied by a national cult which was governed by mythological ritual. And it would be permissible to speak of syncretism only if it were found that Yahweh was included in a pantheon in which he had a definite mythological relationship with the other foreign deities, say Baal.[637]

This critique of Kaufmann's position towards the question of Israelite idolatry in Israel shows the weak and strong points in his reconstruction. In order to have the full picture of Kaufmann's interpretation of the religion of Israel, we shall proceed to highlight his view on Israelite monotheism, apostolic prophecy, and the role of Moses in bringing a new original idea to his people.

5 Israelite monotheism

Kaufmann's understanding of Israelite idolatry certainly prepared the way for his thesis on Israelite monotheism, as Kaufmann believed, that idolatry never existed as a culture phenomenon, while monotheism was a new creation. Moreover, Kaufmann assumed that idolatry was uprooted in pre-exilic Israel.[638] Thus, in his view, certain of the 'idolatries' of Israel were no more than stages left behind.[639] Kaufmann showed that the sin of idolatry was exaggerated and therefore the historicity of the sweeping biblical indictment must be re-examined.[640]

---

636 José Faur, "The Biblical Idea of Idolatry," 3–4.
637 Irving M. Zeitlin, *Ancient Judaism: Biblical Criticism from Max Weber to the Present* (Cambridge: Polity Press, 1991), 190.
638 Kaufmann, *The Religion of Israel*, 134.
639 Kaufmann, *The Religion of Israel*, 137.
640 Kaufmann, *The Religion of Israel*, 134.

More interesting is Kaufmann's contention that there was no sin and the people of Israel were not guilty. He explained how the sins of particular groups were ascribed to the entire people. This is an almost necessary consequence of the biblical postulate that Israel's calamities were caused by its sins.[641] Kaufmann also maintained, "The historiographer could not account for what had taken place – the collapse of Israel's monarchy – without sin. Had there been no sin, he would have had to invent it. Israel's sinfulness is essential to biblical theodicy."[642] Moreover, Kaufmann demonstrated that Baal worship in the Books of Judges and Samuel was not part of the original account but belonged to the schematic editorial framework.[643] This implied, as Kaufmann would have it, that the sin of idolatry "was more of a historiographical necessity than a reality."[644]

Furthermore, Kaufmann sought to prove that popular idolatry was not authentic paganism. He also pointed out that prophetic denunciation against popular idolatry was limited to cult and rites. There were no hints of polemics against the worship of mythological gods, from which he concluded, "Israelite idolatry could never take on the character of a genuine syncretism. For genuine syncretism presupposes an essential parity between the deities to be amalgamated."[645] What was decidedly important was Kaufmann's judgment that idolatry in Israel was a stunted phenomenon that never attained the level of a cultural force. The implications are clear: if idolatry failed to exercise a powerful effect on the faith of the people, it can only be that monotheism stood on a firm ground in ancient Israel. In Kaufmann's view, Israelite monotheism permeated the entire life of Israel. He maintained that monotheism brought about a new conception of God.[646] With all of this in mind, I turn to Kaufmann's interpretation of Israelite monotheism.

---

641 Kaufmann, *The Religion of Israel*, 135.
642 Kaufmann, *The Religion of Israel*, 135.
643 Kaufmann, *The Religion of Israel*, 138.
644 Kaufmann, *The Religion of Israel*, 135. Moshe Greenberg mentioned that Kaufmann "had grave reservations regarding the validity of the biblical denunciation of Israel's apostasy. For he regarded this denunciation as flowing from a theological postulate that tended to distort reality: the need of theodicy. justification of God's judgment upon Israel was a leading motif of biblical thought. The whole historical narrative serves as an explanation for the failure of god's covenant with Israel. In accord with biblical doctrine, that failure must be blamed on human dereliction – hence, the necessity of amassing an overwhelming, decisive indictment against Israel which would leave no doubt about the justice of its fate." See Greenberg, *Studies in the Bible*, 181.
645 Kaufmann, *The Religion of Israel*, 146.
646 Kaufmann, *Toledot* I, 224–245.

5.1 Monotheism and polytheism: two different worldviews

Kaufmann made the point that monotheism and polytheism were two distinct religious categories.[647] Admittedly, Kaufmann's understanding of Israelite monotheism was the most important part of his hypothesis. He postulated the idea that Israelite religion was monotheistic from the very outset. In his reading, historical monotheism began with Moses[648] and was devoid of any polytheistic mythology.[649] Moreover, Kaufmann claimed that the people of ancient Israelite did not understand what was meant by polytheism. The question which must be posed here is how did Kaufmann conceive of monotheism?

In accordance with Kaufmann's perspective, the distinctive characteristic of Israelite religion was the idea of God as supreme over all.[650] The Israelites peculiar conception of God was not an arithmetic matter of counting the number of gods, but the idea that God was the source of all being. In the words of Kaufmann, "The mark of monotheism is not the concept of a god who is creator, eternal, benign, or even all-powerful; these notions are found everywhere in the

---

[647] On monotheism and polytheism in recent scholarship discussion, see Manfred Oeming ed., *Der eine Gott und die Götter: Polytheismus und Monotheismus im antiken Israel* (Zürich: TVZ, 2003). See also Hans-Peter Müller, "Monotheismus und Polytheismus," RGG⁴ (2008), vol. 5, 1459–1462.

[648] Kaufmann referred to different manifestations of Israelite monotheism. There is, for example, what Kaufmann called "primeval monotheism". On this see *Toledot* I, 287–289, 315–320; there is also "cosmic-national monotheism," which appeared in the Torah; compare Kaufmann, *Toledot* I, 612–623; also, idem, *The Religion of Israel*, 163, 404. In addition, Kaufmann found another type of monotheism especially in the wisdom literature, that is, "legendary monotheism". On this see Kaufmann, *The Religion of Israel*, 323. The monotheism of the prophets, or what Kaufmann called "universalistic monotheism," is depicted in prophetic literature. See Kaufmann, *The Religion of Israel*, 403.

[649] Kaufmann was obsessed with the idea that the Hebrew Bible showed absolutely no apprehension of the real character of mythological religion. See Kaufmann, "The Bible and Mythological Polytheism," 181; idem, "The Biblical Age," 13. For a discussion see Benjamin Uffenheimer, "Myth and Reality in Ancient Israel," in *The Origins and Diversity of Axial Age Civilizations* (ed. S. N. Eisenstadt; Albany: State University of New York Press, 1986), 135–168.

[650] The idea of God as supreme overall was criticized by Benjamin Uffenheimer who argued that instead of the conception of God as supreme overall, the notion of God as deliverer was what could have stirred the imagination of the people of Israel. He pointed out, "It is unlikely that a faith in the absolute supremacy and uniqueness of the God of Israel would be the achievement of the people who left Egypt, as Kaufmann implied. An abstract faith of this kind could not have attracted a nation of slaves, whose bondage extended back for several generations. What would have fired the imagination of a nation in those circumstances was the message of deliverance, namely, the concept of a god who would liberate them and lead them to freedom." See Uffenheimer, "Myth and Reality in Ancient Israel," 144–145.

pagan world. It is, rather, the idea of a god who is the source of all being, not subject to a cosmic order, and not emergent from a pre-existent realm; a god free of the limitations of magic and mythology."651 He further maintained, "Even the worship of other supernatural beings, which is for the Bible the essence of idolatry, cannot be considered in necessary contradiction to monotheism."652 This meant that the doctrinal aspect of biblical monotheism was that YHWH was God, there was none else.653 In discussing the name 'YHWH' and its derivation, Kaufmann asserted that YHWH was the symbol of the monotheistic idea for the Torah literature, as for the prophets. In short, to Kaufmann YHWH was 'the God'.654

By contrast, Kaufmann defined polytheism as the belief in gods.655 It should be mentioned that Kaufmann distinguished three elements in polytheism: deification of natural phenomena (sky, earth, moon, and sea, as well as deification of plants and animals, of the dead, of kings and heroes); myth (arose as an outcome of the deification of nature); and deification of material objects (natural or artificial).656 This prompts us to ask about the essential idea of polytheism. In Kaufmann's view, "It is not the plurality of gods per se, then, that expresses the essence of polytheism, but rather the notion of many independent power-entities, all on a par with one another, and all rooted in the primordial realm."657

Thus monotheism and polytheism are essentially different. While the fundamental idea of monotheism is god supremacy, polytheism conceives of god as subordinate to other entities. As mentioned, Kaufmann made a sharp distinction between monotheism and polytheism. He presumed that Israelite monotheism "never really [came] to grips with the essence of polytheism, the belief in mythological gods."658 Kaufmann saw by no means a transition from polytheism to

651 Kaufmann, The Religion of Israel, 29.
652 Kaufmann, The Religion of Israel, 137.
653 Kaufmann, The Religion of Israel, 137.
654 Kaufmann, The Religion of Israel, 229.
655 Kaufmann, The Religion of Israel, 19.
656 For more details see Kaufmann, "The Bible and Mythological Polytheism," 180.
657 Kaufmann, The Religion of Israel, 23. Kaufmann's view of polytheism has been criticized by Mark Smith who wrote that Kaufmann's "sophisticated analysis saddles polytheism with an order to which the gods themselves are subject, in contrast to the monotheistic deity's control over all. He has pointed out that there is little evidence for an independent order having mastery over deities in either Ugaritic or Mesopotamian mythologies." See Mark S. Smith, The Origins of Biblical Monotheism: Israel's Polytheistic Background and the Ugaritic Texts (New York: Oxford University Press, 2001), 12.
658 Kaufmann, "The Biblical Age," 13. A sound critique of Kaufmann's distinction between monotheism and polytheism has been given by Uffenheimer, who posed the following important

monotheism.[659] This was because Kaufmann believed that the perception of the idea of God in monotheism and polytheism represented two different worldviews and made it difficult to think of any kind of historical continuity. Moreover, Kaufmann thought that Israelite monotheism "was an entirely new religious idea, an original creation and one that had no roots in polytheistic civilization."[660] In Kaufmann's opinion, the birth of Israelite monotheism marked the death of paganism in Israel and consequently Israel was not a polytheistic people.[661] In support of his argument, he claimed that biblical authors were unfamiliar with real polytheism. He based this on the idea that the Bible failed to express the real contrast between Israelite religion and mythological polytheism.[662] The Bible is unaware of the nature of pagan religion.[663] Also, the gods and their myths were not a central issue in the religion of YHWH.[664] As an example, Kaufmann referred to the prophet Amos, saying, "Amos, the first known literary prophet, hardly mentions the belief in gods. In 8: 14, he speaks of Ashimah of Samaria; in 5: 26, he names gods that the Israelites 'made' for themselves. Thus the prophet, who is considered by many to have been the first to arrive at pure monotheism, fails entirely to express himself on the nature of the polytheism which he allegedly leaves behind".[665] Kaufmann recapitulated his view as follows:

> The Bible no longer knows what polytheism really is and throughout, from its earliest to its latest parts, represents pagan religion purely as fetishism, as the worship of wood and stone or the host of heaven. Nothing is said of the genuine pagan belief in mythological

---

questions: Does the abyss between polytheism and monotheism not leave any room for historical continuity, or does historical reality know of an in-between phenomenon? Secondly: Does the rationalistic definition of monotheism as a non-mythological creation fit historical reality? See Benjamin Uffenheimer, "Yehezkel Kaufmann: Historian and Philosopher of Biblical Monotheism," *Immanuel* 3 (1973): 9–21.

659 In this context, Uffenheimer aptly remarked that Kaufmann denied the relevance of the principle of emulation for explaining the growth of monotheism. Kaufmann believed that monotheism was a-mythological in essence, as God is not subject to the material laws inherent in matter. Kaufmann drew a sharp difference between polytheism and monotheism that did not allow a transition from a polytheistic-pantheistic-mythological outlook to the monotheistic-transcendent one. According to him, no historical-evolutionary theory can explain the leap over the abyss dividing these two worlds. There is no historical continuity between polytheism and monotheism. Uffenheimer, "Yehezkel Kaufmann: Historian and Philosopher of Biblical Monotheism," 13.

660 Kaufmann, "The Biblical Age," 7–8.
661 *The Religion of Isrcel*, 2–3.
662 Kaufmann, "The Biblical Age,"13.
663 Kaufmann, *The Religion of Israel*, 7.
664 Kaufmann, *The Religion of Israel*, 20.
665 Kaufmann, *The Religion of Israel*, 14.

gods. This can only mean that even the earliest parts of the Bible were created after the death of the gods in Israel, in a monotheistic environment from which mythological polytheism had been uprooted.[666]

Perhaps the most striking feature in Kaufmann's understanding of Israelite monotheism was his insistence that it first appeared as an intuitive creation.[667] He emphasized that Israelite monotheism was not a product of intellectual speculation, or of mystical meditation, in the Greek or Indian manner. According to Kaufmann:

> Israelite monotheism first appeared as an insight, an original intuition...The new religious idea never received an abstract, systematic formulation in Israel. It expressed itself rather in symbols, the chief of which was the image of an omnipotent, supreme deity, holy, awful, and jealous, whose will was the highest law. Taking on popular forms, the new idea pervaded every aspect of Israelite creativity.[668]

Moreover, Kaufmann asserted that monotheism, once it appeared in Israel, dominated the life and the culture of ancient Israel. Monotheism, said Kaufmann, "pervades every aspect of Israel's creativity: legend, cult, ethics, wisdom, priesthood, prophecy, and kingship. It speaks in the history of the nation, and as if from a hidden centre dominates all."[669]

Thus, it appears that Kaufmann's interpretation of Israelite monotheism aimed to prove two things. First, he wanted to connect monotheism with popular religion. In other words Kaufmann endeavoured to attest the popular origin of monotheism, a stage prior to the literary prophets.[670] Second, Kaufmann sought to differentiate Israelite monotheism as a unique phenomenon in its cultural environment. Thus, for Kaufmann Israelite monotheism was essentially a popular creation.[671] He even talked about popular and priestly versions of the monothe-

---

666 Kaufmann, "The Biblical Age," 25.
667 Kaufmann points out that the rise of Israelite religion as a new creation did not originate in the battle with fetishist idolatry; it preceded this battle. For, it was the new religion which put an end to heathenism in Israel and thereby created the necessary conditions for the rise of that lifeless idolatry which the Bible condemns. On this see Kaufmann, "The Bible and Mythological Polytheism," 197.
668 Kaufmann, *The Religion of Israel*, 60.
669 Kaufmann, "The Biblical Age," 13.
670 See Kaufmann, *Toledot* I, 221, 254, 609; see further, idem, *Toledot* II, 239, 299,403.
671 Kaufmann frequently emphasized that Israelite monotheism did not grow out of a polemic against idolatry. At the same time, he refuted the emergence of monotheism in Israel as being the result of prophetic denunciation against national popular religion. See Kaufmann, "The Bible and Mythological Polytheism"; idem, "The Biblical Age," 13. For more in this subject, see Uffenheimer, "Yehezkel Kaufmann: Historian and Philosopher of Biblical Monotheism," 16.

istic idea. In Kaufmann's opinion, pre-exilic monotheism was fostered by priestly and popular circles.[672] Furthermore, Kaufmann affirmed that the monotheistic idea of god is rooted in the popular religion of the people of Israel and was not an invention of the literary prophets.[673] Israelite monotheism was, then, an original creation of the people of Israel.[674]

With respect to Israelite monotheism and its cultural environment, Kaufmann contended that Israelite religion differed fundamentally from the religions of the pagan world. This was a bewildering point of Kaufmann's interpretation. On the one hand, Kaufmann attempted to detach Israelite monotheism from the ideas of the pagan world, while on the other, he sought to place Israelite monotheism as an empirical idea in its historical context.[675] In order to overcome this problem, Kaufmann did two important things. First, he suggested that the religions of Egypt, Babylon and Canaan, in whose midst Israelite religion was born, were highly advanced religions.[676] In the words of Kaufmann:

> Amidst this high cultural environment, Israelite religion was born. Its prehistory is not to be sought in primitive or Bedouin religion, but in the mellowed civilizations of the ancient Near East. Its initial level was not magical, totemistic, animistic, or demonistic; it originated among developed theistic religions.[677]

Kaufmann's next step was to demonstrate that the ancient materials which Israelite religion inherited from the surrounding nations were replaced by Israel's new idea, monotheism. He thought that pagan myth was fundamentally transmuted by the Israelite idea and explained how Israelite religion absorbed foreign materials and made them anew.[678] For example, he described "the magical strand of biblical thought", saying that the ancient materials related to magic became in Israel a vehicle to express a new non-pagan idea. This transmutation of magical materials, according to Kaufmann, was one of the striking features of the history of Israelite religion. [679]As Kaufmann deduced from this process of transformation, "All mythological and magical rationales were replaced by historical

---

672 Kaufmann, *The Religion of Israel*, 162.
673 Kaufmann, "The Biblical Age," 59. As for the monotheistic idea and prophets, see Kaufmann, *The Religion of Israel*, 157, 344, 346.
674 Kaufmann, *The Religion of Israel*, 2.
675 Kaufmann, *The Religion of Israel*, 225–226.
676 Kaufmann, *The Religion of Israel*, 220–223; also, idem, "The Biblical Age," 5–7.
677 Kaufmann, *The Religion of Israel*, 221.
678 Kaufmann, *The Religion of Israel*, 63.
679 Kaufmann, *The Religion of Israel*, 81.

and monotheistic ones."[680] At this point, it is important to mention what Kaufmann called the 'triumph of monotheism'.[681] In his view, pre-exilic Israel must have had a monotheistic faith which grew up within the environment of popular monotheism.[682]

That the monotheistic idea made itself visible in all forms of Israel's life indicated, in Kaufmann's view, that it was a product of Israel's national culture. It was presumably Kaufmann's conviction that Israelite monotheism grew out of the creative spirit of the people of Israel that led him to reject other theories on the history of Israelite religion.[683] As for the origin of Israelite monotheism, Kaufmann pointed out that this question had to be posed inside Israel and in its own culture.[684] To Kaufmann, the question of the origin of Israelite monotheism should start with acknowledging that Israel created a new religious idea. In addition, he emphasized that there was no development from polytheistic and monolatrous stages towards monotheism. Instead, Kaufmann saw the course of Israelite religion as having moved from monotheism to monolatry, not from monolatry to monotheism.[685]

5.2 Apostolic-prophecy and the rise of Israelite religion

In his inquiry into the origins of Israelite religion and the idea of monotheism, Kaufmann relied on two main arguments. First, he developed the idea of 'apostolic-prophecy', which started with Moses. Second, he argued that historical monotheism began with Moses.[686] This meant that "the empirical history of monotheism did not antedate the rise of Israel."[687] Moreover, Kaufmann pointed out that prophecy emerged in Israel long before entry into the land of Canaan. The

---

680 Kaufmann, *The Religion of Israel*, 102; also, idem, "The Biblical Age," 42.

681 Kaufmann, *Toledot* I, 659–660.

682 Kaufmann, *The Religion of Israel*, 133, 134.

683 For example, Kaufmann disputed the theories of Wellhausen, Meyer, Stade and Smend that Israelite religion was at first polytheistic. He also rejected the hypotheses of Sellin, Kittel and Albright that heathen mythology exercised a profound influence on Israelite culture. On this see Kaufmann, "Bible and Mythological Polytheism," 179. In addition, Kaufmann refuted Renan's theory on the Semites and the origin of monotheism. See Kaufmann, *The Religion of Israel*, 61; idem, *Toledot* I, 2–12; also, idem, *From the Secret of the Biblical World*, 256–280.

684 See Kaufmann, *Toledot* II, 23–25.

685 Kaufmann, *The Religion of Israel*, 148.

686 Kaufmann, *Toledot* II, 41.

687 Kaufmann, "The Biblical Age," 15.

beginning of prophecy can be dated back to the period before settlement.[688] In Kaufmann's view, Sinaitic theophany was the source of the people's faith in prophecy. As it appeared in the Book of Deuteronomy, this was the foundation of Israelite prophecy.[689] Moreover, Kaufmann suggested that the distinctive feature of Israelite prophecy was the idea of personal election. The prophet was sent to the people to bring them the word of God and his commands; he was charged with a mission.[690] Kaufmann explained that the verb 'send' was the heart of the divine call to an Israelite prophet. The prophet acted on behalf of God, not of man. His function was not to answer men's inquiries, like the pagan prophet and diviner, but to do and say only that required by God.[691] To Kaufmann, this was a peculiarly Israelite concept. "Israelite prophecy is an Israelite creation."[692] Furthermore, Kaufmann remarked, "What makes the history of Israelite prophecy *sui generis* is the succession of apostles of God that come to the people through the ages."[693] In addition, he found a historical aspect in apostolic prophecy. To quote Kaufmann:

> Ever and from its beginnings it belongs to the religion of YHWH. No apostolic prophet comes to Israel in the name of another god. Apostolic prophecy was always the standard bearer of the faith of YHWH, and its champion in the battle with idolatry. Every large step in the development of the religion of YHWH in Israel took the form of prophecy: the stress on the moral demand of God, the idea of a universal redemption, with Israel playing a central role.[694]

Pursuing this further, Kaufmann maintained that Moses was the first prophet with a mission to a people. The prophetic type of Moses, in Kaufmann's view, belonged to the earliest stage of Israelite prophecy.[695] Moses was an antique model of an apostolic prophet.[696] Thus Kaufmann dated Moses's prophecy, that is, apostolic prophecy, to the earliest phase of Israelite religion. In fact, Kaufmann

---

688 Kaufmann, *The Religion of Israel*, 216.
689 Kaufmann, *The Religion of Israel*, 212.
690 Kaufmann, *The Religion of Israel*, 212.
691 Kaufmann, *The Religion of Israel*, 213.
692 Kaufmann, *The Religion of Israel*, 214. Kaufmann mentioned that the advent of apostolic prophecy was a turning point, a new phenomenon of tremendous import for the future. See Kaufmann, *The Religion of Israel*, 215.
693 Kaufmann, *The Religion of Israel*, 212.
694 Kaufmann, *The Religion of Israel*, 214.
695 Kaufmann, *Toledot* I, 524.
696 Kaufmann, *The Religion of Israel*, 224, 227, 228. Kaufmann compared Moses's prophecy with that of *kāhin* among Arab tribes. See Kaufmann, *The Religion of Israel*, 227–228; also, idem, *From the Secret of The Biblical World*, 64–65.

tried to relate the beginning of Israelite religion with the dawn of the people of Israel through Moses's prophecy. In other words he defined apostolic-prophecy, with Moses, as a peculiarly Israelite phenomenon.[697] In this way, Moses was considered the first apostle-prophet and the father of monotheism, as will be shown.

If monotheism began with Moses, what about the pre-Mosaic period? To put it differently, did monotheism exist during the patriarchal times? In his interpretation of the history of monotheism in Israel, Kaufmann drew attention to certain phenomena which serve as the organic framework to monotheism. These were apostolic prophecy, the battle with idolatry, and the name of YHWH.[698] According to Kaufmann, none of these were known to the patriarchs. Israelite monotheism was, then, post-patriarchal.[699] In Kaufmann's opinion, "What distinguishes the patriarchs is their role as ancestors of the nation that was destined to become monotheistic. The biblical view gives no support to the theory that Abraham originated the idea of the one God or founded a congregation of monotheists."[700] Kaufmann went so far as to say, "The historicity of the biblical tradition concerning the monotheism of the Patriarchs is difficult to determine. History knows only of national cultures and national religions, and historical monotheism existed in antiquity as the national religion of Israel."[701] It was only at the time of Moses that monotheism became the faith of all Israel.[702] Seen from Kaufmann's perspective, monotheism began in Israel with Moses, the creator of an original idea.[703] The monotheism of the patriarchs was "the child of later conceptions – the same that produced the monotheist cast of the primeval legends of Genesis."[704]

---

697 Kaufmann, *Toledot* I, 731–737.
698 Kaufmann, *The Religion of Israel*, 222; idem, "The Biblical Age," 16.
699 Kaufmann, *The Religion of Israel*, 222.
700 Kaufmann, *The Religion of Israel*, 221.
701 Kaufmann, "The Biblical Age," 14.
702 Kaufmann, "The Biblical Age," 14.
703 Kaufmann, *The Religion of Israel*, 227. Kaufmann's position concerning the beginning of monotheism in Israel seems to be close to that of Albright who argued that Israelite monotheism appeared as a new phenomenon. Both Kaufmann and Albright believed that "without monotheism, Israel, as we know it, could not have existed" and that "it was indeed Moses who was the principal architect of Israelite monotheism. See William F. Albright, *Yahweh and the Gods of Canaan: A Historical Analysis of Two Contrasting Faiths* (London: Athlone Press, 1968), 206. For a critique of Kaufmann and Albright, see John J. Collins, *The Bible After Babel: Historical Criticism in a Postmodern Age* (Grand Rapids: Eerdmans, 2005), 99–101. See also H. H. Rowley, "Living Issues in Biblical Scholarship: The Antiquity of Israelite Monotheism," *ExpTim* 61, no. 11 (1949): 333–338.
704 Kaufmann, *The Religion of Israel*, 222.

According to Kaufmann, the message of Moses brought about a religious rev-olution among the tribes of Israel.[705] We have earlier noted that Kaufmann con-nected historical monotheism with the name YHWH as god of Israel and apostol-ic prophecy. Kaufmann added other features such as the election of Israel and the battle with heathendom.[706] He pointed out that the struggle against pagan-ism in Israel started with Moses. In the words of Kaufmann, "That no story of a battle with paganism is recorded before the age of Moses suggests a terminus a quo. Only with Moses does the contrast between the faith of YHWH and pagan-ism appear."[707] In addition, "While Israel, from its beginning regarded itself as the people of YHWH, this tie between people and YHWH did not exist in patri-archal times. It is a fact that apostolic prophecy is formative for the history of Israel from its beginning".[708] Thus, in Kaufmann's view the struggle with pagan-ism and the revelation of the name YHWH to Moses marked the beginning of the monotheistic revolution in Israel.[709]

As a matter of fact, Kaufmann considered Moses to have been the initiator of a new religious idea in Israel:

> Moses is the historical person who first envisioned the peculiar ideas of Israelite religion. His racial stock is of no consequence, the only significant fact being that his new idea was neither Egyptian nor Babylonian. His thought cannot be related to any 'monotheistic ten-dencies' in Egypt or Babylon without distorting it.[710]

Moreover, Kaufmann noted that the message of Moses was a turning point in the history of Israelite religion, believing that it was during the time of Moses that a great transformation occurred. To quote Kaufmann's words:

> With Moses the sin of idolatry – particularly as a national sin – comes into existence. Be-fore, idolatry was nowhere interdicted and punished. The stories depicting idolatry as a na-tional sin presuppose the existence of a monotheistic people. Since such stories begin only with Moses, we infer that it was in his time that the great transformation took place. By

---

705 Kaufmann, "The Biblical Age," 25.
706 Kaufmann, "The Biblical Age," 16.
707 Kaufmann, *The Religion of Israel*, 223.
708 Kaufmann, *The Religion of Israel*, 224.
709 Kaufmann, *The Religion of Israel*, 225.
710 Kaufmann, *The Religion of Israel*, 226. According to Kaufmann, Moses was not a priest and did not perform any priestly activities. On this see Kaufmann, *Toledot* II, 342–346. In addition, Kaufmann rejected the idea that connected Moses with the Midianite priest Jethro. See Kauf-mann, *The Religion of Israel*, 242–244. For further detail about Moses and his message, see Kaufmann, *Toledot* II, 334–348.

making Israel enter a covenant with the one God, he made it a monotheistic people that alone among men was punishable for the sin of idolatry.[711]

6 Summary

We have seen that Kaufmann interpreted monotheism as a product of the creative spirit of the people of Israel. He argued that monotheism and polytheism were two different worldviews. The essential nature of monotheism and polytheism dictated that the gap between them could not be bridged. Israelite monotheism was a unique phenomenon in Israel's history. In fact, Kaufmann sought to demonstrate that Israelite religion was monotheistic from the very beginning. Moreover, he pointed out that monotheism was a folk religion; it was the religion of the entire nation. On the other hand, Kaufmann maintained that pre-exilic Israel was not an idolatrous people. What remained among the Israelites "was vestigial idolatry, a vulgar superstition of the sort that the ignorant level of monotheistic peoples practices to this day."[712] Kaufmann relied on two assumptions in his thesis of the history of monotheism in Israel. He started first by claiming that the Torah contained ancient monotheistic material uninfluenced by prophetic doctrines.[713] His next step was to prove that the books of the Former Prophets contained no evidence whatsoever of religious syncretism.[714] Furthermore, Kauf-

---

711 Kaufmann, *The Religion of Israel*, 230.

712 Kaufmann, *The Religion of Israel*, 142.

713 Kaufmann's contention that the Torah contained ancient materials eas criticized by David Lieber, who found Kaufmann's argument far from convincing for three reasons. As for the first, David Lieber said that the existence of ancient materials in a document is no proof of the antiquity of the document itself. Second, that the documents were uninfluenced by prophetic teachings may simply have been due to the fact that the influence of the prophets was highly circumscribed during the days of the First Temple and did not extend to the circles in which these documents were written. Further, David Lieber pointed out that the materials which were, admittedly, ancient were not unequivocally monotheistic. On this see David Lieber, "Yehezkel Kaufmann's Contribution to Biblical Scholarship," *Journal of Jewish Education* 34, no. 4 (1964): 254–261 (259).

714 Kaufmann's denial of the existence of syncretism in Israel contradicted facts deduced from the Old Testament about Baal worship and at the same time neglected Israelite contact with surrounding peoples. Albright, for example, disputed Kaufmann's unrealistic approach to the history of backsliding in Israel. He wrote, "There was so much exchange of cultural influences between Israel and its neighbours on all sides of its tiny territory, and there were so many irruptions of paganism into Israel, that the ignorance presupposed by Kaufmann's view is simply incredible." See Albright, *Yahweh and the Gods of Canaan*, 173, 180. Also Uffenheimer, "Myth and Reality in Ancient Israel," 135–168.

mann noted that the prophetic denunciation against foreign worship in Israel was exaggerated and therefore cannot be taken seriously as proof of idolatry.

Kaufmann's view on the history of Israelite religion invited attack.[715] Against the scholarly consensus, Kaufmann adopted an uncompromising position concerning the origin of monotheism.[716] Furthermore, Kaufmann was accused of conducting a deductive approach in his reconstruction of the history of Israelite religion.[717] In and his description of monotheism as 'primal intuition' was refuted. Baruch Halpern, for example, pointed out that Kaufmann's analysis of Israelite monotheism was unhistorical, because monotheism for Kaufmann was a constant rather than a variable, a framework not a datum contained.[718] Kaufmann's insistence that Israelite religion remained a single intuition and system of belief that had not undergone changes through the centuries was hard to believe.[719] As David Lieber observed, the exact nature of this 'primal intuition' is not at all clear. He said, "Kaufmann at times definitely implies that it involves the belief in a transcendent, universal deity, who is at once creator, lawgiver, and redeemer. At others, he concedes that these notions were only potentially present in the intuition during the age of Moses, and were actualized during the following centuries."[720] Kaufmann's idealization of the beginning of monotheism in Israel served to enforce his ideas about the creative spirit of ancient Israel. However, it is difficult to maintain that ancient Israelites during the period of Sinai wanderings could have developed a unique idea of God. For that reason, Uffenheimer rightly remarked, "It is unlikely that a faith in the absolute supremacy and

---

715 See, for example, Israel Knohl, *Biblical Beliefs: Limits of the Scriptural Revolution* (in Hebrew) (Jerusalem: Magnes Press, 2007).

716 This could explain why Kaufmann's contribution on the study of Israelite monotheism has been ignored. Kaufmann's view of monotheism was notably absent from the discussion in recent scholarly debate. See, for example, Rainer Albertz, *Geschichte und Theologie: Studien zur Exegese des Alten Testaments und zur Religionsgeschichte Israels* (Berlin: de Gruyter, 2003), 359 – 382. Moreover, when Kaufmann's thoughts on monotheism are treated, it was noted that the complete picture of his position was not presented. See Nathan MacDonald, *Deuteronomy and the Meaning of "Monotheism"* (Tübingen: Mohr Siebeck, 2003), 36 – 40.

717 A detailed analysis of Kaufmann's view on monotheism and a critique of his can be found in Thomas M. Krapf, "Biblischer Monotheismus und vorexilischer JHWH-Glaube. Anmerkungen zur neueren Monotheismusdiskussion im Lichte von Yehezkel Kaufmanns Polytheismus-Monotheismus-Begriff," *Berliner theologische Zeitschrift* 11, no. 1 (1994): 42 – 64.

718 Baruch Halpern, "Brisker Pipes than Poetry: The Development of Israelite Monotheism," in *Judaic Perspectives on Ancient Israel* (ed. Jacob Neusner; Philadelphia: Fortress Press, 1987), 77 – 107 (106 – 107).

719 Norman K. Gottwald, *The Hebrew Bible in its Social World and in Ours* (Atlanta: Scholars Press, 1993), 195.

720 David Lieber, "Yehezkel Kaufmann's Contribution to Biblical Scholarship," 259.

uniqueness of the God of Israel would be the achievement of the people who left Egypt, as Kaufmann implies. An abstract faith of this kind could not attract a nation of slaves, whose bondage extended back for several generations."[721] Perhaps what worried readers of Kaufmann's interpretation of the history of Israelite religion was his insistence on the purity of monotheistic faith in pre-exilic Israel and, the idea that the Biblical writers misunderstood the nature of Israelite idolatry.

Looking to reinforce his thesis on the history of Israelite religion, Kaufmann turned to studying the early traditions of Israel in Canaan. Consistent with his stance, he argued that Israelite religion remained intact. He showed that the course of Israel's history in the premonarchic period attested to the fact that there was no amalgamation between the Israelites and the Canaanites. I shall now focus on the importance of this issue in understanding Kaufmann's structure.

---

[721] Benjamin Uffenheimer, "Myth and Reality in Ancient Israel," 144.

Chapter Six:
Early Israelite History in Canaan

1 Introduction

In the two preceding chapters my aim has been to highlight the main points in Kaufmann's interpretation of Israelite religion. We have seen that Kaufmann proposed that the Torah predated the Prophets and its monotheism was developed before prophetic influence took hold among the people of Israel. Kaufmann's main concern was to demonstrate that the Torah contained ancient and reliable documents that could be used for historical reconstruction. He found that the Torah's literature represented the early stages of Israelite religion. In addition, Kaufmann argued that the sources of the Torah were different expressions of a constant faith.

Having re-examined the date of the sources, especially the Priestly Code, Kaufmann turned to study the basic ideas of Israelite religion. In comparison to all forms of paganism, he contended that Israelite religion developed new religious ideas. Furthermore, he concluded that paganism had been uprooted from Israel since the days of Moses, that is, from its very beginning. Israelite idolatry was not 'authentic paganism', but fetishist worship of lifeless objects. Most important was Kaufmann's conclusion that monotheism was implanted in the Israelite consciousness to such a degree that idolatry was not able to affect the popular religion. In order to strengthen his view on the history of Israelite religion, Kaufmann studied the early history of Israel in Canaan and advanced two points. The first was the idea that the conquest of Canaan took place through massive war. The second point was his assertion that the alleged Israelite-Canaanite amalgamation did not occur. Kaufmann's assumptions, it will be shown, aimed to justify his opinion that the Israelites remained a monotheistic people in Canaan. In addition, Kaufmann wished to prove that Israel's popular religion was not 'Canaanized' and that the Yahweh-Baal hypothesis was inaccurate. Following Kaufmann's steps in interpreting the basic ideas of Israelite religion in order to reconstruct the early history of Israel in Canaan, I shall examine how far he succeeded in his undertaking.

2 The Patriarchal Age

Kaufmann considered the Patriarchal Age to have been the period of confederation of the Israelite tribes, during which he assumed that the ethnic unit of the

Benē-Yiśrāēl was formed. In his view, the patriarchs "are not tribal symbols but historical personages enveloped in legend. They were "princes of God," the venerated leaders of the Hebrew tribes.[722]

Kaufmann was inclined to disregard what happened before Moses. Let us consider, for example, his assessment of the patriarchal age in the history of Israelite religion.[723] He wrote, "The people – the real bearers of historical monotheism – even according to biblical tradition, did not inherit their faith from the patriarchal age."[724]

Not only did Kaufmann neglect the role of the patriarchs in engendering the unique ideas of Israelite religion but he also asserted, "There is no religious contrast between the patriarchs and their surroundings."[725] Conversely, he emphasized that the historicity of Moses was supported by trustworthy historical facts.[726] He said that the appearance of Moses's prophecy marked the beginning of a uniquely Israelite phenomenon.[727] Moses's message, so Kaufmann, brought about a religious revolution among the tribes of Israel.[728]

In reconstructing early Israel, Kaufmann rejected the hypothesis that identified the origin of the Israelite tribes with the appearance of the Hyksos.[729] In his opinion, there was no real similarity between the Hebrew shepherds-turned-slaves who fled Egypt and the Hyksos ruling class who, after a century of rule, were expelled by the Egyptians. The Hyksos military and political organization, with its horses, chariots and city-state, contrasted sharply with the ass-and-camel pastoral culture of the patriarchs. The crucial point in Kaufmann's argument was that the patriarchal time (Jacob and his sons) took place after the events related to the Hyksos, either in Egypt or in Palestine.[730] Likewise, Kauf-

---

722 On this see Kaufmann, *The Religion of Israel*, 219; also, idem, *Toledot* II, 11 – 13, 15 – 19.
723 For Kaufmann's characterization of the patriarchal age, see *Toledot* II, 1 – 33.
724 Kaufmann, *The Religion of Israel*, 222. Kaufmann calls the time before Moses "the patriarchal age". In his reconstruction of the patriarchal tradition, Kaufmann came close to the view of Albright. Compare, William F. Albright, "Moses in Historical and Theological Perspective," in *Magnalia Dei: The Mighty Acts of God: Essays on the Bible and Archaeology in Memory of G. Ernest Wright* (ed. Werner E. Lemke, Patrick D. Miller, and Frank Moore Cross; Garden City: New York, 1976), 120 – 131.
725 Kaufmann, *The Religion of Israel*, 222.
726 Kaufmann, *The Religion of Israel*, 224.
727 Kaufmann, "The Biblical Age," 20.
728 Kaufmann, "The Biblical Age," 24.
729 Kaufmann, *Toledot* I, 5 – 7.
730 Kaufmann, *The Religion of Israel*, 217; see further, idem, *Commentary on Joshua*, 51; see also, *Toledot* II, 4 – 7.

mann refused to identify the Hebrew tribes with *Habiru* groups.[731] He drew attention to the essential contrast between the Israelites tribes and the Habiru in the following manner:

> The Bible speaks of tribes; the Hapiru in Palestine and elsewhere are, for the most part, only mercenaries or slaves. They are rootless migrants, never represented as ethic units on the move in search of tribal territory. What they conquer is for the kings and princes who hire them for the sake of plunder.[732]

According to Kaufmann, the beginning of the people of Israel was as follows: From the beginning of the second millennium B.C., there was a movement of Hebrews into the cultural lands of the Near East.[733] The tribes of Israel belonged to these Hebrew groups.[734] They apparently succeeded in preserving their tribal organization, their pastoral way of life and their cultural traditions. The patriarchal ancestors of Israel – Abraham 'the Hebrew' and his offspring – were evidently of this sort. When they entered Canaan in the second half of the second millennium B.C.E., it was not as soldiers, slaves, or hirelings, but as distinct, independent tribes. A sense of kinship united them, and their common purpose was to find land upon which they could settle.[735] Most important to Kaufmann:

> The tribes did not originate in the desert at all. They came from Babylonia and lived for a while in Upper Mesopotamia, whence they came to Canaan and eventually to Egypt; their stay in the desert after the Exodus was a relatively short affair. During many generations they lived in lands of high culture.[736]

As referred to above, Kaufmann tended to minimize the patriarchal influence on the history of Israelite religion. He suggested that the patriarchs were not monotheistic.[737] This can be seen from his description of Abraham and his religion. Kaufmann wrote:

---

731 *Toledot* II, 328–334. On the question of Habiru and its connection with the history of Israelite tribes see, for example, Moshe Greenberg, *The Hab/piru* (New Haven; American Oriental Society, 1955). For a recent discussion see Oswald Loretz, *Habiru-Hebräer: Eine sozio-linguistische Studie über die Herkunft des Gentiliziums ʿibrî vom Appellativum ḫabiru* (Berlin: de Gruyter, 1984), 1–17.
732 Kaufmann, *The Religion of Israel*, 217; idem, *Commentary on Joshua*, 54–55; *Toledot* II, 2–10; "The Biblical Age." 4–5.
733 Kaufmann, *Toledot* II, 18–25.
734 Kaufmann, *Toledot* II, 11–13.
735 Kaufmann, "The Biblical Age," 4–5; also, idem, *The Religion of Israel*, 218.
736 Kaufmann, "The Biblical Age," 5.
737 Kaufmann, *Toledot* II, 25–32.

Abraham is [...] not represented as the founder of monotheistic religion. He is but a link in the chain of monotheists that goes back to Adam. What distinguishes the patriarchs is their role as ancestors of the nation that was destined to become monotheistic. The biblical view gives no support to the theory that Abraham originated the idea of the one God or founded a congregation of monotheists.[738]

3 Moses

The real beginning of Israel started with Moses. To put it differently, Kaufmann gave credit to the great role of Moses in early Israelite history, believing that it was under his leadership that the Israelite tribes were consolidated. Moses was the first to envisage the unique idea of Israelite religion, monotheism.[739] We have already mentioned that Kaufmann connected historical monotheism with Moses. He further emphasized that the religious transformation of Israel was the lifework of Moses.[740] In the words of Kaufmann:

Moses worked only with a few pastoral tribes, who were strangers in a foreign land. Their culture and religion was an amalgam having no established centre of influence, nor did they have a stable political organization. The national religious message of Moses is what first consolidated them into a people. For at the bottom, the tribal confederation was a free band of believers.[741]

Although Kaufmann emphasized that Moses was a historical figure,[742] he was sceptical about the biblical tradition related to Moses and his message. He wrote, "We do not have a reliable account of the original account of Moses's message. Although the whole of biblical literature is a product of the deep transformation that it brought about, the Bible tells nothing of the course of that transformation."[743] Thus Kaufmann observed that the stories about Moses were not given as a dry historical account, but as liturgical poetry such as in Exod. 3. He described the account given in Exod. 3:1–4:17 as a prophetic legend.[744]

According to Kaufmann, Moses was a leader and judge with political authority like Deborah, Gideon, Samson and Samuel.[745] Moreover, Kaufmann affirmed,

738 Kaufmann, *The Religion of Israel*, 221.
739 Kaufmann, *Toledot* II, 36.
740 Kaufmann, *The Religion of Israel*, 225.
741 Kaufmann, *The Religion of Israel*, 231, n. 8.
742 Kaufmann, *Toledot* II, 37–40.
743 Kaufmann, *The Religion of Israel*, 230.
744 Kaufmann, "The Biblical Age," 16; also, idem, *Toledot* II, 38.
745 Kaufmann, *The Religion of Israel*, 227; see further, idem, *Toledot* II, 45, 68–70.

"Moses does not act as a priest. It is in the role of a prophet that he performs cultic acts."[746] In the same line, Kaufmann refuted the Kenite-Midianite hypothesis that connected Moses and his message with the cult of a god of Sinai or Kadesh.[747] In Kaufmann's opinion, Moses' special connection with Kadesh was a romance of modern midrashists.[748] The best way to have a true understanding of Moses' figure would be through considering the picture of the pre-Islamic Arab *Kāhin*. In the words of Kaufmann:

> Like the *Kāhin*, Moses is not connected with an established temple or cult. Whether Moses was ever himself a *Kāhin* or not, he seems to have grown up among a family of such seers, and this surely affected him. The ancient Hebrew *Kāhin* – clairvoyant – was the social type that served as the vehicle of his appearance as prophet and leader.[749]

As far as Moses is concerned, it seems quite clear that Kaufmann aimed to associate the historical context of Israelite religion with Moses.[750] In so doing, he first connected the rise of Israelite religion with apostolic prophecy, the first representative of which was Moses.[751] Secondly, as mentioned, Kaufmann argued that historical monotheism began with Moses. Thus, Kaufmann viewed Moses's message as the true beginning of Israelite monotheism. With Moses, the name YHWH was first conceived of as a symbol of the monotheistic idea.[752] Moreover, it was during the Mosaic period that the struggle against paganism and the idea of Yahweh as a jealous God appeared.[753] "With the coming of Moses," said Kaufmann, "the

---

746 Kaufmann, "The Biblical Age," 21. It should be mentioned that Kaufmann argued against the claims which attributed a cultic or priestly profession to Moses. In addition, Kaufmann asserted the superiority cf Moses to Aaron in the Priestly Code. In Kaufmann's view, Moses was depicted in P as a prophet who stood at the head of the P's camp. In the camp itself, the priest has no authority. It was Moses who dispatched the spies, who sent Phinehas with the sacred vessels and trumpets to the war with Median. In sum, Moses appeared in P as a prophet-leader not a priest. On this see Kaufmann, *The Religion of Israel*, 185; also, idem, *Toledot* II, 342–346.
747 As for the relation with the Midianites, Kaufmann maintained that "nowhere is Israel ever said to have entered the territory of Midian. The contact with Jethro and the Kenites is made in the desert between Egypt and Midian…nor is there any shred of evidence in the later history which points to a religious affinity between Midian and Israel". See Kaufmann, *The Religion of Israel*, 244.
748 Kaufmann, *The Religion of Israel*, 242–244; also, idem, *Toledot* II, 334–348.
749 Kaufmann, *The Religion of Israel*, 227. See further Albright, "Moses in Historical and Theological Perspective," 128.
750 Kaufmann, *Toledot* II, 41.
751 Kaufmann, *Toledot* II, 37.
752 Kaufmann, *The Religion of Israel*, 229.
753 kaufmann, *The Religion of Israel*, 223, 224; idem, *Toledot* II, 55.

contrast between Israel and its God and the pagan world suddenly manifests itself in its full proportions."[754] In this way Kaufmann tried to find different factors that could be used to connect the beginning of Israelite religion and history with Moses. In short, Kaufmann evidently considered Moses to be the founder of Israel and its religion.[755]

With regard to the Exodus tradition and the events connected with it, Kaufmann, in general, regarded these as historical fact, but he was sceptical concerning the theophany on Mount Sinai.[756] In Kaufmann's view, "The account of what occurred at Sinai has been preserved in several versions, all wreathed in legend."[757] Again, Kaufmann asserted that the appearance of monotheism in Israel was bound up with the events of the Exodus and Moses.[758] In this context, it has been noted that Kaufmann exalted Moses's leadership and ascribed the liberation of the Israelite tribes to him. To Kaufmann, Moses saved the Hebrew tribes from imposed forced labour in Egypt and fulfilled the longing of his tribesmen for freedom.[759] As he put it, "It was [Moses] prophetic genius that transformed the liberation of the tribes into the birth of a nation, an event which proved to be one of the crucial junctures of human history".[760]

To sum up, we noted that Kaufmann mentioned three features of Israelite religion that first appeared with Moses and the Exodus: The name YHWH as God of Israel, the struggle against paganism, and Moses as the first apostolic prophet. In Kaufmann's opinion, these decisive phenomena brought about a religious revolution among the tribes of Israel, and polytheism perished forever from Israel.[761] This means that according to Kaufmann's construction, Israel remained a monotheistic people and Israelite religion underwent no radical changes through the centuries.[762] The transition from paganism to monotheism occurred very early. As Kaufmann pointed out, "The passage from paganism to monotheism occurred at the time of the Exodus and Israel never retraced its steps to return to its former religious stage."[763] In this way, Kaufmann demonstrated that Israelite religion

754 Kaufmann, "The Biblical Age," 16.
755 Kaufmann, "The Biblical Age," 15.
756 See Kaufmann, *Toledot* II, 67.
757 Kaufmann, *The Religion of Israel*, 233. See also Yaacov Shavit and Mordechai Eran, eds., *The Hebrew Bible Reborn: From Holy Scripture to the Book of Books: A History of Biblical Culture and the Battles over the Bible in Modern Judaism* (Berlin: Walter De Gruyter, 2007), 255.
758 Kaufmann, "The Biblical Age," 15.
759 Kaufmann, "The Biblical Age," 15.
760 Kaufmann, "The Biblical Age," 15.
761 Kaufmann, "The Biblical Age," 25.
762 Kaufmann, *The Religion of Israel*, 134.
763 Kaufmann, "The Biblical Age," 77.

began its first historical phase with Moses.[764] Once monotheism emerged amidst the Israelites at the time of Moses, Israelite religion never stepped back to idolatry.

As referred to earlier, Kaufmann rejected the hypothesis which placed the origins of the Israelites and their religion in the desert. To Kaufmann, there was no evidence that biblical tradition located any of the ancestors of Israel in the desert. He mentioned that Abraham, Isaac, and Jacob had wandered in Canaan, but never stayed at Kadesh. In Kaufmann's opinion, the Israelites had no historical connection with Kadesh nor with anywhere else in the desert.[765] In addition, Kaufmann asserted that the Israelite tribes, after moving out of Egypt had marched forward with the aim of occupying Canaan.[766] Further, the conquest and settlement of Canaan could not be separated from the liberation process of the Israelite tribes. Without the settlement in Canaan, said Kaufmann, the Exodus from Egypt would seem to present an insignificant incident.[767] Connecting all of this with Moses and the Israelite religion, Kaufmann contended:

> The desire of the tribes to return to Canaan, memories of which were still alive among them, was at the bottom an ethnic-political one. Yet under prophetic inspiration, it too became a religious ideal. Possession of the land is the earliest eschatology motif of Israelite religion. It is the ultimate goal of the people, and its attainment is promised by God.[768]

Kaufmann's view can be summarized as follows: the Israelites were not desert nomads and did not trace their origin back to the desert. While their most exalted religious memories are associated with the time of wandering, this period is uniformly represented as one of hardship and suffering. Moses could hardly have stirred a people who lived for generations in Canaan and Egypt by the promise of bringing them into the wilderness.[769]

Having outlined the main features of Israel's early history before the period of conquest, one could safely conclude that Kaufmann's entire case presupposed his interpretation of Israelite religion as monotheistic. We have seen how Kaufmann started by arguing that Moses waged a war against paganism in Israel and it ceased to exist. Moses's religious idea was entirely new and caused a revolution among the tribes of Israel.[770] Kaufmann went further and maintained

---

764 Kaufmann, *Toledot* II, 41.
765 Kaufmann, *Toledot* II, 65–66.
766 Kaufmann, *Toledot* II, 65–66.
767 Kaufmann, *Toledot* II, 78.
768 Kaufmann, *The Religion of Israel*, 241.
769 Kaufmann, *The Religion of Israel*, 232–233.
770 Kaufmann, *Toledot* II, 53–57.

that the Sinai episode was a temporary situation and the desert had no connection with Israel's origin. As it seems to me, Kaufmann wished to assert that the Israelite tribes remained a purely monotheistic people. Considering this, it becomes clear why Kaufmann wrote two commentaries on Joshua and Judges. He was attempting to show that the account given in Joshua and Judges was a reliable description of the conquest and reflected early Israelite history in Canaan. What is decidedly important is Kaufmann's attempt to prove that the Israelite religion in Canaan remained intact, i.e. that significant Yahweh-Baal worship never existed. In order to support his assumptions, Kaufmann was obliged to prove that the Israelites lived in Canaan in isolated areas away from the influence of the Canaanites. With this in mind, I show in the following that Kaufmann, sought to reinforce his hypothesis about Israelite religion and monotheism through his reconstruction of conquest and settlement tradition.

4 Inquiry into the traditions of conquest and settlement

It is worth mentioning that the tradition concerning the possession of land of Canaan by the Israelite tribes was and still is a disputed issue.[771] There are three main hypotheses that explain the conquest and settlement.[772] I am concerned, however, to shed light on Kaufmann's reconstruction of the conquest and settlement traditions. This section aims to reveal the importance of this subject in understanding Kaufmann's theory on the history of ancient Israel and its religion. It should be mentioned that Kaufmann devoted the last ten years of his life to investigating the traditions of conquest and settlement in Canaan. In doing so he pursued two objectives: firstly, Kaufmann was searching for what

---

[771] For example, Martin Noth affirmed, "Owing to the lack of information, it is impossible to come to any firm conclusion one way or the other." See Martin Noth, *The History of Israel*, 72. In this context, George Mendenhall wrote, "There is no problem of biblical history which is more difficult than that of reconstructing the historical process by which the Twelve Tribes of ancient Israel became established in Palestine and northern Transjordan." See George E. Mendenhall, "The Hebrew Conquest of Palestine," *The Biblical Archaeologist* 25, no. 3 (1962): 65–87 (66). Walter Kaiser also emphasized, "The story of Israel's entrance and occupation of the land is the most difficult problem in the whole history of Israel in the scholarly world of the 20th century." See Walter C. Kaiser, *A History of Israel: From the Bronze Age through the Jewish Wars* (Nashville, Tenn.: Broadman & Holman Publ., 1998), 131.

[772] On this see Manfred Weippert, *Die Landnahme der israelitischen Stämme in der neueren wissenschaftlichen Diskussion: Ein kritischer Bericht* (Göttingen: Vandenhoeck & Ruprecht, 1967). For a discussion see Richard S. Hess, Gerald A. Klingbeil, and Paul J. Ray eds., *Critical Issues in Early Israelite History* (Winona Lake: Eisenbrauns, 2008).

he considered to be the historical foundations of Israelite history. Secondly, because the structure of Kaufmann's hypothesis required further support, he viewed the traditions of conquest and settlement as reliable and the conquest as having been conducted by all Israelite tribes.[773] My discussion starts by giving the reasons why Kaufmann examined this subject. Next, I consider some factors that characterized Kaufmann's reconstruction, such as his distinguishing between conquest and settlement as belonging to two different periods, the Israelite's relationship with the Canaanites, and the utopian concept of the land of Israel. Lastly, I will offer a critique of Kaufmann's picture of the conquest and settlement.

Instead of proceeding to complete his massive multi-volume *Toledot*, Kaufmann turned to studying the books of Joshua and Judges. He gave two reasons for changing his direction. First, Kaufmann said that the duty of Jewish Bible scholars was to write commentaries on biblical books, especially those related to the 'land', because there were so few of these in Hebrew. As for the second reason, Kaufmann sought to illuminate what he thought to be the fascinating beginning of biblical history and to affirm the historicity of ancient Israelite traditions after their having been 'misappropriated' by non-Jewish research.[774]

The beginning of Kaufmann's works in this respect was a monograph written in Hebrew entitled (*Ha-Sippur ha-Mikra'i al Kibbush ha-Arez*- The Biblical Account of the Conquest of Palestine)[775]. The intention of Kaufmann's book was to refute the hypotheses of Alt[776], Noth[777] and other such approaches concerning the biblical material dealing with the conquest of Palestine and the division of the land among the twelve tribes.[778] In 1959, Kaufmann wrote a commentary on the book of Joshua, in which he argued for the credibility of Joshua's account of the conquest.[779] At the same time Kaufmann rejected any theory that consid-

---

773 Kaufmann, *The Biblical Account of The Conquest of Palestine*, 91.
774 On this see Menahem Haran, *Yehezkel Kaufmann Jubilee Volume*, xi; see further the preface provided by Greenberg to Kaufmann's reprinted edition of *The Biblical Account* (1985), 10.
775 The Hebrew version was published in Jerusalem in 1956.
776 Albrecht Alt, "Israels Gaue unter Salomo," in *Alttestamentliche Studien R. Kittel zum 60. Geburtstag dargebrach* (BWANT 13; Leibzig, 1913), 1–19; idem, "Judas Gaue unter Josia," *PJB* 21 (1925), 100–117; idem, "Die Landnahme der Israeliten in Palästina," in *Kleine Schriften* I (1925), 89–125.
777 Martin Noth, "Studien zu den historischen-geographischen Dokumenten des Josuabuches," *ZDPV* (1953): 185–255; idem, *Das Buch Josua* (HAT 1, no 7; Tübingen, 1938).
778 On this see C. A. Simpson, "Reviews," *The Journal of Theological Studies* VI, no 2 (1955): 257–258. See also G. Ernst Wright, "Book Review: The Biblical Account of the Conquest of Palestine," *JBL* 75, no. 2 (1956): 54–155.
779 Kaufmann, *Commentary on Joshua*, 59–62.

ered the process of conquest to have been a gradual penetration. Pursuing his work further, Kaufmann two years later dedicated an article representing his overall view on the traditions of early Israelite history in Canaan.[780] In 1962 he completed this series with a commentary on the book of Judges.[781] In effect, Kaufmann's commentary was an attempt to establish that the conquest and settlement represented two different periods and that Joshua's war of national conquest differed from the tribal wars that had been conducted by individual tribes during the period of Judges.

Kaufmann certainly realized the importance of the traditions of conquest and settlement in understanding Israel's early history. His interest in this subject indicated that he was aware of many of the biblical criticism positions that he, with his arguments, had undertaken to dispute. Again, as referred to above, Kaufmann's aim was to reinforce his thesis concerning Israelite religion and monotheism.[782] This can be seen in a letter to Moshe Greenberg, in which Kaufmann wrote, "These books [Joshua and Judges] recount the beginnings of the people of Israel, and so their testimony is decisive for the beginning of Israel's faith as well...There are pre-monarchic narratives here, although biblical criticism refuses to acknowledge the fact, since that would demolish its position."[783] It means that Kaufmann's theory on the history of Israelite religion compelled him to uphold the basic validity of the biblical account of the conquest.[784]

---

780 See Kaufmann, "Traditions Concerning Early Israelite History in Canaan," *Scripta Hierosolymitana* 8 (1961): 303–334.

781 Kaufmann, *Commentary on Judges* (Jerusalem: Ḳiryat Sefer, 1962).

782 H. L. Ginsberg mentioned that Kaufmann had explained to him in a letter that his commentaries on the books of Joshua and Judges, the sources of knowledge of the earliest period of Israel's history, were meant to reinforce the essential theses of his History of Israel's Religion. On this see H. L. Ginsberg, "Yehezkel Kaufmann, 1889–1963," *Reconstructionist* 29, no. 14 (1963): 27–29.

783 Greenberg, *Studies in the Bible*, 179. See further Kaufmann, *The Biblical Account* (1985), 10; also, idem, "The Biblical Age," 28.

784 As Stephen Geller rightly remarked, "Only the annihilation of the Canaanites in the areas of mass Israelite settlement will insure that total spiritual isolation needed to defend his chaste dichotomies." See Stephen Geller, "Wellhausen and Kaufmann," *Midstream* 31, no. 10 (1985): 39–48 (45).

5 The narrative of the conquest

Kaufmann credited the biblical account of the conquest as given in Joshua and Judges.[785] To him, the narrative of the conquest is not a late composition invented by scribes or part of the deuteronomistic redaction.[786] Kaufmann, in effect, sought to overcome the problem of a deuteronomistic redaction of the historical books by distinguishing between 'early' Deut (chs.1–11) which forms the basis of the book, and 'late' Deut (chs.12–26), which contains legislation about the unification of the cult.[787] In Kaufmann's opinion, the historical philosophy of the book of Deuteronomy had no original connection with the idea of unification of the cult and was older than it.[788] Therefore, Kaufmann contended that the former prophets did not really belong to a historical deuteronomistic work. To quote Kaufmann:

> In the former prophets the idea of the unification of the cult appears only from 1Ki 3:2 onwards. Before this reference, there is no mention of it. There is no contact in style and subject-matter with Deut, but – only with the early Deut, more precisely – only with the chapters forming the framework in which the unification of the cult is not mentioned at all. It follows that the deuteronomistic elements in Josh and Ju is early and has no connection with the 7th century.[789]

With regard to Joshua's stories of the conquest, Kaufmann maintained that they corresponded to real incidents.[790] Thus, for example, Kaufmann accepted that Jericho was taken by a military campaign[791] and that the story of Ai in Joshua (chs. 7–8) was genuine and had to be considered the first battle fought by the Israelite tribes in the land of Canaan. Moreover, both Jericho and Ai served as the basis for further campaigns. According to Kaufmann, who seems to have only retold the biblical story of the conquest, the issue was decided in two

---

785 Although Kaufmann recognized the similarity between Joshua and Judges and the sources of the Torah, he contended that "affinity with the literature of the Pentateuch cannot decide the question of the date of the composition of Josh and Ju. This date is to be fixed by the internal evidence." On this see Kaufmann, *The Biblical Account*, 7. For more discussion on the relationship of Joshua to the pentateuchal documents, see Kaufmann, *Commentary on the Book of Joshua*, 12–15 and 31–33.
786 Kaufmann, *Commentary on the Book of Joshua*, 6–9.
787 Concerning the relationship between the Book of Deuteronomy and Josiah's reform, see Kaufmann *The Religion of Israel*, 172–175.
788 Kaufmann, *Commentary on Joshua*, 5–7.
789 Kaufmann, *The Biblical Account*, 4–7.
790 Kaufmann, *Commentary on Joshua*, 61.
791 Kaufmann, *Commentary on Joshua*, 99.

great battles: one with a southern, the other with a northern coalition of kings. The central highlands were conquered and their population was annihilated or expelled.[792] This meant that dating the stories of Joshua was not a problem for Kaufmann, who suggested that the book of Joshua "was composed at the beginning of the period of the Judges, at the time of Dan's migration to the north."[793] The author of the book of Joshua, wrote Kaufmann, "had possessed various written sources such as the 'Book of Jashar', list of portions, and a list of boundaries and cities which contained the cities of Ephraim and Manasseh. He also had a priestly scroll about the events of the conquest and the distribution of the land, containing a list of priestly and Levitical cities."[794]

As for the narrative of the conquest in the Book of Judges, Kaufmann's analysis shows that he accepted the stories as presented in the book. He identifies two literary strata in the Book of Judges: Judg 1; Judg 3–21. To Kaufmann, each literary stratum bore the stamp of historical fact. The first contained the story of the war of conquest and the second described the liberation war.[795] However, Kaufmann distinguished the stories of Judges from the pragmatic framework of the book, the latter of which he believed to be religiously motivated. He further noted that the purpose of this framework was to explain the events against the background of the sins of idolatry and the worship of Baal, which were the characteristic issues during the period of Judges.[796]

In Kaufmann's reading, the Book of Judges is characterized by two features. First, there is the worship of Baal, which was not mentioned in the Torah, nor in Joshua's book. It first appeared in Judges 2:13, which means that the idea of Baalism and Ashtoreth was manifested only in the literature of the period of Judges.[797] Secondly, Kaufmann found that the problems of complete conquest and loss of the remaining land were distinctive to the Book of Judges.[798] He thus concluded that the idea of losing the land and its association with the sin of idolatry had not occurred before the Book of Judges or after it; it was a dead issue after

792 Kaufmann, *The Religion of Israel*, 255.
793 Kaufmann, *The Biblical Account*, 97.
794 Kaufmann, *The Biblical Account*, 97–98.
795 According to Kaufmann, the Book of Judges is a literary unit and cannot be seen as a process of revision and redaction (national, deuteronomic, priestly, theocratic). On this see Kaufmann, *Commentary on Judges*, 20–21.
796 Kaufmann, *Commentary on Judges*, 23–25.
797 Kaufmann, *Commentary on Judges*, 33.
798 For a discussion of the problem of unconquered land, see Rudolf Smend, "Das uneroberte Land," in *Zur ältesten Geschichte Israel, Gesammelte Studien*, Bd. 2 (München: Kaiser, 1987), especially 226–227.

the period of Judges.[799] To Kaufmann, this indicated that the stories in the Book of Judges were a reliable description of events that took place during the Judges era.[800] As for the date of the Book of Judges and its composition, Kaufmann wrote, "The Book of Judges presents a picture of ups and downs, of sin and repentance, of many struggles... it exalts the monarchy, and we may assume that it was compiled in the early period of the monarchy."[801]

From the literary analysis of the Books of Joshua and Judges, it seems quite clear that Kaufmann regarded the narrative of conquest as valid. In this respect, it remains to examine the relationship between Joshua's account of conquest and its parallel in Judges 1. To Kaufmann, Judges 1 was a historical continuation of the Book of Joshua. Judges 1 was an ancient document, belonging to the early part of the period of the Judges.[802] In Kaufmann's opinion, "Judg1 is a story of fragmentary excerpts about the wars of the tribes which followed the wars of Joshua. The tribes are already in occupation each of its own 'lot', but they were compelled by certain circumstances to renew the wars on the national level."[803] In support of his view, Kaufmann noted that the sin of idolatry which would befall the Israelites in the future is absent from the horizon in Judges 1.[804] As Kaufmann pointed out, Judges 1 did not know the sin of idolatry in the period of Judges. Rather Judges 1 referred to a generation without sin, that is, the generation of Joshua.[805]

Thus, Kaufmann presumed that the biblical account of conquest in Joshua and Judges represented the reality of events. Basically, he sought to provide an alternative view to the prevailing one. Although he recognized the need for biblical criticism, he accused it of distorting the facts. As he put it:

> The higher criticism has sought by all the means in its power to obscure [the] monumental evidence. It has everywhere discovered the finger marks of editors, inserters, supplementers and later hands, later patriots, and so on and so forth, who, from ulterior motives and through misunderstanding the text etc., made it into a confused patchwork.[806]

---

799 Kaufmann, *Commentary on Judges*, 33.
800 Kaufmann, *Commentary on Judges*, 33.
801 Kaufmann, *The Biblical Account*, 63. Kaufmann wrote, "The background of the Book of Judges, including its historiographical evolution of the era, is undoubtedly the idealization of the kingdom." See Kaufmann, *History of the Religion of Israel, vol. IV: From the Babylonian Captivity to the End of Prophecy*, 36.
802 Kaufmann, *The Biblical Account*, 82–86; idem, *Commentary on Judges*, 14–16.
803 Kaufmann, *The Biblical Account*, 86.
804 Kaufmann, *Commentary on Joshua*, 47.
805 Kaufmann, *Commentary on Joshua*, 47.
806 Kaufmann, *The Biblical Account*, 62.

In Kaufmann's view, biblical scholars had deliberately blurred the original account of conquest. He wrote, "[Scholars] have recourse to fanciful inventions in the manner of the midrash exegesis by 'allusion'. Here analysis is not sufficient for their purpose. A 're-creation' is required, an imaginative reconstruction of the whole book."[807] As a result, Kaufmann rejected any explanations that had been given to the problem of conquest and settlement. For instance, he regarded the deuteronomistic redaction of Joshua and Judges as baseless.[808]

In addition, Kaufmann took issue with the Alt-Noth hypothesis that described the stories of Joshua and Judges as etiological legends.[809] These stories, according to Kaufmann, and contrary to Alt-Noth, were not "aetiological legends," but Israelite. If they were "aetiological", then, they were Israelite solutions to aetiological problems.[810] Furthermore, Kaufmann did not accept the idea that the land was occupied gradually over time, believing instead that it was taken by military campaigns.[811] He also maintained that the Israelites were united into a confederation of tribes before entering the land of Canaan. We have already mentioned that he rejected the idea that the Israelites remained in the desert as individual tribes. According to Kaufmann, the absence of friction between the Israelite and the Bedouin tribes of the desert meant that they spent the period which preceded the conquest under a league of tribes.[812] With this in mind, one can safely say that Kaufman counted entirely on the biblical account concerning the conquest and settlement in Canaan.

6 Conquest and settlement: two different periods

Surprisingly enough, while acknowledging that the stories of the Conquest were shrouded in a mist of legend, Kaufmann still believed that it was possible to reconstruct the actual march of events.[813] According to Kaufmann, the course of conquest was as follows:

> Since the invading Israelites encountered neither Egyptians nor Philistines, their entry into Canaan must have taken place when the Egyptian rule was near its end, but before the Phil-

---

807 Kaufmann, *The Biblical Account*, 65.
808 Kaufmann, *Commentary on Joshua*, 7 – 8.
809 Kaufmann, *The Biblical Account*, 70 – 74.
810 Kaufmann, *The Biblical Account of The Conquest of Palestine*, 78.
811 Kaufmann, *The Religion of Israel*, 254 – 255. For more discussion see Kaufmann, *Toledot* II, 92.
812 Kaufmann, *The Religion of Israel*, 241 – 242; also, idem, *Toledot* II, 88 – 89.
813 Kaufmann, *The Biblical Account*, 91.

istines had become a military power. The time of the Egyptian weakness between the region of Merneptah (1235–1227) and Ramses III (1195–1164), or perhaps during the latter is indicated. The Canaanite city-states were disunited. Although they surpassed Israel in material and armaments, the Israelite tribes were united and animated by the zeal of a new religion. The Canaanite resistance was sufficiently serious to cause the invoking of a *ḥerem;* it was unable, however, to prevent the Israelite occupation of the country.[814]

Kaufmann went further, describing the route of conquest as follows:

The war of conquest begins with the crossing of the Jordan. The camp is at Shittim (Josh. 2:1) on the plains of Moab, in the portion of Gad. Therefore, the natural crossing-point for the tribes is close to Jericho. The war advances by stages along the line Jericho-Ai-Gibeon-Beth-horon-Emeq Ayalon, and thence to the Shephelah. In other words, it is fought on the borders of Ephraim, Benjamin and Dan, passing from there to the border of Judah. The route of conquest is drawn by objective military factors. All this has no connection with Benjamin and the shrine at Gilgal.[815]

According to Kaufmann's analysis, there were different types of wars conducted by the Israelite tribes. The narrative from Num. 21–2 Sam. 23 should be divided into three groups: 1) The first group (Num. 21–Jud. 1) included wars of conquest; 2) The second group (Jud. 3–1 Sam. 31) referred to the war of liberation; 3) The third group (2 Sam.1: 24–1 Kgs. 1: 11) was that of imperial wars.[816] In Kaufmann's opinion, these three categories of war represented three different periods: 1) The period of conquest of the land (Moses, Joshua, Caleb); 2) The period of Judges (Othaniel to Saul); 3) The monarchic period from Saul onwards.[817] Moreover, Kaufmann explained that the Canaanites were the main enemy in the war of conquest, while the Philistines were the oppressors in the wars of liberation. As for the third period, which he labelled "David's wars", it was distinguished by the absence of *Ḥerem*.[818]

In this way, Kaufmann separated the war of conquest from those which took place during the period of Judges and after it.[819] To put it differently, Kaufmann

---

814 Kaufmann, *The Religion of Israel*, 254–255.
815 Kaufmann, *The Biblical Account*, 70.
816 Kaufmann, "Traditions Concerning Early Israelite History in Canaan," 323.
817 Kaufmann, "Traditions Concerning Early Israelite History in Canaan," 304.
818 Kaufmann, *Commentary on Judges*, 5.
819 Weinfeld pointed out that "Kaufmann is, of course, correct in maintaining that pre-deuteronomic traditions similarly distinguished between wars of conquest and defensive wars. But these traditions do not conceive the two types of warfare as characterizing two distinct historical periods. Judg. 1, for example, alludes to wars of conquest (vv. 1–26) and defence (vv. 27–36; see particularly v. 34) as being waged in the same period. The period of Joshua is not depicted as one of conquest alone, nor is the post-Joshua period only one of defensive wars against Canaan-

differentiated the conquest period from that of the Judges. In his view, the war of settlement was characterized by its local and tribal elements. By contrast, Joshua's war was marked by its national character.[820] For the significance of these different types of war in understanding the overall structure of Kaufmann's analysis, let us examine them more closely.

With regard to the war of conquest, Kaufmann asserted that it was waged mainly against the Canaanites. The narrative of that war is set forth from Num. 21–Judg 1.[821] Moreover, the war of conquest had geographical limits, from the River Jordan to the sea and from the southern wilderness to the Euphrates River or the border into Hamath. More important, as Kaufmann pointed out, the war of conquest was characterized by an absence of the Philistines.[822] Furthermore, Kaufmann maintained that throughout the war of conquest, the Israelites were the aggressors and the Canaanites were always on the defensive.[823]

The second type of war, that is, the liberation war, is described in the narrative between Judg. 3 and 1 Sam. 31. To Kaufmann, this war was quite different from that of conquest. He argued that its objective was not the conquest of territory for ethnic settlement and it had no pre-established geographical limits. In Kaufmann's opinion, the war of liberation belonged to the period of Judges and was conducted after the conquest of the land. This war was carried on against surrounding enemies, including Aram, Ammon, Moab, Edom, Amalek and Midian. The objective of fighting was not to conquer land or to expand the portion already under control, but to remove the yoke of foreign rule or to liberate the land from oppression. According to Kaufmann, the Philistines became the chief military opponent during the war of liberation. David first appeared on the stage of history as the conqueror of Goliath, the Philistine (1 Sam. 17).[824] Thus Kaufmann remarked that the Philistine factor was the scarlet thread running through the period after the conquest of the land.[825]

---

ite pressure. The pre-deuteronomic traditions refer both to Canaanite pressure during Joshua's lifetime (Josh. 17: 14–18) and to campaigns of conquest not undertaken under his leadership (Judg. 1: 1–26)." On this see Moshe Weinfeld, *Deuteronomy and the Deuteronomic School* (Oxford: Clarendon Press, 1972), 14.

820 Kaufmann distinguished between the stories of Joshua and those of Judges. He said that the local and tribal elements could be easily recognized in the Book of Judges. Conversely, Kaufmann contended that in Joshua the tribes had not yet occupied their portions. The tribes were still an army in camp. On this see Kaufmann, *The Biblical Account*, 65.

821 Kaufmann, "Traditions Concerning Early Israelite History in Canaan," 304.

822 Kaufmann, "Traditions Concerning Early Israelite History in Canaan," 305.

823 Kaufmann, "Traditions Concerning Early Israelite History in Canaan," 305.

824 Kaufmann, "Traditions Concerning Early Israelite History in Canaan," 306–308.

825 Kaufmann, "Traditions Concerning Early Israelite History in Canaan," 308.

The wars of empire, or as Kaufmann called them, "the accounts of David's imperial wars," are to be found in 2 Sam. These wars were mainly conducted against the Philistines, Moabites, Ammonites, Aramites, and Edomites. They began first as wars of liberation, but soon changed into wars of imperial conquest. In Kaufmann's view, David did not expand the area of Israel's ethnic settlement, but subdued enemy peoples, imposing upon them servitude and the "bringing of gifts" (2 Sam. 8). Accordingly, this period was characterized by a neglect of the old command regarding the complete destruction of the Canaanites.[826]

In addition to the three above-mentioned kinds of war, Kaufmann mentioned another which he called 'the last war of conquest'. The account of this war is in Judg. 1: 22–26 and concerns the capture of Bethel. In Kaufmann's opinion this last war marked the end of the conquest. He claimed that after the last war of conquest, there was not a single narrative similar in type to the accounts of the wars of conquest. This meant, according to Kaufmann, that the conquest of the land by the tribes of Israel ended with the taking of Bethel in the generation of Caleb.[827] Furthermore, Kaufmann drew attention to Judg 1: 19, 21, 26–35, and what he referred to as 'the wars of tribute'.[828] He found in this account a list of gaps pertinent to the period between the wars of conquest and the wars of liberation. To Kaufmann, the list of gaps in Judges 1 precisely fixed the places from which the Canaanites had not been driven out. He maintained that this list of gaps was the summing-up at the end of the period of conquest, the period of the wars of Joshua's and Caleb's generation.[829] Kaufmann noted that the list involved only 'Canaanites', like all of Judges 1, that the Philistines were not mentioned, and that Dan was still settled in the west.[830] This indicated to Kaufmann that Judges 1 was older than the song of Deborah. He concluded that the list of gaps in Judges 1:22–26 meats that the 'real land' of Israel was conquered before the period of Judges.[831]

At the end of his analysis, Kaufmann arrived at the idea that the 'war of tribute' marked the end of the war of conquest. Further, Kaufmann contended that collecting tribute from the Canaanites was a new phenomenon, peculiar to the period after the conquest of Bethel. The war of tribute was not mentioned in the narratives of the wars of Moses, Joshua and Caleb. Moreover, the limited

---

826 Kaufmann, "Traditions Concerning Early Israelite History in Canaan," 308.
827 Kaufmann, "Traditions Concerning Early Israelite History in Canaan," 308–309.
828 Kaufmann, "Traditions Concerning Early Israelite History in Canaan," 309.
829 Kaufmann, "Traditions Concerning Early Israelite History in Canaan," 310–311.
830 Kaufmann, "Traditions Concerning Early Israelite History in Canaan," 312.
831 Kaufmann,"Traditions Concerning Early Israelite History in Canaan," 313.

area of the wars of tribute proved that the land had already been conquered. The relationship with the Canaanites had changed and entered a new phase. As mentioned, the war of conquest had been pursued in order to seize Canaanite land from which the Canaanites were expelled, whereas the purpose of the war of tribute was to impose forced labour upon the Canaanites without driving them out.[832]

Thus, Kaufmann detached the time of conquest from that of settlement by distinguishing the different types of war. The first referred to a national war that was carried on by all the tribes and was waged mainly against the Canaanites, while the second took place at a time when the tribes were forced under certain circumstances to fight in order to secure their heritage. Admittedly, Kaufmann's distinction of the different types of war and his eccentric analysis was problematic and raised several questions. For example, he did not make sufficiently clear the issue of tribal boundaries and portions assigned to each tribe.[833] Furthermore, he did not answer the question of why the list of cities mentioned in Joshua did not fit the actual division of the land between tribes. In order to deal with these issues, Kaufmann created a new concept regarding the land in which Israel had settled, namely, that of the utopian land of Israel.

7 Utopian land of Israel

As mentioned, Kaufmann hypothesized that the Israelite tribes, in contrast to other groups, fought to meet their need for land. Once their aim was achieved by the conquest of Transjordan and central Palestine, the desire for further land expansion came to an end.[834] As he put it, "The hope of conquering the ideal land of Israel gradually came to be a utopian dream. When the task of conquest passed from the united camp into the hands of the individual tribes, the idea of the complete conquest of the land of Canaan was in effect foregone."[835] Kaufmann attempted to show that the biblical books after that of Judges did not make any mention of the problem of the incomplete conquest of Canaan. So Kaufmann:

---

832 Kaufmann, "Traditions Concerning Early Israelite History in Canaan," 313–314.
833 According to Kaufmann, "The tribal portion, actually and ideally, is an ethnic, not a political, entity." See Kaufmann, *The Biblical Account*, 25.
834 Kaufmann, *Toledot* II, 91–95.
835 Kaufmann, *The Religion of Israel*, 255.

> The problem of the complete conquest of Canaan was a *forgotten problem* in later genera-
> tions. It was considered *for the last time* in Ju 2–3, and thenceforth *the question disappeared*
> *forever!* Neither David nor Solomon, nor anyone after them, aspires to carry out Joshua's
> national testament. No prophet, no patriot, no dreamer of dreams demands the 'comple-
> tion' of the Conquest.[836]

Thus, Kaufmann sought to solve the problem of incomplete conquest by adopt-
ing the idea of the *utopian land of Israel*. He wrote, "Throughout the Pentateuch,
Josh, and Judges runs an unreal utopian conception of the land of Israel..."[837] According to Kaufmann, this ideal land had boundaries at once much wider or
much narrower than the boundaries that correspond with either 'the settled
area of Palestine' or David's or Solomon's kingdom.[838] Moreover, Kaufmann
drew attention to many maps of the land of Canaan. He pointed out that the
Bible referred to five different conceptions of the land of Israel, reflecting
changes in the historical situation, i.e. 1) The land of Canaan, or the land of
the patriarchs; 2) Moses' land of Israel; 3) Joshua's land of Israel; 4) The land
of the real Israelite settlement; and 5) The kingdom of Israel. The first four conceptions are ethnographic, the fifth imperialistic.[839]

The first map is called the land of Canaan. According to Kaufmann the land
of Canaan was promised to the patriarchs as in the Pentateuch from Gen. 12 to
Num. 26. This land did not include Transjordan. It was characterized by the absence of the Philistines and was conceived as the future ethnic territory of Israel.[840] The second map is known as Moses' land of Israel. Its description is found
in Num. 21:21–35 and represents the greater land of Israel. It appeared at the
time of Moses, who was forced under the pressure of Reuben and Gad to assign
them Transjordan. As Kaufmann deduced, this meant that Moses gave the Israelites possession of territory which had not been promised to the patriarchs.[841]

The third map is named Joshua's land of Israel. To Kaufmann, the wars of
conquest gave rise to this new conception of Joshua's land, manifested as a dominant idea in Josh 1–Judg 3. Pursuing this further, Kaufmann observed that a
most significant ethnographical change occurred in Joshua's land, namely the
Philistines of the Pentapolis made their appearance here after Joshua's
wars.[842] Moreover, Kaufmann described Joshua's land as a dynamic territorial

---

836 Kaufmann, *The Biblical Account*, 62.
837 Kaufmann, *The Biblical Account*, 46.
838 Kaufmann, *The Biblical Account*, 48.
839 Kaufmann, *The Biblical Account*, 48, 48–54.
840 Kaufmann, *The Biblical Account*, 48–51.
841 Kaufmann, *The Biblical Account*, 51–52.
842 Kaufmann, *The Biblical Account*, 52–53.

unit, the boundaries of which were considered temporary. The conception of this land was ethnic, not imperialistic. Within it, a special class of *enslaved* Canaanites came into being, *the Gibeonites*.[843] Kaufmann thus concluded that Joshua's land should be considered a peculiar conception of its own time. There was no mention of it in the Pentateuch, and by the time of the Judges it was already outdated.[844]

The fourth map is called the real land of Israel.[845] Kaufmann mentioned that this new map of the land came into being as a result of the wars in the period of Judges. It represented an area of ethnic Israelite settlement on both sides of the River Jordan. He described the real land of Israel as a static ethnic area with a clearly determined shape. Its borders were entirely new, being neither those of the ideal land of Canaan, nor yet those of the land of Joshua. Its full extent was marked by the new expression "from Dan to Beersheba which appears for the first time in Ju 20.1."[846] The last map of the land, that of the Kingdom of Israel, is associated with monarchy. It emerged with the establishment of David's kingdom. Kaufmann mentioned that the basis of David's empire stood on the real land of Israel but its boundaries stretched beyond. New regions were added, not as areas of ethnic Israelite settlement, but as provinces of imperialistic rule. These included the coast, Edom, Moab, Ammon and Aram.[847]

We note that Kaufmann recognized the traditions of conquest and settlement as given in the books of Joshua and Judges. Having outlined the different maps of the land of Canaan, Kaufmann came to the following conclusion:

> We find a clear line of development from Gen 15 to Ju 3. We see how the ancient aspiration to occupy the land of Canaan swerves through its collision with reality at the end of Moses's life; how it is refracted in the time of Joshua; how it is mutilated in the period of the Judges; and how the hope of its complete realization is finally abandoned at the end of that period. Each of these maps reflects a stage in Israel's history, and each is balanced by a corresponding stratum in the ancient biblical literature. Each stage has a corresponding and different 'map' of the land of Canaan and of Israel.[848]

843 Kaufmann, *The Biblical Account*, 52–53.
844 Kaufmann, *The Biblical Account*, 56–57.
845 See Kaufmann, *Commentary on Joshua*, 7–8.
846 Kaufmann, *The Biblical Account*, 53–54.
847 Kaufmann, *The Biblical Account*, 54.
848 Kaufmann, *The Biblical Account*, 61–62.

8 Israelites and the Canaanites

Kaufmann's description of the different maps of the land of Canaan poses questions regarding the relationship of the Israelites with the indigenous inhabitants. Kaufmann insisted that the Israelite tribes, as pure monotheistic people, remained faithful to Yahweh and their religion retained its peculiar features in Canaan. He supported his view by arguing that the Israelite tribes had succeeded in keeping possession of the land of Canaan by means of a massive, destructive war. Thus, Kaufmann argued, the wars in the period of Judges created new conditions on both sides of the Jordan, where an area of ethnic Israelite settlement was shaped.[849] In Kaufmann's opinion, this was possible only by means of great national wars.[850] He further emphasized, "At no stage was the conquest of the land a process of peaceful settlement. It did not produce a national and cultural intermingling."[851] More illuminating is "that the Canaanite factor had been liquidated in the real land of Israel as early as the beginning of the period of Judges."[852] To Kaufmann, "A Hebrew settlement in Palestine before the conquest is a figment of scholarly imagination."[853]

In Kaufmann's interpretation, the four definite Canaanite wars took place after Judges 1. These wars happened in different places: in Laish-Dan, in the valley of Esdraelon, in Jebus-Jerusalem, and in Gezer. Kaufmann emphasized that these four wars were determined by the conditions of the period after the conquest.[854] To Kaufmann, there were no Canaanites in the land of Israel after the invasion of the conquest. He even denied that the cities mentioned in the book of Judges, i. e. Succoth, Penuel, Thebez and Kirjath-Jearim, were Canaanite

---

849 Kaufmann, *The Biblical Account*, 53.
850 See Kaufmann, *Toledot* II, 91.
851 Kaufmann, *The Biblical Account*, 91. In Kaufmann's view, "The peaceful theory makes the tradition of early history of Israel dark riddle." On this see Kaufmann, "Traditions Concerning Early Israelite History in Canaan," 327 – 330; idem, *From the Secret of the Biblical World*, 85, 86.
852 Kaufmann, *The Biblical Account*, 91; also, idem, *The Religion of Israel* 247 – 254, where Kaufmann explained the conception of *Ḥerem*.
853 Kaufmann, *The Religion of Israel*, 218. Kaufmann asserted that there was neither ethnographic conquest nor real settlement at the time of Patriarchs as can be inferred from the patriarchal literary stratum. Moreover, he pointed out that the first story of conquest and settlement was to be found in Num. 21; 32 which tells the conquest of Transjordan. The conquest stratum differs from that of Patriarchs. For the patriarchal stratum is characterized by peace and wandering without having the idea of national land, whereas the conquest stratum is distinguished by its war and national settlement. On this see Kaufmann, *Commentary on Joshua*, 52 – 54.
854 Kaufmann, "Traditions Concerning Early Israelite History in Canaan," 314.

cities.[855] It follows that the Canaanite factor disappeared after the war of conquest. Kaufmann subscribed to the idea that the real land of Israel was conquered at the beginning of the period of Judges. He noted, "In the days of Deborah, the Canaanites were active in the Valley of Esdraelon, the only large Canaanite enclave. But from that time on there was no longer a Canaanite front."[856] The Canaanites disappeared from the scene after the war in Esdraelon. Seen from Kaufmann's perspective, "The song of Deborah gives a clear and instructive geo-ethnic description which explains the disappearance of the Canaanite from after that struggle."[857]

In light of Kaufmann's understanding, the question which then arises is whether a peaceful coexistence was possible between the newcomers and the inhabitants of the land? To put it differently, did Kaufmann envision a kind of amalgamation between Israelite and Canaanites? We read in Kaufmann's books such statements as, "The biblical records give no support to the view that a general ethnic and cultural amalgam of peoples took place in Israelite Palestine. Nor is there any trace of a mass assimilation of Canaanites into Israel".[858] And, "There was no peaceful or intermingling relationship with Canaanites during the time of Judges. If this had been so, the Canaanites would have shared the Israelites' suffering at the hands of their enemies and would have been their natural allies in the wars of liberation".[859] Kaufmann's answer, I would say, fits well with his overall interpretation of the history of Israelite religion. He assumed that the relationship with the Canaanites was decided by the law of Ḥērem,[860] accord-

---

855 Kaufmann, "Traditions Concerning Early Israelite History in Canaan," 321.

856 Kaufmann, "Traditions Concerning Early Israelite History in Canaan," 321.

857 Kaufmann, "Traditions Concerning Early Israelite History in Canaan," 321; also, idem, *Commentary on the Book of Judges*, 39.

858 Kaufmann, *The Religion of Israel*, 248.

859 Kaufmann, "Traditions Concerning Early Israelite History in Canaan," 322; see further, idem, *Commentary on Judges*, 12 – 13.

860 Kaufmann disagreed with those who consider the Ḥērem in Josh as a deuteronomistic construction. On Kaufmann's reading, the Ḥērem idea is older than and predates Deuteronomy. Kaufmann said that this idea occurs in all sources of the Torah (Exod. 23: 23, 27 – 33; 34: 11 – 16; Num. 33:51 – 56). Moreover, he contended that the notion that the Israelite would destroy the Canaanites was not a product of the 7th century. He claimed that a close analysis of the literature showed that the Canaanites had been expelled from the real land of Israel. As can be seen from the Book of Judges, the Canaanites remained only in small enclaves. Saul chased the Gibeonites but did not fight Canaanites. According to Kaufmann, the destruction of Canaanites as attested by Ḥērem idea was not a racial territorial but a religious necessity in order to prevent Israelite apostasy. This religious-culture necessity was required to annihilate the Canaanite idolatry (Ex 23:24; Num 33:52; Deut 7:5. In Kaufmann's view, Ḥērem was necessary to uproot idolatry from of the land. On this see Kaufmann, *Commentary on Joshua*, 82 – 85.

ing to which the Canaanite must be completely destroyed.[861] As for the effect of *Ḥērem*, Kaufmann wrote:

> Terrible as it was, the *Ḥērem* had important social and religious consequences; Israel did not assimilate the indigenous population. Materially this brought about a marked decline. At the same time, it provided Israel's new religious idea with an environment in which to grow free of the influence of a popular pagan culture.[862]

In order to strengthen his view, Kaufmann mentioned several differences that distinguished the Israelites from the Canaanites. For instance, the tribes did not adopt the military art of iron chariots from the Canaanites; the Israelite army was a force of swordsmen.[863] Moreover, the Israelites did not take over the Canaanites' form of political organization, the city-state. Instead, as Kaufmann pointed out, the tribe was the political unit of the Israelites.[864] Furthermore, Kaufmann believed that there was no Canaanite influence on Israelite religion.[865] He contended:

> "The Israelites in Canaan were a people distinct ethnically and culturally. Their vitality was the wellspring of an original national culture, and every aspect of their life became an embodiment of the monotheistic idea. Canaan provided the geographical setting in which a monotheistic civilization could flourish."[866]

According to Kaufmann, there was no reason to overstate the changes that occurred in the life of the Israelite tribes after settlement in Canaan. The Israelite tribes had not been totally nomads and they were familiar with the new conditions brought forth by settlement in Canaan. So in the sphere of religion, for example, Kaufmann contended that the Israelite tribes practiced religious rites that were connected with the fertility of the soil, without being influenced by Canaanite religion. He wrote, "Having settled in Canaan, Israel became an agricultural na-

---

861 For more on Kaufmann's view concerning the whole destruction of the Canaanites, see Kaufmann, *Toledot* I, 644–657. Kaufmann's theory about the whole destruction of the Canaanites according to *Ḥerem* law was justified by Zeitlin, who regarded this theory as historical fact. See Irving M. Zeitlin, *Ancient Judaism: Biblical Criticism from Max Weber to the Present*, 146–148.
862 Kaufmann, *The Religion of Israel*, 254.
863 Kaufmann, *The Biblical Account*, 90.
864 Kaufmann, *The Biblical Account*, 90.
865 Kaufmann, *The Biblical Account*, 90.
866 Kaufmann, "The Biblical Age," 32.

tion, and naturally enough its religion adapted itself to this change."[867] As Kaufmann explained:

> In Canaan, Israel's cult became the cult of farmers, and the bulk of its rites related to the land and its products. This does not necessarily imply a fundamental change from the religion of shepherds to that of farmers. For the tribes had been half-nomads; they also tilled the soil, though not bound to a specific territory. Presumably they farmed occasionally in Egypt and in the wilderness, which has tillable soil and in which agricultural festivals are celebrated to the present time. The agricultural element in Israel's cult need not, therefore, be less primary than the pastoral.[868]

Before closing this part, it might be useful to shed light on Kaufmann's portrayal of the period of Judges. In Kaufmann's analysis, the period of Judges can be recognized in the literary stratum from Judg 2–1 Sam 12. This segment of literature cannot be regarded as the result of literary redaction, nor did it consist of tribal legends.[869] Rather, it represented the life of Israelite tribes in the premonarchic period. As Kaufmann put it, "Our knowledge of the premonarchic age (Joshua, Judges, 1 Samuel 1–12) is based upon contemporaneous materials. They may be taken, therefore, as a faithful mirror of the condition of the people in that age."[870] In Kaufmann's opinion, the period of Judges as depicted in Judg. 2–1 Sam. 12 was a result of the great events of the period of Moses and Joshua. During the period of Judges, the Israelite tribes "had a political organization before the monarchy, though it is difficult to detect because of its 'spiritual' character."[871] Authority was divided between two institutions: the secular, primitive democracy of the elders and the authority of the Judges, men of the spirit, messengers of God.[872]

With regard to the institution of the Judges, Kaufmann maintained that it developed in Canaan and it "is a typical and peculiarly Israelite expression of its early monotheism."[873] He also affirmed that "it never created a political body. But it was a well-established functioning idea".[874] Moreover, Kaufmann asserted, 'The authority of the Judges was not viewed as secular, or merely political, but as

---

867 Kaufmann, "The Biblical Age," 37.
868 Kaufmann, *The Religion of Israel*, 259–260.
869 Kaufmann, *Commentary on the Book of Judges*, 44.
870 Kaufmann, "The Biblical Age," 33.
871 Kaufmann, *The Religion of Israel*, 256.
872 Kaufmann, *The Religion of Israel*, 256–257.
873 Kaufmann, "The Biblical Age," 39.
874 Kaufmann, "The Biblical Age," 39.

deriving from the kingship of god."[875] Connecting the period of Judges with one
of the basic ideas of Israelite religion, namely apostolic prophecy, Kaufmann
contended that the idea of apostle-Judges had its origin in "a historical experience that implanted in the people the firm faith that YHWH would always
send it apostle-saviours in time of need. Thus the line of Judges properly begins,
not with Othniel and Ehud, but with Moses and Joshua."[876] As for the role of
Judges, Kaufmann wrote:

> The circle of the Judges was dependent on their personality and on circumstances. There is
> no reason to suppose that they were merely local heroes who were later given national sta-
> tus by the editor of the book of Judges. At the early time, there was no definite boundary
> between local and rational events. Under certain conditions a famous prophet, seer, or
> fighter might extend his influence among several or even all of the tribes.[877]

As we have seen, Kaufmann had enough reasons to ascribe the change in the life
of the Israelite tribes in the land of Canaan to what he called *natural internal evolution*.[878] Therefore, it comes as no surprise that Kaufmann saw the relationship
between the Israelites and Canaanites as one of complete separation: "Neither in
population nor in culture did a Canaanite-Israelite amalgam come into being."[879]
This implies that Kaufmann denied any Canaanite influence on the religion of
Israel. In Kaufmann's thinking, the period of Judges "was a highly creative
one, and its creations for the most part bear the impress of the monotheistic
idea. As for the idolatry of the time, it was but a superficial phenomenon with
no deep or lasting effect."[880]

The foregoing discussion brings into focus some significant aspects of Kaufmann's reconstruction of the early history of Israel. It shows how the idea of the
conquest of Canaan played a central role in Kaufmann's presentation of ancient
Israel. For this reason, I would suggest that Kaufmann's study of the books of
Joshua and Judges was an essential part of his endeavour to establish the historical foundations of Jewish history.

As mentioned, Kaufmann began his study of Jewish history early in 1928. He
began with an investigation of the problem of the Jewish Diaspora, the results of

875 Kaufmann, "The Biblical Age," 39.
876 Kaufmann, "The Biblical Age," 40; also, idem, *Commentary on Judges*, 43–44; idem,
"Probleme der israelitisch-jüdischen Religionsgeschichte I," 27.
877 Kaufmann, *The Religion of Israel*, 257. For more details see Kaufmann, *Commentary on the
Book of Judges*, 36–37, 42–43, 46.
878 Kaufmann, "The Biblical Age," 37.
879 Kaufmann, "The Biblical Age," 31.
880 Kaufmann, "The Biblical Age," 44.

which appear in a four-volume book entitled (גולה ונכר/Exile and Alienation). Kaufmann employed a socio-historical method to reveal the role of religion in ensuring the survival of the Jews. In pursuit of this work, he turned to the Bible to obtain new evidence to support his thesis on Israelite religion, writing eight volumes comprising some 2,600 pages, in which he hypothesized that Israelite religion was monotheistic from its inception. He argued, as previously indicated, that pentateuchal sources, especially "P," are a true reflection of pre-exilic Israel. Certainly, Kaufmann hoped to provide a fresh approach that would revive the old view of premonarchic Israel, after a preponderance of scholars had come to regard this period as non-historical. In order to validate his assumptions, Kaufmann wrote two commentaries on Joshua and Judges with the hope of connecting the origin of Israelite religion with the tradition of conquest and settlement.

In evaluating Kaufmann's ideas concerning early Israelite tradition in Canaan, it seems that only a few biblical scholars concurred with Kaufmann's line of argument.[881] Kaufmann's theory that Canaan was conquered by massive and destructive war is untenable. His historical reconstruction involves many problematic issues, contradicting results produced by literary and historical criticism of the Hebrew Bible. It also ignores historical facts supported by archaeological evidence. John Bright, for example, said, "From a methodological point of view is the fact that there lies at the basis of Kaufmann's work a literary criticism which is, to say the least, eccentric."[882] Similarly, Harrison pointed out, "There is a certain unconscious inconsistency in the general approach adopted by Kaufmann towards his sources materials."[883] De Vaux, too, criticized Kaufmann's approach for neglecting findings on the history of traditions, the achievements of historical criticism, and the results of archaeological discoveries.[884] Fur-

---

881 Manfred Weippert pointed out that Kaufmann's thesis was isolated from the scholary discussion on the question of Conquest. See Manfred Weippert, Die Landnahme der israelitischen Stämme in der neueren wissenschaftlichen Diskussion: ein kritischer Bericht (Göttingen: Vandenhoeck & Ruprecht, 1967), 7, 14. Kaufmann's view, however, was taken up by Irving M. Zeitlin, *Ancient Judaism*, 123 – 146.
882 John Bright, *Early Israel in Recent History Writing: A Study in Method* (London: SCM press, 1956), 67 – 78 (73).
883 R. K. Harrison, *Introduction to the Old Testament* (London: The Tyndale Press, 1969), 378.
884 Roland de Vaux, *The Early History of Israel*, 2: *To the Period of the Judges* (trans. David Smith; London: Darton, Longman & Todd, 1978), 477 – 478. See also J. L. McKenzie, "Book Review: The Biblical Account of the Conquest of Palestine," *Catholic Biblical Quarterly* 17, no. 1 (1955): 95 – 97. However, it should be mentioned that Kaufmann did refer to archaeological evidence but he minimised its importance in understanding the problem of conquest. He wrote, "Archaeology provides only information concerning the cities and their construction, the culture

thermore, Kaufmann's uncritical use of biblical tradition invited attack. Thus, for example, Niels Peter Lemche noted that, "Kaufmann's version of the Israelite conquest, which slavishly followed the biblical version, could hardly be called a rationalistic paraphrase of the Old Testament".[885]

In addition, both Alt and Eissfeldt recognized problematic issues in Kaufmann's literary analysis.[886] Alt mentioned that Kaufmann tried to isolate the books of Joshua and Judges by means of literary examination.[887] He pointed out that Kaufmann's view on the composition of Deuteronomy did not offer enough explanation to the problem.[888] By the same token, Eissfeldt criticized Kaufmann's attempt to validate the credibility of the biblical narratives. He noted that Kaufmann utilized literary and historical methods to connect the events from Exodus to the period of Judges.[889] Even Moshe Greenberg, who accepted some of Kaufmann's thinking, considered Kaufmann's approach of leaping from literary criticism to historical reconstruction to be most questionable.[890]

In essence Kaufmann took the religious and historical value of the Hebrew Bible for granted. He accepted the results of literary criticism only when it accorded with his assumptions. Thus, for example, he rejected deuteronomistic layers in the Books of Joshua and Judges. His position with regard to the authority of biblical tradition became more and more fundamentalist. In point of fact, Kaufmann sought to interpret Israel's history as a thing apart. He used specific expressions such as (popular culture יצירה עממית), (האומה של היצירה כח creative force of the nation) to show that Israel's particular history was a unique creation of the people of Israel.[891] This can be seen in Kaufmann's interpretation of conquest. He wrote, "Conquest can be understood only as the finger of God – a sign

---

of the land, but does not provide epigraphic material about Israel at the time of conquest. Furthermore, the archaeology does not give reliable evidence which can be used as argument against the biblical account concerning the conquest." On this see Kaufmann, *Commentary on Joshua*, 67–73; also, idem, *The Religion of Israel*, 146–147.

885 Niels Peter Lemche, *The Israelites in History and Tradition* (London: SPCK, 1998), 142.

886 Kaufmann replied to the critique of Alt and Eissfeldt, emphasizing that he did not reject biblical criticism in itself, but rather what Kaufmann called (השתוללות- lack of restraint). Kaufmann believed that this kind of criticism had been applied with regard to Joshua. On this see Kaufmann, *Commentary on Joshua*, 21.

887 See Kaufmann's response to Alt's claim about the conquest and deuteronomic redaction in Kaufmann, *Commentary on Joshua*, 4–5.

888 Albrecht Alt, "Utopien," *ThLZ* (1965): 521–528.

889 Otto Eissfeldt, "Die Eroberung Palästinas durch Altisrael," in *Kleine Schriften* III (Tübingen: Mohr, 1966), 367–383 (380–381).

890 See his preface to the reissued print of Kaufmann, *The Biblical Account*, 11.

891 Kaufmann, *From the Secret of the Biblical World*, 18–26.

that Jehovah is God in the heavens and on the earth beneath (Josh. 2.11), and that the 'living God' is in the midst of Israel (Josh. 3.10). This idea is not 'local'. It is Israelite, Israel's original idea."[892] As I understand it, Kaufmann's entire case presupposed that just as the monotheistic idea marked the beginning of Israel on the stage of history, so the traditions of conquest and settlement likewise represented the beginning of Israel's history in its land. My conclusion is that Kaufmann, in an attempt to strengthen his hypothesis on the religious history of early Israel, correlated the religion of Israel with the tradition of conquest and settlement. Thus Kaufmann made the point that the monotheistic faith of Israel could not be separated from its early traditions.

---

892 *The Biblical Account*, 74.

Chapter Seven:
Sources of Kaufmann's Exegetic Approach

1 Introduction

We have seen that Kaufmann's reconstruction of the history of early Israel was strongly influenced by his premises on the beginning of Israelite monotheism. He developed a model according to which Israelite religion was monotheistic at the outset and never deviated through the course of Israel's history. Moreover, it was Kaufmann's enthusiasm in producing a new model of interpretation to the history of Israelite religion that led him to counterargue diverse other methods and numerous approaches that he tirelessly endeavoured to refute. In his approach, Kaufmann combined historical investigation with sociological analysis. Also recognizable in his method are the thoughts of a philosopher and a nationalist.

Although Kaufmann accepted the major principles that have been long established by historical critical methods, his works on the Hebrew Bible was often described as a fundamental critique of classical criticism.[893] Kaufmann worked to provide a different paradigm which could replace the dominant view on biblical research. In the introduction to his opus magnum *Toledot*, Kaufmann emphasized that his study „is a fundamental critique of classical criticism. It seeks to draw ultimate conclusions, to suggest a new position in place of the prevailing one."[894] In what follows I consider Kaufmann's methods of interpretation. My inquiry starts with an outline of Kaufmann's stance towards biblical criticism. I then explore the sources of Kaufmann's exegetical approach, and followed with an examination of his premises and assumptions.

2 Kaufmann and biblical criticism

Before proceeding to discuss Kaufmann's stance towards biblical criticism, it is important to draw attention to the crucial role of text and literary criticism in biblical research. In 1924 Hugo Gressmann wrote:

---

893 Job Y. Jindo rejected the view that Kaufmann's work was merely a critique of German biblical scholarship. See Job Y. Jindo, „Revisiting Kaufmann: Fundamental Problems in Modern Biblical Scholarship from Yehezkel Kaufmann's Criticism of Wellhausen," *Journal of the Interdisciplinary Study of Monotheistic Religions* 3 (2007): 41–77 (43). Against this proposition, see Stefan Schreiner, „Kaufmann, Yehezkel," RGG[4] , vol. 4 (2008): 906–907.
894 Kaufmann, *Toledot* I, vi; also, idem, *The Religion of Israel*, 1.

Wer die Quellenkritik und ihre Ergebnisse nicht anerkennen will, hat die Pflicht, die ganze bisherige Forschung als Sisyphusarbeit aufzuzeigen, wenn er als wissenschaftlicher Mitarbeiter gewertet werden will...Textkritik und Literarkritik sind nach wie vor die Grundlagen, ohne die nur märchenhafte Luftschlösser gebaut werden können, Hypothesen ohne wissenschaftliche Bedeutung.[895]

Gressmann's words show the importance of source critical approach and its results. To begin with, Kaufmann did not reject the historical critical method. Unlike some of his contemporary Jewish Bible scholars such as Benno Jacob [1862–1945] and Umberto Cassuto [1883–1951], Kaufmann worked with the results brought forth by historical criticism. However, Kaufmann sought to correct what he felt to be misguided biblical criticism.[896] It was said of him:

Kaufmann does not blindly accept the conclusions of the various schools of Biblical scholarship, and when he is sceptical about some of the more "definite" conclusions of Bible criticism, it is not as a result of renewed conservatism but rather as a critic of the criticism which became widespread in the more general sphere of Biblical scholarship.[897]

In his commentary on the Book of Joshua, Kaufmann asserted that although biblical criticism was based on sound arguments, it came to counter-productive conclusions.[898] Kaufmann went even further, saying that biblical criticism "underrated the historical worth of biblical traditions."[899] He described how biblical scholarship interpreted a given biblical text: "The habit of developing far-reaching theories from a novel exegesis of an isolated passage – usually an obscure one at that – and of reaching large conclusions literally from jots and tittles, is deeply ingrained in biblical scholarship."[900]

Furthermore, Kaufmann contended that biblical scholarship failed to appreciate what he called "monumental evidence," and the "monumental fact" of Is-

---

895 Hugo Gressmann, „Die Aufgabe der Alttestamentlichen Forschung," *ZAW* 42 (1924): 1—33 (2 – 3).
896 In the judgment of Israel Eldad, Kaufmann waged a crusade to save the Bible "from the hand of the malicious Bible critics". On this see Yaacov Shavit, *The Hebrew Bible Reborn: From Holy Scripture to the Book of Books*, 394.
897 Ephraim E. Urbach: *Collected Writings in Jewish Studies* (ed. Robert Brody and Moshe D. Herr; Jerusalem: Hebrew University, Magnes Press, 1999), 495.
898 Kaufmann, *Commentary on Joshua*, 15 – 19. Moshe Greenberg noted that Kaufmann's commentary on Joshua and Judges was spiced with a large dose of pungent criticism and denunciation of the ways of contemporary (especially European) scholarship. See Greenberg, *Studies in the Bible*, 176.
899 Kaufmann, *The Religion of Israel*, 1.
900 Kaufmann, *The Religion of Israel*, 3.

raelite religion and biblical literature. As for Israelite religion, Kaufmann wrote, "Enthralled by pagan stereotypes, biblical scholarship has failed to appreciate the significance of this monumental testimony to the radically non-pagan character of Israelite folk culture."[901] With respect to biblical literature, it would be sufficient here to mention one example of Kaufmann's analysis. In his interpretation of the composition of first Isaiah, Kaufmann claimed, "Criticism, notwithstanding its preoccupation with the ideology, the style, and the historical allusions of Isaiah 1–33, has failed to take account of the monumental fact that the whole bears a unique ideological stamp that sets it apart from the rest of biblical literature."[902]

It should be noted that Kaufmann's position towards biblical scholarship accorded well with his grave reservations concerning the way that Christian scholars perceived Judaism. To illustrate, I refer to Kaufmann's words:

> Christian scholarship has occupied itself through the ages with the differences between Christianity and Judaism, and tried to explain the separation in terms of different beliefs, and religious attitudes. Judaism is said to be a religion of fear and of law, its god a dreaded sovereign-king. Christianity, on the other hand, is a religion of love and grace, its god a merciful, loving father. Judaism is ritualistic and concerned with 'physical purity': Christianity is a religion of faith demanding spiritual and moral virtue. Judaism is community oriented, societal: Christianity individual-personal. Judaism is impersonal law and covenantal-national. Christianity is personal, universalistic, human.[903]

Kaufmann's literary analysis of the Pentateuch sheds more light on his stance towards biblical criticism. The first book of Kaufmann's *Toledot* is almost entirely dedicated to an inquiry into the pentateuchal literature. In more than 200 pages, he expounds his position on the relation of the Torah to classical prophecy, the law corpora, the Book of Deuteronomy, the antiquity of the Priestly Code, and the composition of the Pentateuch.[904] As for the Torah and prophecy, Kaufmann proposed that the Torah predated prophecy.[905] He believed that the religious horizon of the Torah represented the early stages of Israelite religion and was not influenced by the doctrine of literary prophets.[906] With regard to the legal corpora, Kaufmann distinguished three legal materials in the Torah: the code of Exodus

---

901 Kaufmann, *The Religion of Israel*, 93.
902 Kaufmann, *The Religion of Israel*, 380. See also Kaufmann's view of conquest and his analysis of Joshua and Judges in *The Biblical Account*, 87–91.
903 Kaufmann, *Christianity and Judaism: Two Covenants* (Jerusalem: Magnes Press, Hebrew University, 1988), 17–18.
904 Kaufmann, *Toledot* I, 23–220.
905 See Chapter 4 above.
906 *Toledot I*, 23–46; and Chapter 4 above.

(JE); the Priestly Code (P), chiefly in Exodus, Leviticus, and Numbers; and thirdly, the laws of Deuteronomy (D).[907] In Kaufmann's opinion, "The mutual independence of these codes is evident from their duplications, discrepancies, and
distinct terminology and style."[908] In this context, it should be mentioned that
Kaufmann supported the documentary hypothesis and its division of the sources
into J, E, D, and P with the exception that P preceded D.[909] Kaufmann argued that
P owed nothing to D's characteristics and therefore it must not be regarded as
merely an expansion of D's laws. Moreover, Kaufmann affirmed that P reflected
the pre-exilic situation when the Israelites were a military rather than ecclesiastical congregation.[910]

Respecting the composition and development of the Torah literature, Kaufmann identified two periods:

> The period of the composition of the Torah literature and the age of the formation of the
> Torah book. The first is an age of variegated, many-styled creativity. The second is an
> age of collection and ordering. The legal corpora were composed and fixed before the for-
> mation of the book. The boundary between the two periods – the end of the creation of the
> Torah literature, and the beginning of the formation of the book – was the reform of Josiah,
> inspired and guided by the Torah book found in the temple.[911]

In addition, Kaufmann distinguished the following literary strata:

> Genesis 1–11 (Near-Eastern materials; folkloristic naiveté; no revelation); Genesis 1–49 (the
> book of formative acts and words; no prophecy); JEP (Genesis-Numbers; no trace of deu-
> teronomic ideas); Deuteronomy – II Kings (the influence of the idea of centralization is ap-
> parent); The laws of JE; The laws of P; The laws of D; The Torah-group (Genesis – II Kings;
> no trace of the influence of literary prophecy) ;The literary prophets (the climax of biblical
> religion); The Hagiographa, the postexilic portions of which show a synthesis of the ideas
> of the Torah and prophets.[912]

---

907 Kaufmann, *Toledot* I, 47–80.
908 Kaufmann, *The Religion of Israel*, 166.
909 For more discussion see Greenberg, "A New Approach to the History of the Israelite Priesthood," 41. See further Harrison, *Introduction to the Old Testament*, 75, 378. See also Edward L.
Greenstein, *Essays on Biblical Method and Translation* (Atlanta: Scholars Press, 1989), 15. Gottwald, *The Hebrew Bible in its Social World and in Ours*, 196. Yaacov Shavit, *The Hebrew Bible
Reborn*, 394.
910 See Kaufmann, *Toledot* I, 113–142.
911 Kaufmann, *The Religion of Israel*, 172.
912 Kaufmann, *The Religion of Israel*, 208; idem, *Toledot* I, 211.

Thus, according to Kaufmann, the absence of any hint that literary prophecy influenced the Torah stratum (Genesis – II Kings) indicated that this literary stratum was composed before and independently of the literary prophecy. Moreover, Kaufmann drew attention to the fact that there was no mention whatsoever of the influence of D on JEP, which meant that this literary stratum (JEP) was shaped before the idea of unification of the cult and had no impact on the life of the nation. Furthermore, Kaufmann argued that the two literary strata of (Gen. 1–11) and (Gen. 1–49) contained ancient materials that belonged to the period before the rise of Israelite prophecy, namely, before 'the Exodus from Egypt.'[913]

What is of crucial importance for Kaufmann's literary analysis is the dating of the Priestly Code and his examination of the relation between the Torah and prophecy.[914] He endeavoured to show that monotheism appeared in Israel's earliest literature, before the period of classical prophecy.[915] Kaufmann believed that the prophets did not bring about a new religion but only emphasized the moral factors of existing Israelite religion.[916] Kaufmann, in fact, was concerned to prove the authenticity of the Torah literature as a source for history. Thus, he argued, the Pentateuch sources, especially the priestly source, contained ancient materials dated back to pre-exilic times. In the words of Kaufmann:

> The development of Israelite faith was, indeed, more ramified and intricate than either tradition or modern criticism has recognized. A stratum of tradition, independent of literary prophecy, is evident in the literature of the Torah-group. From the viewpoint of the evolution of Israelite religion this stratum belongs not after, but before literary prophecy. It is the literary product of the earliest stage of Israelite religion.[917]

Having re-examined the relationship of the Torah and prophecy, Kaufmann was able to arrive at a far-reaching conclusion. As Moshe Greenberg rightly remarked:

> An important consequence of Kaufmann's historical reconstruction is the separation of some basic concepts and institutions from literary prophecy. Monotheism, generally conceded to be fully developed in P, becomes independent of and anterior to literary prophecy. Similarly the deuteronomic reform is dis-attached from prophetic agitation.[918]

---

913 Kaufmann, *Toledot* I, 211.
914 See Chapter 4 above.
915 Kaufmann, *The Religion of Israel*, 153, 157.
916 See Chapter 4 above.
917 Kaufmann, *The Religion of Israel*, 165–166.
918 Greenberg, "A New Approach to the History of the Israelite Priesthood," 46.

Though Kaufmann acknowledged the need for literary criticism and seemed to have reckoned on most of its results, he nevertheless, developed a different understanding of its task.[919] At first, Kaufmann welcomed attacks on what he called "the faulty and ridiculous application of [literary] criticism by scholars."[920] Thus, for example, Kaufmann claimed that the insistence of biblical criticism on assigning the Priestly Code to the circumstances of the Second Temple produced fictitious results.

According to Kaufmann, biblical critics deliberately distorted the historical facts of Israel's history.[921] In other words, Kaufmann only supported the criticism that fit well in his reconstruction of the history of ancient Israel.[922] To make this point clear, I refer to Kaufmann's interpretation of Gideon's battle with Baal (Judg. 6). This example shows that Kaufmann at times ignored the obvious meaning of the text. The story of Gideon's battle with Baal indicates that there was an Israelite cult of a Canaanite deity – which calls into question Kaufmann's insistence that early Israelite religion was in no way contaminated by the Canaanites. As Moshe Greenberg observed, "Kaufmann tried, for a time, to deny the plain sense by interpreting the battle as raging over the proper epithets of YHWH. Only later, in his commentary to Judges, did he allow that 'perhaps there were some Canaanite vestiges in Ophrah'."[923]

It seems that Kaufmann did not question the historicity of the biblical account concerning Israel's history. As Norman Gottwald points out, "While disavowing biblical literalism, at every crucial turning point in his argument he employed biblical materials as though they presented a reliable historical account. What the Bible says about Moses, Exodus, and Conquest is accepted by Kauf-

---

919 This puzzling position of Kaufmann was criticized by John Bright (*Early Israel in Recent History Writing*, 73) and Roland de Vaux (The Early History of Israel, 2: To the period of the Judges, 674).

920 See Kaufmann, *The Biblical Account*, 3. Kaufmann labelled the works of biblical critics as scholarly romancing, creative imagination of modern biblical scholarship, or common mistake[s] of biblical scholarship. On this see Kaufmann, *The Religion of Israel*, 108, 118, 383. It is also noted that Kaufmann criticized the historical inquiries of biblical critics either for their preconceived notions or because of their way of applying the method of historical criticism. Kaufmann, for example, rejected the historical reconstructions of Alt and Albright. In his opinion, both Alt and Albright adhered much more closely to the data in their present form, showing little of the imaginative and detective-like approach advocated, say, by Collingwood in the reconstruction of history from documents. On this see Greenberg, *Studies in the Bible*, 184.

921 Kaufmann, *Commentary on Joshua*, 15.

922 Consider, for example, Kaufmann's interpretation of the Book of Hosea. See Kaufmann, *The Religion of Israel*, 368–377.

923 Kaufmann *Toledot* II, 143. Also Greenberg, *Studies in the Bible*, 185.

mann as more or less straightforward history."[924] Thus, though Kaufmann claimed to work with the historical critical method, he nevertheless inclined to a traditional interpretation of Scripture. We can safely say that Kaufmann saw the method of literary criticism as a suitable approach insofar as it did not contradict what he considered to be the historical testimony of biblical literature.

Another distinctive aspect of Kaufmann's analysis is that he gave priority to literary sources.[925] Most of Kaufmann's conclusions about the history of ancient Israel and the nature of Israelite religion was based on results derived directly from analysis of biblical literature.[926] In his illustration of the method of investigation employed in *Toledot*, Kaufmann wrote, "Especially significant are the inferences to be drawn from the ideological constants of the literary corpora, from the leading motives of the various strata, from the several crystallizations of the historical tradition."[927] Thus Kaufmann equated the historical information gained from literary sources with findings of archaeology and epigraphy. According to his understanding, the historical information acquired from analysis of biblical literature was "the literary equivalent of geological stratification, and [was] as conclusive as the material remains of buildings, inscriptions, artefacts, and pottery."[928]

It turns out that Kaufmann did not refute the historical-critical method at all. He sought, in fact, to refine some of the historical results that had been produced historical criticism.[929] As for the method of textual criticism, it is surprising that Kaufmann did not, except for a few instances, build his arguments on evidence

---

924 Gottwald, *The Hebrew Bible in its Social World and in Ours*, 196.

925 Thomas Krapf pointed out that Kaufmann worked with the literary documents as the basic source for his interpretation. He also mentioned that Kaufmann was gifted with an historical sense of biblical text. In addition, Krapf noted that although Kaufmann employed the historical critical method, he knew the traditional exegesis of *p'schat*. On this see Thomas M. Krapf, *Die Priesterschrift und die vorexilische Zeit: Yehezkel Kaufmanns vernachlässigter Beitrag zur Geschichte der biblischen Religion*, 56 – 59, and 109 – 110.

926 In his assessment of Kaufmann's approach, Moshe Greenberg wrote, "If at times the guiding principle of biblical criticism appears to be "since the text says so it must be otherwise," the net effect of Kaufmann's approach is to make him [...] the advocate of the text. And this tendency grew to its fullest expression in the commentaries to Judges and Joshua." See Greenberg, *Studies in the Bible*, 185.

927 Kaufmann, *Toledot* ⁻, ix; also, idem, *The Religion of Israel*, 3.

928 Kaufmann, Toledot, ix; see further Kaufmann, *The Religion of Israel*, 3.

929 See Joseph Blenkinsopp, "Pentateuch," in *The Cambridge Companion to Biblical Interpretation* (ed. John Barton; Cambridge, Cambridge University Press, 1998), 181 – 197 (182).

derived from textual variants.[930] This can be seen, for example, in Kaufmann's literary analysis of the Book of Hosea. He divided the book into two literary units: first Hos. 1–3, and second Hos. 4–14. Attempting to place the date of Hos. 1–3 before King Jehu destroyed the Baalistic cult (2 Kgs 10:28), Kaufmann sought to place first Hos. 1–3 in the time of Jehoram, son of Ahab (853–42 B.C.), by disputing the Masoretic reading 'house of Jehu' in 1:4 and maintaining that the original reading was 'house of Jehoram'. Kaufmann considered there was some slight support for this because of Septuagint's 'Judah' for 'Jehu'. Kaufmann then concluded that first Hosea was a product of pre-classical prophecy.[931] On the other hand, it has been observed that Kaufmann's approach paid little attention to the method of form criticism. He even rejected the Scandinavian school and its claims that Torah and prophecy became written literature only in late times. In Kaufmann's judgment, the position of this school concerning "how the Torah came into being is quite unclear in details".[932] Kaufmann went further and maintained that the religio-historical views of the oral tradition school "are even more paganistic than those of the classical criticism."[933]

From this, it follows that Kaufmann viewed the biblical literature as providing a reliable description of the history of ancient Israel and its religion. The literature of the Torah, particularly its main source the Priestly Code, was the literary product of the earliest stage of Israelite religion, the stage prior to literary prophecy.[934] He credited the Torah as reflecting the historical reality of the premonarchic period. In Kaufmann's assessment, "The whole political background of the Torah's narratives, laws, and songs points to the preconquest period."[935] Moreover, Kaufmann considered the conquest account, as given in Joshua and Judges, as being the true representation of Israel's early tradition in Canaan, not literary invention.[936] Here one cannot fail to detect the two significant pillars of Kaufmann's reconstruction: re-examination of the relationship between Torah and prophecy, and reliability of early Israelite tradition in Canaan. These two factors lay at the root of Kaufmann's hypothesis on the history of ancient Israel.

---

930 Kaufmann makes only few references to LXX. He refers to the Septuagint version of 1 Sam 14: 41, saying that the Hebrew text may be restored on the basis of the LXX. On this see Kaufmann, *The Religion of Israel*, 92.
931 Kaufmann, *The Religion of Israel*, 370. See also Hyatt, "Yehezkel Kaufmann's View of the Religion of Israel," 55.
932 Kaufmann, *The Religion of Israel*, 156, no. 1.
933 Kaufmann, *The Religion of Israel*, 156, n.1. See further Hyatt, "Yehezkel Kaufmann's View of the Religion of Israel," 55.
934 Kaufmann, *The Religion of Israel*, 2.
935 Kaufmann, *The Religion of Israel*, 203.
936 Kaufmann, *Commentary on the Book of Judges*, 18–29.

3 Kaufmann's exegetical approach

As in the case of every hypothesis, so with Kaufmann there must be a theoretical basis underlying his thoughts. In order to understand Kaufmann's thinking, it is important to place his contributions in the intellectual and cultural setting of his time. Kaufmann's exegetical approach showed that different streams of thought shaped his paradigm. Some of Kaufmann's ideas were influenced by the works of his predecessors. For example, Kaufmann apparently inherited the Jewish rationalist tradition that was initiated by Maimonides in medieval times and further elaborated in the beginning of 20th century by the German-Jewish philosopher Herman Cohen. Moreover, one cannot fail to notice the impact of Wilhelm Dilthey and Max Weber on Kaufmann's phenomenological and socio-historical interpretation of the history of Israelite religion. In addition, Kaufmann's understanding of Israelite religion as a product of Israel's national spirit seems to reflect the romantic trend and Jewish nationalism of his time. In what follows I aim to clarify the different lines of thought that shaped Kaufmann's interpretation of the history of ancient Israel and its religious development.

3.1 Jewish rationalism

It has been noted that Kaufmann's view on prophecy, concept of God and monotheism connected him to the rationalistic trend of Jewish thought.[937] The beginning of this rational tendency can be traced back to Maimonides's *Guide for the Perplexed Reason*, which discusses the relation of philosophy to religion.[938] Yet it was in Hermann Cohen's book, *Religion der Vernunft aus den Quellen des Judentums*, that the rationalist stream of Jewish thought flourished. Kaufmann's *Toledot*, especially in his interpretation of the origin of Israelite monotheism, followed the lead of Jewish rational thinking.

---

[937] Benjamin Uffenheimer, "Some Reflections on Modern Jewish Biblical Research," in *Creative Biblical Exegesis: Christian and Jewish Hermeneutics Through the Centuries* (ed. Benjamin Uffenheimer, Henning Graf Reventlow; JSOTSup 59; Sheffield: JSOT Press, 1988), 161–174. For Jewish nationalism, see E. Schweid and L. Levin, *The Classic Jewish Philosophers from Scadia Through the Renaissance* (Leiden: Brill, 2008).

[938] On Maimonides's approach see Salo W. Baron, "The Historical Outlook of Maimonides," in *History and Jewish Historians: Essays and Addresses* (Philadelphia: Jewish Publication Society of America, 1964), 109–163.

Kaufmann's ideas on prophecy seem to build on the rationalistic tradition that goes back to Maimonides.[939] Thus, in his interpretation of Israelite prophecy, Kaufmann used the idea of the 'apostle-prophet' or 'messenger-prophet,' which he considered to be a peculiar Israelite phenomenon.[940] As Kaufmann put it, "The highest form of Israelite prophecy – the apostle-prophet – is, [...] a peculiarly Israelite conception."[941] Kaufmann's characterization of Israelite prophecy as something entirely new connected him with the thoughts of Maimonides, who said, "Yet that an individual should make a claim to prophecy on the ground that God had spoken to him and had sent him on a mission was a thing never heard of prior to Moses our Master."[942] Moreover, Kaufmann believed that the essential characteristic of Israelite prophecy was the proclamation of the 'word of Yahweh'. The effect of the 'spirit of Yahweh' on people, which leads them to a state of ecstasy, is regarded in the Old Testament not as the cause of prophecy, but at the very most, as a by-product of prophetical experience.[943] In this respect, Menahem Haran drew attention to the impact of Maimonides's philosophy on Kaufmann, "Perhaps it would not be an exaggeration to say that, as far as Kaufmann is concerned, his view is at least in some way a transformation [...] of the old rationalistic definition which Maimonides gave to the phenomenon of prophecy."[944]

In addition, it may be noted that Kaufmann's definition of Israelite monotheism came close to the views of Maimonides and Herman Cohen. The contributions of their interpretation are fundamental to our understanding of Kaufmann's system. Both Maimonides and Cohen emphasized the transcendent character of God, which Kaufmann saw as the basic idea of Israelite religion. The uniqueness of the conception of God was, according to Kaufmann, the essence of Israelite religion and its monotheistic idea. He wrote, "The doctrinal aspect of biblical monotheism is that YHWH is God, there is none else."[945] Kaufmann's position in this regard reminds us of Maimonides, "who objected to any corporeal concept

---

939 For more discussion of Maimonides, see David Hartman, *Maimonides: Torah and Philosophic Quest* (Philadelphia: Jewish Publ. Soc. of America, 1976). See also James A. Diamond, "Concepts of Scripture in Maimonides," in *Jewish Concepts of Scripture: A Comparative Introduction* (ed. Benjamin Sommer; New York: New York University Press, 2012), 123 – 138.
940 Kaufmann, *Toledot* I, 686 – 737; also, idem, *The Religion of Israel*, 212 – 216.
941 Kaufmann, *Toledot* I, 511; idem, *The Religion of Israel*, 94.
942 Moses Maimonides, *The Guide of the Perplexed* (trans. by Shlomo Pines; Chicago: University of Chicago Press, 1963).
943 Kaufmann, *Toledot* I, 528, 511 – 530; idem, *The Religion of Israel*, 97 – 101.
944 Menahem Haran, "From Early to Classical Prophecy: Continuity and Change," *Vetus Testamentum* 27, no. 4 (1977): 385 – 397 (396).
945 Kaufmann, *The Religion of Israel*, 137.

of God."[946] On the other hand, Hermann Cohen preceded Kaufmann in emphasizing the non-mythological character of Israelite monotheism with its idea of transcendence.[947] Benjamin Uffenheimer aptly summed up the views of the three Jewish thinkers Maimonides in the following manner:

> All three aspired to cancel, or at least mitigate, the importance of irrational elements in monotheism. Maimonides fiercely objected to the sensual concept of god. The tool he used was philosophical Midrash, by means of which he identified the anthropomorphic images of god with the abstract concepts of the Aristotelian system. Hermann Cohen, on the other hand, who was forced to acknowledge these images as they were, cancelled their importance by means of historical criticism, that is to say he considered them to be desiccated pre-historic remains of monotheism. Kaufmann made a fundamental distinction between abstractness and transcendence. Biblical faith is not a philosophical one, since it is the outcome of popular intuition; it therefore contains no abstractions, but does have transcendence in its aim to elevate God above and beyond the world.[948]

A clear presentation of Kaufmann's rationalism is manifested in his explanation of the birth of monotheism in Israel as a new idea. Kaufmann wrote:

> The birth of an original, genial creation, of an individual or of a society, is not susceptible of 'explanation'. The rise of every new and original idea is a marvel, any 'explanation' of which is bound to be specious and superficial. True, a historian is obligated to explain the phenomena, but this obligation involves too the determination of what he is unable to explain.[949]

Clearly, in working out his hypothesis on the history of Israelite religion, Kaufmann followed the line of Jewish rational tradition. Though this stream of thinking went back to medieval Jewish philosophy, it flourished in the German-speaking world during the nineteenth and beginning of the twentieth century as part

---

946 See Uffenheimer, "Some Reflections on Modern Jewish Biblical Research,"169.

947 Kaufmann worked out Cohen's ideas and gave them empirical and an historical philological basis. For more on the relationship between Kaufmann and Cohen, see Eliezer Schweid, "Biblical Critic or Philosophical Exegete? The Influence of Herman Cohen's The Religion of Reason on Yehezkel Kaufmann's History of Israelite Religion," (Hebrew) *in Massuot: Studies in Qabbalah and Jewish Thought in Memory of Professor Efraim Gottlieb* (ed. Michal Oron and Amos Goldreich; Jerusalem: Mosad Bialik, 1994), 414–428.

948 Benjamin Uffenheimer, "Yehezkel Kaufmann. Historian and Philosopher of Biblical Monotheism," *Immanuel* 3 (1973): 9–21 (17).

949 Kaufmann, *Toledot* II, 41. Translation is taken form Greenberg, *Studies in the Bible*, 184.

of the *Wissenschaft des Judentums*.[950] In point of fact, Kaufmann attempted to translate this inherited rationalism into the language of empirical history. With the aim of confirming the biblical picture of Israelite religion, Kaufmann employed a socio-historical analysis to place the ideas of Israelite religion into the framework of history. This can be seen in Kaufmann's endeavour to transfer the rational thoughts of Hermann Cohen into a language of history. As Uffenheimer explained:

> Kaufmann in effect translated the inherent rationalism of ninetieth-century research on Judaism, as defined and reflected in Herman Cohen's philosophical work, *Religion der Vernunft aus den Quellen des Judentums*, into the language of historical-philological exegesis. In contradiction to Cohen's spiritual and universalistic interpretation of prophetic and Jewish religion, Kaufmann strives to restore to the Bible the concrete basis out of which it has been stripped.[951]

3.2 In search of the nation

Romanticism is the second stream of thought from which Kaufmann derived his ideas. Furthermore, the first decades of the twentieth century witnessed a growing movement of Jewish nationalism. The writings of Jewish thinkers and the Hebrew literature of that time addressed the issues of nation, land, culture and religion. A number of Jewish intellectuals began to pay more attention to national matters and were concerned with the problem of Jewish existence in diaspora. Some of them tried to connect the Jewish situation in diaspora with the whole national past of the Jewish people. Kaufmann certainly developed his ideas within the intellectual atmosphere of his time. As his early writings on Jewish history indicate, Kaufmann was concerned with national matters. In his first major work *Golah ve- Nechar (Exile and Alienation*[952]*)*, Kaufmann expounded the problem of the historical fate of the Jewish people as follows:

---

950 For more discussion see Thomas M. Krapf, "Some Observations on Yehezkel Kaufmann's Attitude to Wissenschaft des Judentums," *Proceedings of the Eleventh World Congress of Jewish Studies*, vol. 2 (Jerusalem: World Union of Jewish Studies, 1994): 69–76.
951 Uffenheimer, "Myth and Reality in Ancient Israel," 136–137.
952 It should be mentioned that Kaufmann's *Gola ve-Nechar* contained the theoretical assumptions underlying much of Kaufmann's historiography. Zevit mentioned that Kaufmann's *Toledot*, which began to be published in 1935, may be considered as an extended footnote to his four-volume historical-sociological study of the Jewish people which was written in the tradition of mainline European, nationalist historiography. On this see Ziony Zevit, *The Religions of Ancient Israel: A Synthesis of Parallactic Approaches*, 43–44.

Why did Israel tread a unique historical path which no other nation or tongue in the world trod? The question, clearly, is at once speculative and practical: it inquiries into the past, but its eyes are on the present and future. Its beginnings are in historical and archaeological study, but its end is a complex of agonizing and painful problems of life.[953]

Throughout his writings, Kaufmann attempted to reply to this question. He studied all issues related to Jewish history at his time, including the problem of exile, the essence of Judaism, the causes of anti-Semitism, and the relation between Judaism and other religions, especially Christianity.[954]

Dealing with these issues, Kaufmann found himself in the company of Jewish thinkers who had raised similar questions concerning Jewish history. Laurence Silberstein pointed out that Kaufmann's writings were ideologically "best understood within the context of Jewish nationalist thought. Like Pinsker, Ahad Haam, Dubnow, and Herzl, Kaufmann's perception of the social and cultural condition of the Jewish people was rooted in nationalist presuppositions concerning the nature of the Jewish group and the meaning of Jewish history."[955] Moreover, Kaufmann's perception of the Jewish problem connected his ideas with the thoughts of Ahad Haam (1856–1927), the leading spokesman of Jewish cultural nationalism, and the Jewish historian and nationalist Simon Dubnow (1860–1941).[956] The strong impact that the teachings of Ahad Haam and Dubnow had on Kaufmann is evidenced by the fact that the majority of his writings between 1914 and 1928 were devoted to a critique of their ideas. Accordingly, as Laurence Silberstein remarked, any attempt to understand Kaufmann's view on Jewish history and nationalism must begin with a brief discussion of these two men.[957]

Furthermore, Kaufmann's view of religion and historiosophy presupposed the influence of the ideas of Ahad Haam. Kaufmann's first article in 1914 was

---

953 Kaufmann, *Golah ve-Nechar* I, 1. See further Laurence J. Silberstein, *History and Ideology: The Writings of Y. Kaufmann* (unpublished Ph.D. dissertation, Brandeis University, 1971).
954 Efraim Shmueli, "The Jerusalem School of Jewish History: A Critical Evaluation," *Proceedings of the American Academy for Jewish Research* 53 (1986): 147–178 (148).
955 Laurence J. Silberstein, "Historical Sociology and Ideology: A Prolegomena to Yehezkel Kaufmann's Golah v'Nekhar," in *Essays in Modern Jewish History: A Tribute to Ben Halpern* (ed. Frances Malino; Rutherford: Fairleigh Dickinson UP, 1982), 173–195 (174).
956 Arnold Band suggested that Kaufmann's original interest in Biblical studies derived from his critique of Ahad Ha'am and the other "evolutionists" among nineteenth century writers. His work, then, carried back into the life of ancient Israel the same trends which were apparent in its later history. On this see David Lieber, "Yehezkel Kaufmann's Contribution to Biblical Scholarship," *Journal of Jewish Education* 34, no. 4 (1964): 254–261 (261).
957 Laurence J. Silberstein, "Religion, Ethnicity, and Jewish History: The Contribution of Yehezkel Kaufmann," *Journal of the American Academy of Religion* 42, no. 3 (1974): 516–531 (520).

mainly a critique of Ahad Haam's view on Judaism.[958] In his attempt to find a solution for the problem of the Jewish diaspora, Ahad Haam proposed a nationalist conception of Judaism and Jewish history which became one of the dominant intellectual trends among Eastern European Jews in the early twentieth century.[959] In the view of Ahad Haam, Judaism developed as a result of the inherent need for self-preservation of the Jewish people, having to overcome the persisting threat of possible ethnic extinction.[960] Simon Dubnow followed the lead of Ahad Haam and sought to translate the ideas of Jewish nationalism into a comprehensive interpretation of Jewish history. He suggested that the secret of Jewish national survival was to be found in the nation's ability to establish autonomous Jewish communities in the diaspora.[961] Yehezkel Kaufmann, while building upon the ideas of his predecessors, argued for the centrality of Judaism as religion in understanding the fate of the Jews. However, Kaufmann's view differed from those of Ahad Haam and Dubnow. Kaufmann asserted that it was "Judaism alone, and not gentile hatred or a reified national will to survive, that accounted for the remarkable preservation of Jewish national consciousness in exile."[962]

3.3 Religion and the quest for the original idea

Kaufmann believed in the power of religion.[963] He proposed that religion alone could account for the survival of the Jews in the diaspora.[964] He further maintained that religion enabled the Jewish people to preserve their identity as a distinct minority in foreign lands. As Kaufmann put it:

---

958 Kaufmann, "The Judaism of 'Ahad Ha-'am," *HaShiloah* (1914). See further Job Y. Jindo, "Revisiting Kaufmann: Fundamental Problems in Modern Biblical Scholarship. From Yehezkel Kaufmann's Criticism of Wellhausen," *Journal of the Interdisciplinary Study of Monotheistic Religions* 3 (2007): 41–77.
959 Laurence J. Silberstein, "Religion, Ethnicity, and Jewish History: The Contribution of Yehezkel Kaufmann," 520.
960 Job Y. Jindo, "Revisiting Kaufmann," 44.
961 Laurence J. Silberstein, "Religion, Ethnicity, and Jewish History," 520–521.
962 Ismar Schorsch, "The Last Jewish Generalist," *AJS Review* 18, no. 1 (1993): 39–50 (43).
963 "Religion, for Kaufmann, was one of the givens in all cultures. He explained it from a socio-anthropological perspective as what a people does as a result of its ideas about its relationship to the sphere of the unseen in existence, whether it is magic or sacrifice or prayer". On this see Ziony Zevit, *The Religions of Ancient Israel: A Synthesis of Parallactic Approaches*, 43–44.
964 Job Y. Jindo, "Recontextualizing Kaufmann: His Empirical Conception of the Bible and Its Significance in Jewish Intellectual History," *The Journal of Jewish Thought and Philosophy* 19, no. 2 (2011): 95–129 (105). See also M. Brenner, *Jüdische Geschichte lesen: Texte der jüdischen Geschichtsschreibung im 19. und 20. Jahrhundert* (München: Beck, 2003), 214–215.

Religion absorbed all of the Hebrew national foundations. Because of its powerful influence in the life of the nation, it served to strengthen the national foundations even in exile. Religion gave the nation a mysterious national life in place of the actual national life that it had lost. It gave it a sacred land, a sacred state and a sacred language in place of the secular land, state and language that had been lost.[965]

Religion, in Kaufmann's view, created the people. He recognized its importance in shaping the history of the Jewish people. For this reason, Kaufmann undertook to study the social and historical function of religion.[966] Emphasizing the central role of religion in Jewish history, Kaufmann wrote:

> In every generation religion was the first and only cause for Israel's separateness in the diaspora...To this cause were added, it is true, other ephemeral causes which stamped their imprint on Israel's life in different periods. But were it not for the functioning of this primary force, there would have been no place for the functioning of the ephemeral factors.[967]

Having discovered that religion moulded the destiny of the Jews through the centuries, Kaufmann turned to the Bible, which he thought to be the historical foundation of Jewish history. It is worth mentioning that Kaufmann's works on the Hebrew Bible cannot be separated from his early writing on Jewish history.[968]

---

965 Kaufmann, "Democratic Nationalism" (Hebrew) *HaShiloah* (1914), 294 (Translation from Laurence J. Siberstein, "Religion, Ethnicity, and Jewish History," 521.

966 "Although Kaufmann made no reference to Durkheim, Rudolph Otto, or Weber, there were many similarities between his interpretation of religion and that found in their writings. Once again, his lack of specific references made it impossible to establish, with any degree of certainty, a definite relationship. Nevertheless, it is certainly clear that, in portraying religion as a major social and historical force, Kaufmann was following in the footsteps of a group of historians and social theorists that included Fustel de Coulanges, Marx, Durkheim, and Weber." See Laurence J. Silberstein, "Historical Sociology and Ideology: A Prolegomena to Yehezkel Kaufmann's Golah v'Nekhar,"186.

967 Kaufmann, "The National Will to Survive," (Hebrew) *Miklat* 4 (June–August 1920), 192. See further Laurence J. Silberstein, "Religion, Ethnicity, and Jewish History: The Contribution of Yehezkel Kaufmann," 522.

968 Moshe Greenberg rightly pointed out that "Kaufmann believed the singularity of Jewish existence to be determined by the peculiar character of Judaism; but that in turn was rooted in the unique faith of the Bible. Hence, he was inevitably led back to the biblical age in his search for understanding the motives of Jewish history." On this see Greenberg, *Studies in the Bible*, 176. Similarly, Uffenheimer observed that "Kaufmann, the sociologist, the philosopher of national revival, struggling with the questions of the present and future, became a Bible scholar, for he discovered that one can understand the character of this people only by a careful study of the Bible. This gave rise to his great scholarly work, The History of the Faith of Israel." See Uffenheimer, "Yehezkel Kaufmann: Historian and Philosopher of Biblical Monotheism," 10.

In his *Toeldot* the major contribution on the history of Israelite religion, Kaufmann set about to prove that Israel's religion was not the product of gradual development, as most biblical critics would have it. Instead, Kaufmann argued that Israelite religion expressed the national culture of the people of Israel and could be explained according to evolution hypothesis. He defined the religion of Israel as folk-religion, a product of the national spirit of the people of Israel.[969]

In his discussion on the origin of cultural creativity, Kaufmann rejected all suggestions and definitions of culture that ignored the role of spirit, *ruah*. In Kaufmann's thinking, Israelite religion began as a new, intuitive idea. It grew up out of the (creative spirit of the people of Israel- רוח יוצר של ישראל).[970]

According to Kaufmann, neither idealism nor materialism could explain the origin of cultural creativity.[971] Kaufmann believed that both idealism and materialism overshadowed the basic problem, that is, in "the infinitive diversity of cultural forms" (האין-סופי של רבוי צורות היצירה התרבותית).[972] In Kaufmann's interpretation, the source of cultural creativity was to be found in "the creative force of the spirit" (היוצר של רוח האדם כח).[973] Furthermore, Kaufmann drew attention to what he called "the concealed secret, a secret of the spirit" (סוד,סוד טמיר הרוח), which explains the geniality of individuals.[974] As for national creativity, Kaufmann mentioned that this could be measured according to the "internal force concealed in the culture". Thus, for example, Kaufmann contended that although ancient Israel and Greece had no political or economic impact, the inner force of their culture could not be denied.[975] He came up with the idea that each ethnic group was the subject of a particular formulation of the creative spirit.[976] Kaufmann then made the point that neither circumstances nor conditions could

---

969 Kaufmann, *From the Secret of the Biblical World*, 11 – 33.

970 The Talmudic scholar Ephraim E. Urbach pointed out, "Yehezkel Kaufmann's theories on "the popular religion" of monothesitic faith, on the "spirit of the nation," and on a "folk-inspired Book of Genesis" are no more lucidly phrased than the very similar expressions found in Zuns's writing, but in the case of the former they lack the spark of innovation." See Ephraim E. Urbach, *Collected Writings in Jewish Studies*, 504.

971 Kaufmann, *From the Secret of the Biblical World*, 11 – 19. To Kaufmann, "the concept of culture refers not to norms, customs, patterns of behavior, or practical arts, but rather to the totality of ideas and values created by the human spirit and transmitted from one generation to another." See Laurence J. Silberstein, "Historical Sociology and Ideology," 184.

972 Kaufmann, *From the Secret of the Biblical World*, 11.

973 Kaufmann, *From the Secret of the Biblical World*, 12.

974 Kaufmann, *From the Secret of the Biblical World*, 13.

975 Kaufmann, *From the Secret of the Biblical World*, 15.

976 Kaufmann, *From the Secret of the Biblical World*, 16.

answer the question of cultural creativity, but only the creative spirit.[977] By "spirit" Kaufmann meant "the creative potential in humans through which they intuit and gain insight about the essence of things."[978]

Now we may ask how Kaufmann connected the concept of *ruah* as the source of cultural creativity with the history of Israelite religion. This may be answered by considering his view of "idea" (אידיה). For Kaufmann, the basic "idea" of Israelite religion was the notion of a supreme God.[979] The religion of Israel was essentially the creation of this intuitive idea.[980] In this way, Kaufmann found the link between "idea" or Israelite religion and "the people", of Israel.[981] In his Golah ve- Nechar study, Kaufmann connected the religion as an idea with the creative spirit of the people of Israel. As Zion Zevit pointed out, Kaufmann argued (1) that a people, groups of individuals living together, have a consciousness, (2) that the contents of this consciousness are "ideas", and (3) that culture is the actual expression of these ideas.[982]

Kaufmann explained how the new religious idea, once it appeared in Israel's history, took different forms and pervaded all aspects of culture. In the words of Kaufmann:

> It is similar to the development of a plant or an animal from a seed to its species: all the stages of growth are concealed in the seed, and they emerge, one by one, from the potential to the actual. In the ancient days of Israel, a new religious idea was planted which fertilized the nation's cultural creativity. Over the generations this idea brought forth from the potential to the actual that which was hidden in it. Everything that the nation created, throughout its history, bore the stamp of this idea. Times change and it remains; symbols change and it appears within all of them, for it was the idea that existed at the outset.[983]

This new religious idea was monotheism.[984] Seen from Kaufmann's perspective, Israelite monotheism was a new cultural creation, a product of the creative spirit

---

977 For Kaufmann's characterization of spirit *ruah*, see Kaufmann, *From the Secret of the Biblical World*, 11–13, 20–21, and 16–17.
978 See Job Y. Jindo, "Revisiting Kaufmann," 60.
979 Kaufmann, *The Religion of Israel*, 60.
980 Kaufmann, *From the Secret of the Biblical World*, 31, 54, 57, 64; idem, "Israelite Religion," *Encyclopaedia Biblica*, 740–741.
981 For the connection between Israelite religion and Israelite culture, see Kaufmann, *From the Secret of the Biblical World*, 28–31.
982 Kaufmann, *Golah ve-Nechar* I, 30. See further Zion Zevit, *The Religions of Ancient Israel*, 44.
983 *From the Secret of the Biblical World*, 59. Translation from Ehud Luz, "Jewish Nationalism in the Thoughts of Yehezkel Kaufmann," 180–181.
984 For the beginning of Israelite monotheism as an idea, see Kaufmann, *Toledot* I, 1–12. In this context, Laurence Silberstein pointed out that "Kaufmann's conception of 'idea' emerges

of the people of Israel.[985] Thus Kaufmann associated the spirit *ruah* and *idea*, that is, he connected the spirit of the people with its religious idea, monotheism.[986] The new religious idea, monotheism, began with Moses. According to Kaufmann, Moses was the first to discover this novel idea which caused a religious revolution in the life of the Israelite tribes.[987]

With Moses as creator of the religious idea in ancient Israel, we come to a very interesting point in Kaufmann's interpretation of the history of Israelite monotheism. Although Kaufmann put forward the notion that monotheism first began as a breakthrough in history, he nevertheless wondered why it first appeared with Moses. As Kaufmann put it:

> Why and how the new religious idea of a transcendent divine will was born in the mind of Moses cannot be known. It could not be known even if more had come down to us concerning that revelation than a beautiful and wondrous fabric of legend. Only with regard to the social-historical background of that revelation is it possible to say something on the basis of the biblical evidence.[988]

---

most clearly in his interpretation of Israelite religion. To him, the essential element in religion is neither the ritual nor the experiential dimension, but the basic idea that is embodied in the religion. Accordingly, the essence of Israelite religion is the idea of one God who is supreme over nature. This idea, in turn, may be contrasted with the essential idea of pagan religions wherein the gods are considered to be subservient to nature." On this see Laurence J. Silberstein, "Historical Sociology and Ideology: A Prolegomena to Yehezkel Kaufmann's Golah v'Nekhar," 185.
985 Kaufmann, *From the Secret of the Biblical World*, 22 – 25. Uffenheimer observed that Kaufmann in his definition of monotheism as a new religious idea "took the leap from empirical history to philosophical anthropology by sequestering monotheism from the field of development in time and putting it in the sphere of the 'creative spirit' of the nation." See Uffenheimer, "Yehezkel Kaufmann: Historian and Philosopher of Biblical Monotheism," 13 – 14. For different understandings of monotheism in modern Jewish thought see, Nathan Rotenstreich, "Jewish Thought," in *Nineteenth Century Religious Thought in the West* III (ed. Ninian Smart: Cambridge: Cambridge University Press, 1985), 76 – 82.
986 For monotheism as a product of creative spirit, see Kaufmann, *From the Secret of the Biblical World*, 22, 24, 26; for monotheism as intuitive idea, see pages 31, 54, 57, 64.
987 Kaufmann, *From the Secret of the Biblical World*, 24.
988 Kaufmann, *Toledot* II, 45, translation from Greenberg, *Studies in the Bible*, 184. As might be noted, although Kaufmann considered the dawn of Israelite monotheism to be a new intuitive idea, he inclined to explain its manifestation within a socio-historical context. In effect, Kaufmann wanted to interpret Israelite's monotheism in its historical-culture framework. Thus, he wrote, "The question of the formation of ancient Israelite culture—more specifically, of the Israelite faith—for the scholar who seeks to remain within the boundaries of appearance [i.e., the boundaries of empirical investigation], is a cultural-historical question, and it must be discussed in the way manifestations of cultural creativity are generally discussed." On this see Kaufmann, *Toledot* I, 32. For a full treatment of this subject, see Job Y. Jindo, "Recontextualizing Kaufmann: His Empirical Conception of the Bible and Its Significance in Jewish Intellectual History," 95 –

However, Kaufmann stated that the new religious idea was transmitted to the people of Israel through Moses by "objective spirit" (רוח אובייקטיבי).[989] More to this point, Kaufmann maintained that every genuine spirit that affected society and left an imprint in its life was likely to be preserved for the next generation. He suggested that language, religion, art, leadership, justice, etc. were treasures of constant cultural value, of objective spirit which was transmitted from one generation to another.[990] In this way, Kaufmann propounded that monotheism was born in Israel as the "objective spirit," first discovered by Moses, who conveyed it to the people of Israel. The new religious idea permeated the life of the nation and shaped its culture.[991] Thus Kaufmann explained the central and fundamental part of religion in the history and culture of the people of Israel:

> Absolute spirit as an eternal force, 'national spirit' as an unfolding of a single 'idea' or 'principle', the notion of a unified 'soulness' embodied in a cultural body; all of these are metaphysical concepts that are not the result of empirical historical inquiry. But the creative spirit, the creative power of the ethnic group or nation, the power of objectified spirit to stamp its imprint, shape cultural values and form symbols; all of these are, without any doubt, part of empirical, historical experience.[992]

In line with his stance, Kaufmann distinguished monotheism from the other religious ideas surrounding it. According to Kaufmann, the fundamental idea of Israelite monotheism was the non-mythological conception of God. This was the essential difference that precluded a transition or development from polytheism to monotheism. Furthermore, Kaufmann showed that the polytheistic philosophy even at its highest level did not arrive at the basic idea of Israelite mono-

---

125. Job Y. Jindo claimed that Kaufmann sought to investigate Israelite religion according to the general principles of empirical analysis. He remarked that "while Kaufmann espoused the notion of the Bible as a product of the *ruah le'umi* of ancient Israel, he insisted on using the term *ruah* (spirit or mind: cf. *Geist* in German) only in the empirical sense and not in a speculative Hegelian or romanticist sense (cf. *Volksgeist*), which was how the term was usually used among Jewish thinkers of this period." See Job Y. Jindo, "Recontextualizing Kaufmann: His Empirical Conception of the Bible and Its Significance in Jewish Intellectual History," 104.

989 Kaufmann, *From the Secret of the Biblical World*, 21.

990 Kaufmann, *From the Secret of the Biblical World*, 20.

991 It has been noted that Kaufmann's view presupposes the philosophy of Dilthey. Thus, Job Y. Jindo remarked, "In Diltheyan terms, Kaufmann conceived of the Bible as a cultural expression that manifests a lived experience of ancient Israel and sought to explore how the monotheistic mind obtained a deeper insight into the structures and functioning of the world and life, as contrasted to the mindsets of those in surrounding polytheistic cultures." See Job Y. Jindo, "Recontextualizing Kaufmann," 109.

992 Kaufmann, *From the Secret of the Biblical World*, 21. Translation form Laurence J. Silberstein, "Historical Sociology and Ideology," 186.

theism. Therefore, Kaufmann concluded that monotheism was an absolute primal idea and an entirely new conception that could be elucidated in terms of an historical development that grew out of idolatry.[993]

As I see it, Kaufmann, in effect, sought to explain the monotheistic idea as a cultural expression of ancient Israel. He clearly declared, "The monotheistic idea was not only born in Israel's initial period, but that already then it had affected a far-reaching revolution in the spirit of the people. It did not make its appearance as the esoteric doctrine of a select circle, but became at once the basis of a new culture for the whole nation."[994]

We have seen that Kaufmann emphasized the role of ideas in history and culture.[995] He started by confirming the role of *ruah* as the origin of cultural creativity and then explained how this *ruah* was embodied in cultural ideas. Pursuing this further, he argued that the history of Israelite religion must be grasped in the light of its unique religious idea, that is, monotheism. Yet, Kaufmann's interpretation found no support and his thoughts remained in the air. There are, at least, two problematic issues in Kaufmann's proposition. First, Kaufmann's usage of terms like *ruah*, along with what he called collective spirit, to describe the rise of Israelite religion seems to ignore Israel's historical position in the desert of Sinai. For this reason, Shelomo Dov Goitein criticized Kaufmann for applying expressions such as "spirit of the nation" (רוח האומה) and "primal popular creation" (יצירה באשית עממית). He declared that science could not recognize these terms because they were not understandable and did not provide enough explanation for the emergence of Israelite religion.[996] Similarly, the Talmudic scholar Ephraim Elimelech Urbach pointed out that Kaufmann employed words like "popular creation" (יצירה עממית) and "creative force of the nation" (כח היצירה של האומה) to explore the origin of monotheism. He said that Kaufmann seemed to have ignored the phenomenon of revelation and used Hegelian terms which could not explain the dawn of monotheism in the Sinai desert.[997] On the other hand, the Jewish scholar Armand Kaminka called attention to Kaufmann's interpretation of Israelite religion, which he described like an "external event

---

993 Kaufmann, *From the Secret of the Biblical World*, 23.

994 Kaufmann, "The Bible and Mythological Polytheism," 197.

995 Kaufmann's assumption regarding the role of idea in history, as Laurence Silberstein noted, "provided the basis for his critique of the Marxist interpretation of history in which he argued that ideas, rather than socio-economic relations, comprise the substructure of society." See Laurence J. Silberstein, "Historical Sociology and Ideology," 184.

996 Shelomo Dov Goitein, *Davar* 6 (1937); see further Kaufmann, *From the Secret of the Biblical World*, 26.

997 Efraim Urbach, "Neue Wege der Bibelwissenschaft," 2, 3.

that exceeded the law of nature".[998] He accused Kaufmann of employing ambiguous expressions such as "popular legend" (האגדה העממית) and "creative popular spirit" (יצירת הנפש העממית).[999] In response to Kaminka's claim, Kaufmann proclaimed that the monotheistic idea grew out of the genius of Moses. Kaufmann went further and maintained that the new religious idea prospered through the teachings of the prophets, priests, and poets of Israel. It was embodied in the kingdom of God, deeds of kings, and in the destiny of the entire nation. Kaufmann then concluded that the new religious idea was crystallized in the culture and history of the nation of Israel.[1000] According to a sound critique of Kaufmann's view, "Kaufmann had in effect replaced a transcendental view with a meta-historical view; namely, he had replaced revelation with a collective genius."[1001]

The second flaw in Kaufmann's system of interpretation is related to his concept of Israelite monotheism as an intuitive idea. We have demonstrated that Kaufmann dated the intuition of the monotheistic idea to the desert period. He implemented a sociological interpretation to argue that monotheism was a creation of the collective folk spirit of the people of Israel. Moreover, he insisted that monotheism as a new religious idea had no antecedent in world history.[1002] Following this, Kaufmann contended that with the appearance of monotheism the world divided into two parts: that of the idolatrous and that of the Israelite world.[1003] The notion of a supreme and transcendent god manifested only in Israel as an intuitive idea.[1004]

We then note how Kaufmann underlined the role of a new religious idea in shaping the history of Israel. More interesting is Kaufmann's view, "You cannot investigate the historical development of religious belief if you do not assume, from the outset, the existence of a particular idea that gives the development significance and direction."[1005] My impression is that Kaufmann, in his emphasis on the creative genius of the people of Israel, claimed too much for the people of Israel and too little for God. He credited "the Israelites with an extraordinary capacity for intuiting and responding to abstract ideas—a point, by the way,

998 Armand Kaminka, *Moznaim* 8 (1939): 469–476.
999 See further Kaufmann *From the Secret of the Biblical World*, 285.
1000 Kaufmann, *From the Secret of the Biblical World*, 26.
1001 Yaacov Shavit and Mordechai Eran, *The Hebrew Bible Reborn: From Holy Scripture to the Book of Books*, 395.
1002 Kaufmann, *Toledot* I, 254.
1003 Kaufmann, *From the Secret of the Biblical World*, 28.
1004 Kaufmann, *From the Secret of the Biblical World*, 31, 54.
1005 See Ehud Luz, "Jewish nationalism in the thought of Yehezkel Kaufmann," 181.

which is contrary to the Biblical story."[1006] With this borne in mind, it would be no exaggeration to suggest that Kaufmann enslaved himself to the origin of monotheistic idea in Israel. Therefore, his interpretation of the beginning of Israelite religion as a new intuitive insight seems to be unwarranted.

[1006] David Lieber, "Yehezkel Kaufmann's Contribution to Biblical Scholarship," 259.

Chapter Eight:
Moving between Wellhausen and Kaufmann

1 Introduction

In the following pages I discuss several issues related to the models constructed by Wellhausen and Kaufmann for the history of Israel. This will include an analysis of their respective views concerning religion, history and biblical texts. Some reiteration of their thoughts may be inevitable here. Israel's religious history will be scrutinized for its importance in understanding the nature of the disagreements between Wellhausen and Kaufmann. In addition, I highlight points of contact between these two scholars concerning the question and the writing of history. In order to fully comprehend how Wellhausen and Kaufmann evaluated the role of the prophets, priests, and monarchy in Israel's history, I dedicate more space to their notion of theocracy and its relation to these institutions. I also seek to answer the question of how they perceived this combination of religious and political elements in Israel's history in order to determine whether they viewed the tradition of ancient Israel historically or more influenced by religious dogma. At the end of my discussion, I look into Wellhausen's and Kaufmann's presuppositions with the aim of understanding how their underlying premises determined the direction of thoughts. This will be followed by an evaluation of their contributions.

2 Setting the scene

As mentioned in the introduction to this study, both Wellhausen and Kaufmann contributed to our understanding of the history of ancient Israel and its religious history. However, they did not stand alone in this respect. Wellhausen worked from the hypotheses of the great biblical scholars of the 19th century and developed a historical synthesis on the history of ancient Israel. With an awareness of Wellhausen's contribution and different positions in biblical research, Yehezkel Kaufmann introduced his *Toledot* as follows:

> Biblical scholarship finds itself today in a peculiar position. There is a view of the history of biblical religion to which the body of biblical scholars subscribe; precisely why this view prevails, however, is not at all clear. At the end of the last century Julius Wellhausen formulated the now classic theory of the evolution of the literature and of the religion of Israel…Wellhausen's arguments complemented each other nicely, and offered what seemed to be a solid foundation upon which to build the house of biblical criticism. Since then,

> however, both the evidence and the arguments supporting this structure have been called into question and, to some extent, even rejected.[1007]

In this telling quotation, several things are to be observed. Kaufmann drew attention to the dominant view in biblical criticism. He characterized Wellhausen's hypothesis in biblical literature and religion as "evolution theory". Moreover, Kaufmann conceded that Wellhausen's arguments offered a solid foundation, but called for a reassessment of Wellhausen's legacy. This shows us that Kaufmann was concerned at the outset with Wellhausen's theory. In his appraisal of Kaufmann's position, Isaac Leo Seeligmann pointed out that Kaufmann's *Toledot* was basically directed against classic criticism of the Hebrew Bible as represented by Wellhausen. Seeligmann mentioned that Kaufmann was preoccupied with issues related to history, history of religion, and biblical literature.[1008] To do more justice to Kaufmann, it should be said that he touched upon all issues in the study of the Hebrew Bible. This appeared in his *Toledot*, which is a massive treatment of the history of Israelite religion, history and biblical literature. Furthermore, Kaufmann investigated many questions related to early Israelite tradition in Canaan in two commentaries on Joshua and Judges. In dealing with these issues, Kaufmann found himself in the company of biblical scholars and it was Wellhausen with whom he entered into discussion and controversy.[1009]

Kaufmann's critique of Wellhausen centres mainly on the history of Israelite religion and development of biblical literature.[1010] As for the history of Israelite religion, Kaufmann rejected Wellhausen's hypothesis regarding the origin of Israelite monotheism. In his opinion, Israelite religion was monotheistic from its very beginning, In contrast to Wellhausen's proposition that ethical monotheism first appeared with the prophets, Kaufmann contended that the prophets had taken popular monotheism, which developed in Israel prior to the classical prophets, for granted. Respecting biblical literature, we note that Kaufmann ac-

---

1007 Kaufmann *Toledot* I, ה; idem, *The Religion of Israel*, 1.
1008 Isac Leo Seeligmann "Yehezkel Kaufmann," in *Yehezkel Kaufmann Jubilee Volume: Studies in Bible and Jewish Religion* (ed. Menahem Haran; Jerusalem: Magnes Press, 1960), x.
1009 See David Noel Freedman, "Review: The Religion of Israel, from Its Beginnings to the Babylonian Exile by Yehezkel Kaufmann," *JBL* 81, No. 2 (1962): 185–190.
1010 Patrick D. Miller pointed to the significant contribution of Kaufmann, especially when compared to American biblical theology. He wrote, "Both affirmed a focus on the historical over the natural and the mythological. Kaufmann and Wright saw the Wellhausenist approach to Israel's literature and religion as radically wrong and set that approach as a principal target of attack." See Patrick D. Miller, *Israelite Religion and Biblical Theology: Collected Essays* (Sheffield: Sheffield Academic Press, 2000), 147.

cepted Wellhausen's division of the sources of the Pentateuch but he reversed their chronological order. Kaufmann dated the Priestly Code before Deuteronomy and placed the Torah before the literary prophets.[1011] In what follows I point out some aspects that I believe are particularly pertinent to an understanding of the real divide between Wellhausen and Kaufmann. I start by examining their view on the history of Israelite religion, and follow with an outline of their respective histories of ancient Israel and then an examination of their views concerning the authority of the biblical text.

3 Wellhausen and Kaufmann: Similarities and differences

3.1 Religious history of ancient Israel

The most important area of confrontation between Wellhausen and Kaufmann lay in their understanding of religious development in ancient Israel. Wellhausen studied the religion of ancient Israel with the aim of determining the main lines of its development. Kaufmann, too, hoped to arrive at the basic character of Israelite religion. While Wellhausen insisted that the course of Israelite religion showed a remarkable change from the religion of people to the religion of law, Kaufmann strongly rejected the definition of religion in terms of evolution. Moreover, their different conceptions of God in Israel's religion and the beginning of monotheism increased the divide between the theories of Wellhausen and Kaufmann.

According to Wellhausen, Israel's religion was a product of its history. He put forward the idea that religion shaped the nation's experience and moulded its subsequent history. As Wellhausen put it:

> The foundation upon which, at all periods, Israel's sense of its national unity rested was religious in its character. It was the faith which may be summed up in the formula, Jehovah is the God of Israel, and Israel is the people of Jehovah. Moses was not the first discoverer of this faith, but it was through him that it came to be the fundamental basis of the national existence and history.[1012]

Though Wellhausen emphasized the central role of religion in Israel's history, he did not, to be sure, overstate its substance. Wellhausen believed that religion in ancient Israel was the natural impulse of the people. Early Israelite religion did

---

1011 See Chapter 4 above.
1012 Wellhausen, *Prolegomena*, 433.

not arise out of theoretical dogmas or spiritual thoughts. Instead, Wellhausen asserted that its function was to answer questions brought about by everyday life. Early Israelite religion, like other religions, was not based on special revelation:

> Es kann keine Frage sein, daß die alten Israeliten unter Religion wesentlich den Opferdienst verstanden. Aber dadurch unterschieden sie sich nicht von anderen Völkern, der Kultus beruht nicht auf besonderer Offenbarung und datiert nicht erst aus der mosaischen Zeit.[1013]

Kaufmann, though he developed his own understanding, held Wellhausen's view on the fundamental part of religion in the history of ancient Israel. However, Kaufmann disregarded Wellhausen's assumption on the nature of early Israelite religion. In Kaufmann view, early Israelite religion was not naïve or spontaneous. Its conduct was a reflection of the affairs of life. According to Kaufmann, religion came from the power of a new idea. This new idea, with its potential force, changed the life of the people. Kaufmann contended that a new religious idea cannot be simply connected with the life of the people. In supporting his view, Kaufmann gave two examples taken from Christianity and Islam. He proposed that the new religious ideas of these two religions were not part of the life of the people, but yet they had changed their lives and history. Likewise, the ideas of the Israelite religion marked a new beginning.[1014] Kaufmann exaggerated the emergence of religion as a new perceptive idea. So Kaufmann wrote:

> We should clearly think of religion as a product of intuitive ideas. Religion includes beliefs and views about the world. But its way, – at least in ancient times – was not to rephrase these concepts in theoretical notions. It expresses itself by signs and symbols. The historian can reveal the "essence" of these ideas and formulate them in abstract ideas. But the way by which these ideas were manifested is not abstract.[1015]

Whether it was natural impulse or intuitive idea, it appears that Wellhausen and Kaufmann agreed with the pivotal role of religion in ancient Israel. They differed, however, in interpreting its basic character. Whereas Kaufmann looked for pure beginning and of true faith, Wellhausen was obsessed with natural and spontaneous life at the beginning. To further illustrate this point, let us consider their perception of the god of ancient Israel. In Wellhausen's interpretation, Jehovah was not the almighty god of the world.[1016] "Der Gott Israels war nicht der All-

---

1013 Wellhausen, *Israelitische und jüdische Geschichte*, 16.
1014 Kaufmann, *Toledot* II, 111–113.
1015 Kaufmann, *From the Secret of the Biblical World*, 30.
1016 Of the name Jehovah, Wellhausen explains, "Der Name Jahve scheint zu bedeuten: er fährt durch die Lüfte, er weht." See Wellhausen, *Israelitische und jüdische Geschichte*, 23.

mächtige, sondern nur der mächtigste unter den Göttern. Er stand neben ihnen
und hatte mit ihnen zu kämpfen; Kamos und Dagon und Hadad waren ihm
durchaus vergleichbar, minder mächtig, aber nicht minder real wie er selber."[1017]
Moreover, Wellhausen pointed out the essential character of Yahweh as warrior
god. "Jahve war das Feldgeschrei dieser kriegerischen Eidgenossenschaft, der
kürzeste Ausdruck dessen, was sie unter sich einigte und gegen außen schied.
Israel bedeutet "El streitet" und Jahve war der streitende El, nach dem die Nation
sich benannte."[1018] More revealing is Wellhausen's assertion that the Israelites'
perception of their God was not entirely different from that of other nations. It
was only later in the course of Israel's history that the conception of the deity
changed. To quote Wellhausen:

> The relation of Jehovah to Israel was in its nature and origin a natural one; there was no
> interval between Him and His people to call for thought or question. Only when the exis-
> tence of Israel had come to be threatened by the Syrians and Assyrians, did such prophets
> as Elijah and Amos raise the Deity high above the people, sever the natural bond between
> them, and put in its place a relation depending on conditions, conditions of a moral char-
> acter.[1019]

By contrast, Kaufmann built his theory of the history of Israelite religion on the
idea of a Supreme god. Disagreeing with Wellhausen's proposition, Kaufmann
stressed everywhere that the essential idea of Israelite religion was its conception of god.[1020] He articulated this understanding in the following way:

> The essential idea of the religion of Israel which distinguishes it from the religions of the
> world is the idea of God above all. The idea is of God who controls everything and is not
> subject to supra power which connects Him with mythology and magic. The key of the re-
> ligion of Israel is: Yahweh is God. It is not the idea of numbers which sees God as one of
> many, but the idea of absolute sovereignty. This idea frees the God from mythology, magic,
> and paganism. This is what makes the Israelite religion unique in its origin and essence.[1021]

Going back to Wellhausen, we note that he ascribed the major change in the concept of god in Israel to the prophets. In Wellhausen's view it was not until the
time of the prophets that the moral aspect in the religion of Yahweh appeared.
The prophet Amos was the first to introduce the idea of the righteousness of god:

1017 Wellhausen, *Israelitische und jüdische Geschichte*, 29.
1018 Wellhausen, *Israelitische und jüdische Geschichte*, 23.
1019 Wellhausen, *Prolegomena*, 417.
1020 Kaufmann, *Toledot* I, 227.
1021 Kaufmann, "The Religion of Israel," in *Encyclopaedia Biblica*, 729–730.

> Nach dem populären Glauben war Jahve durch den Kultus an Israel gerufen wurde weil er nur dort mit seinem Namen bekannt war, nur dort angerufen wurde, nur dort seine Wohnung und seine Altäre hatte. Dieses Band durchschneidet Amos. Jahve ist kein Gott, der der Opfer und Gaben bedarf, der sich durch sie bestechen läßt, der um des Kultus willen blindlings die Partei seiner Verehrer und guten Bekannten ergreift. Was er von Israel verlangt, ist etwas Allgemeingültiges, nämlich die Gerechtigkeit.[1022]

As mentioned, Wellhausen argued that Yahweh was not a universal god from the beginning. Yahweh was conceived in Israel as the god of their nation. The idea that Yahweh was god for the whole world came late. For Wellhausen, it would have been strange for Moses to have introduced a new conception of god to his unknowing people:

> Jahve war nicht von jeher der Weltgott und wurde dann der Gott Israels, sondern er war von Haus aus der Gott Israels und wurde dann (sehr viel später) der Weltgott. Mit dem, aufgeklärten Gottesbegriff hätte Moses den Israeliten einen Stein statt eines Brotes gegeben.[1023]

Kaufmann, too, shared Wellhausen's view that Yahweh was a notional god of Israel. However, Kaufmann offered a new explanation as to the national character of Yahweh[1024]. He proposed that Yahweh was conceived in Israel as a national god because he revealed himself only to the Israelites and therefore had become "known" (נודע) to them. Yahweh did not dismiss other nations, but his name and the Torah were "unknown" (נעלם) to them. Thus did Kaufmann dispense with the problem of the universal concept of Yahweh, by suggesting that Yahweh was *known* in Israel and *unknown* to other nations.[1025]

To go into more depth on the differences between Wellhausen and Kaufmann, we should consider their respective views on monotheism. According to Wellhausen, the religion of Israel changed in the course of its history. Only gradually did the religion of Israel drag itself up from heathenism. As Wellhausen put it, "Die israelitische Religion hat sich aus dem Heidentum erst allmählich emporgearbeitet; das eben ist der Inhalt ihrer Geschichte. Sie hat nicht mit einem

---

1022 Wellhausen, *Grundrisse zum Alten Testament*, 91.
1023 Wellhausen, *Grundrisse zum Alten Testament*, 20.
1024 It should be mentioned that Kaufmann criticized Martin Buber for accepting the developmental theory concerning the conception of God. According to Kaufmann, this theory put forward the idea that until the Israelites entered into Canaan God was conceived as God of shepherds and afterwards he became God of farmers in the land. The developmental theory postulated that until the time of Amos there was no "lord of history", and that other nations had their own gods. Even during the exile, there was no "god of the universe". The real universalism began only with second Isaiah. See Kaufmann, *From the Secret of the Biblical World*, 269.
1025 Kaufmann, *From the Secret of the Biblical World*, 41.

absolut neuen Anfang begonnen."[1026] Kaufmann, in contrast, contended that monotheism was not a product of Israel's history and did not grow up gradually. Rather, it was monotheism that shaped the entire history of Israel. As I see it, this main contention between Wellhausen and Kaufmann is pertinent to religious development. To put it another way, Kaufmann rejected the evolutionary theory, arguing that it did not fit the peculiar character of Israelite religion.[1027] He believed that monotheism emerged in Israel as an entirely new, intuitive idea, a groundbreaking product with no precedent.

To really understand Wellhausen and Kaufmann's views on the history of religious development in ancient Israel, we should examine how they arrived at such different conclusions. Based on his dating of the sources of the Pentateuch to different historical periods, Wellhausen concluded that Israelite religion had passed through various stages of development.[1028] Wellhausen's idea of religious development, however, did not mean that he understood the different phases of Israelite religion in terms of evolutionism.[1029] He built a structure according to which the course of Israelite religion moved from the popular belief of the people, where nothing seems to have been prescribed or fixed, to a stage where Israelite religion became the religion of the law. Between the two phases of ancient Israel and Judaism, Wellhausen regarded the prophetic religion as a transitional period.[1030] Thus he divided the history of Israelite religion into three periods according to which the religion of Israel went through successive stages, each of which bears the stamp of its time. The implication of Wellhausen's structure is clear. The religion of early Israel was characterized by close connection with the life and daily affairs of the people. Post-exilic Judaism was, in contrast, a complete degradation of spontaneity and naturalness. Judaism, in Wellhausen's

---

1026 Wellhausen, *Israelitische und jüdische Geschichte*, 32.

1027 Benjamin Mazar pointed out that although Kaufmann did not say so explicitly, he nevertheless "accepts the view of modern research as to the general ways of development: discontinuous development, invisible processes, and sudden revelation of the new". See Benjamin Mazar, *Judges* (The World History of the Jewish People 3; London: Allen, 1971), 219.

1028 For Wellhausen's view on the history of Israelite religion, see Chapter 2 above.

1029 See Hans G. Kippenberg, *Die Entdeckung der Religionsgeschichte: Religionswissenschaft und Moderne* (Munchen: Beck, 1997), 101.

1030 Wellhausen differentiated between the religion of early Israel or pre-prophetic religion, prophetic religion, and the religion of Judaism. He credited the prophetic reformation for introducing the moral and ethical dimensions to the religion of Yahweh. However, Wellhausen was aware that the prophets did not entirely transform the old practice of the people into a new form of religion. Herbert Hahn pointed out that Wellhausen felt strongly that post-exilic Judaism rather than prophetic religion was the antithesis of the early religion of Israel. See Herbert F. Hahn, "Wellhausen's Interpretation of Israel's Religious History," 301.

view, separated life from religion and became immersed in rituals and ceremonies. Having distinguished the religion of early Israel from Judaism, Wellhausen deduced that monotheism was a product of Israel's history and, therefore, it did not exist from the very beginning.[1031]

Kaufmann challenged Wellhausen's hypothesis regarding the history of Israelite religion. Kaufmann was convinced that the basic character of Israelite religion remained intact.[1032] That is why he argued for religious *revolution* instead of religious *evolution*. In his view, religious diversity in ancient Israel did not account for different beliefs, nor did it presuppose stages of development. To Kaufmann, all forms of Israelite religion were the creation of the people of Israel.[1033] As mentioned, Kaufmann regarded the sources of the Torah as different manifestations of one basic and unified faith.[1034] In a telling quotation, Kaufmann propounded his view about the course of religious development in Israel as follows:

> Israelite religion did not, of course, spring full-blown into existence. Like every cultural phenomenon, it underwent an evolution in time. It arose in the wilderness, took on new forms in Canaan, and reached a climax in the middle of the eighth century with the rise of classical prophecy. After the destruction of the Temple, it evolved forms enabling it to exist apart from its land. It developed a new doctrine of retribution. A stage was reached when it declared war upon the religion of the heathen and aspired to become a universal religion. But this development was organic, like that of a living organism, all of whose stages are latent in the seed but appear only gradually, one by one. In the life of Israel the seed of a new religious idea was sown in antiquity; throughout the ages this idea continued to realize and embody in new forms the latent possibilities it harboured.[1035]

Although Kaufmann speaks about evolution and development, he seems to have worked out a different understanding of these two terms. He did not refute the idea of development in itself, but he did not regard development as progress.[1036] Moreover, Kaufmann tended to understand Israel's religious history in terms of

---

1031 Wellhausen continued the same line of thought in his Arabic and Islamic studies. He assumed that religion moved from particularism and polytheism to monotheism. On this see Wellhausen, *Reste arabischen Heidentums* (Berlin: Reimer, 1897), 217. However, Uffenheimer criticized Wellhausen's view on monotheism, maintaining that Wellhausen's method "was based on the assumption that monotheism is basically an intellectual theory, arrived at by contemplation and speculation on the part of a small elitist group, the prophets, who fervently opposed the commonly accepted crude and primitive folk religion, pagan by nature..." See Uffenheimer, "Myth and Reality in Ancient Israel," 150.
1032 Kaufmann, "The Biblical Age," 14.
1033 See Chapter 5 above.
1034 See Chapter 4 above.
1035 Kaufmann, "The Biblical Age," 14.
1036 Kaufmann, *Gola VeNackar* I, 36.

development not *evolution*. That is to say Kaufmann recognizes a change in the history of Israelite religion that kept the "seed" of religious idea intact. For him, the history of Israelite religion was the historical development of one basic idea that was monotheism.[1037] As it seems to me, Kaufmann embraced an ambivalent view concerning the history of Israelite religion. On the one hand, he claimed that Israelite religion bore no relation to surrounding cultures and that its monotheistic idea was completely different from pagan religions. On the other hand, he saw the development of Israelite religion as something that occurred in history, not as *progress or evolution*, but rather a *revolution*. Kaufmann's doctrine remains unchanged; Israelite monotheism was an entirely new religious idea unknown to other peoples or religions.[1038]

Kaufmann's chief objection to religious evolution accorded well with his interpretation of the history of Israelite religion.[1039] He asserted that the religion of Israel did not take the route from national-polytheistic religion to monolatry and monotheism.[1040] Kaufmann's view was based on two assumptions. First, he contended that myth was absent from the historical development of Israelite religion.[1041] Second, he put forward the idea that the biblical literature did not know the pagan doctrine of belief in gods. Paganism in Israel, said Kaufmann, was conceived of as fetishism. Kaufmann, then, concluded that polytheism

---

1037 Peter Slyomovics, "Yehezkel Kaufmann's Critique of Wellhausen: A Philosophical-Historical Perspective (in Hebrew)" *Zion* 49 (1984): 61–92 (79).

1038 Thomas Krapf noted that Kaufmann distinguished between primitive religion and higher religion. According to Krapf, this implied that Kaufmann might have employed the evolutionary view. In addition, Krapf remarked that Kaufmann's interpretation of the beginning of Israelite religion alluded to the evolutionist conception, especially when considering Kaufmann's view that Israelite religion emerged within the high culture and civilization of Babylon, Egypt, and Canaan. On this see Thomas M. Krapf, *Yehezkel Kaufmann: Ein Lebens- und Erkenntnisweg zur Theologie der Hebräischen Bibel*, 101–104. Moshe Greenberg, in contrast, supported Kaufmann's understanding of the history of religious development. He wrote, "Kaufmann's inclination to interpret the atypical in the light of the typical has resulted in the charge that he is anti-evolutionary, that he sees without perspective. It is true that he denies an evolution from the pagan to the Israelite conception of deity. The biblical monotheistic idea is, for him, a new intuition or reality, not an arithmetic matter of diminishing the number of the gods... but in tracing the evolution of the monotheistic idea itself in Israel, Kaufmann has outdone his critics." See Greenberg, *Studies in the Bible*, 182.

1039 It is worth noting that Kaufmann rejected the theories of Herbert Spencer and Tylor on the history of religion, see Kaufmann, *Toledot* I, 286.

1040 On this see Kaufmann, *Toledot* I, 590–591, 612–622, 677–684.

1041 Ithamar Gruenwald called for a reconsideration of the relationship between myth and monotheistic religion. He argues that myth occupies a central position at the heart of religion. On this see Ithamar Gruenwald, "God the 'stone/rock': Myth, Idolatry, and Cultic Fetishism in Ancient Israel." *Journal of Religion* 76, no 3 (1996): 428–449.

was, in essence, mythological. Thus, he deduced that the monumental feature of Israelite religion was the absence of mythological polytheism.[1042] More revealing was Kaufmann's claim that there was no struggle against mythological gods in Israelite religion.[1043]

Furthermore, Kaufmann attempted to invalidate the assumption that popular religion was idolatrous. In order to connect the popular faith with the national culture of Israel, Kaufmann envisaged the idea of a "creative force of national spirit".[1044] Kaufmann sought to prove that the development of Israelite religion was not a gradual process. Rather, the history of Israelite religion was a reflection of an organic embodiment of a basic idea.[1045] This embodiment was in itself a development. Kaufmann went further to maintain that monotheism in Israel was not merely a notion or thought, nor a theological-philosophical dogma, but an essential idea of popular culture, a complete perception of the world. He then deduced that it was out of this new religious idea that the peculiar character of Israel's culture came into being.[1046]

Kaufmann's denial of Wellhausen's hypothesis on religious evolution in ancient Israel related to his objection to the literary development of the Hebrew Bible. Kaufmann relied on the assumption that the Torah preceded the literary prophets and therefore its religious horizon was prior to the prophetic doctrines.[1047] Opposing the critical view, Kaufmann challenged the traditional viewpoint and put the biblical literature in the order of Torah, Prophets and Historiography. This meant, according to Kaufmann, that Israel's earliest stage of religious history was to be traced back to the Torah. Furthermore, Kaufmann proposed that the Torah, along with the historical books, developed independently of the literary prophets. He concluded that the historical horizon of the Torah-

---

1042 Kaufmann "The Bible and Mythological Polytheism," 179–197.
1043 Kaufmann, *From the Secret of the Biblical World*, 38–39.
1044 See Chapter 7 above.
1045 Kaufmann, "The Biblical Age," 14.
1046 Although Kaufmann seemed to have pictured the history of Israelite religion as something out of the laws of nature, he nevertheless sought to connect it with historical conditions. He said that the embodiment of Israel's religious idea depended on the historical conditions of each period. But in the spiritual history, so Kaufmann, we have to consider this idea as an independent force. This was the case with regard to the basic idea of the early history of Israel's faith. For a discussion see Kaufmann, *Toledot* I, 11.
1047 For a discussion on Kaufmann's view about prophecy and its impact on his interpretation of Israelite religion, see Uffenheimer, "Yehezkel Kaufmann: Historian and Philosopher of Biblical Monotheism," 14–15.

group differed from prophetic ideas,[1048] reflecting the priestly and popular religion of the people.[1049]

It turns out that Kaufmann underestimated the impact of prophetic doctrines on the history of Israelite religion, especially in its formative period, that is, the age prior to classic prophecy.[1050] Kaufmann's far-reaching conclusion was that the prophets and their beliefs were immersed in popular religion and built upon it. It is, then, no surprise that Kaufmann dated the monotheistic idea to the desert period. This idea originated in the history of Israel from its very beginning and the prophets took the popular monotheism for granted.[1051] Kaufmann took issue with what he called the school of Wellhausen, which bound the rise of monotheism in Israel to the prophets. In Kaufmann's words:

> The opinion that it was the prophets who formulated the monotheistic explanation of the catastrophe is based on the assumption of the school of Wellhausen that prophecy preceded the law, which assumption is specious. The priestly-popular religion which is crystallized in the Pentateuch preceded classical prophecy...the people remained faithful to the ancient monotheistic belief.[1052]

1048 According to Kaufmann, "Classical prophecy sprang from the soil of Israel's popular monotheism... was rooted in and grew out of the early religion. It does not so much repudiate the popular religion as rise above it...from the popular religion classical prophecy received its idea of the one God..." See Kaufmann, *The Religion of Israel*, 344. Moreover, Kaufmann emphasized that the classical prophets created a new literature, but that they were steeped in the literature of the past. In Kaufmann's view, Jeremiah was strongly influenced by Deut and Ezekiel by the Priestly Code. See Kaufmann, *The Religion of Israel*, 344–345.

1049 Kaufmann distinguished between two periods in the history of monotheism: the time of the popular religion which embodied the literature of the Torah, and the prophetic religion which appeared in the prophetic books. See Kaufmann, *Toledot* I, 623.

1050 Kaufmann contended that Israelite religion was a popular religion in the pre-exilic period. This would mean that the prophets had no influence on the monotheistic idea as depicted in the Torah-group. Kaufmann went further and maintained that the Books of Job, Proverbs and Psalms were pre-exilic products that did not contain prophetic influence. According to Kaufmann, the implication of this was that the Torah-group, Psalms, Job and Proverbs dated from the First Temple period. All of this indicates and confirms the popular character of Israelite religion. See Kaufmann's introduction to the second volume of *Toledot*.

1051 Kaufmann described the religion of Israel as "folk religion," not a product of an elite group. He rejected Wellhausen's judgment that the prophets rebelled against the popular religion of the people. In Kaufmann's mind, the prophets accepted the same belief in Yahweh. The contribution of the classic prophets, from Amos onwards, lay mainly in their ethical interpretation of the tradition. See Uffenheimer, "Yehezkel Kaufmann: Historian and Philosopher of Biblical Monotheism," 15. See further Greenberg, *Studies in the Bible*, 179. See also Ziony Zevit, *The Religions of Ancient Israel*, 44–45.

1052 Kaufmann, *History of the Religion of Israel, vol. IV: From the Babylonian Captivity to the End of Prophecy*, 22.

In contrast to Wellhausen who regarded Isaiah's prophecy as a radical change from the old popular religion,[1053] Kaufmann gave credit to the popular belief, considering it the main stream from which the prophets derived their religious ideas. The fundamental point that Kaufmann strove to establish was that popular religion should not be taken as naïve and idolatrous, as critical scholarship would have it, but as a monotheistic religion. Kaufmann supported this premise through his interpretation of the nature of popular idolatry and paganism.[1054] Differing from the view of Wellhausen, that the prophets repudiated the idolatrous elements of their popular religion,[1055] Kaufmann contended that idolatry had been a mere superficial phenomenon and not fundamental to the religion of the people.[1056]

Moving from this basic difference between Wellhausen and Kaufmann regarding religious development in ancient Israel, we turn to another aspect of their respective views, the relationship between Israelite religion and Canaanite religion. According to Wellhausen, Canaanite religion strongly affected the reli-

---

1053 Wellhausen, "Israel," 485.

1054 D. R. Dumm makes a good point in his observation that Kaufmann admitted that Israel was guilty of idolatry but maintained that it was not the idolatry of paganism. In Kaufmann's thinking, "The popular idolatry that prophetic books depict is thus a magical, fetishist, non-mythological worship of images, 'gods they knew not,' imported from abroad." See Kaufmann, *The Religion of Israel*, 144. This means that Israel's infidelity was therefore limited to the area of cult and rite and did not involve an acceptance of the basic postulate of paganism. The principle argument offered for this claim was the fact that the prophets consistently attacked idolatrous rite rather than myth. On this see D. R. Dumm "Book Review," *CBQ* 23 (1961): 68 – 69. Furthermore, Nahum Saran explained Kaufmann's view on the nature of popular religion, maintaining that idolatry at no time had any popular roots, no syncretism. He went onto say that the religious derivations were very limited in scope and restricted to the cult and ritual, and had very little bearing on the belief in monotheism. This indicates that Israelite idolatry was not authentic polytheism but vestigial idolatry, a vulgar phenomenon, superficial and devoid of creative force. On this see Nahum Sarna, "From Wellhausen to Kaufmann," 74.

1055 Wellhausen, *Israelitische und jüdische Geschichte*, 110.

1056 Kaufmann minimized the significance of the idolatrous practices found in pre-exilic Israel. He argued that until the exile, no foreign gods in the Book of Kings had been worshiped in the north. In Judah there was, during the time of Athaliah (Jezebel's daughter), one temple and one priest to Baal (2kig. 11: 18). Until the days of Manasseh, so Kaufmann, the presence of foreign gods and attempts to extirpate them were recorded only for the royal city. Consequently, Kaufmann concluded "The biblical arraignment is exaggerated; sins of particular groups are ascribed to the entire people...the historiographer could not account for what had taken place – the collapse of Israel's monarchy – without sin. Had there been no sin he would have had to invent it." Another point that was made by Kaufmann was that a careful evaluation of the prophetic denunciation was required, before it could be used as a historical record. See Kaufmann, *The Religion of Israel*, 134 – 135.

gion of Yahweh. Wellhausen believed that the cultural contact with the Canaanites had a deep effect on the sphere of religious worship as well.[1057] As Wellhausen put it, "The cultus, as to place, time, matter, and form, belonged almost entirely to the inheritance which Israel had received from Canaan; to distinguish what belonged to the worship of Jehovah from that which belonged to Baal was no easy matter."[1058]

Kaufmann, an advocate of the uniqueness of Israelite religion, developed a different understanding. He minimized the influence of Canaanite religion on the religion of Israel.[1059] His basic tenet was that Israelite religion remained intact and there was no foreign impact on its essential features.[1060] Moreover, Kaufmann disputed syncretism in the form Yahweh-Baal. He further accused the adherents of this view of distorting the history of Israelite religion. This, however, did not prevent Kaufmann from acknowledging the existence of what he called the fossil remains of pagan nations.[1061] Nevertheless, Kaufmann maintained that idolatry did not grow to be a popular or national faith in Canaan.[1062] Because the

---

1057 Wellhausen, *Israelitische und jüdische Geschichte*, 44–48.

1058 Wellhausen, "Israel," 469.

1059 Kaufmann restricted the Canaanite's influence on Israelite religion to the period before settlement. Thus, Kaufmann for example, wrote "Israel's sacrificial terminology (and surely its practice as well) was influenced by the Canaanites. These influences may be assumed to have been absorbed by the tribes during their wanderings in Canaan in patriarchal times." See Kaufmann, *The Religion of Israel*, 220.

1060 In support of his position, Kaufmann put forward the hypothesis of a total destruction of the Canaanites. In his view, "...biblical sources do not refer Israel's apostasy to the influence of domestic Canaanites. This has been shown to be in harmony with other lines of evidence pointing to the historicity of the biblical tradition that the Canaanites were subject to the Ḥērem." See Kaufmann, *The Religion of Israel*, 254.

1061 According to Kaufmann, "The religion of YHWH could take hold of the people only after overcoming the ancient faith, and the fossil remains of pagan notions that have been preserved in the Bible testify that it was never wholly eradicated." See Kaufmann, *The Religion of Israel*, 8, 20, 114.

1062 Kaufmann arguments can be summed as follow: 1) In the Former Prophets to 1 Kgs 16 (Ahab-Jezebel), there are no hints at popular worship of Baal. The story of Joash (Judges 6) is an individual episode and cannot be used as strong evidence. Moreover, Kaufmann insisted that none of the Judges was engaged in a conflict against Baal's worship; 2) There is no single story in the Bible that refers to the influence of Canaanite idolatry within the real land of Israel; 3) The only mention of the impact of Canaanite's idolatry is found in (Judg 3:5 – 6), only as historical framework. Here the story hints at the Canaanite who lived outside the boundaries of the real land of Israel; 4) The Bible does not know mythological polytheism, but only fetishist idolatry. The religious revolution demolished the idolatry and replaced it with monotheistic faith. For more discussion see Kaufmann, *The Religion of Israel*, 138–141; also, idem, *Commentary on the Book of Judges*, 34–35; idem, *Commentary on Joshua*, 85.

monotheistic idea was ingrained in Israelite faith, idolatry was destroyed in one fell swoop. More important was Kaufmann's view that the battle was directed against the idolatrous cult only, not against the myth.[1063] Interestingly, Kaufmann put forward the idea that idolatry in Israel was a result of biblical historiography.[1064] He went on to say that even the literature of the pre-exilic period was basically monotheistic.[1065]

As for the history of worship in ancient Israel, it is clear that Wellhausen did not differentiate the Israelites from their neighbours. He wrote, "Im ganzen und großen ist der Kultus der Brauch aller Welt, seit Noah, ja seit Kain und Abel; der Unterschied ist nur, daß die Israeliten ihn dem Jahve, die anderen Völker anderen Göttern weihen. Das ist die alte, gesunde volkstümliche Betrachtungsweise."[1066] By contrast, Kaufmann made a sharp distinction between Israelite worship and that of other nations. Moreover, he pointed out that Israel's religion, in comparison to the pagan religion, "is entirely ignorant of the close relationship between magic and the gods; it knows nothing of the cosmic-mythological basis of the pagan cult; it has no appreciation of the symbolic value of Images."[1067]

Kaufmann, then, was repudiating the early beginnings of Israel's faith (against idolatry and myth), whereas Wellhausen was contextualizing it. This is another example of how Wellhausen and Kaufmann understood differently the nature of Israelite religion. While Wellhausen tended more to interpret Israelite religion in its context, Kaufmann preferred to put Israel's religion in opposition to its environment. In other words, Wellhausen held that the history of Israelite religion was the history of interaction and assimilation with Canaanite

---

1063 Kaufmann, *Toledot* I, 685. Kaufmann paid much more attention to the problem of mythology and its relation to the religion of Israel. Thus, Kaufmann wrote "In contrast to the philosophic attack on Greek popular religion, and in contrast to the later Jewish and Christian polemics, biblical religion shows no trace of having undertaken deliberately to suppress and repudiate mythology. There is no evidence that the gods and their myths were ever a central issue in the religion of YHWH. And yet this religion is non-mythological." See Kaufmann, *The Religion of Israel*, 20.
1064 Kaufmann, *Toledot* II, 160.
1065 Kaufmann, *Toledot* II, 238. According to Kaufmann, the biblical period did not know idolatry. Kaufmann contended that biblical scholarship did not understand the nature of the biblical age. He argued that scholars did not comprehend the secret of the basic phenomenon of the Israelite religion. As a result, so Kaufmann, instead of accepting the idea that the biblical age was a monotheistic period, scholars used to label it as idolatrous. On this see Kaufmann, *From the Secret of the Biblical World*, 33.
1066 Wellhausen, *Israelitische und jüdische Geschichte*, 17.
1067 Kaufmann, *The Religion of Israel*, 19–20.

religion.[1068] Kaufmann, on the other hand, disputed that there was an amalgamation of Israelite religion with other religions which in his opinion were paganistic.

Wellhausen built his structure of interpretation on the basis of the relationship of Yahweh to his people. As Wellhausen put it, "Jahve der Gott Israels und Israel das Volk Jahves – das ist zu allen Zeiten der kurze Inbegriff der israelitischen Religion gewesen."[1069] With the appearance of this relation, so Wellhausen, "beginnt die Geschichte Israels."[1070] This was the constitution of Israelite religion which relied on a natural relationship. The later national unity of the Israelites was the outcome of religion. In Wellhausen's words:

> Es wurde späterhin auf einen bestimmten Akt der Bundschließung zurückgeführt, während es ursprünglich als natürlich galt, nicht als vertragsmäßig und lösbar. Die Teile waren älter als das Ganze, das Volk. Die Stämme und Geschlechter wurden zu einer nationalen Einheit zusammengefaßt durch die Religion, durch Jahve.[1071]

With this borne in mind, one cannot fail to notice that the history of Israelite religion, according to Wellhausen, shows the passage from the religion of the people to the higher level of prophetic doctrine about the god of the world. Wellhausen described this move as follows:

> Jahve hat einen Kampf zu bestehen gehabt mit den anderen Mächten, mit denen er sich anfangs vertrug, und hat sie überwunden. Und er selbst ist in diesem Kampfe gewachsen...erst beim Untergangs des Volks, der von den Propheten vorausempfunden wurde, erhob er (Jahve)sich über dessen Grenzen zum Gott der Menschenwelt und der Welt überhaupt. Erst dann wurde er für seine Person ganz unabhängig vom Kultus.[1072]

Looking for the history of religion in the sphere of human creativity, Kaufmann evaluated the character of Israelite religion in quite different manner. The natural and naive features that Wellhausen ascribed to the early phase of Israelite re-

---

1068 Wellhausen emphasized that the people of Israel had taken up the Canaanite's culture and religion. He wrote, "Diese Veränderung ihres Lebens beeinflußte auch ihre Religion. Wie sie die Wohnstätten und Höfe, die Felder und Gärten, die Keltern und Tennen von ihren Vorgängern übernahmen, so auch die Heiligtümer, die sogenannten Bamoth, mit ihrem Zubehör nicht selten wohl auch mit ihren alten Priesterfamilien." See Wellhausen, *Grundrisse zum Alten Testament*, 82.

1069 Wellhausen, *Grundrisse zum Alten Testament*, 73.

1070 Wellhausen, "Die Israelitisch-Jüdische Religion," in *Die Kultur der Gegenwart: Ihre Entwicklung und ihre Ziele* (ed. Paul Hinneberg; Berlin: Teubner, 1906), 1–40 (8).

1071 Wellhausen, „Die Israelitisch-Jüdische Religion," 8.

1072 Wellhausen, *Grundrisse zum Alten Testament*, 80–81.

ligion were absent from Kaufmann's construction. In Kaufmann's view, Yahweh was a supreme god from the very beginning. He asserted that Israelite religion emerged out of original spirit and its monotheistic idea was a product of Israel's national culture.[1073] Kaufmann further contended that Israel's culture was never idolatrous and, therefore, monotheism could appear only among non-idolatrous people.[1074]

While Wellhausen distinguished different stages in the religious history of early Israel, Kaufmann spoke about a persistent faith that remained unaltered.[1075] To further illustrate this point, we note that Wellhausen differentiated between pre-prophetic religion in its primitive perception of Yawheh and prophetic religion which emphasized the aspects of ethics and righteousness. In addition, Wellhausen degraded Judaism which replaced the natural religion of early Israelites with institutions and binding laws. Kaufmann utterly denied Wellhausen's structure, maintaining that the history of Israelite religion was the history of monotheism. Throughout its course, so Kaufmann, the basic idea of Israelite religion underwent no changes.

It thus appears that Wellhausen differentiated a bit too much between ancient Israel and Judaism, whereas Kaufmann was determined to find Judaism in ancient Israel. To put it differently, Wellhausen spoke too much about Judaism and too little about Israel. Kaufmann, in contrast, focussed too much on Israel but little on Judaism. As I see it, Wellhausen began at the end whereas Kaufmann looked at the beginning. There is, however, one further point that deserves mention. Wellhausen regarded Deuteronomy, which crowned the work of the prophets, as a transitional period between Israel and Judaism. Kaufmann, on the other hand, was in favour of one basic and constant line of belief that persisted throughout the centuries, that is monotheism.

We should also note that their respective views on Israel's religious history were related to their understanding of Israel's history. Wellhausen reconstructed different stages of both Israel's religion and history. Kaufmann, in contrast, inclined to interpret Israel's history and religion as based on a firm idea, that is,

---

1073 Kaufmann, *From the Secret of the Biblical World*, 22–23.

1074 Kaufmann, *Toledot* I, 736.

1075 Peter Slyomovics points out that Kaufmann, unlike Wellhausen and Hegel, did not distinguish different categories of ideas. He mentions that Kaufmann regarded paganism and monotheism as two different types of religions that represented two contrasting worldviews. He suggests that Kaufmann did not discuss monotheism as something developed out of polytheism, but focused on the basic ideas of both religions. See Peter Slyomovics, "Yehezkel Kaufmann's Critique of Wellhausen," 74. See further Kaufmann, *From the Secret of the Biblical World*, 54.

monotheism from the beginning. As we shall see, these two opposite views reflect different understandings of history and religion.

3.2 History and history writing

The reader of Wellhausen's *Israelitische und jüdische Geschichte* will realize immediately that Wellhausen was very critical regarding the biblical account of Israel's history. In less than 50 pages, Wellhausen outlined Israel's history from the beginning to the rise of monarchy. This, of course, was because Wellhausen had downgraded the credibility of the biblical narrative, especially those parts belonging to the Jewish tradition of the post-exilic time. Kaufmann, on the other hand, recounted Israel's history from the patriarchal period to the dawn of monarchy in more than 150 pages.[1076] In dealing with the biblical texts Kaufmann began with an assumption of their basic truthfulness. To some extent, Kaufmann was uncritical of biblical texts.

We note that Wellhausen's history of ancient Israel before the Exile contained three main features. First, Wellhausen considered that Moses was the culture-hero creator of the nation of Israel. The second was Wellhausen's premise of the fusion of the Hebrew tribes with the Canaanites and acceptance of their culture. Wellhausen's third point was the emergence of monarchy and the beginning of Israel's political history with Saul and David. According to Wellhausen, the patriarchal stories did not reflect authentic information about the earliest history of Israel. He assumed that Israel had not become a real people until the days of Moses. According to Wellhausen, Israel's history began with Moses.[1077] It was under Moses's leadership that Israel continued to be moulded. Moses was the first to elicit the feeling of Israel's national unity. "It was also [Moses] who maintained it in life and cherished its growth."[1078]

Following this further, Wellhausen wrote that the next great step in ancient Israel's history took place in the land of Canaan. However, he asserted, the tribes entered into Canaan as nomads in search of pasture, not as the elected people with a divine promise. The most important change occurred in the life of the early Israelites when they assimilated with Canaanite and accepted their culture. In Wellhausen's words, "The Hebrews learned to participate in the culture of the

---

1076 Kaufmann, *Toledot* II.
1077 Wellhausen, *Israelitische und jüdische Geschichte*, 23, 28.
1078 Wellhausen "Israel," 434.

Canaanites, and quietly entered into the enjoyment of the labours of their predecessors."[1079]

The third and most important phase in Israel's history started with monarchy. Wellhausen was impressed by figures such as Saul and David who "made out of the Hebrew tribes a real people in the political sense."[1080] Wellhausen further maintained:

> It was they [Saul and David] who drew the life of the people together at a centre, and gave it an aim; to them the nation is indebted for its historical self-consciousness. All the order of aftertimes is built up on the monarchy; it is the soil out of which all the other institutions of Israel grow up.[1081]

This so far is Wellhausen's sketch of the history of Israel up to monarchic period. Comparing Wellhausen's picture of early Israel with that of Kaufmann, we observe several things. Kaufmann accepted Wellhausen's view that Israel's history began with Moses, but differed from him in a few details. Thus, for example, Kaufmann did not entirely deny the patriarchs as historical figures, but he questioned their monotheistic faith.[1082] Moses, according to Kaufmann, introduced a religious revolution.[1083] It is here that we notice the cleft that separates the views of these two giants. Although Wellhausen credited Moses as being the founder of Israel and its religion, he did not overstate the content of his message.[1084] Kauf-

---

1079 Wellhausen "Israel," 434, 446.

1080 Wellhausen, *Prolegomena*, 413.

1081 Wellhausen, *Prolegomena*, 413.

1082 According to Kaufmann, historical monotheism began with Moses. He claimed that the patriarchal stratum signified their existence as "wanderings families." In point of fact, Kaufmann rejected the view that held the patriarchs to be later-constructed figures or "projections" of monarchic times, as Wellhausen would have it. He affirmed that the tribal element was prior to the patriarchs. On this see Kaufmann, *Commentary on Joshua*, 50–56. Furthermore, Kaufmann propounded that the Israelite tribes of the "Sons of Jacob" appeared at early times and the stories that narrate the lives of the patriarchs found its place among them. See Kaufmann, *Toledot* II, 15–16.

1083 Kaufmann, *The Religion of Israel*, 227.

1084 According to Wellhausen, "To Moses, who had been the means of so brilliantly helping out of their first straits the Hebrews who had accompanied him out of Egypt, they naturally turned in all subsequent difficulties; before him they brought all affairs with which they were not themselves able to cope. The authority which his antecedents had secured for him made him as matter of course the great national 'Kadhi' in the wilderness." See Wellhausen, *Prolegomena*, 434.

mann, in contrast, said that monotheism began with Moses and that he was the first apostle prophet with a mission.[1085]

Furthermore, Kaufmann refused to regard Israel as a primitive, natural or ethnic community. In his view, Israel was a child of prophecy.[1086] Unlike Wellhausen, who suggested that the history of ancient Israel did not rest on covenant theology or principles of Mosaic Law, Kaufmann contended that Israel became a nation through a covenant based on a divine law.[1087] To quote Kaufmann:

> Covenant imposed a new moral responsibility on the tribes in addition to and beyond that of the individual. Having been elected *en masse*, and having heard together the divine moral commands, the people as a whole become answerable for their moral state. An intensification of moral demands is the outcome of the prophetic and communal nature of the Sinaitic Covenant.[1088]

Again, Kaufmann's picture of Israel's history was based on the early dating of monotheism. This was why, for instance, Kaufmann supported the invasion theory according to which Canaan was conquered by massive war. In Kaufmann's thinking, it was the *Ḥērem* war that enabled the monotheistic people to settle in Canaan. Kaufmann the goes too far, in my opinion, by maintaining that the monarchy grew out of the monotheistic idea.[1089] David, according to Kaufmann, was a political figure and his kingdom was *hesed Elohim*.[1090] Thus, while Wellhausen was impressed by the monarchy along with its figures (Saul and David) and institutions, we find that Kaufmann exalted apostle-prophecy as a new religious phenomenon out of which the unique monotheistic idea unfolded.

It is quite clear that both Wellhausen and Kaufmann agreed on the beginning of Israel's early Moses history but differed about the character of Moses, his people and about what happened thereafter. Wellhausen felt, "Wir haben allerdings nur eine dunkle Kunde von Moses, keine authentischen Zeugnisse, am wenigsten von seiner Hand."[1091] To Kaufmann, the authenticity of Moses was

---

1085 In Kaufmann's view, the stories about Moses demonstrated that the Israelites did not know Yahweh in Egypt. The people of Israel were not a monotheistic people before Moses. The monotheistic belief was limited to individual patriarchs, while the rest of the people were pagans…It was during the time of Moses that historical monotheism could be dated. Hence Kaufmann concluded that the monotheistic revolution of the Torah told reliably of events as they happened among the tribes of Israel. See Kaufmann, *Toledot* II, 36.

1086 Kaufmann, "The Biblical Age," 24.

1087 Kaufmann, "The Biblical Age," 24.

1088 Kaufmann, "The Biblical Age," 24.

1089 Kaufmann, *Toledot* II, 109.

1090 Kaufmann, *Toledot* II, 170, 171.

1091 Wellhausen, *Grundrisse zum Alten Testament*, 73.

vouched for by reliable tradition derived from biblical literature.[1092] Whereas Wellhausen did not see anything unique in premonarchic Israel except for the figure of Moses as founder of a nation, Kaufmann talked about covenant, apostle prophecy, and above all monotheism as a primal intuition in Israel's history. In contrast to Wellhausen, who affirmed that Israel first developed in Canaan and its real history began with David, Kaufmann contended that the Israelite tribes entered into a covenant with Yahweh and were given a divine promise to settle in the land of Canaan.

As for the question of their view on history, both Wellhausen and Kaufmann posed very stimulating questions about history and history writing. Wellhausen's famous statement "History, it is well known, has always to be constructed...The question is whether one constructs well or ill."[1093] Though this seems to present a complete understanding of the task of the historian, Wellhausen did not intend to stop there. In his investigation of the beginning of Israel's history, Wellhausen would end the second chapter of *Israelitische und jüdische Geschichte* with the following words:

> Warum die israelitische Geschichte von einem annähernd gleichen Anfange aus zu einem ganz andern Endergebnis geführt hat als etwa die moabitische, läßt sich schließlich nicht erklären. Wohl aber läßt sich *eine Reihe von Übergängen* beschreiben, in denen der Weg vom Heidentum bis zum vernünftigen Gottesdienst, im Geist und in der Wahrheit, zurückgelegt wurde.[1094]

In his explanation of the uniqueness of Israelite religion,[1095] Kaufmann raised a question similar to that of Wellhausen. But while Wellhausen recognized "eine

---

1092 Kaufmann, *Toledot* II, 37 – 40, 334 – 348; idem, *From the Secret of the Biblical World*, 60 – 61.

1093 Wellhausen, *Prolegomena*, 367.

1094 Wellhausen, *Israelitische und jüdische Geschichte*, 33. (Emphasis is mine).

1095 Judging from his interpretation of Israelite religion, Kaufmann's approach to the history of ancient Israel seems to reflect the metaphysical point of view. This appeared in his explanation of the role of what he called "creative spirit" (רוח יוצר). For more on this subject, see Kaufmann, *From the Secret of the Biblical World*, 14, 16, 20 – 21, 27 – 28. In what seems to be a support of Kaufmann's position, Menahem Haran argued that Kaufmann did not represent his idea in metaphysical way. Haran pointed out that Kaufmann's conception of *spirit* meant that it could not be revealed by scientific research. See Menahem Haran, "On the Border of Faith", 54. Moreover, Eliezer Schweid mentions that Kaufmann by characterizing the function of the creative spirit as national consciousness had transformed the idealistic-metaphysic conception into a sociological anthropological one. See Eliezer Schweid, "Biblical Critic or Philosophical Exegete? The Influence of Herman Cohen's The Religion of Reason in Yehezkel Kaufmann's History of Israelite Religion," 424. In the same context, Slyomovics remarks that Kaufmann's definition of *ruah* as primal intuition ex nihilo referred to the influence of Hermann Cohen's philosophy. In addition, Slyomovics

Reihe von Übergängen," Kaufmann spoke about "an ultimate mystery". As Kaufmann put it:

> Why was Israel thus unique among all the peoples in its religious world view? The believer answers: Israel was chosen; the empirical historian can only say: here is revealed the creative genius of the nation. Neither answer is completely satisfying, for no creation of the spirit can be completely explained; there is an *ultimate mystery* which always eludes us. We may be able to describe the historical circumstances of its appearance; that is the most we can hope for.[1096]

Comparisons between Wellhausen and Kaufmann such as the one above illustrate their common ground as well as their differences. Thus for example Wellhausen wrote that Israel's history trod a different path from that of the Moabites which "ultimately could not be explained" (*läßt sich schließlich nicht erklären*). One can find a similar formulation by Kaufmann, who drew attention to the "ultimate mystery" that marked Israel's religion. Nevertheless, Wellhausen and Kaufmann sensed something quite different in Israel's history. Wellhausen thought of it as a "series of transitions" (*eine Reihe von Übergängen*).[1097] Kaufmann, on the other hand, appeared reluctant to accept the notion of change or transition.[1098]

Perhaps we could say that both Wellhausen and Kaufmann realized the difficulties of the historical reconstruction of ancient Israel. Nevertheless, they gave deep thought to dealing with the problems. Wellhausen provided two useful insights for grasping the history of ancient Israel. With the first, he called for critical reading of the text and analysis of its tendency. This was based on Wellhausen's conviction that "no fancy is pure fancy; every imagination has underlying it some elements of reality by which it can be laid hold of, even should these only

---

mentioned that Kaufmann did not connect the definition of *ruah* to development. Here, Slyomovics noted that the real divide between Kaufmann on the one hand, and Wellhausen and Hegel on the other, could be detected. For a discussion see Peter Slycmovics, "Yehezkel Kaufmann's Critique of Wellhausen," 73. Job Y. Jindo presupposes a different understanding of Kaufmann. He points out that Kaufmann studied history "on the basis of verifiable facts, by applying a constant set of principles deduced from the observation of general cultural and religious phenomena. Kaufmann's empirical approach, however, was different from that of other empiricists, who would reject transcendental and metaphysical components all together. Kaufmann did not deny the existence of the transcendental and the metaphysical, but rather chose not to discuss them in his study of history." See Job Y. Jindo, " Revisiting Kaufmann," 61.
1096 Kaufmann, "The Biblical Age," 14. (Emphasis is mine).
1097 Wellhausen, *Israelitische und jüdische Geschichte*, 33.
1098 Kaufmann, "The Biblical Age," 14.

be certain prevailing notions of a particular period."[1099] His second insight was the application of analogy, as can be deduced from his statement "Die israelitische Geschichte wird erst dadurch zu einer wirklichen Geschichte und bleibt nicht außerhalb aller Analogie mit der Geschichte der ganzen übrigen Menschheit."[1100]

Kaufmann, on the other hand, acknowledged the limitation of historical studies in explaining unique phenomena.[1101] Attempting to explain the rise of monotheism with Moses, he declared "Why and how this idea arose in his mind we do not know. We should not know even if we possessed more than those remarkable legends relating the revelation made to Moses. It is possible, however, to delineate the social and historical background of that revelation."[1102] Similarly, Kaufmann described how it was difficult to explain some mysterious "sparks" of original creativity. He argued that monotheism was something that could and need not be explained by historical studies.[1103] For this reason, Kaufmann called for inquiry into the idea after its emergence, not into its motives.[1104] In describing the emergence of monotheism, Kaufmann wrote:

> Monotheism... was "created by the unique and creative word." It sparked like lightning inside the intuitive consciousness of the tribes that had left Egypt or in the intuitive vision of the first prophet-messenger, Moses. It is impossible to 'explain' this spark of striking and original creativity. The birth of every novel and original idea happens with a mysterious spark, and therefore, any attempt to explain it is inconsequential-imaginative.[1105]

In order to have a complete understanding of Wellhausen and Kaufmann, we should highlight their positions regarding how Israel's history is treated in the Hebrew Bible. It is known that Wellhausen regarded the Book of Chronicles as "a second history running parallel with the Books of Samuel and Kings."[1106]

1099 Wellhausen, *Prolegomena*, 161.
1100 Wellhausen, *Grundrisse zum Alten Testament*, 81.
1101 Menahem Haran, "On the Border of Faith," 54.
1102 Kaufmann, *The Religion of Israel*, 227.
1103 Job Y. Jindo, "Revisiting Kaufmann," 64.
1104 Thomas Krapf points to three characteristics of Kaufmann's approach: 1) the central place of metaphysics in the biblical religion; 2) denial of evolution; 3) "the creative spirit" as the significant factor in the human history. On this see Thomas M. Krapf, *Yehezkel Kaufmann: Ein Lebens- und Erkenntnisweg zur Theologie der Hebräischen Bibel*, 43.
1105 Kaufmann, *Toledot* II, 41. Menahem Haran, "On the Border of Faith," 54. Translation is taken from Job Y. Jindo, "Revisiting Kaufmann," 64.
1106 According to Wellhausen, "When the narrative of Chronicles runs parallel with the older historical books of the canon, it makes no real additions, but the tradition is merely differently

Wellhausen assumed that Israel's past was remoulded in the Book of Chronicles in accordance with the ideology of the priestly writing. [1107]As Wellhausen put it:

> The Books of Samuel and of Kings were edited in the Babylonian exile; Chronicles, on the other hand, was composed fully three hundred years later, after the downfall of the Persian Empire, out of the very midst of fully developed Judaism. We shall now proceed to show that the mere difference of date fully accounts for the varying ways in which the two histories represent the same facts and events, and the difference of spirit arises from the influence of the Priestly Code which came into existence in the interval.[1108]

Kaufmann worked with a different understanding of biblical historiography. He avoided talking about any kind of recasting or reshaping of the tradition under the influence of a dominant view or ideology, as Wellhausen did. Instead, Kaufmann built his view of biblical historiography on the basis of how Israel's destiny was depicted in the biblical literature. This is apparent in Kaufmann's distinction between former prophets and literary prophets. Thus Kaufmann explained that the historiography of these two groups was not similar. In the former prophets the decisive factor which led to catastrophe was the sin of idolatry and the worship of Baal, whereas in the literary prophets the moral-religious factor was the cause of destruction. Kaufmann went further and said that even the Book of Kings, which told the story of destruction, did not recognise moral sin but was only concerned with idolatry as the primary cause of destruction.[1109]

Furthermore, Kaufmann proposed that biblical historiography started during the period of Judges. In his view, actual documentation began early in the period of Judges, not during monarchy.[1110] According to Kaufmann, the Torah represented the period of poem and legend, but historical writings appeared with the Book of Joshua. He deduced that historical literature emerged in Israel during the period of Judges.[1111] Seen from Wellhausen's perspective, the literary period

---

coloured, under the influence of contemporary motives. In the picture it gives, the writer's own present is reflected, not antiquity." See Wellhausen, *Prolegomena*, 211.

1107 For a discussion of Wellhausen's view on Chronicles, see Eugene Ulrich ed., *Priests, Prophets, and Scribes: Essays on the Formation and Heritage of Second Temple Judaism in Honour of Joseph Blenkinsopp* (Sheffield: JSOT Press, 1992), 37–39.

1108 Wellhausen, *Prolegomena*, 171.

1109 Kaufmann, *Commentary on Judges*, 30.

1110 In Kaufmann's view, the divine will was the subject of history. He believed that the history of Israel was the history of the word of God. The God of Israel was manifested in the events of Israel's history and therefore these events became history. See Kaufmann, *Toledot* II, 153.

1111 Kaufmann, *Toledot* II, 154.

of Israel could hardly have started before the ninth century BCE.[1112] Here we notice that Wellhausen and Kaufmann worked from a different understanding of biblical historiography and literature.

Wellhausen and Kaufmann also elucidated the Exile and its effect on Israel's history and religion in quite opposite ways. From Wellhausen we read in his *Prolegomena:*

> The Babylonian exile, which violently tore the nation away from its native soil, and kept it apart for half a century, a breach of historical continuity than which it is almost impossible to conceive a greater. The new generation had no natural, but only an artificial relation to the times of old; the firmly rooted growths of the old soil, regarded as thorns by the pious, were extirpated, and the freshly ploughed fallows ready for a new sowing.[1113]

Here Wellhausen is referring to the fundamental changes that take place in the history of the nation. More important is Wellhausen's confirmation that the Exile brought about discontinuity with the past. Wellhausen, in effect, differentiates between the Israel of pre-exilic times, with its natural and spontaneous faith, and the Judaism of post-exilic times as an artificial religion.[1114] Looking at Kaufmann's position, we find that he agreed that exile influenced Israelite religion; "It was not only the people that went into exile, but their religion as well."[1115] However, Kaufmann insisted that even after the loss of nationhood, Israelite religion was still able to retain its peculiar character. In Kaufmann's view, the Exile had no great effect on faith in Yahweh.[1116] He maintained that the exiles were a monotheistic people.[1117] Moreover, Kaufmann argued, "It was precisely in exile that the full stature of Israelite religion began to manifest itself."[1118] He summed up his view in this regard as follows:

1112 Wellhausen proposed that the golden age of Hebrew literature dated from the period of the Kings and Prophets which preceded the dissolution of the two Israelite kingdoms by the Assyrians. See Wellhausen, *Prolegomena*, 9.
1113 Wellhausen, *Prolegomena*, 28.
1114 It has been said that "Wellhausen used the exile as a defining event in his analysis of Israelite religion and the composition of the Bible. Wellhausen's historical and literary analyses helped elevate the exile to its dominating role in biblical criticism. One biblical scholar has even suggested that it would be fair to say that Wellhausen discovered the exile." See William M. Schniedewind, *How the Bible Became a Book: The Textualization of Ancient Israel* (Cambridge: Cambridge University Press, 2004), 140.
1115 kaufmannm, "The Biblical Age," 76.
1116 Kaufmann, *The Religion of Israel*, 440–441.
1117 Kaufmann, *The Religion of Israel*, 102.
1118 Kaufmann, *The Religion of Israel*, 450–451.

Although its national and territorial basis had been destroyed, its inner strength remained undiminished. Diaspora gradually assimilated the foreign, pagan culture, but did not accept pagan religion...it testifies to the distinctiveness of Israelite religion, to its vitality, which proved to be independent of time and place and unabated by pagan civilization.[1119]

3.3 Authority of biblical texts

The question to be discussed in this section is whether the biblical text can be used for writing about ancient Israel? We have seen throughout my discussion of Wellhausen and Kaufmann that they agreed on the beginning of Israel's history with Moses but parted ways regarding what happened afterwards. They shared the view that religion determined Israel's history but differed on dating the rise of monotheism in Israel. Both accepted the source analysis approach, but they diverged concerning the chronology of the sources and the dates of their composition.

It should be mentioned that the literary question of the Pentateuch has been and still is the decisive factor in reconstructing Israel's history and the development of Israelite religion.[1120] Biblical scholars vary in their opinions as to whether the literary traditions of early Israel can be used for historical purposes or if they offer an unrealistic description of the genuine history of ancient Israel. Both Wellhausen and Kaufmann agreed that Israel's literary tradition was the main source for writing about ancient Israel. They depended on data and insights gained from literary investigation. The literary strata that Wellhausen and Kaufmann identified in the Old Testament were similar; with the exception that Kaufmann discerned Near Eastern materials in Genesis.[1121]

In the course of his scholarly career, Wellhausen worked on the literary sources of the Hebrew Bible, the New Testament and Islam. The results he gained from critical analysis of the pertinent sources were later used to write the history of Israel, Christianity, and early Islam. As for Kaufmann, we note that he devoted the first book of *Tcledot* to the literary problem of the Pentateuch. However, the literary question of the Pentateuch was not the starting point of Kaufmann's career. He, nevertheless, turned to studying the Bible with the hope of refining the

1119 Kaufmann, "The Biblical Age," 77.
1120 For recent discussion on this issue, see Reinhard G. Kratz, "The Pentateuch in Current Research: Consensus and Debate," In *The Pentateuch: International Perspectives on Current Research* (ed.Thomas B. Dozeman, Konrad Schmid and Baruch J. Schwartz; Tübingen: Mohr Siebeck, 2011), 31–61.
1121 Kaufmann, *The Religion of Israel*, 208.

results of historical criticism.[1122] It is true that Kaufmann's innovations lay primarily in his study of Israelite religion and the origin of monotheism. But he realized that this quest was linked with source analysis and literary criticism of the Pentateuch. In what follows I aim to show how Wellhausen and Kaufmann dealt with the question of literary sources of the Pentateuch. I also consider their views on the authority of the biblical text.

As mentioned, both Wellhausen and Kaufmann recognized the source-critical approach of documentary hypothesis.[1123] The real divide between them was not about the content of the Pentateuchal sources but their historical order. The main features of Wellhausen's hypothesis on the history of the Pentateuch/Hexateuch are as follows: Wellhausen identified four sources in the Pentateuch: J (9th century BCE), E (8th century BCE), D (7th century BCE), P (6th or 5th century BCE). According to Wellhausen's analysis, the Jehovist (JE) was a purely historical document and legal material was incorporated into it in a second stage.[1124] Moreover, Wellhausen followed de Wette's lead, that Deuteronomy was promulgated in Josiah's time. As for the dating of P's materials, Wellhausen ascribed them to the post-exilic period.

As far as Kaufmann was concerned, he accepted the documentary hypothesis in its classic formulation.[1125] Kaufmann had no quarrel with Wellhausen's analysis of the content and the narrative framework of the sources.[1126] What

---

1122 Kaufmann, *The Religion of Israel*, 1.

1123 It is worth noting that Kaufmann criticized the Scandinavian school and its religious-historical views; "How this school conceives the manner in which the Torah came into being is quite unclear in details. Particularly erroneous is their view that Torah and prophecy became written literature only in late times." See Kaufmann, *The Religion of Israel*, 156, n.1. For a discussion of the "documentary hypothesis" as paradigm in Old Testament Scholarship, see Rolf Rendtorff, "The Paragidm is Changing: Hopes and Fears," *Biblical Interpretation*, 1, 1 (1993): 34–53.

1124 Wellhausen, "Pentateuch and Joshua," 506.

1125 Umberto Cassuto mentioned that Kaufmann recognized the documentary hypothesis but challenged some of its basic premises. As he puts it, "Kaufmann successfully opposes a given portion of its concepts, as he does in his valuable studies on the history of the Israelite religion, still accepts the fundamental principle of the customary division of the text according to sources, and bases his views thereon." See Umberto Cassuto, *The Documentary Hypothesis and the Composition of the Pentateuch: Eight Lectures* (Jerusalem: Magnes Press, 1961), 8.

1126 There are, however, few instances in which Kaufmann disagreed with Wellhausen regarding the narrative framework of the biblical books. For example, against Wellhausen (Die Composition des Hexateuchs, 128–129) that Joshua (chs.14–17) composed from two different traditions, Kaufmann argued that (Josh.14: 1) is a continuation of (Josh.13: 32) and there is no place for (Joshu.18: 1). Kaufmann also rejected Wellhausen's interpretation of (Josh. 19). For more on this issue, see Kaufmann, *Commentary on Joshua*, 172, 228.

Kaufmann rejected was Wellhausen's order of the sources and the dating of the Torah's literature. Kaufmann explained his position regarding biblical criticism so:

> Such of its findings as the analysis of three chief sources in the Torah (JE, P, and D) have stood the test of inquiry and may be considered established But its basic postulate – that the priestly stratum of the Torah was composed in the Babylonian exile, and that the literature of the Torah was still being written and revised in and after the Exile – is untenable.[1127]

Interesting is that Kaufmann diverged here from Wellhausen's view on the compositional date of the Pentateuchal documents. His analysis of the pentateucal sources sought to reverse Wellhausen's order, going back to pre-Wellhausen's time. Thus, according to Kaufmann, the JEP sources were composed before the seventh century. With regard to Deuteronomy Kaufmann contended, "It has long been recognized that there is an *early nucleus* in Deut and that only the legislation about the *unification of the cult* can be assigned to the 7th century."[1128] The implication of Kaufmann's thoughts is clear: none of the sources was composed during or after the exile. In Kaufmann's view, P was not aware of D's centralization and therefore it must "have been composed before the age of Hezekiah."[1129] More important was Kaufmann's conclusion that "Josiah's age marks the beginning of the emergence of the Torah book out of the Torah literature."[1130]

As for the legal corpora in the Pentateuch, we find that Wellhausen identified the following codes:

1127 Kaufmann, *The Religion of Israel*, 1.
1128 Kaufmann, *The Biblical Account of the Conquest of Palestine*, 4. John Bright criticized Kaufmann's distinction between 'early Deut' and 'late Deut', writing "Now it seems to me that this represents not only an abandonment of the accepted results of criticism, but an abandonment of sound critical method as well. For to distinguish between an 'early Deut' and a 'late Deut' in the manner that Kaufmann does, and to assert that such a style might have been written at any period, means no less than to discard style as an effective tool of the critical method." See John Bright, *Early Israel in Recent History Writing*, 74.
1129 In his opposition to Wellhausen's late dating of P, Kaufmann argued, "The idea that P is dominated by the exilic mood of national guilt is wrong. That mood brought into prominence the new cult forms of confession and prayer without sacrifice often illustrated in Daniel, Ezra, and Nehemiah. These are not found in P. The sins that P's sacrifices atone for are unwitting transgressions of the individual and the community, especially sins involving impurity (Lev. 4–5; Num. 15:25; cf. Lev. 16: 16ff.). The sin offering, an innovation of P according to Wellhausen, is brought only for unwitting sins and has no reference to the historical sin of the nation. P knows of no special rite for atoning national sin." See Kaufmann, *The Religion of Israel*, 205–206, n. 16.
1130 Kaufmann, *The Religion of Israel*, 209; also, idem, *Toledot* I, 212.

> Es sind jedoch verschiedene legislative Schichten im Pentateuch zusammengestellt, die si-
> naitische, die deuteronomische und die priesterliche. Sie ergänzen sich nicht, sondern folgen
> auf einander; die priesterliche fußt auf der deuteronomischen, diese auf der sinaitischen. Sie
> sind aus einem geschichtlichen Prozeß erwachsen und bezeichnen dessen Stadien.[1131]

Kaufmann found, like Wellhausen, that "there are three legal corpora, differing from one another in their general style and juristic terminology, containing parallel and at times contradictory laws."[1132] Moreover, Kaufmann conceded, "The present Torah book was not in pre-exilic times canonical and binding upon the nation. The literature that was to become incorporated in the Torah existed in various documents and versions."[1133] Kaufmann also acknowledged that "Deuteronomy was promulgated in the reign of Josiah, and that the Torah as a whole was promulgated and fixed in the time of Ezra-Nehemiah."[1134]

We should now ask what the points of dispute between Wellhausen and Kaufmann actually were. As far as the biblical literature is concerned, Kaufmann rejected Wellhausen's characterization of the Torah's literature as a later priestly formulation of prophetic teaching.[1135] Kaufmann undertook to invalidate Wellhausen's position by arguing that the Torah was a product of Israel's earliest literature, a stage prior to literary prophecy.[1136] In his discussion of the relationship between Torah and prophecy Kaufmann arrived at the following conclusions:

> 1. In the historical books of the Torah group, literary prophecy is never mentioned; 2. In
> none of the books of the Torah group is there an awareness of the ideas originated by
> the literary prophets regarding the history of Israel, the relation of morality to cult, and es-
> chatology; 3. The idea of a central, chosen sanctuary, one of the pervading themes of the
> Torah literature, is absent in pre-Deuteronomic prophecy. The Josianic reform has, there-
> fore, no roots in literary prophecy, though it does in the Torah literature.[1137]

It must be emphasized that Wellhausen was impressed by the teachings of the prophets, who stressed the significance of morality over rituals.[1138] It is also true that Wellhausen placed the Prophets before the Torah. However, and this point seemed to have been overlooked, Wellhausen did not exaggerate the reli-

---

1131 Wellhausen, *Israelitische und jüdische Geschichte*, 15.
1132 Kaufmann, *The Religion of Israel*, 156.
1133 Kaufmann, *The Religion of Israel*, 156.
1134 Kaufmann, *The Religion of Israel*, 157.
1135 Kaufmann, *The Religion of Israel*, 157.
1136 For a discussion of Kaufmann's view, see Efraim Urbach, "Neue Wege der Bibelwissenschaft".
1137 Kaufmann, *The Religion of Israel*, 165.
1138 Wellhausen, *Israelitische und jüdische Geschichte*, 106, 168, 174.

gion of the prophets.[1139] We read in *Prolegomena*, "The prophets did not form the tradition at first, but came after, shedding upon it their peculiar light. Their interest in history was not so great that they felt it necessary to write it down; they only infused their own spirit into it subsequently."[1140] Here we should examine Wellhausen's assertion that the prophets had less interest in writing down the tradition.

According to Wellhausen there had not been a written Torah in pre-exilic Israel. As Wellhausen put it, "What distinguishes Judaism from ancient Israel is *the written Torah*."[1141] This does not mean that Wellhausen denied the existence of the Torah. As he clearly put it, "Ancient Israel was certainly not without God – given basis for the ordering of human life; only they were not fixed in writing."[1142] The central point in Wellhausen's system was that the Torah existed in ancient Israel, but not as fixed laws. To illustrate, I quote Wellhausen:

> Much greater importance is attached to the special Torah of Jehovah, which not only sets up laws of action of universal validity, but shows man the way in special cases of difficulty, where he is at a loss. This Torah is one of the special gifts with which Israel is endowed (Deuteronomy xxxiii. 4); and it is entrusted to the priests, whose influence, during the period of the Hebrew kings...rested much more on this possession than on the privilege of sacrifice. The verb from which Torah is derived signifies in its earliest usage to give direction, decision.[1143]

In addition, Wellhausen's interpretation of the Torah in ancient Israel as sets of instructions instead of prescribed laws was based on the fact that he dated much of the legal materials in the Pentateuch to the post-exilic period. Thus, Wellhausen's structure about dating the priestly materials became more coherent as it accorded with his view that the Torah was not written law in early Israel. Referring to its late composition, Wellhausen affirmed, "The Priestly Code is the quintessence not of the oral tradition, but of the tradition when already written down."[1144]

1139 Rudolf Smend drew attention to Wellhausen's awareness "that prophecy could make one forget the historical role played by other factors, especially the priesthood." See Rudolf Smend, *From Astruc to Zimmerli: Old Testament Scholarship in Three Centuries* (Tübingen: Mohr Siebeck, 2007), 100.
1140 Wellhausen, *Prolegomena*, 29.
1141 Wellhausen, *Prolegomena*, 410.
1142 Wellhausen, *Prolegomena*, 393.
1143 Wellhausen, *Prolegomena*, 394.
1144 Wellhausen, *Prolegomena*, 336.

In contrast to Wellhausen, who suggested that the Torah functioned in early Israel only to provide decisions, Kaufmann, insisted that the Torah as a book of binding law appeared in pre-exilic Israel. He wrote:

> The first book of Torah...was Deuteronomy. The law of JE and P is the background of the account of Josiah's Passover (II Kings 23:21–3); in accord with D's provisions Josiah did away with the ancient home sacrifice of JE and P. A covenant was concluded with the people to observe the newly discovered Torah book; henceforth, the book was accepted as binding divine law.[1145]

Assuming the validity of Kaufmann's analysis we could ask what the condition of material preserved in the JEP was if Deuteronomy was the first book of the Torah. Kaufmann answered this question so:

> We cannot know; apparently it was still on individual scrolls. P was probably also extant in several versions, one of which was the basis of the laws of Ezekiel. Concerning the principles of selection, no more can be said than that whatever was believed to be the genuine word of God was incorporated, intact and unrevised, into the new book; the rest was suppressed. The ancient priestly materials transmitted from early times were added to the corpus of Deuteronomy. Since Deuteronomy claimed to have been the last words of Moses, the priestly corpus was arrayed before it.[1146]

In addition, Kaufmann pointed out that the legal corpora were fixed early. They were combined, however, only after their formation was completed. As Kaufmann further mentioned, "Already in early times the sources were quasi-canonical, so that later one hesitated to alter them. This diffidence reached its peak in the age of the compilation of the Torah book."[1147] Against the view that the post-exilic time was a period of writing down the traditions, Kaufmann contended, "The age of Restoration was an age of compilation, not of edition and revision, let alone of innovation."[1148]

Thus, while Wellhausen argued that the early tradition of ancient Israel was reworked during the second commonwealth, Kaufmann emphasized, "The founders of post-exilic Judaism were not the composers, but merely the collectors of the Torah literature. They did not alter anything of what they 'found written,' much less add to it."[1149] Moreover, Kaufmann tells us about ancient material that had survived intact:

1145 Kaufmann, *The Religion of Israel*, 208.
1146 Kaufmann, *The Religion of Israel*, 211.
1147 Kaufmann, *The Religion of Israel*, 209.
1148 Kaufmann, *The Religion of Israel*, 210.
1149 Kaufmann, *The Religion of Israel*, 193.

The Torah literature was crystallized at the latest by the beginning of the monarchy. It alludes briefly to the new political institution of kingship, but did not flourish on its soil. The ideas, the religious and political symbols of the Torah were fully formed by the time of the early monarchy. The literature continued, of course, to develop and pass through successive formulations; but, the symbols and ideals of early times remained intact.[1150]

That the Torah was formed during the early monarchic period, as Kaufmann would have it, contradicts Wellhausen's assumption that during the post-exilic time there had been an "artificial reawakening of dry bones, especially by literary means."[1151] Here Wellhausen was referring to the work of the Chronicler which he described as follows:

Like ivy it overspreads the dead trunk with extraneous life, blending old and new in a strange combination. It is a high estimate of tradition that leads to its being thus modernised; but in the process it is twisted and perverted, and set off with foreign accretions in the most arbitrary way.[1152]

Looking back we find that Wellhausen arrived at his theory on literary and religious development in ancient Israel via three steps. He first compared the laws of Pentateuch with religious practice as depicted in the historical and prophetic book. The purpose of this was to define what came first – law or prophets. As for the second step, Wellhausen examined the interrelationship of the legal corpora to determine the sequence of the various laws. The last step was to study the historical tradition preserved in Judges, Samuel and Kings and then compare them to the book of Chronicles. Having achieved this task Wellhausen reached the following conclusion:

In the Chronicles the pattern according to which the history of ancient Israel is represented is the Pentateuch, i.e. the Priestly Code. In the source of Chronicles, in the older historical books, the revision does not proceed upon the basis of the Priestly Code, which indeed is completely unknown to them, but on the basis of Deuteronomy. Thus in the question of the order of sequence of the two great bodies of laws, the history of the tradition leads us to the same conclusion as the history of the cultus.[1153]

Wellhausen, then, built a structure according to which the historical order of the pentateuchal sources was JE, D, and P. In Wellhausen's view, the literary development went hand in hand with the religious history of ancient Israel. Wellhau-

---

1150 Kaufmann, *The Religion of Israel*, 204, 202–203.
1151 Wellhausen, *Prolegomena*, 227.
1152 Wellhausen, *Prolegomena*, 227.
1153 Wellhausen, *Prolegomena*, 294.

sen's system, however, did not convince Kaufmann, who had great reservations regarding the chronological order of the sources and its implication for the history of Israelite religion. Although Kaufmann worked with literary criticism of the Pentateuch, he nevertheless questioned some of its findings. According to Kaufmann, "We cannot say exactly when in pre-exilic times JE or the ground form of D or P was composed. The various forms of ancient Israelite creativity developed alongside each other; they cannot be forced into an artificial pattern of evolution."[1154] Furthermore, Kaufmann did not regard the literary traditions of ancient Israel as unrelated or disparate literary pieces. He objected to the fragmentation of biblical literature and called for the following methodological issue to be considered:

> The literature of Israel has Judean and Ephraimitic, popular and priestly, early prophetic and sapiential elements. It is futile to attempt to fix the date of this material by comparing the customs and beliefs which have accidentally been preserved in the historical books with those of the Torah. For what seem to be the products of various ages may in fact have been concurrent developments of different places and circles.[1155]

Here we come up against a fundamental difference between Wellhausen and Kaufmann. Although the foregoing discussion seems to concentrate primarily on issues related to a literary problem, the main question is a methodological and philosophical one. Wellhausen's vision assumed diachronic stages. Kaufmann's approach, however, was synchronic.

As can be deduced from their respective histories, both Wellhausen and Kaufmann agreed that Israel's literary tradition was the key to reconstructing Israel's religion and history. When Wellhausen announced that he could understand Hebrew antiquity without the book of the Torah, he meant that the Torah had ceased to deliver historical information about ancient Israel. The implications of this are clear. Wellhausen's dating of the priestly materials in the Torah to the post-exilic period meant that he dispossessed pre-exilic Israel of basic concepts and institutions. For example, the monotheism of the Torah would be a later formulation and the sacred institutions, as predicted in the Torah, a product of the Jewish traditions of the Second Temple.

Kaufmann was certainly aware of the consequences to the history of Israelite religion of a late dating of the Torah.[1156] This appears, for example, in Kauf-

---

1154 Kaufmann, *The Religion of Israel*, 291.
1155 Kaufmann, *The Religion of Israel*, 291.
1156 We should remind ourselves that the aim of Kaufmann's literary analysis of the sources was to prove that the Torah contained ancient materials predating literary prophecy. He strove to prove that the pentateuchal sources (including the language, style and content) belonged to

mann's contention, "It is a basic tenet of the critical view of the history of Israel-ite religion that no monotheistic literature dates to the preprophetic period."[1157] This indicates that Kaufmann focused on the main line of Wellhausen's argu-ments, which connected the later date of the Torah with the later appearance of monotheism in Israel. And this meant, consequently, the lack of monotheistic literature at the beginning of Israel.[1158] Kaufmann criticized Wellhausen's prem-ise and sought to replace Wellhausen's system with his own. In so doing, Kauf-mann claimed that the legislative portion of the Torah predated literary prophe-cy. This, in turn, enabled Kaufmann to maintain that literary prophecy could not be used as an ideal source for reconstructing early Israelite religion. Consistent with this argument, Kaufmann assumed that the biblical literature form Gene-sis–2 Kgs was a complete literary stratum. Within this bulk of literature there were no hints as to the historical view of the prophets.[1159] Kaufmann further noted, "The classical prophets created a new literature, but they [were] steeped in the literature of the past."[1160] Moreover, Kaufmann showed that popular-priestly monotheism developed independently of the influence of the literary prophets. Building on this, Kaufmann affirmed that without this fundamental fact, we would not be able to understand the history of Israelite religion.[1161]

So far, what divided Wellhausen and Kaufmann concerned the historical order of the sources and the relationship between the Torah and prophecy. We turn now to examining their views on the authority of the biblical text. The schol-arly career of Julius Wellhausen as well as the subject matter with which he was involved, indicate that he was interested in the text and textual criticism.[1162]

---

the very beginning of Israelite religion. He even contended that the book of the Torah was his-torical proof of the early stage of Israelite monotheism – the stage prior to classical prophecy. Kaufmann also maintained that ancient materials in which the monotheistic idea could be as-certained existed in early Israel. On this see Kaufmann, *Toledot* I, 220.

1157 Kaufmann, *The Religion of Israel*, 153.

1158 Kaufmann, *Toledot* I, 13.

1159 Kaufmann, *Toledot* I, 45.

1160 Kaufmann, *The Religion of Israel*, 344.

1161 Kaufmann, *Toledot* II, 239.

1162 It was Wellhausen's interest in textual and literary criticism that gave the impression that he was mainly a philologist, not an historian. On this see, for example, Hermann Cohen, "Julius Wellhausen: Ein Abschiedsgruß", in *Jüdische Schriften*, vol. 2, 463 – 468 (463). Wellhausen him-self stated, "Ein Philologe bin ich eigentlich nicht." See Rudolf Smend, *Julius Wellhausen: Ein Bahnbrecher in drei Disziplinen*, 7. In a prestigious study about Wellhausen's principles of history writing, Boschwitz distinguished between the task of a philologist and that of an historian as follows, "Die Philologie geht vom Text aus und kehrt zum Text zurück. Die Historiographie aber drängt weit hinaus über den 'Text': über dessen Mitteilungswillen hinaus, ja diesem entge-gen, erstrebt sie ein neues eigenes Ganzes, in dem die Quellen verschwinden." For a discussion of

Wellhausen's concern with a critical approach to the text began early in 1871, as revealed in the title of his book *Der Text der Bücher Samuelis*. Pursuing his critical studies further, Wellhausen focused on the text of the Old Testament with the aim of establishing what he called the "original text" (ursprünglicher Text).[1163] This was the main task that Wellhausen hoped to accomplish in *Die Composition des Hexateuchs*. His *Prolegomena* was clearly the sum of his previous critical studies on the Hexateuch. In this ground-breaking work Wellhausen made it clear that *"texts give evidence for what they imply; not for what they say."*[1164] Thus, in numerous instances Wellhausen referred to texts that had been "corrupted".[1165] He also remarked, "Interpolation has already crept into the text of Samuel."[1166] As a literary critic, Wellhausen preferred the individual narrative, i. e. "What is essential and original is the individual element in the several stories; the connection is a secondary matter, and only introduced in the stories being collected and reduced to writing."[1167] Wellhausen, in effect, sought to make the text of the Hebrew Bible readable and suitable for historical purposes.[1168]

Whereas Wellhausen read and reconstructed the text from the perspective of historical criticism, Kaufmann read and understood it from within the Jewish historian's perspective. To put it another way, while Kaufmann claimed that he applied the historical-critical method, he nevertheless seems to have accepted the plain sense of the text.[1169] Kaufmann was convinced that the biblical texts provided historical information, even if they contained differences and inconsistencies.[1170] For more illustration of this point I quote Kaufmann, who conceded that

---

Wellhausen's usage of text for the sake of history, see Friedemann Boschwitz, *Julius Wellhausen: Motive und Maßstäbe seiner Geschichtsschreibung*, 7 – 8.

1163 See, for example, Wellhausen, *Die Composition des Hexateuchs*, 31, 42, 120.

1164 Wellhausen, *Prolegomena zur Geschichte Israels* (1905), 316. Also Thomas L. Thompson "Lester Grabbe and Historiography: An Apologia," *SJOT* 14 (2000): 140 – 161 (147).

1165 Wellhausen, *Prolegomena*, 266, 267.

1166 Wellhausen, *Prolegomena*, 177.

1167 Wellhausen, *Prolegomena*, 335.

1168 It would not be an exaggeration to say that Wellhausen tortured the text for the sake of history. In this context, Weidner observed, "Wellhausens Kritik ist daher vor allem destruktiv, allerdings destruiert er, trotz seiner historischen Methode, nicht historisch den Autor wie seine Vorgänger, sondern richtet sich gegen den Text selber und dessen Aussage." See Daniel Weidner, "Geschichte gegen den Strich bürsten: Julius Wellhausen und die jüdische Gegengeschichte," 31.

1169 This can be seen in his commentaries on Joshua (1959) and Judges (1962), in which Kaufmann was an advocate of the texts.

1170 Eliezer Schweid pointed out that for Kaufmann contradictions played no important role in changing the meaning of the text. He remarked that Kaufmann credited the text of the Torah as

the book of the Torah, "[was] compiled from ancient scrolls, embodying divergent and at times mutually contradictory matter."[1171] Kaufmann nonetheless
maintained "The Torah is a monument to the diffidence of an age which
dared not alter a jot or tittle of, much less add anything to, the ancient revelation."[1172] In addition, he minimized the impact of what he called "extreme
text-criticism" on the history of Israelite religion. He felt that reading too
much into the text could not solve complex issues. As he put it:

> The further analysis of the various editions or recensions of each source rarely leaves the
> realm of speculation. Without having demonstrated that ancient Hebrew writers ordered
> their writings in a logical manner, did not include explanatory comments and repetitions,
> etc., text critics regard lack of logical order, explanations, and repetitions as signs of com-
> pilation, expansion, and edition. Furthermore, the degree of compositeness alleged by ex-
> treme text-criticism gives cause to doubt that even the keenest critic could successfully un-
> ravel so intricate a skein. Be that as it may, such analysis has little bearing on the larger
> questions of the history of Israelite religion.[1173]

As if this were not enough, Kaufmann went further and condemned the Bible
scholars who "discover everywhere duplications, contradictions, derangements
of sequence etc., and 'emend'. According to them, the text has been tampered
with by the first, second, and third hands of 'redactors' and 'expanders'."[1174]
Seen from Kaufmann's perspective, "It does not occur to scholars that the biblical author wrote in an entirely different way, and not according to the schema of
a Latin composition."[1175] However, Kaufmann's position towards textual criticism
did not mean that he radically rejected the historical-critical method. He informs
us, "The search for 'sources' was based on some objective factor, or at least, constituted an attempt to achieve a certain degree of objectivity."[1176] What Kaufmann refuted, however, was analysis based on "considerations which are purely
subjective and [of] the dogmatic assumptions of some personal theory which the

---

being authentic. He also noted that Kaufmann like, Hermann Cohen, considered that the differences in language, style, and duplications were not enough to evaluate the text. The idea and the
content of the text had to be taken into account. See Eliezer Schweid, *A History of Modern Jewish
Religious Philosophy*, vol. 5 (In Hebrew) (trans. Leonard Levin; Supplements to the Journal of
Jewish Thought and Philosophy 14; Leiden; Brill, 2011), 157.
1171 Kaufmann, *The Religion of Israel*, 448.
1172 Kaufmann, *The Religion of Israel*, 448.
1173 Kaufmann, *The Religion of Israel*, 156.
1174 Kaufmann, *The Biblical Account*, 2.
1175 Kaufmann, *The Biblical Account*, 2–3.
1176 Kaufmann, *The Biblical Account*, 3.

text must be made to fit."[1177] In his appraisal of Kaufmann's approach, Moshe Greenberg wrote:

> Kaufmann's great strength lay unquestionably in the philosophic, analytic sphere – in the discrimination, interrelation, and development of ideas. His strictly historical and philological contributions, though often containing valuable and suggestive insights, generally lack the same creative brilliance. Here the critic comes to the fore, exposing the weakness in the theories of his predecessors, rather than the master-builder. His historical and exegetical work is similar in that both aim to make sense out of the given data with a minimum of recourse to extrinsic sources. Kaufmann endeavours to show the given in the most plausible light, and while he does not hesitate to emend, rearrange, or excise texts when he feels it necessary, he has done more than most modern scholars to make the biblical text cohere without such recourse.[1178]

We thus note that while Wellhausen attempted to reconstruct the text in order to make it more consistent for historical purposes, Kaufmann felt that the text enabled us to understand Israel's history without exercising too much criticism of its content. In other words, if Wellhausen's reconstruction can be described as an attempt to grasp history through criticizing the thoughts expressed in the text, Kaufmann, in contrast, insisted that the historian should accept what the text said. It is here, as I see it, that the real divide between Wellhausen and Kaufmann can most clearly be observed. The former was a critical scholar working deep under the surface of the text, whereas the latter credited the authority of the text without being critical of its content.[1179]

1177 Kaufmann, *The Biblical Account*, 3.
1178 Greenberg, *Studies in the Bible*, 184.
1179 If one follows Menahem Haran's distinction between criticism and exegesis, it can be said that Wellhausen applied the critical method, whereas Kaufmann reckoned on the traditional exegetical view. According to Haran, the fundamental difference between exegesis and criticism is that "criticism interprets the history of Israel and of biblical literature as resulting from historical conditions, whereas in exegesis such factors have no importance for the comprehension of Scripture...the postulates of criticism, which are inextricably bound to its secular essence, are its lifeblood and from their efficacy it functions, whereas in exegesis they are non-existent. It is no wonder, therefore, that exegesis terminates without crossing the threshold of criticism, while the latter takes up only where exegesis has concluded its task." See Menahem Haran, "Midrashic and Literal Exegesis and the Critical Method in Biblical Research," in *Studies in Bible* (ed. S. Japhet; ScrHier 31; Jerusalem: Magness, 1986), 45–56 (37). Converesly, Job Y. Jindo, suggested that Kaufmann did not follow traditional exegetes. See Job Y. Jindo, "Recontextualizing Kaufmann: His Empirical Conception of the Bible and Its Significance in Jewish Intellectual History," 111.

Consequently, the structures that Wellhausen and Kaufmann built were logical consequences of their methodological premises.[1180] However, the common thing between Wellhausen and Kaufmann was, as mentioned earlier, their reliance on literary sources as the starting point for reconstructing Israel's religion and history. That is to say, the respective histories of Wellhausen and Kaufmann were based on data deduced from Israel's literary tradition. Both paid less attention to either the pre-literary stage or to external and extra-biblical sources. We have also seen that Wellhausen and Kaufmann agreed that the sources of the Pentateuch were the authoritative text for writing about ancient Israel. Moreover, both Wellhausen and Kaufmann shared the common view that biblical literature was bound up with Israel's religion and history.

Having demonstrated the main similarities and differences between Wellhausen and Kaufmann, their positions can be summarized as follows. It has been shown that both Wellhausen and Kaufmann accepted the basic premises of the critical source analysis approach. However, while Wellhausen characterized the age before the 9th century BCE as the non-literary period,[1181] Kaufmann argued that Israel's historical literature began early during the period of Judges.[1182] Furthermore, we have made it clear that while Wellhausen assigned the larger part of Torah literature to the exilic and post-exilic period, Kaufmann placed the whole of the Torah literature in pre-exilic Israel. What divided the thinking of these two scholars was the order of the composition of pentateuchal sources and the results drawn from it.[1183] Wellhausen, in accordance with his literary criticism, questioned the historical dating of the law and ascribed it to the Second Temple period. Kaufmann, in contrast, worked out a different hypothe-

---

1180 Nahum Sarna pointed out that Wellhausen's and Kaufmann's results were the natural outcome of their methodology. As he put it, "Wellhausen's system is quite logical; his documentary hypothesis and his chronological order for the sources led him drastically to reconstruct the history of Israel's religion. To him it was clear that Israel was not a monotheistic people until the end of the biblical area. Kaufmann, too, is perfectly logical. His reversal of Wellhausen's chronology leads him to the opposite conclusion. Israel was a monotheist people from its very inception and the whole of biblical literature is a product of a monotheistic environment." See Nahum Sarna, "From Wellhausen to Kaufmann," 70.
1181 According to Wellhausen, the Hebrew literature first flourished after the Syrians had been repulsed. However, Wellhausen asserted, "Writing of course had been practiced from a much earlier period, but only in formal instruments, mainly upon stone.". He further wrote, "The question why it was that Elijah and Elisha committed nothing to writing, while Amos a hundred years later is an author, hardly admits of any other answer than that in the interval a non-literary had developed into a literary age." See Wellhausen, "Israel," 464–465.
1182 Kaufmann, *Toledot* II, 154.
1183 Kaufmann, *Toledot* I, 22.

sis. He argued that the law was formulated prior to literary prophecy and, therefore, reflected the earliest stage of Israelite religion.[1184]

Wellhausen and Kaufmann did, however, share common ground. They attempted to reconstruct Israel's history and religion based on evidence from
"within". That is, they seem to have taken on the inside paradigm, according
to which Israel's history was to be interpreted in the light of materials derived
from Israelite tradition, i. e. literary sources. Having reached this point, we can
safely say that both Wellhausen and Kaufmann followed the inside approach,
but while Kaufmann accepted it as given, Wellhausen turned this account on
its head.

1184 On Kaufmann's reading "The prophets told the realistic history of Israel after its electing
and the giving of the law...the prophets are the necessary completion and indispensable historical explanation of the Torah..." See Kaufmann, *History of the Religion of Israel, vol. IV: From the
Babylonian Captivity to the End of Prophecy*, 490.

Chapter Nine:
Early Israel: Priestly Ideal or Prophetic Theocracy?

1 Introduction

As can be drawn from the foregoing discussion, both Wellhausen and Kaufmann had some points in common: i. e. religion as the decisive factor in Israel's history, Moses's time marking the beginning of Israel as a nation, and literary tradition as the point of departure in reconstructing the history of ancient Israel. It has been shown that Kaufmann's dispute with Wellhausen revolved around the central question of dating the Priestly Code.[1185] But the controversy between Wellhausen and Kaufmann extended to more than this. Let us consider the question of whether post-exilic theocracy reflected on the priestly writings. In my view, answering this question would help us to have a more comprehensive picture of the actual divide between Wellhausen and Kaufmann. There are, to be sure, several issues connected with this question, for example, the beginning of institutions in ancient Israel and the role of priests and prophets. All of these points are interrelated and should therefore be examined carefully.

In support of his argument for the late dating of the Priestly Code, Wellhausen called attention to P's negative attitude towards monarchy. For Wellhausen this implied a rejection of institutions that were not administered by the law and the Torah. Wellhausen, thus identified P with the conditions of post-exilic times, when the Jewish community was governed by high priests under foreign domination. Wellhausen arrived at the idea that the Priestly Code represented the theocratic ideal of the Second Temple.

[1185] It should be mentioned that much of the criticism from Jewish scholars against Wellhausen's hypothesis centered on his dating the Priestly Code. The best-known example in this regard is the work of David Hoffmann (*Die Wichtigsten Instanzen gegen die Graf-Wellhausensche Hypothese*) who in 1903 provided a comprehensive criticism of Wellhausen's hypothesis. Following the lead of Hoffmann, many Jewish scholars (Yehezkel Kaufmann, Menahem Haran, Jacob Milgrom, and Israel Knohl) argued for the antiquity of P. They started a line of criticism against Wellhausen's hypothesis, investigating the social background of P and D (Weinfeld, 1972) or focusing primarily on linguistic issues (Hurvitz, 1982). For a discussion see Rudolf Smend, *Epochen der Bibelkritik*, 209. Erich Zenger, "Priesterschrift" *TRE* 27 (1997): 435–446. Also Henning G. Reventlow, *Epochen der Bibelauslegung*, vol.4, 409. Benjamin Sommer, *Jewish Concepts of Scripture*, 226. On Jewish biblical criticism, see Hans-Joachim Bechtoldt, *Die jüdische Bibelkritik im 19. Jahrhundert* (Stuttgart: Kohlhammer, 1995), 414–423.

Opposing Wellhausen's view, Kaufmann worked with a different understanding of the Priestly Code. Kaufmann contended that P, like all sources of the Pentateuch (JE and D), reflected the life of the people of Israel in the pre-exilic period. He rejected Wellhausen's claims that P reflected the post-exilic theocracy. In Kaufmann's words:

> Die „Theokratie" des P ist nicht der nachexilischen, sondern derjenigen des JE ähnlich, wenn auch, wie gesagt, priesterlich gefärbt. Sie ist Prophetokratie und nicht Hierokratie; ihren Mittelpunkt bildet das Orakelzelt eines Kriegsvolkes und nicht die deuteronomische Opferstätte einer Kultusgemeinde. Man kann in P das „Spiegelbild" der nachexilischen Zeit nur dann finden, wenn man Kriegslager und Offenbarung außer acht läßt, dann die Gesetzgebung des P im Anschluß an das Judentum deuteronomisiert und das Orakelzelt in eine deuteronomische Opferstatte verwandelt und so das „Spiegelbild" der nachexilischen Gemeinde in P künstlich selbst hineinprojiziert. In Wirklichkeit aber ist das Verhältnis des P zu dieser Gemeinde genau dasselbe, wie das der anderen vordeuteronomischen Quellen des Pentateuchs.[1186]

While it is true that the controversy between Wellhausen and Kaufmann starts with the historical placing of the Priestly Source[1187], it extends to cover other issues and therefore has more important implications for the history of ancient Israel. When we consider their perception of the theocratic idea, the following crucial questions arise: Did theocracy exist in ancient Israel? What is meant by theocracy? Did pre-monarchic Israel form any political organization? Most important, how did they distinguish pre-exilic Israel from post-exilic Judaism? Consideration of these questions sheds light on the structures built up by Wellhausen and Kaufmann. In what follows I focus on these issues and to show their impact on understanding the historical reconstruction of Wellhausen and Kaufmann.

As far as the theocratic idea is concerned, Kaufmann paraphrases Wellhausen's view as follows:

> The ideal government of early times was monarchic; the priests were under the monarchy, merely royal appointees. But P depicts Israel in the Mosaic age as a theocratic church, centred about a tabernacle and headed by the high priest, Aaron. For P, the monarchy was a deflection from the theocratic ideal. But a priestly theocracy did not exist in Israel before

---

1186 Kaufmann, „Probleme der israelitisch-jüdischen Religionsgeschichte I," 43.
1187 Kaufmann was not the first to take issue with Wellhausen's later dating of the Priestly Code. A number of scholars (W. Graf Baudissin, Eduard Riehm, Franz Delitzsch, and Nöldeke) have questioned the lateness of P's dating. For a discussion see Raymond F. Surburg, "Wellhausenism Evaluated after a Century of Influence," 85. Also Ernest W. Nicholson, *The Pentateuch in the Twentieth Century: The Legacy of Julius Wellhausen.*

the Exile. It was the Persian domination that enabled it to develop. P, thus, reflects the situation and ideal of post-exilic times.[1188]

Kaufmann's exposition of Wellhausen's hypothesis on P as a reflection of post-exilic times contains four significant points that involve most of the relevant issues raised in this study. One point is related to Wellhausen's premise that monarchy was the ideal institution in early Israel. The second has to do with the status of priests in ancient Israel before the exile. The third point involves Wellhausen's assertion that P depicted Israel as a theocracy. Fourth, and perhaps most important, is the notion that priestly theocracy did not exist in pre-exilic Israel. Kaufmann challenged all of these assumptions. He favoured the idea that neither pre-exilic Israel nor post-exilic Judaism knew the "theocratic ideal," as Wellhausen would have it. In Kaufmann's reading, the ideal ruler of pre-monarchic Israel was a saviour-judge representing the kingdom of God. Referring to this ideal ruler, Kaufmann coined the term "Prohetokratie" (prophetic theocracy), which in his view described the pre-monarchic institution.

2 Early theocracy

Wellhausen took to heart the idea of theocracy and its importance in understanding the character of historical development of ancient Israel.[1189] It should come as no surprise that Wellhausen dedicated an appropriate place in his *Prolegomena* to investigating the theocratic idea.[1190] Even in the introduction of *Prolegomena* we read:

1188 Kaufmann, *The Religion of Israel*, 155.

1189 Wellhausen built on his forerunners, especially de Wette and Vatke. Rudolf Smend points out that Wellhausen based his view of theocracy on Vatke's conception "mit weniger philisophischer und mehr historischer Präzision als sein Vorgänger." On this see Rudolf Smend, *Die Mitte des Alten Testaments* (Theologische Studien 101; Zürich: EVZ-Verlag, 1970), 60. For de Wette and Vatke's interpretation of theocracy and its relation to Wellhausen's reconstruction see, Wolfgang Hübener, "Die verlorene Unschuld der Theokratie," in *Religionstheorie und politische Theologie*, Bd. 3: *Theokratie* (ed. JacobTaubes; München, 1987), 29–64. See further Daniel Weidner, "Geschichte gegen den Strich bürsten: Julius Wellhausen und die jüdische Gegengeschichte," 54.

1190 For Wellhausen's understanding of theocracy, see Ernst M. Dörrfuss, *Mose in den Chronikbüchern: Garant theokratischer Zukunftserwartung* (Berlin: De Gruyter, 1994), 64–76. Dörrfuss points out that Wellhausen attempted to coin new terms in order to be able to describe the development of the theocratic idea. Moreover, he mentions that Wellhausen had a problem with

> It was according to the mode furnished by [Priestly Code] that the Jews under Ezra ordered
> their sacred community, and upon it are formed our conceptions of the Mosaic theocracy,
> with the tabernacle at its centre, the high priest at its head, the priests and Levites as its
> organs, the legitimate cultus as its regular function.[1191]

In this quote Wellhausen is saying that Mosaic theocracy, which was created by
the Priestly Code, was a product of the Jewish traditions of the exile.[1192] Moreover, Wellhausen gives us a few characteristics of this theocracy: the people became a sacred community which was ruled by high priests and centred on the
legitimate cultus. Having examined the history of worship and history of tradition, Wellhausen titled the last chapter of *Prolegomena* "The Theocracy as Idea
and as Institution." His central argument was that "in ancient Israel the theocracy never existed in fact as a form of constitution. The rule of Jehovah is here an
ideal representation; only after the exile was it attempted to realise it in the
shape of a Rule of the Holy with outward means."[1193] "Nor," he further maintained, "did the theocracy exist from the time of Moses in the form of the covenant, though that was afterwards a favourite mode of regarding it."[1194]

Wellhausen was convinced that Mosaic theocracy was a later construction
estranged from the reality of ancient Israel. In his thinking, theocracy was by
no means the starting point of Israel's history, but rather its artificial and secondary product. "The Mosaic theocracy, the residuum of a ruined state, is itself not
a state at all, but an apolitical artificial product created in spite of unfavourable
circumstances by the impulse of an ever-memorable energy: and foreign rule is
its necessary counterpart.[1195] Wellhausen went on more about this, affirming that

---

the term 'theocracy,' as can be deduced from the different expressions he used to explain this
concept: i.e. first and second theocracy; old and new theocracy.
1191 Wellhausen, *Prolegomena*, 8–9.
1192 For Wellhausen's understanding of the theocratic idea in Israel's history, see Horst Hoffmann, *Julius Wellhausen: Die Frage des absoluten Maßstabes Seiner Geschichtsschreibung*, 6–23.
Hoffmann gave a detailed description of Wellhausen's different types of theocracy: ancient theocracy found in ancient Israel; hierocracy of post-exilic times; nomocracy of Judaism and Talmud as in rabbinic literature and Christian theocracy.
1193 Wellhausen, *Prolegomena*, 411.
1194 Wellhausen, *Prolegomena*, 417.
1195 David Polish comments on Wellhausen's view that theocracy never existed in fact as a
form of constitution as follows: Wellhausen "argues that a presupposition for a theocratic system
must be a centralized state that is sufficiently well organized to support and administer such a
system, and such a state did not exist in the time of the Judges. Yet the state was a 'new creation'
during the reigns of Saul and David, owing nothing to the 'mosaic theocracy' when the relation
of Jehovah to Israel was…a natural one (with) no interval between Him and His people to call for

"Mosaic theocracy appears to show an immense retrogression."[1196] The nature of ancient Israelite history did not fit with the conditions of Mosaic theocracy. As Wellhausen put it:

> To anyone who knows anything about history it is not necessary to prove that the so-called Mosaic theocracy, which nowhere suits the circumstances of the earlier periods, and of which the prophets, even in their most ideal delineations of the Israelite state as it ought to be, have not the faintest shadow of an idea, is, so to speak, a perfect fit for post-exilian Judaism, and had its actuality only there. [1197]

Theocracy, then, appeared after the Exile and, "It is from that time that it is transported in an idealised form to early times."[1198] Wellhausen assumed that nothing was instituted at the outset of Israel's early history.[1199] The question that then arises is whether, if theocracy did not exist in ancient Israel in the form of a constitution or covenant, what then was the nature of early theocracy? When Wellhausen described theocracy in ancient Israel, he talked about theocracy in "a certain sense" (in einem gewissen Sinne).[1200] According to Wellhausen, theocracy in ancient Israel was not a ready-made institution, but expressed the full penetration of religion and life. As he put it:

> Dennoch kann die Theokratie in einem gewissen Sinne als der charakteristische Ausgangspunkt der israelitischen Geschichte festgehalten werden. Nur nicht als ein Gemächt, als eine fertige Anstalt, die plötzlich den Israeliten in der Wüste aufgezwungen wird. Nicht als ein geistliches Wesen, das dem natürlichen Volkstum fernsteht und den Gegensatz von Heilig

---

thought or question." On this see David Polish, *Give Us a King: Legal Religious Sources of Jewish Sovereignty* (Hoboken: Ktav Pub. House, 1989), 34

1196 Wellhausen, *Prolegomena*, 422.

1197 Wellhausen, *Prolegomena*, 150–151.

1198 Wellhausen, *Prolegomena*, 256.

1199 Ronald Clements explained Wellhausen's position as follows: "Wellhausen showed that, on the evidence of OT witness to Israel's life during the period of the monarchy, *the nation had not functioned at that time as such a priestly theocracy.* On the contrary this theocracy was an ideal, a pattern fastened onto a picture of the past. The more reliable evidence of the nation's beginnings in the Books of Judges and Samuel showed a much more primitive organization, and confirmed the view that the idea of a Jewish theocracy, centered upon a law given to Moses, was a post-exilic creation which had only arisen once Israel had lost its own national existence." See Clements, *A Century of Old Testament Study*, 11.

1200 Horst Hoffmann pointed out that this theocracy extended to the early stages of Israel's history back to the time of Moses. He quoted Wellhausen's *Israelitische und jüdische Geschichte* "…in der bewegten Zeit, die dem Auszuge aus Ägypten voraufging, und während des Aufenthaltes in der Wüste, der darauf folgte, entstand der Bund der Stämme, die später das Volk Israel ausmachten." See Horst Hoffmann, *Julius Wellhausen: Die Frage des absoluten Maßstabes seiner Geschichtsschreibung*, 6. 66.

und Profan in schärfster Ausbildung voraussetzt. Vielmehr gerade umgekehrt als die engste Durchdringung der Religion und des Volkslebens, des Heiligen und des Nationalen, erwachsen aus vorhandener Wurzel und auf gegebener Grundlage fortbauend.[1201]

More important is Wellhausen's affirmation that Moses did not introduce a new constitution, but maintained the old one, which consisted of a system of families and clans.[1202] To Wellhausen, Moses was not preoccupied with or interested in spiritual and theoretical questions but practical issues:

> Mit theoretischen Wahrheiten, nach denen nicht die mindeste Nachfrage war, befaßte er [Moses] sich nicht, sondern mit praktischen Fragen, die bestimmt und notwendig durch die Zeit gestellt wurden. Jahve der Gott Israels bedeutete also nicht, daß der allmächtige Schöpfer Himmels und der Erden vorerst nur mit diesem einen Volke einen Bund geschlossen hätte zu seiner Erkenntnis und Verehrung. Es bedeutete…nur daß die nationale Aufgaben, innere und äußere, als heilige erfaßt wurden, und daß der Gott die Einheit des Volkes war.[1203]

On the other hand, Wellhausen referred to what he called "the real meaning of theocracy".[1204] In his view, "actual and legal existence (in the modern sense) was predicable only of each of the many clans; the unity of the nation was realised in the first instance only through its religion. It was out of the religion of Israel that the commonwealth of Israel unfolded itself, not a *holy* state, but *the* state."[1205] It requires little imagination to see that Wellhausen inclined towards an early theocracy which was not based on institutions, "Die Theokratie, kann man sagen, entstand als Komplement der Anarchie."[1206] More revealing

---

1201 Wellhausen, *Israelitische und jüdische Geschichte*, 20 – 21.
1202 Wellhausen, *Israelitische und jüdische Geschichte*, 20 – 21.
1203 Wellhausen, *Israelitische und jüdische Geschichte*, 32.
1204 According to Wellhausen, "War and the administration of justice were regarded as matters of religion before they became matters of obligation and civil order; this is all that is really meant when a theocracy is spoken of. Moses certainly organised no formal state, endowed with specific holiness, upon the basis of the proposition "Jehovah is the God of Israel;" or, at all events, if he did so, the fact had not in the slightest degree any practical consequence or historical significance." See Wellhausen, "Israel," 436.
1205 Wellhausen, "Israel," 436.
1206 Wellhausen, *Grundrisse zum Alten Testament*, 20. Wellhausen's inclination towards early theocracy becomes clear when he connected ancient Israelite theocracy to Islamic theocracy, "Die muslimische Theokratie wurde nicht durch eine Organisation von besonderer Heiligkeit abgestempelt; in dieser Hinsicht hatte sie keine Ähnlichkeit mit der jüdischen nach dem Exil. Es gab keinen Priesterstand, keinen Unterschied von Klerus und Laien, von geistlichen und weltlichen Geschäften." He further writes, "Nur die alte israelitische Theokratie weist eine grosse Ähnlichkeit mit der arabischen auf, obwohl ihr allerdings der Gedanke ursprünglich fern lag, dass

about Wellhausen's view was his assertion that the idea of *nation*, not the *law*, was more important at the beginning of Israel's history:

> In the older Hebrew literature the founding of the nation and not the giving of the law is regarded as the theocratic, creative act of Jehovah. The very notion of the law is absent: only covenants are spoken of, in which the representatives of the people undertake solemn obligations to do or leave undone something which is described in general terms.[1207]

These in sum were Wellhausen's thoughts on the theocratic idea in ancient Israel. As mentioned, Wellhausen situated Mosaic theocracy in the reality of the post-exilic period. Wellhausen, in fact, differentiated between the Mosaic theocracy based on institution and law and the early theocracy that presupposed a very natural beginning of the nation.[1208] He considered pre-monarchic Israel to have been a period when theocracy as a constitution did not form a part of ancient Israel. In Wellhausen's view, the elders were the actual rulers of the tribes without a need for a centralized state or constitutional laws. According to Wellhausen's assumption, this meant the lack of hierocratic organization during the time preceding the rise of Israelite monarchy.

3 Prophetic theocracy

Precisely opposed to Wellhausen's view regarding the absence of any organization, which included all Israel, Kaufmann developed his hypothesis on pre-monarchic Israel.[1209] In Kaufmann's view, there had been certainly a kind of spiritual and political rule in early Israel before the rise of monarchy.[1210] In

---

der richtige theokratische Herrscher der Prophet und nicht der König sei." See Wellhausen, *Das arabische Reich und sein Sturz* (Berlin: Reimer, 1902), 6.

1207 Wellhausen, *Prolegomena*, 347.

1208 Smend, like Wellhausen, asserted "Die Theokratie war im alten Israel eine andere als im Judentum". See Rudolf Smend, (sen.), "Über die Genesis des Judentums," *ZAW* 2 (1882): 94–151 (95).

1209 Kaufmann argued for the antiquity of the Book of Joshua, which belongs to prophetic theocracy. See Kaufmann, *Commentary on Joshua*, 21

1210 According to Kaufmann the roots of this system were established even before the settlement. He said, "The very institution of judges and its underlying concept of the "Kingdom of God" rest on the faith in a succession of messengers of God. The early kingdom of God is founded on the expectation that what happened – God's sending a savior to Israel – will be repeated when the need arises (cf. e. g., Judg. 6: 13). The source of this expectation must lie in the period before the judges, that is, in the period before the settlement." See Kaufmann, *The Religion of Israel*, 216.

explaining the conditions that led to the establishment of such a system Kaufmann wrote:

> The time was marked by a strong and simple faith in the nearness of YHWH, a direct con-
> tinuation of the feeling in Moses' time. The God who had revealed himself to Israel in a
> mighty act of redemption continued to show himself near. The concrete expression of
> this faith was the succession of saviours raised up by YHWH in Israel-prophets, Nazirites,
> and mighty men. The whole period of the judges is an embodiment of this idea. The tribes
> do not go the way of their neighbours and establish a monarchy, because they believe sim-
> ply and strongly that YHWH rules them through his messengers. From Moses to Samuel,
> apostles of God hold national-political leadership; they represent the kingdom of God,
> the visible embodiment of God's will in the world.[1211]

Against Wellhausen's claim that monarchy was preceded by a period of unrest
and affliction[1212], Kaufmann spoke of a national-political system consisting of
saviour-judges as apostles of God.[1213] Here, as I see it, Kaufmann was certainly
following the perspective of the biblical account, especially the Books of Joshua
and Judges. In Kaufmann's view, the tribes of Israel gained their political unity
under the leadership of men of God.[1214] Kaufmann labelled the Israelite polity
that existed before monarchy as "prophetic theocracy" (Prophetokratie), by
which he meant that the apostle-prophet played a political role in pre-monarchic
Israel. However, Kaufmann distinguished this prophetic rule from priestly government:

> Die Theokratie der Urzeit ist nicht Hierokratie, sondern Prophetokratie. Nicht Priester,
> sondern Propheten standen an der Spitze des Volkes in der Urzeit, Gesandte Jahwes, die das
> Volk im Kriege und im Frieden anführten. Die „Richter", von Josua bis Samuel, sind Nach-
> folger Moses, nicht Aarons.[1215]

When did this "Prophetokratie" emerge? According to Kaufmann, the prophetic
kingdom of God appeared before the rise of monarchy. He contended that this
prophetic theocracy was a political system, but based on the will of God who

---

1211 Kaufmann, *The Religion of Israel*, 256.
1212 Wellhausen doubted the central authority in the period of the Judges. He proposes, "Judi-
cial competence resided at that time chiefly in the smallest circles, the families and houses.
These were but little controlled, as it appears, by the superior power of the tribe, and the
very notion of the state or of the kingdom did not as yet exist." See Wellhausen, *Prolegomena*,
413.
1213 Kaufmann, *The Religion of Israel*, 216, 256–258.
1214 Kaufmann, *The Religion of Israel*, 262.
1215 Kaufmann, „Probleme der israelitisch-jüdischen Religionsgeschichte I," 27.

would send saviours to his people. Kaufmann further declared that the nature of ancient Israelite theocracy was not a mixture of political life with national matters or the unification of the sacred with the national, as Wellhausen would have it.[1216] Moreover, Kaufmann held that early Israelite theocracy did not know a mixed priestly-kingly rule or kingly-godly dominion like that which existed among pagan people. Rather, theocracy in ancient Israel was the rule of prophet-judges.[1217]

In addition, Kaufmann made the point that prophetic theocracy derived its authority from the Kingship of God.[1218] As he put it:

> Under normal circumstances the primitive democracy of the elders sufficed for the government of the tribes. But in periods of stress it was inadequate, and then the hidden kingdom represented by inspired men, God-sent saviours, revealed itself... The authority of the judges was not viewed as secular, or merely political, but as deriving from the Kingship of God .. This is the early Israelite theocracy – a prophetic theocracy, with inspired men at its head, as contrasted with the later priestly theocracy of Second Temple times.[1219]

Thus the divergence between Wellhausen and Kaufmann concerning the theocratic ideal is obvious. While Wellhausen regarded the theocratic ideal during the period of Judges as being a later construction of the priestly ideal, Kaufmann assigned the appearance of theocratic rulers to the time of Judges, not as a priestly ideal, but as a prophetic ideal.[1220] This reveals a fundamental difference be-

---

1216 Here Kaufmann is referring to Wellhausen's statement "Der wirkliche Sinn der Theokratie ist demnach, daß Krieg und Recht Religion waren, ehe sie Zwang und bürgerliche Ordnung wurden." See Wellhausen, *Israelitische und jüdische Geschichte*, 27.
1217 Kaufmann, *Toledot* I, 698.
1218 Here we note the earlier dating by Kaufmann of the kingship of Yahweh to the pre-monarchic period. This seems to contrast with Wellhausen, who dated the kingship of Yahweh to the time of Saul and David, "The kingship of Jehovah, in that precise sense which we associate with it, is the religious expression of the fact of the foundation of the kingdom by Saul and David." See Wellhausen, *Prolegomena*, 414. For a discussion of this subject, see Ludwig Schmidt, "Königtum: II Altes Testament," *TRE* 19 (1990): 323–345.
1219 Kaufmann, "The Biblical Age," 39–40. Kaufmann contended that this kind of prophetic rule could be traced back among the tribes of *benē aber* and the Arab tribes. This was taken by Kaufmann as evidence to support the historicity of the tradition concerning the prophetic theocracy in Israel. Kaufmann argued that figures such as poets or priest-seers existed among the Arab tribes and occupied a prominent position, leading their people at times of war. They were also judges. See Kaufmann, *Toledot* I, 700–701.
1220 Benjamin Uffenheimer accepted Kaufmann's contention. He points out, "Wellhausen misinterpreted the very nature of that ideal. There was nothing in common with the career of the judges and the rule of the high priest in the Second Temple period. The latter were the official representatives of the institutional temple cult, enjoying hereditary succession, and were con-

tween Wellhausen and Kaufmann on this issue. According to Wellhausen, except for the time of Moses, the whole period before Saul and David was not a source of historical reconstruction. For Wellhausen, with the monarchy came the true political beginning of Israel. Kaufmann, on the other hand, reversed Wellhausen's historical reconstruction of ancient Israel, dating the rule of the prophetic ideal to pre-monarchic times. To go into more depth on the dispute between Wellhausen and Kaufmann over the phases of historical development of ancient Israel, we turn to their concepts of the theocratic ideal.

4 Theocratic ideal

The theocratic ideal was the main subject of Kaufmann's first contribution to biblical studies. The first heading of Kaufmann's article in the *Zeitschrift für die alttestamentliche Wissenschaft* was "Das sogenannte theokratische Ideal des Judentum."[1221] Kaufmann introduced the topic by referring to Wellhausen's hypothesis and its consequences with regard to understanding the history of Israelite religion. He wrote:

> Seit den Ausführungen Wellhausens in seinen „Prolegomena zur Geschichte Israels" über das Wesen der jüdischen Theokratie ist die Idee vom theokratischen Ideal des Judentums – das wird man wohl sagen, dürfen – zur leitenden Idee der modernen Wissenschaft der israelitisch-jüdischen Religion geworden. Das theokratische Ideal sei die große Wasserscheide der israelitisch-jüdischen Religionsgeschichte. Das wesentliche Merkmal dieses Ideals sei die Ablehnung des Königtums als Sünde und Abfall von Jahwe und die Verherrlichung der „Gottesherrschaft", d. h. der Priesterherrschaft. In der „Theokratie" wird das Volk durch die Kultusgemeinde verdrängt, an deren Spitze ein Priesterfürst steht. Dieses Ideal sei in der Grundschrift des Pentateuchs, im Priesterkodex, am reinsten dargeboten. Die Theokratie wird da in die Urzeit verlegt. Vom Königtum will diese Schrift nichts wissen…Nun hat aber die Theokratie in Wirklichkeit die Fremdherrschaft, die dem Judentum die Sorge um die irdischen Angelegenheiten abgenommen hat, zur Voraussetzung. Das theokratische Ideal konnte sich also erst in nachexilischer Zeit entfalten. Damit wäre für die Wissenschaft ein fester Punkt gewonnen, von dem aus sich die ganze Entwicklung der israelitisch-jüdischen Geschichte überblicken läßt.[1222]

---

cerned primarily with the cult and everything pertaining to the status of the priesthood. The judges, on the other hand were not theocratic rulers in the ritual sense, and in fact did not even rule in succession; their status, unlike that of the high priests, did not depend upon lineage." On this point see Benjamin Uffenheimer, *Early Prophecy in Israel* (transl. from the Hebrew by David Louvish; Jerusalem: Magnes Press, Hebrew University, 1999), 208 – 212 (208).

1221 Kaufmann, "Probleme der israelitisch-jüdischen Religionsgeschichte I," 23 – 32.
1222 Kaufmann, „Probleme der israelitisch-jüdischen Religionsgeschichte I," 23 – 24.

In this telling and comprehensive quotation, Kaufmann sums up issues related to our discussion. Perhaps more important is Kaufmann's observation that the theocratic idea was crucial to understanding Israelite religion and Judaism. Thus Kaufmann paraphrased Wellhausen's views, drawing attention to several things: 1) the negative attitude of theocracy towards monarchy; 2) the role of priesthood within theocracy 3) the people of Israel transformed into a cultic community as part of the theocratic ideal of post-exilic time; 4) theocracy as presented in its purest form in the Priestly Code of the Pentateuch; 5) foreign domination as the presupposition for theocracy; 6) theocracy as a product of the post-exilic setting. These points almost cover the main arguments of Wellhausen's construction of the theocratic ideal in Israel's history. In his attempt to counter Wellhausen's hypothesis, Kaufmann posed pivotal questions. For example, Kaufmann wondered whether Judaism had really cherished such a theocratic ideal. Did post-exilic Judaism know a theocratic or hierocratic constitution? Did Judaism view hierocracy as an ideal and strive towards it? In Kaufmann's estimation, the hierocratic ideal was not part of the history of Judaism:

> Die Quellen belehren uns, daß es nicht der Fall war. Man hat die Hierokratie samt deren Voraussetzung, der Fremdherrschaft, als schmachvolle Wirklichkeit empfunden, sehnte sich aber nach etwas anderem. Daß diese Wirklichkeit dem Judentum zum idealen Vorbild werden konnte, erscheint daher als ausgeschlossen.[1223]

The respective views of Wellhausen and Kaufmann become clear when examining such issues as the theocratic ideal, monarchy and theocracy, the role of priests and prophets, theocracy and the Priestly Code. All of these themes are interconnected and therefore require careful consideration. For example, Wellhausen relates P's document to post-exilic reality because of its rejection of monarchy. Kaufmann likewise connects the theocratic idea with prophecy, challenging the role of priests in the Jewish polity.

The concept of the theocratic ideal existed in both Wellhausen's and Kaufmann's construction of the history of ancient Israel and Judaism, but they differed as to the nature of the governing persona in this ideal. In Wellhausen's view the priest is the ideal theocratic leader of a people who are under foreign domination. Kaufmann, in contrast, argued that the ideal theocratic authority was a prophetic government ruling before the rise of monarchy. Wellhausen, as mentioned, was convinced that theocracy did not appear as an institution in ancient Israel. As he put it, "The theocratic ideal was from the exile onwards the centre of all thought and effort, and it annihilated the sense for objective

---

1223 Kaufmann, „Probleme der israelitisch-jüdischen Religionsgeschichte I," 24.

truth, all regard and interest for the actual facts as they had been handed down."[1224] Furthermore, Wellhausen made clear the point that theocracy became hierocracy in the Second Temple period. He advanced the idea that early theocracy "in a certain sense" (in einem gewissen Sinne), became hierocracy through Josiah's reform. This hierocracy turned into a "developed theocracy" for the Jewish exiles as expressed in the Book of Ezekiel and the priestly writings. In Wellhausen's words, "Ein verbannter Priester, Ezechiel, hatte den Anfang gemacht, ein Bild von ihr, wie sie gewesen war und wie sie sein sollte, aufzuzeichnen, als Programm für die zukünftige Herstellung der Theokratie."[1225] Wellhausen then concluded, "Die Theokratie ist Hierokratie geworden und bedeutet die Herrschaft des Heiligen in der Gemeinde."[1226]

Rebutting Wellhausen's premises, Kaufmann gave many instances in which the Hebrew Bible betrayed no knowledge of hierocratic ideals.[1227] Moreover, Kaufmann contested Wellhausen's characterization of Ezekiel as the father of theocracy, pointing out that Ezekiel had no idea about the rule of priests.[1228] In Kaufmann's view, Ezekiel envisioned in his eschatological oracles (נָשִׂיא) a king from the house of David (44: 3; 45: 6).[1229] Kaufmann further pointed out that Ezekiel did not even mention the high priest. Thus, according to Kaufmann, "The idea that Ezekiel fathered the theocratic polity of later Judaism is absurd. He anticipated not a hierocracy, but a visionary kingdom of God."[1230] It is here that we can clearly see how far Kaufmann's view differed from that of Wellhausen, who, in describing Ezekiel's theocracy, wrote:

> An ein jüdisches Weltreich denkt er nicht, überhaupt nicht an ein Reich, sondern nur an eine Kultusgemeinde. Die Theokratie ist Sion. Aber Sion ist nicht mehr wie in Isa. 11 die Stadt Davids, wo gutes Regiment und Recht und Friede herrscht, sondern die Stadt des Tempels, wo Jahve so verehrt wird wie es seiner Heiligkeit entspricht.[1231]

1224 Wellhausen, *Prolegomena*, 161.
1225 Wellhausen, *Israelitische und jüdische Geschichte*, 167.
1226 Wellhausen, *Israelitische und jüdische Geschichte*, 168.
1227 R. Thompson sums up Kaufmann's view as follows: "Priestly rule is found neither in Ezekiel (whose head was a prince), nor in Haggai-Zechariah (where the high priest is subordinate to Zerubbabel), nor in Chronicles (whose hero was David), nor in Ezra (who was a scribe), nor in P (whose Aaron was subject to the prophetic Moses). See R. J. Thompson, *Moses and the Law in a Century of Criticism since Graf*, 120–123.
1228 Kaufmann, *Toledot* I, 689.
1229 Kaufmann, "Probleme der israelitisch-jüdischen Religionsgeschichte I," 24.
1230 Kaufmann, *The Religion of Israel*, 443.
1231 Wellhausen, *Israelitische und jüdische Geschichte*, 147.

When Wellhausen conducted a literary criticism of the Book of Judges, he found that Chapters 19–21 contradicted the general tendency prevailing in the period of Judges.[1232] This appears, according to Wellhausen, in the usage of particular terms such as עדה ('ēdā, congregation) to describe the people of Israel. In Wellhausen's thinking, this characterization fits the conditions of post-exilic times, when the Jews lived as a sacred assembly. Building on this, Wellhausen contended that these chapters had been edited to match the theocratic ideal of the Priestly Code. To quote Wellhausen:

> Die Einheit Israels ist eine kirchliche, das handelnde Subjekt ist die Versammlung des Volkes Gottes… oder, wie der gewöhnliche Ausdruck lautet, die Gemeinde; als habe es damals nicht tausende von Sakralvereinigungen, sondern nur eine einzige gegeben, denn עדה im technischen Sinn ist keine politische, sondern eine sakrale Gemeinde. Es hat alles einen gesalbten, aber nicht prophetisch – außerordentlichen, sondern gesetzlich – ordnungsmäßigen religiösen Anstrich.[1233]

Kaufmann, on the other hand, rejected Wellhausen's assumption that a theocratic ideal was reflected in the Book of Judges.[1234] He asserted that Israel was depicted, in all sources including "P", as a people not a congregation.[1235] The 'ēdā of "P" is not an ecclesiastical community, but a military camp.[1236] In Kaufmann's view, the עדה of Judges (chs.20–21) refers to primitive Israelite democracy.[1237] According to Kaufmann's interpretation, ancient Israel was represented from its beginning to the dawn of monarchy as an assembled group of people governed by a prophetic theocracy whose leader was a messenger-saviour.[1238]

1232 Wellhausen, *Die Composition des Hexateuchs*, 229–233.

1233 Wellhausen, *Die Composition des Hexateuchs*, 229.

1234 Kaufmann, *Commentary on the Book of Judges*, 45.

1235 According to Kaufmann, the Jewish community עדה at the time of the Second Temple was not a prophetic theocracy for Prophecy had already ceased. In the Hellenistic period, however, the high priest was the head of the Jewish community. According to Kaufmann therefore, it could be said that during the Hellenistic period the Jewish community was a priestly theocracy. Yet, this was not the case in the Persian period, when the people were under the rule of a Persian governor. See Kaufmann, *Commentary on the Book of Joshua*, 18.

1236 Kaufmann, *The Religion of Israel*, 185. See further Moshe Greenberg, "A New Approach to the History of the Israelite Priesthood", 41.

1237 Kaufmann, *Commentary on Judges*, 280. As for Judges (ch.19) Kaufmann observed that theocracy was basically connected to the persona of the prophet or the priest. This chapter, so Kaufmann, contained not the slightest reference to either prophets or priests. See Kaufmann, *Toledot* II, 398.

1238 Kaufmann, *Commentary on Joshua*, 18–20; idem, *Commentary on Judges*, 279–280; also *The Religion of Israel*, 257

Wellhausen, however, gave another example that shows a tendency to idealize the notion of a theocratic rule. He deemed the references concerning the rejection of monarchy in (Judg. 8: 22–23) and (1 Sam 8–12) to be a reflection of priestly and theocratic redaction.[1239] In contrast to Wellhausen, Kaufmann held that anti-monarchic passages "refer to the historical moment of the beginning of the monarchy."[1240] Kaufmann went on to maintain that even in post-exilic times, national and eschatological ideas were bound up with monarchy.[1241] He came to the conclusion that a priestly rule along the lines envisioned by Wellhausen never existed.[1242]

Wellhausen built his view on the assumption that monarchy was the ideal government in ancient Israel. He wrote in Prolegomena, "In the eyes of Israel before the exile, the monarchy is the culminating point of the history, and the greatest blessing of Jehovah."[1243] Moreover, Wellhausen illustrated how the people of early Israel were indebted to the monarchy and its founders: "The ancient Israelites were as fully conscious as any other people of the gratitude they owed to the men and to the institutions by whose aid they had been lifted out of anarchy and oppression, and formed into an orderly community, capable of self-defence."[1244] Following this further, Wellhausen showed that this theocracy was arranged on a quite different footing from the model favoured by early Israelites. Thus, Wellhausen explained the rejection of monarchy in I Samuel as follows:

> The position taken up in the version of I Samuel vii. viii. x. 17 seq. xii., presents the greatest possible contrast to this way of thinking. There, the erection of the monarchy only forms a worse stage of backsliding from Jehovah. There can be no progress beyond the Mosaic ideal; the greater the departure from it the greater the declension.[1245]

In quite the opposite direction, Kaufmann claimed that ascribing the rejection of monarchy in Judges and I Samuel to the conditions of the Second Temple theocracy blurred the facts and distorted the history.[1246] In Kaufmann's reading there

---

1239 Wellhausen, *Die Composition des Hexateuchs*, 222, 241–243.
1240 Kaufmann, *The Religion of Israel*, 264.
1241 Kaufmann, "The Biblical Age," 81.
1242 Kaufmann, *Toledot* I, 687.
1243 Wellhausen, *Prolegomena*, 253.
1244 Wellhausen, *Prolegomena*, 254.
1245 Wellhausen, *Prolegomena*, 254.
1246 Kaufmann examined the anti-monarchic references in Judges, I Samuel and Hosea and concluded that each of these was making reference to a contemporary historical situation and was not an insertion reflecting later times. For example, Kaufmann mentioned that there was no ideological connection between these references. Hosea refers to the political situation

was no hint in these books of the supposed ideal rule of priests. Kaufmann elaborated that the "Kingdom of Yahweh", like in the cases of Gideon and Samuel, had nothing to do with the priestly rule, as Kaufmann noted that Gideon's story contained no references to the priesthood. Moreover, Kaufmann mentioned that in the stories of Samuel and Saul, Samuel did not appear as a priest fighting for the rule of priests, but rather as a prophet and a judge. In addition, Kaufmann showed that Hosea, who rejected monarchy, did not make a claim for priestly rule. Hosea, according to Kaufmann, fought against the rule of priesthood (4:4).[1247]

Consequently, Kaufmann deduced that the rejection of the monarchical system was not directed against any one monarchy as such, but was rather the positive and idealistic belief in the rule of a saviour-judge who was to rule by the divine will. From Kaufmann's point of view, this appeared correct when we consider that this rejection of the monarchy ceased with the conviction that the rule of judges was close to its end.[1248] Kaufmann summed up his position in this regard in the following:

> The isolated passages in which kingship is opposed do not, therefore, represent an ideology that prevailed in Israel at any time after the establishment of the monarchy. The origin of this hostility must be sought in the pre-monarchic period. That Hosea 13: 10 f. cannot be its source is clear not only because the attitude there expressed bore no ideological fruit in later literature and thought, but also from the very language of the passage. The people's request for a king is cited in the phraseology of I Samuel, but with one telling divergence: Hosea's Israel asks for "king and officials" *(Śārim)* (cf. also 8:4). Alongside the king, sharing his authority, appears the bureaucracy of the later monarchy. To the writer of I Samuel 8, however, *Śārim* do not yet hold any important positions in their own right; they are merely the king's "servants" *('abādim,* vs. 14). The people ask only for a king, and in the sequel, the king alone is spoken of. Here the conditions of the early monarchy are reflected.[1249]

of the late kingdom, when the rule of *sarem* increased. This is not the case in the books of Judges and Samuel which represented the pre-monarchic period when monarchy began to take the place of prophetic rule. See Kaufmann, *Toledot* I, 697 – 698.

1247 Kaufmann, *Toledot* I, 694 – 708. In fact, Kaufmann strove to make the point that the prophets and judges from Moses to Samuel were against monarchy, not the rule priests (Aaron, Eliezer, Ali, Sadok). For Kaufmann this meant that the kingdom of Yahweh was not a priestly kingdom but a prophetic one.

1248 Kaufmann, *Toledot* II, 103.

1249 Kaufmann, *The Religion of Israel*, 264.

As for the relationship of the Priestly Code and theocracy, Wellhausen pointed out that the theocracy of P was a hierocracy.[1250] It should be mentioned here that Wellhausen understood theocracy as a hierocratic system.[1251] Within this system the high priest occupied the most prominent position and became the actual ruler of the people. As Wellhausen put it:

> Die Ämter der Theokratie waren in den Händen der Priester und des mit ihnen zusammenhängenden Adels; das allein entsprach der Verfassung, der Thora. In der Theokratie mussten die weltlichen Funktionen im Schlepptau der heiligen gehen, der oberste Priester war das Staatsoberhaupt und so fort.[1252]

Wellhausen further wrote of the high priest, "As the head of the priesthood, he is head of the theocracy, and so much so that there is no room for any other alongside of him; a theocratic king beside him cannot be thought of (Numbers xxvii. 21)."[1253] More revealing was Wellhausen's assumption that by means of genealogy the Chronicler created an epoch of the high priests:

> The Chronicler gave a corresponding number of high priests to the twice twelve generations of forty years each which were usually assumed to have elapsed between the Exodus and the building of Solomon's temple, and again between that and the close of the captivity; the official terms of office of these high priests, of whom history knows nothing, have taken the place of the reigns of judges and kings, according to which reckoning was previously made (1Chronicles v. 29, seq.).[1254]

1250 This can be adduced from Wellhausen's affirmation: "Der Priesterkodex fordert nun aber nicht, wie die Theokratie sein soll, sondern er beschreibt, wie sie ist." See Wellhausen, *Israelitische und jüdische Geschichte*, 169.

1251 Hübener points out that Wellhausen "kann und will Theokratie nur als entwickelte hierokratische Organisation denken und findet unter dieser Perspektive vor dem Königtum zwangsläufig nichts als Anarchie." See Wolfgang Hübener,"Die verlorene Unschuld der Theokratie," 33.

1252 Wellhausen, *Die Pharisäer und die Sadducäer*, 26.

1253 Wellhausen, *Prolegomena*, 150. In Wellhausen's view, it was Ezekiel who opened the way towards hierocracy: "The hierocracy towards which Ezekiel had already opened the way was simply inevitable. It took the form of a monarchy of the high priest, he having stepped into the place formerly occupied by the theocratic king. As his peers and at his side stood the members of his clan, the Levites of the old Jerusalem, who traced their descent from Zadok (Sadduk)..." On this see Wellhausen, "Israel," 495.

1254 Wellhausen, *Prolegomena*, 151. Kaufmann reacted to Wellhausen's assumption "Daß die Annahme Wellhausens falsch ist, erhellt daraus, daß der Chronist bis zum ersten Tempelpriester 15 statt 12 Priester zählt. Unbegreiflich ist es aber, wie aus der Tatsache, daß der Chronist unter hundert anderen genealogischen Listen auch eine Priesterliste bringt, geschlossen werden kann, daß die "Amtsdauer dieser Hohenpriester ... an die Stelle der Regierung der Richter und Könige" getreten sei. Weder in der Chronik selbst noch irgendwo anders wird eine derartige Ära ge-

In addition, Wellhausen drew attention to the utter indifference of the Priestly Code towards all state and national matters.[1255] He summed up aptly how hierocracy took the place of monarchy and the high priest of "P" took the place of the king:

> The post-Deuteronomic legislation is not addressed to the people, but to the congregation; its chief concern is the regulation of worship. Political matters are not touched upon, as they are in the hands of a foreigner lord. The hierocracy is taken for granted as the constitution of the congregation. The head of the cultus is the head of the whole; the high priest takes the place of the king.[1256]

The position taken by Wellhausen as to the idealized high priest of "P" – the hierocratic ideal – was severely refuted by Kaufmann. Moreover, Kaufmann wondered how Wellhausen was able to mislead the biblical scholars for such a long time, convincing them that the high priest of "P" stood at the head of his people as the symbol of priestly dominion during the Second Temple.[1257] Consistent with his stance, Kaufmann rejected the view that there was a connection between the priestly ideal of "P" and the position of priests in the age of the Second Temple.[1258] In Kaufmann's view, the position of the high priest in "P" was as follows:

> The idealized high priest of P stands, not in the place of, but beside the prophet-judge. His authority is founded on his oracle, the Urim, which is of crucial and living significance to P, as can be seen from Num. 27: 21. P also assigns to the priest a role in war; at the command of the prophet leader he accompanies the army into battle bearing the holy vessels and trumpets (Num. 31:6).[1259]

Against Wellhausen's proclamation that the offices of the theocracy were in the hands of the priests, Kaufmann put forward the idea that the high priest of "P" never embodied a prominent leadership. He further maintained that even inside

---

braucht. Der vermeintliche Beleg aus MC 2: 26…beruht auf einer unmöglichen Deutung dieser Stelle: die Amtszeit des Ahimelech kann unmöglich als die Zeit des Pontifikats seines Sohnes gelten." See Kaufmann, "Probleme der israelitisch-jüdischen Religionsgeschichte I," 26.

1255 In Wellhausen's words, "Sehr bezeichnend ist die völlige Gleichgültigkeit des Priesterkodex gegen alles Staatliche und Nationale. Die Funktion der Theokratie ist der Kultus, mit der Regierung hat sie nichts zu tun, weil dieselbe wesentlich der Fremdherrschaft überlassen ist.' See Wellhausen, *Israelitische und jüdische Geschichte*, 20, n.1.

1256 Wellhausen, "Israel," 499.

1257 Kaufmann, *Toledot* I, 138.

1258 Kaufmann, *The Religion of Israel*, 187. For a discussion see Moshe Greenberg, "A New Approach to the History of the Israelite Priesthood," 41–47.

1259 Kaufmann, *The Religion of Israel*, 186.

the temple, the high priest had no leading position. Thus, according to Kaufmann:

> Der Hohepriester ist in P, wenn man so sagen darf, eines der allerheiligsten Kultstücke; eine leitende Funktion wird ihm aber nicht zugedacht. Nicht nur wird in P nirgends ein Versuch gemacht, „ihm weltliche Macht zu vindizieren" (WELLHAUSEN, Prolegomena, S. 147), sondern auch im Tempel selbst hat er keine leitende Stellung. Mose allein richtet alles im Auftrage Jahwes ein, besetzt alle Ämter, weiht nicht nur Aaron ein, sondern auch dessen Söhne, usw. (Ex· 25 ff.). Mose allein beaufsichtigt das Heiligtum, und alle, auch Aaron, müssen vor ihm Rechenschaft ablegen (Lev 10 ie f.). Der Hohepriester ist hier in keinem Sinne der Vorsteher des Volkes, und nicht ihm gehorcht man in diesem Kriegslager. Der Prophet ist hier der alleinige Oberbefehlshaber.[1260]

Unlike Wellhausen, who held that the high priest had a privileged position during the Second Temple period, Kaufmann made it evident that priests were thrust aside. There are two other important points in Kaufmann's rejection of Wellhausen's system. As to the first, Kaufmann asserted that it had never been thought that the priesthood was a continuation of the monarchy. The second point was Kaufmann's observation that Judaism did not calculate time according to the rulerships of the high priests. As Kaufmann put it:

> Merkwürdig ist, daß in der großen religiösen Bewegung des Frühjudentums die amtierende Priesterschaft so gut wie gar keine Rolle spielt. Nehemia war kein Priester, und Esra wirkte als Schriftgelehrter und nicht als amtierender Priester. Die Hohepriester wurden zur Seite gedrängt. Später, als das Priesterfürstentum nun einmal da war, betrachtete wohl das Volk die Hohepriester als seine Vorsteher. Niemals galt aber nach genuin jüdischer Auffassung das Priesterfürstentum als legitime Fortsetzung des Königtums. Das Judentum hat nicht einmal die Namen der Hohepriester aufbewahrt. Es ist höchst charakteristisch, daß das Judentum keine Zeitrechnung nach Hohepriestern kennt.[1261]

Kaufmann, then, was convinced that neither in the pre-exilic nor during Second Temple period did the hierocratic ideal exist.[1262] He showed that the Hebrew

---

1260 Kaufmann, „Probleme der israelitisch-jüdischen Religionsgeschichte I," 28–30. In the same context, Kaufmann affirmed „Und es ist lehrreich genug, daß die 'theokratische' Chronik die Einrichtung des Tempelkultes nicht auf Zadok, den Ahnherrn der nachexilischen Priesterfürsten, sondern auf den König David zurückführt." On this see Kaufmann, „Probleme der israelitisch-jüdischen Religionsgeschichte I," 25.

1261 Kaufmann, „Probleme der israelitisch-jüdischen Religionsgeschichte I," 25–26.

1262 Kaufmann, "Probleme der israelitisch-jüdischen Religionsgeschichte I," 27. When Kaufmann said that Israel did not know the hierocratic ideal even in post-exilic times, he quoted Ezr–ix 8–9; Neh. ix 36f. and Neh. ix as a whole. J. G. Vink points out "both texts are Maccabean and cannot be quoted for the relevant Persian period." See J. G. Vink, "The Date and Origin of the

Bible did not mention anywhere a hierocratic ideal that rejected monarchy in favour of theocracy:

> Von einem hierokratischen Ideal im Sinne einer Ablehnung des Königtums zugunsten einer Priesterherrschaft findet sich somit im AT gar keine Spur. Die „Theokratie" des P (wie des Pentateuchs überhaupt) ist keine Hierokratie, sondern Prophetokratie. In dieser Theokratie spiegelt sich weder die Wirklichkeit noch das Ideal der nachexilischen Zeit wider.[1263]

This controversy between Wellhausen and Kaufmann concerning the position of the high priest in theocracy raises several questions: When did the institution emerge in ancient Israel? Why did monarchy occupy such an important place in Wellhausen's historical reconstruction? What is meant by Kaufmann's prophetic theocracy? Who did Kaufmann regard as the founder of ancient Israelite polity?

Wellhausen makes the point clear that sacred institutions did not exist in pre-monarchic Israel. As he clearly stated, "Es findet sich überhaupt keine Organisation, die das ganze Volk umfaßt."[1264] Moreover, Wellhausen's historical reconstruction of early Israel shows that he did not take seriously the biblical stories from the pre-monarchic period. Wellhausen, however, did refer to the old traditions that consider the whole period before monarchy as anarchic:

> Die Dauer der Periode zwischen Saul und Moses läßt sich noch schlechter veranschlagen, da die sogenannten Richter in eine ganz künstliche Sukzession mit ebenso künstlicher Chronologie gebracht sind. Die ältere Tradition betrachtet den ganzen Zeitraum nur als ein vorübergehendes anarchisches Interregnum.[1265]

This brings us to the central idea in Wellhausen's structure. This is Wellhausen's distinction between a non-institutional stage and a later institutional one. According to Wellhausen, the first stage emerged before the exile. At that time neither priests nor prophets had gained exclusive authority:

> Ein Priester und Prophet ist Reichsverweser, er hat keine äußeren Machtmittel zur Verfügung und dennoch unbedingte Autorität, als Stellvertreter Jahves. Jahve sorgt für alles; seine Untertanen haben weiter nichts zu tun, als sich seiner Verehrung zu widmen und den Mahnungen seines Stellvertreters zu folgen.[1266]

Priestly Code in the Old Testament," in *The Priestly Code and Seven Other Studies* (Brill: Leiden, 1969), 9, n. 2.

1263 Kaufmann, „Probleme der israelitisch-jüdischen Religionsgeschichte I," 31.

1264 Wellhausen, *Israelitische und jüdische Geschichte*, 19.

1265 Wellhausen, *Israelitische und jüdische Geschichte*, 9.

1266 Wellhausen, *Israelitische und jüdische Geschichte*, 20.

Wellhausen worked with the idea that the prophets did not turn the tradition upside down, nor did they bring about a new constitution: "The theocracy as the prophets represent it to themselves is not a thing essentially different from the political community, as a spiritual differs from a secular power; rather, it rests on the same foundations and is in fact the ideal of the state."[1267] In Wellhausen's thinking, the prophetic ideas were part and parcel of common reality, a completely profane life:

> Die Propheten waren bis auf die Zeit des Deuteronomiums keine Praktiker; sie schufen ihren Ideen keine Organe, mit denen sie in die gemeine Wirklichkeit hätten eingreifen können. Ein reales und völlig profanes Volksleben mit seinen Einrichtungen und Ordnungen ging fertig neben ihnen her; auch wenn sie gewollt hätten – was aber nicht der Fall war –, so hätten sie gar nicht freies Feld gehabt zur Einführung eines platonischen Staates.[1268]

Wellhausen's far-reaching outlook was that the authority of the priests in pre-exilic Israel had not been derived from the law or based on a theocratic regime.[1269] In Wellhausen's view, the priestly Torah was a prepolitical institution. He showed that the authority of the priestly Torah was restricted to certain individuals. Wellhausen wrote:

> The execution of their decisions did not lie with them; they could only advise and teach. Their authority was divine, or, as we should say, moral, in its character; it rested upon that spontaneous recognition of the idea of right which, though unexpressed, was alive and working among the tribes – upon Jehovah Himself – who was the author of this generally diffused sense of right, but revealed the proper determinations on points of detail only to certain individuals. The priestly Torah was an entirely unpolitical or rather prepo-

---

1267 Wellhausen, *Prolegomena*, 414. In his comments on (Isaiah i. 21–27) Wellhausen wrote, "The state the prophet has before his eye is always the natural state as it exists, never a community distinguished by a peculiar holiness in its organisation. The kingdom of Jehovah is with him entirely identical with the kingdom of David; the tasks he sets before it are political...He is unconscious of any difference between human and divine law..." On this see Wellhausen, *Prolegomena*, 415.

1268 Wellhausen, *Die Pharisäer und die Sadducäer*, 14.

1269 According to Wellhausen, the priests had gained exclusive legitimacy only later on. He distinguished three main phases in the history of the priesthood in Israel; 1) an early stage without a fixed hereditary priesthood or legislative prescription for such; 2) growth of influence, power, and centralization of the priesthood under the monarchy, with the priests in the late monarchy constituting a clerical order, hereditary in numerous families; (3) in the post-exilic period, the picture of which is preserved in P, a theocracy under priests and Levites with the Aaronid priests dominating, the Levites generally becoming temple servants, and the high priest functioning as head of worship and head of the nation. See, in particular, Patrick D. Miller, "Wellhausen and the History of Israel's Religion," 69.

litical institution; it had an existence before the state had, and it was one of the invisible foundation pillars on which the state rested.[1270]

Thus so far we have seen Wellhausen's characterization of the non-institutional stage in the history of ancient Israel. As for the institutional phase, he went on to say that its birth-throes began in Deuteronomy and the full shape of this transition was reflected in the Priestly Code.[1271] The situation of the Israelites in post-exilic times favoured the emergence of institutions. According to Wellhausen's explanation, only institutions could meet the reality of the Second Commonwealth; the prophetic ideas were not sufficient for the needs of these times. As Wellhausen formulated it:

> Circumstances favoured the design, and this was the great point. As matters then were, the reconstitution of an actual state was not to be thought of, the foreign rule would not admit of it (Ezra iv. 19 seq.). What plan was to be taken, what materials to be used for such a building as the times allowed? The prophetic ideas would not serve as building stones; they were not sufficiently practical. Then appeared the importance of institutions, of traditional forms, for the conservation even of the spiritual side of the religion.[1272]

The setting of institutions back in time to the Mosaic period was a later work of scribes. As a result of their work, Wellhausen declared, monarchy was deprived of its splendid image. In Wellhausen's words:

> It naturally never came into the heads of these epigoni to conceive that the political organisation and centralisation which the monarchy called into being provided the basis for the organisation and centralisation of the worship, and that their church was merely a spiritualised survival of the nation. What is added to Moses is taken away from the monarchy.[1273]

The implication of Wellhausen's thoughts is clear; institutions priestly or prophetic, did not exist in pre-exilic Israel. There was no exclusive authority derived from the priestly Torah or inspired by the theocracy of the prophets. Contrary to Wellhausen, Kaufmann ascribed to priests and prophets a greater share in ancient Israelite polity. Thus Kaufmann contended that the office of apostle-proph-

---

1270 Wellhausen, "Israel," 436.
1271 Wellhausen, *Prolegomena*, 38.
1272 Wellhausen, *Prolegomena*, 420.
1273 Wellhausen, *Prolegomena*, 256. Wellhausen's words imply that the cult took the place of the monarchy; "This would seem to suggest that the cult took on some of the monarchy's political functions." On this see Jeremiah W. Cataldo, *A Theocratic Yehud? Issues of Government in a Persian Province* (New York: Clark, 2009), 127.

et, which began with Moses and extended to the monarchy, constituted the basis of Israelite polity. In addition, Kaufmann asserted that the role of the priests was complementary to that of the prophets. Moreover Kaufmann, unlike Wellhausen, acknowledged the importance of the period preceding the monarchy. He claimed that the period of Judges presented the Kingdom of God, when ancient Israel was under the leadership of the prophet-judges.[1274] The feeling at this time, in Kaufmann's view, was that the time of Joshua and Judges was a continuation of Moses's prophecy. From Moses to Samuel and Saul, apostle-prophet carried out a national-political function.[1275] In Kaufmann's thinking, the period of Judges began early with Moses and Joshua. He described the institution of Judges as follows:

> When we inquire as to the origin of this institution we can find but one answer: a historical experience that implanted in the people the firm faith that YHWH would always send it apostle-saviours in time of need...the institution of the Judges thus reflects the marvellous religious idealism that prevailed in Israel after the revolution of Moses' time.[1276]

This implied, in Kaufmann's interpretation, that institutions existed in pre-monarchic Israel and the authority of the judges constituted a political system. Kaufmann called this system "primitive-democracy," distinguishing it from theocracy. He went on to say that priests were not part of this secular political system. However, Kaufmann pointed out that this primitive polity aside, the judges were the actual rulers of the people of Israel under the Kingdom of God.[1277]

With reference to the position of the priesthood in ancient Israel, Kaufmann presented it as being far more loyal and creative than prevalent literary criticism deemed it.[1278] Thus Kaufmann exalted the role of the priests in the history of religious development.[1279] He puts forward the idea that the reform movement in

---

1274 Kaufmann, *The Religion of Israel*, 264.
1275 Kaufmann, *Toledot* II, 117.
1276 Kaufmann, "The Biblical Age," 40–41.
1277 Kaufmann, *Toledot* II, 96.
1278 Kaufmann ascribes to the priests a great role in the religious life of the people of Israel in the pre-exilic period. He maintained that their credibility was based on the Torah. Kaufmann even noted that the Torah's literature was a product of the priestly-popular Torah. See Kaufmann, *Toledot II,* 299–300. See further Moshe Greenberg, "A New Approach to the History of the Israelite Priesthood."
1279 Kaufmann stressed the role of the priesthood in the history of Israelite religion. He pointed out that with the appearance of monotheism, the priesthood worked in harmony with prophecy. Furthermore, Kaufmann emphasized that the priesthood grew normally with monotheism and shared with prophecy in creating the world of new religion. This seems to be a denial of Wellhausen's proposition that, with the growth of the priesthood in ancient Israel, religion

Josiah's time was initiated within priestly circles.[1280] In addition, Kaufmann contended that priests occupied a highly regarded position in pre-state times and that their influence remained effective during the monarchic period.[1281] Moreover, the leading position of the priests depended on their oracles.[1282] However, Kaufmann challenged the primacy of the priesthood in ancient Israelite theocracy. He declared that nowhere was an attempt made by the priests to establish a priestly rule. In Kaufmann's words:

> Der Oberpriester ist bei der Königswahl ebenso maßgebend wie der Oberbefehlshaber des Heeres (I Reg 1:7; 2: 36 f.). Ein Hohepriester hat in Judäa einmal sogar einen Staatsstreich durchgeführt (II Reg.11). Die Priester haben jedoch in Israel wohl niemals danach gestrebt, eine eigentliche Priesterherrschaft zu gründen. Das priesterliche Ideal war: hohes Ansehen im Staate, namentlich als Orakelpriesterschaft; eine führende Stellung neben den politischen Leitern des Volkes.[1283]

Unlike Wellhausen, who thought that loss of political independence and rejection of the monarchy were preconditions for theocracy, Kaufmann hypothesized that an authentic prophetic institution existed in pre-monarchic Israel. According to Kaufmann, a large section of the literature between Exod. 2–1 Sam. 12 referred to the time that preceded the rise of monarchy. Kaufmann labelled this period the prophetic theocracy. It persisted to the time of Saul and ended with the period of judges. According to Kaufmann, the prophetic theocracy ceased thereafter and became part of early history. No attempt was made to renew it. It belonged to the past of "ancient history." The end of this prophetic theocracy is recounted in 1 Sam. 12.[1284] Following this further, Kaufmann remarked that a negative attitude towards monarchy was manifested in this section of the literature. This appears, for instance, in Judg. 8: 22–23; 1 Sam 8: 4–22; 10: 18–19. An equally negative attitude towards monarchy can also be recognized between Judges 8 and 1 Samuel 12. Only in Hos. 13: 10–11 does this attitude appear once again.

---

had become estranged from its natural soil and was merely a practice of ritual observances. See Kaufmann, *Toledot* II, 83–84.
1280 In contrast to Wellhausen, who ascribed the reform movement to the prophets as embodied in the program of Deuteronomy, Kaufmann said, "We search in vain for a specific prophetic element in [Josiah's] several acts." See Kaufmann, *The Religion of Israel*, 163; also, idem, *Toledot* II, 484–485.
1281 Kaufmann, "Probleme der israelitisch-jüdischen Religionsgeschichte I," 31.
1282 Kaufmann, "Probleme der israelitisch-jüdischen Religionsgeschichte I," 31.
1283 Kaufmann, „Probleme der israelitisch-jüdischen Religionsgeschichte I," 31.
1284 Kaufmann, *Commentary on Joshua*, 18.

However, Kaufmann pointed out that the triumph of monarchy was the prevailing belief in Israel's history. There was no attempt to invalidate it.[1285]

Kaufmann rejected the view that theocracy came to Israel as a new concept, replacing kingship.[1286] In his eyes, the Israelite kingdom of God was a historical phenomenon and not a result of later theocratic Judaism, as Wellhausen would have it.[1287] Furthermore, Kaufmann showed that Wellhausen's notion of connecting the ancient Kingdom of God with later theocracy damaged the theory at its most elemental level. In Kaufmann's structure, the prophetic kingdom of God preceded the monarchy, whereas priestly rule post-dated it. He went on to argue that in the ancient kingdom of God, hope was invested in the apostle-judges, while in theocracy expectation was focused on the king whose would reinstate the Davidic Kingdom. Kaufmann's far-reaching conclusion was that the apostle-judges appeared before the rule of kings. The prophetic kingdom of God did not display itself in Israel's later history – not in reality or in the messianic vision.[1288]

Seen from Kaufmann's perspective, "several political upheavals were instigated by the prophets."[1289] This seems to contradict Wellhausen, who stated:

> The majority of the prophets were not revolutionists; rather in fact were they always too much inclined to prophesy in accordance with the wishes of the party in power. Besides, in ordinary circumstances their influence was inferior to that of the priests, who were servants of royalty at the chief sanctuaries, but everywhere attached to the established order.[1290]

Unlike Wellhausen, Kaufmann credited the prophets, not the priests, with establishing the religious foundations of the Jewish polity.[1291] Kaufmann differentiated

---

1285 Kaufmann, *Commentary on Joshua*, 18. Kaufmann summed up his view: "The early Israelite theocracy did not on principle repudiate kingship in favor of the rights of the people, God, priest, or prophet. It was the natural effect of the idea of apostolic prophecy on ancient Hebrew society, whose government – a primitive democracy of tribal elders – left room for the leadership of men of God." See Kaufmann, *The Religion of Israel*, 262.
1286 David Polish, *Give Us a King*, 39.
1287 Kaufmann said that Wellhausen's understanding was derived from his interpretation of the theocratic ideal of Second Temple Judaism. Kaufmann claimed that Judaism did not consider the priestly rule to be a continuation of the ancient Kingdom of God, nor did it regard itself as the Kingdom of Israel. See Kaufmann, *Toledot* I, 687, 691.
1288 Kaufmann, *Toledot* I, 707 – 708.
1289 Kaufmann, "The Biblical Age," 48.
1290 Wellhausen, "Israel," 468.
1291 David Polish, *Give Us a King*, 38.

between two types of theocracy; prophetic theocracy and hierocracy. In his view, the prophet was leader of the people, general, judge and king. As he put it:

> Die Einsicht in den Unterschied zwischen den beiden Arten von „Theokratie" ist von grundlegender Bedeutung. Die Hierokratie ist die organisierte Kultusgemeinde mit ihrem Priester an der Spitze, der die Fremdherrschaft die Sorge um das Weltliche abgenommen hat. Die Prophetokratie dagegen ist das im heiligen Kriege mit seinen Feinden liegende Volk, das ein gottbegeisterter Führer befehligt. Der Prophet der Urzeit ist Volksführer, Feldherr, Richter, König.[1292]

Furthermore, Kaufmann contended that biblical criticism misconceived the actual divergence between ancient prophetic theocracy and priestly theocracy. He maintained that Bible scholars have confused theocracy as found in the books of Torah, Joshua, Judges and Samuel with the priestly theocracy of the Second Temple. According to Kaufmann, this way of thinking distorted the facts by detaching ancient phenomenon from its historical context in the time before monarchy and transferring it to later times.[1293] He therefore called for a proper understanding of the prophetic character of theocracy. In his words:

> Man verkennt das Wesen des „theokratischen" Ideals des AT (und des Judentums überhaupt), wenn man seinen prophetischen Grundcharakter übersieht – das Wort „prophetisch" freilich in einem etwas weiteren Sinne genommen. Die „Theokratie" ist nicht bloß eine fromme Gemeinschaft schlechthin, sondern eine Gemeinschaft, in der sich Jahwe fortwährend offenbart.[1294]

It must be borne in mind that Wellhausen distinguished between pre-exilic Israel and the Jewish community of the Second Temple. Put simply, Wellhausen separated Israel's political history up to the exile from the non-political Jewish community of the post exilic-period. He built his understanding of the Second Temple period on three assumptions: 1) since the exile, the Jews were hardly a nation;[1295] 2) the religious community of the Second Temple was cut off from

---

1292 Kaufmann, „Probleme der israelitisch-jüdischen Religionsgeschichte I," 27.

1293 Kaufmann, Commentary on Joshua, 19.

1294 Kaufmann, „Probleme der israelitisch-jüdischen Religionsgeschichte I," 27.

1295 According to Wellhausen, "Seit dem Exil waren die Juden kaum eine Nation mehr, eher eine über die ganze Welt verbreitete Sekte, die hauptsächlich durch die Religion zusammengehalten wurde, und erst in zweiter Linie durch das Blut, welches obendrein an sich als Bindemittel nie genügt hätte, hätte es nicht zugleich religiösen Werte gehabt." See Wellhausen, Die Pharisäer und die Sadducäer, 95.

the nation's past;[1296] 3) most of what had been recorded in the Old Testament was a product of the post-exilic period.[1297] Moreover, Wellhausen made reference to the group of prophetic priests from Ezekiel to Ezra, who had been the first scribes transforming the traditions of pre-exilic history.[1298] Following this further, Wellhausen identified the two Jewish parties of the Second Commonwealth. To him, the Pharisees were a theocratic group who relied on the Torah, whereas the Sadducees were a political party.[1299] With all of this in mind, Wellhausen arrived at the idea that theocracy as an institution was "the residuum of a ruined state,"[1300] a secondary product of Israel's history that matched the conditions of the Jewish community of the Second Temple. More important was Wellhausen's assertion that "theocracy" encompassed ideas such as "church". In Wellhausen's words, "As a matter of taste it may be objectionable to speak of the Jewish church, but as a matter of history it is not inaccurate, and the name is perhaps preferable to that of theocracy, which shelters such confusion of ideas."[1301]

In Kaufmann's understanding of Israel's history, there had been no such gap separating the people of Israel from the traditions of Judaism. He conceived of Israel and Judaism as two embodiments of one authentic and historical tradition of the people of Israel. In Kaufmann's thinking, the vacuum created by the destruction of the First Temple did not divide the records of Israel's history into dif-

---

1296 Jon L. Berquist made the point that the desire of the exiles to detach themselves from the nation's past was complemented by external factors. He writes, "In Wellhausen's view, the internal, intentional aspect of the separation did not conflict with external circumstances. The two were complementary. The internal factors caused the Jerusalemites to abhor the establishment of a new state, and this matched Persian policy, which would not allow such independent political activity anyway." See Jon L. Berquist, *Judaism in Persia's Shadow: A Social and Historical Approach* (Minneapolis: Fortress Press, 1995), 4.

1297 "Was im Alten Testament noch heute wirkt und ohne historische Vorbildung genossen werden kann, ist zum größeren Teil Erzeugnis der nachexilischen Zeit." See Wellhausen, *Israelitische und jüdische Geschichte*, 193.

1298 "An der Spitze dieser Bewegung standen die prophetischen Priester, welche die ersten Schriftgelehrten wurden. Sie haben die äusserlichen Trümmer der vorexilischen Theokratie konserviert, indem sie diese Erzeugnisse religiöser Naivität tränkten mit der Innerlichkeit und dem pathetischen Ernste der Propheten." See Wellhausen, *Die Pharisäer und die Sadducäer*, 13.

1299 It has been said that Wellhausen, "by identifying the Sadducees with the party of the Hasmonaeans and the Pharisees with the supporters of theocracy, [he] had left himself little to account for the apocalyptic and revolutionary activities of the Pharisees." See Arnaldo Momigliano, "Religious History without Frontiers: J. Wellhausen, U. Wilamowitz, and E. Schwartz," *History and Theory* 21, no. 4 (1982): 49–64 (54).

1300 Wellhausen, *Prolegomena*, 422.

1301 Wellhausen, *Prolegomena*, 422.

ferent entities.[1302] Moreover, Kaufmann refuted Wellhausen's supposition that the post-exilic Jews were a religious community. He asserted that the conscious-ness of Jewish exiles as a people never stopped. Thus, Kaufmann pointed out, "In keinem Zeitpunkte ist das nachexilische Judentum bloß Sekte gewesen; es war immer Volk und empfand immer als Volk."[1303]

In contrast to Wellhausen, who hypothesized that theocracy emerged in post-exilic times because conditions were suitable for the appearance of such an in-stitution, Kaufmann made it evident that the theocracy of the Second Temple was imposed upon the Jewish people.[1304] Kaufmann further showed that the post-exilic theocracy was the product of external factors, not a fulfilment of the internal ambition.[1305] In his assessment of the conditions of the Jewish com-munity of the Second Temple, Kaufmann declared that the community did not favour staying in exile and hoped to return; "Their national and eschatological ideals were bound up with Jerusalem and the dynasty of David."[1306] He recog-nized that there was no real break in their history, affirming the continuity of their traditions from pre-exilic Israel to post-exilic Judaism. Kaufmann found support for his view for example in the continuous survival of the messianic idea, pointing out that the Kingdom of David remained the ideal of Judaism. He felt that the messianic idea proved that Judaism did not recognize a theocrat-ic ideal. Even in the apocalyptic literature, it retained the political hope of David and his kingdom.[1307] Thus Kaufmann drew attention to the idealized portrayal of the Davidic kingdom in the Book of Chronicles as the "culmination of Israel's history."[1308]

Wellhausen, we may say, overemphasized the notion of the state; in effect, he equated theocracy with the state. He wrote, "The theocracy was the state of itself; the ancient Israelites regarded the civil state as a miracle, or, in their

---

[1302] David Polish observes that Kaufmann, "challenges the Wellhausen theory that the de-struction of the First Temple represented the watershed dividing Jewish history, separating the record of Jewish people as national entity from that of the 'Jewish church'." See David Polish, *Give Us a King*, 39.

[1303] Kaufmann, "Probleme der israelitisch-jüdischen Religionsgeschichte I," 31.

[1304] Kaufmann, *Toledot* I, 688–689.

[1305] Kaufmann, *Toledot* I, 688–689. Uffenheimer pointed out that Kaufmann in "his analysis of Second Temple Commonwealth sources showed that submission to the Persian yoke was never more than the outcome of a sober realistic appreciation of the situation; nowhere in the literature do we find that appreciation elevated to the level of a theopolitical or eschatolog-ical ideal." See Benjamin Uffenheimer, *Early Prophecy in Israel*, 206.

[1306] Kaufmann, "The Biblical Age," 81.

[1307] Kaufmann, *Toledot* I, 690–691.

[1308] Kaufmann, *Toledot* I, 690.

own words, a help of God."[1309] However, Wellhausen made it quite clear that the state owed nothing to Mosaic theocracy. He maintained that neither a centralized state nor a theocratic ideal existed in premonarchic Israel. It is exactly here that we detect a fundamental divide between Wellhausen and Kaufmann. According to Kaufmann, the appearance of the ideal government was not a utopian creation of the authors of the Second Commonwealth, as Wellhausen would have it. Rather, it was "a vision firmly anchored in the social realities of the period of the Judges; it was in fact, a major factor in forging those realities."[1310] Wellhausen, in contrast, assumed that it was out of anarchy that monarchy emerged as a "natural creation".[1311] Kaufmann contended that an ideal prophetic leader from the time of Moses onwards inspired the people and the political organization during the whole period before the rise of monarchy.[1312] We thus see that Kaufmann's model of an ideal saviour-judge who established the polity of ancient Israel in the pre-state period was completely at odds with Wellhausen's assertion that pre-monarchic Israel was just an idea. In the words of Wellhausen:

> Israel ist kein Organismus, zu dessen regelmäßigen Funktionen etwa die Kriegführung gehörte; Israel ist nur eine Idee. Und Israel als Idee ist gleichbedeutend mit Jahve; nur daß Jahve mehr ist als eine Idee und dem Wunsche die Macht zur Verfügung stellen kann.[1313]

Furthermore, Wellhausen considered theocracy in the form of an institution to be historically impossible in ancient Israel.[1314] He noted that the term theocracy was

---

1309 Wellhausen, *Prolegomena*, 414.
1310 Uffenheimer drew attention to Buber's and Kaufmann's similarities and differences with regard to the social ideal in the time of Judges. See Benjamin Uffenheimer, *Early Prophecy in Israel*, 208–210.
1311 "Thus, for Wellhausen, it would have been impossible for the monarchic Israelite state to have been patterned after a Mosaic theocracy. The central, executive power that was necessary for a theocracy did not exist beforehand." See Jeremiah W. Cataldo, *A Theocratic Yehud? Issues of Government in a Persian Province*, 126.
1312 As David Polish points out, "Kaufmann's prophetic theocracy involves the redemption of the people and its restoration. This has been and is recurrently brought about by God's prophet-messenger whose task is to reconstitute the nation in the spirit of the god who sends". He further adds, "The implications of Kaufman's theocracy are far-reaching. Kaufmann rejects the brand of theocracy that is dependent on national disaster in favor of one whose criterion is national renewal. But even more, he restores the synthesis of Jewish politics and Jewish religion through the action of the divinely commissioned messenger. He is not a political agent alone. He is a person of prophetic and spiritual power." See David Polish, *Give Us a King*, 38.
1313 Wellhausen, *Israelitische und jüdische Geschichte*, 37.
1314 Reinhard Kratz sums up the history of the term theocracy, its connotation by Josephus and Wellhausen, and its different interpretations in the following manner: "Josephus (AP II 184–189)

first coined by Josephus and did not occur in the Old Testament. Moreover, he remarked that the theocracy of ancient times was a form of particularism. Regarding the meaning of "theocracy" Wellhausen wrote:

> Er ist erst von Josephus gebildet und kommt im Alten Testament nicht vor; dort ist nur vom Volke, nicht vom Reiche Jahves die Rede. Die Theokratie ist in der alten Zeit nichts weniger als Hierokratie; weder steht ein Hohepriester an der Spitze, noch ein Priesterkönig nach Art des Melchisedek; gerade der gänzliche Mangel einer Unterscheidung zwischen Geistlich und Weltlich ist charakteristisch. Sie besteht überhaupt nicht in einer besonderen Organisation. Das alte Stamm- und Geschlechterwesen bleibt zunächst völlig in Kraft, eine lose Aristokratie der Ältesten, eine Art milder Anarchie, die man patriarchalisch zu nennen pflegt... Die Theokratie ist nichts weiter, als das, was man früher Partikularismus zu nennen pflegte. Die heiligen Angelegenheiten sind die nationalen. Die Gottheit hat es nicht mit dem einzelnen Menschen und nicht mit der Welt zu tun, sondern mit einem bestimmten durch das Blut zusammengehaltenen Kreise, mit dem Volk Israel.[1315]

Kaufmann disagreed with Wellhausen and his followers with regard to their use of the theocratic idea to map out different phases of Israel's history and the development of biblical literature.[1316] He also disputed Josephus's description of the character of Jewish theocracy,[1317] arguing that it should not be taken as representing original Jewish thinking.[1318] Consequently, Kaufmann constructed a model of prophetic theocracy extending from the time of Moses to the emergence

---

und Julius Wellhausen folgend, wird der Begriff in der alttestamentlichen Forschung gerne *promiscue* mit ‚Hierokratie' verwandt und ist geradezu zum Synonym für das Judentum im Zeitalter des Zweiten Tempels geworden. Gegen diese Auffassung hat man unter Hinweis auf die neueren epigraphischen Funde verschiedentlich eingewandt, daß Juda in der Perserzeit keineswegs als Theokratie oder Hierokratie sondern als persische Provinz organisiert gewesen und also nicht von Priestern, sondern einem Statthalter regiert worden sei. Erst in hellenistischer Zeit könne man von einer Art Theokratie oder Hierokratie sprechen. Beides ist richtig und falsch zugleich. Soweit es die politische Verfassung Judas betrifft, ist den Kritikern Recht zu geben, soweit es aber das Selbstverständnis des Judentums anbelangt, haben eher Josephus und Wellhausen das Richtige getroffen, nur daß sie wie ihre Kritiker der Suggestion der jüdischen Tradition erlagen und den Fehler begingen, die politische Verfassung Judas mit dem in der Überlieferung formulierten Selbstverständnis des Judentums gleichzusetzen". On this see Reinhard G. Kratz, *Das Judentum im Zeitalter des Zweiten Tempels* (Tübingen: Mohr Siebeck, 2004), 183.

1315 Wellhausen, „Die Israelitisch-Jüdische Religion," in *Die Kultur der Gegenwart: Ihre Entwicklung und ihre Ziele*, 6.

1316 Kaufmann, *Toledot* I. 688.

1317 Benjamin Uffenheimer accepted 'Kaufmann's view in this regard. He points out, "The mistaken use of the word 'theocracy' in reference to a priestly-aristocratic regime entered scholarly literature under the influence of Josephus." See Benjamin Uffenheimer, *Early Prophecy in Israel*, 208.

1318 For more on this issue, see Kaufmann, *Toledot* I, 693 – 694, no.7.

of the monarchy. Whereas Wellhausen tended to regard theocracy as the hierocratic rule of priests, and saw this as emerging after the destruction of the First Temple, Kaufmann insisted that theocracy as the hierocratic rule of priests did not exist in either pre-exilic Israel or in the early Judaism of the Second Temple. In other words, Wellhausen made a distinction between early theocracy (in einem gewissen Sinne) in pre-exilic Israel and theocracy as in the form of hierocracy which arose in post-exilic times. Kaufmann proposed that theocracy in Israel existed from the time of Moses to the monarchy in the form of prophetic theocracy. In Kaufmann's opinion, hierocracy appeared only in the late Judaism of the post-exilic period.

We have seen that Wellhausen treated the notion of theocracy as a more historical development resulting from political conditions, while Kaufmann's prophetic theocracy was a religious phenomenon built on the foundations afforded by the belief in God's deliverance of his people.[1319] Theocracy existed, according to Wellhausen, in a time when the people were detached from the soil of their original national existence. Moreover, Wellhausen maintained that religion in premonarchic times had a pre-institutional phase. He also made the point that monarchy was not like a holy state, but simply the state – which in itself was holy. Kaufmann's view, almost static, did not envision such a divide between religion and political history. Rather, Kaufmann advocated the idea that Israelite religion remained the source of Israel's entire history, regardless of whether that history was in a pre-state, exilic or post-exilic period, or even in diaspora. On the whole, for Wellhausen state and religion were one; the state was holy. Therefore, the religious organization, namely "P" was derived from it; for Kaufmann, on the contrary, the religion of "prophecy" had priority over the state.

5 Premises and assumptions

Three preconceptions underlay Wellhausen's system of thought. First, one can hardly fail to notice Wellhausen's negative attitude towards the Pharisees in his assessment of the Jewish parties of the Second Temple period. Second, Wellhausen disregarded rabbinic sources and never made them the starting point of inquiry. Third, his *Prolegomena* reflected a programmatic polemic against "law" and Judaism. What concerns us here is to show how these assumptions shaped

---

1319 Kaufmann pointed out that God sent messengers to save his people. According to Kaufmann, the Exodus from Egypt was considered to be the first example of prophetic theocracy. In the course of time, the office of those messengers gained a political authority. See Kaufmann, *Toledot* I, 701–703.

Wellhausen's view on the history of Israel. In his study on *Pharisees and Saddu-cees* 1874, Wellhausen described the Pharisees as follows:

> Also die Pharisäer unterschieden sich vom Volke nicht durch den absonderlichen Inhalt ihres Wollens, sondern vielmehr durch den Grad ihres Eifers und ihrer Konsequenz in den gemeinsamen Bestrebungen der Bürger des heiligen Gemeinwesens. Sie waren mit anderen Worten innerhalb der Theokratie die theokratische Partei.[1320]

Thus, according to Wellhausen, the Pharisees were a theocratic group within the Jewish theocracy. Wellhausen stated that the Pharisees stood opposed to worldly people. As he put it, "Die Pharisäer standen einerseits den Weltmenschen feindlich gegenüber, andererseits aber schieden sie sich auch sehr von der Menge die vom Gesetz nichts wußte, und vergalten ihr die Verehrung, die sie ihnen zollte, mit unverhohlener Verachtung."[1321] Wellhausen's conception of the Jewish parties in post-exilic times strongly influenced his reconstruction of history. Hans Liebeschütz made the point that Wellhausen's view of the Jewish parties was influenced by his understanding of the situation in post-exilic times. That is to say Wellhausen saw the Sadducees as being the real representatives of actual social conditions, while the Pharisees presented the religious trend that shaped the future of the people.[1322] Moreover, Rudolf Smend remarked that Wellhausen severely criticized the Pharisees and the rabbis.[1323] He quotes Wellhausen:

> Gesetze sind nach Ezechiel dazu da, daß man dadurch mag leben. Damit wird über das System der pharisäischen Satzungen der Stab gebrochen. Das Leben wurde dadurch nicht gefördert, sondern behindert und eingeengt. Die Gesellschaft wurde eine Karikatur durch die angeblich göttlichen und in Wahrheit absurden Ziele, die ihr gesteckt wurden.[1324]

1320 Wellhausen, *Die Pharisäer und die Sadducäer*, 20.
1321 Wellhausen, *Israelitische und jüdische Geschichte*, 283.
1322 Hans Liebeschütz, *Das Judentum im deutschen Geschichtsbild von Hegel bis Max Weber* (Schriftenreihe wissenschaftlicher Abhandlungen des Leo-Baeck-Instituts 17; Tübingen: Mohr, 1967), 246. Liebeschütz pointed out that Wellhausen rejected Geiger's description of the Pharisees as a patriotic party. See Liebeschütz, *Das Judentum im deutschen Geschichtsbild von Hegel bis Max Weber*, 247, 248.
1323 Rudolf Smend, *Epochen der Bibelkritik: Gesammelte Studien* 3 (Beiträge zur evangelischen Theologie 109; München: Kaiser, 1991), 198.
1324 Wellhausen, *Israelitische und jüdische Geschichte*, 283–284.

Wellhausen refers here to two aspects that characterized the Pharisees: their existence as a theocratic group and the "System of Pharisaic Ordinances" (System der pharisäischen Satzungen). It was Wellhausen's assessment of the character of the Pharisees that led scholars to assume that his subsequent study of the law in the Old Testament was influenced by his view of the Pharisees. In his estimate of Wellhausen's hypothesis on the "Law", the Jewish Bible scholar Moshe Weinfeld wrote:

> Wellhausen's opinion about pharisaic theocracy, which was the subject of his study in 1874 – four years before the *Prolegomena zur Geschichte Israels* was published – influenced deeply his views about the Priestly Code in the Pentateuch. Since pharisaic doctrine is based on the Torah...Wellhausen logically looked for the origin of P in a proto-pharisaic environment.[1325]

What Wellhausen remarked about the Pharisees was intrinsic to his understanding of the situation in post-exilic time. This is clear from Wellhausen's evaluation of Jewish sources dated from that period. He was convinced that rabbinic sources could hardly deliver reliable information on the history of ancient Israel. Judging from his experience, Wellhausen cautioned, "Nach den Forschungen der jüdischen Gelehrten zu schlissen... muss die geschichtliche Ausbeute aus dem Thalmud gering sein"[1326] In this context Hans Liebeschütz pointed out that Wellhausen did not make use of rabbinic sources, including the Talmud and Mishnah in his reconstruction, because he did not trust these sources for historical writing.[1327]

Having reviewed Wellhausen's assumptions concerning the Jewish parties of the Second Temple, we turn to Wellhausen's attitude towards the law and Judaism. Wellhausen's labelling of Judaism as a "religion estranged from the heart," shows his antipathy to the law and Judaism. He felt strongly the differences between the religion of ancient Israel and the prescribed law of Judaism, the prod-

---

1325 Moshe Weinfeld, "Julius Wellhausen's Understanding of the Law of Ancient Israel and its Fallacies," in *Shnaton: An Annual for Biblical and Ancient Near Eastern Studies* 4 (ed. Moshe Weinfeld; Jerusalem: Magness Press, 1980), 62–93.
1326 Wellhausen, *Die Pharisäer und die Sadducäer*, 130. Perhaps this could explain why Wellhausen shifted to Arabic and Islamic studies.
1327 Liebeschütz notes that Wellhausen had never used the literature of Judaism as source material for reconstructing early Christianity. See Liebeschütz, *Das Judentum im deutschen Geschichtsbild*, 248, 253, 259, 261. In contrast, Moshe Weinfeld contends that Wellhausen's weakness in rabbinic Judaism prevented him from comprehending the essence of the Torah and its reception in Judaism. See Moshe Weinfeld, "Wellhausen's Understanding of the Law of Ancient Israel and its Fallacies."

uct of the Second Temple period. In Wellhausen's view, these two different worlds, Israel and Judaism, lay far apart:

> Als willkürlicher Abfall kann der Abstand nicht betrachtet werden, der das alte Israel, das fromme ganz ebenso wie das gottlose, nicht bloß von den Forderungen, sondern auch von den Voraussetzungen des Gesetzes trennt. Es ist ein allgemeiner Abstand zweier verschiedener Welten. Wohl gibt es genug Vergleichungspunkte zwischen der älteren Praxis und dem Gesetze.[1328]

Perhaps more informative is Wellhausen's representation of the "law" of the Pentateuch/Hexateuch as church history (*Kirchengeschichte*) as opposed to the *Weltgeschichte* of the history books. He describes it as the dichotomy between holiness and nature. In Wellhausen's words:

> Sobald wir aus dem Pentateuch (oder richtiger dem Hexateuch, denn das Buch Josua gehört inhaltlich mit den fünf Büchern Moses zusammen) heraustreten, kommen wir mit den Büchern der Richter, Samuelis und die Könige in eine ganz andere Sphäre. Statt der Kirchengeschichte setzt mit einem Mal die Weltgeschichte ein, die Heiligkeit hört auf und die Natur beginnt, es ist der Abstand zweier verschiedener Welten.[1329]

Wellhausen's obsession with examining the antithesis between the religion of ancient Israel and Judaism started quite early. In 1879, Wellhausen wrote, "Seit zehn Jahren haben mich geschichtliche Studien ausschließlich im Anspruch genommen, Judentum und altes Israel in ihrem Gengensatze."[1330] In Wellhausen's view, the law was what divided Israel from Judaism. Judaism was the religion of the law. As Wellhausen found, "The law thrusts itself in everywhere; it commands and blocks up the access to heaven; it regulates and sets limits to the understanding of the divine working on earth. As far as it can, it takes the soul out of religion and spoils morality."[1331]

It was the "law" then that made Judaism an artificial product of history. Wellhausen went even further to say that Judaism under the influence of the law took on "an entirely different physiognomy from that of Hebrew antiquity."[1332] Based on this, Wellhausen portrayed Judaism in the following manner:

> It is not easy to find points of view from which to pronounce on the character of Judaism. It is a system, but a practical system, which can scarcely be set forth in relation to one leading

1328 Wellhausen, *Israelitische und jüdische Geschichte*, 15–16.
1329 Wellhausen, *Grundrisse zum Alten Testament*, 69.
1330 In a letter to J. Olshausen. On this see Rudolf Smend, *Epochen der Bibelkritik*, 189.
1331 Wellhausen, "Israel," 509.
1332 Wellhausen, "Israel," 508.

thought, as it is an irregular product of history. It lives on the stores of the past, but is not simply the total of what had been previously acquired; it is full of new impulses, and has an entirely different physiognomy from that of Hebrew antiquity, so much so that it is hard even to catch a likeness. Judaism is everywhere historically comprehensible, and yet it is a mass of antinomies.[1333]

Challenging Wellhausen's hypothesis on the history and character of Judaism, Kaufmann took a different direction. He started by emphasizing that Judaism was a religious-historical phenomenon.[1334] Its origin was rooted in the ideas of the pre-exilic religion, both priestly and prophetic.[1335] Contrary to Wellhausen's conviction that there was little connection between the religion of Israelite antiquity and the Jewish traditions of the Second Temple, Kaufmann insisted that a continuity existed between the viewpoint of the Torah and that of later Judaism. Kaufmann did not question the biblical order that placed the Torah before the prophets. In discussing the history of Israelite religion, he described the relationship of the Torah, prophets and Judaism to one another as follows:

There is thus a recognizable development between the viewpoint of the Torah and that of later Judaism. In between have come the prophets with their insistence on the conditional value of the cult. Later Judaism incorporated the prophetic view in its evaluation of the cult, but the Torah shows no influence of the prophetic idea.[1336]

Kaufmann, unlike Wellhausen who held that Judaism had become detached from the past, maintained that it built on the ancient Israelite religion. Furthermore, he believed that it was during the Second Temple period that faith in Yahweh ripened: "Religious creativity did not cease. On the contrary, it was destined to reach heights that the pre-exilic age had never dreamed of. But it took on a new form, an elaboration of and at all times a dependence upon the legacy of the past."[1337]

In addition, Kaufmann resisted the claim that Judaism had become immersed in the law and rituals and had given away the prophetic emphasis on

---

1333 Wellhausen, "Israel," 508–509. Reinhard G. Kratz rightly observed that Wellhausen's attitude towards Judaism wavered between appreciation and antipathy ('zwischen Zuneigung und Abneigung'); according to Kratz, Wellhausen said that he felt repelled and time and again attracted ('abgestoßen und immer wieder angezogen'). On this see Reinhard G. Kratz, "Eyes and Spectacles," 396.
1334 Menahem Haran points out that Kaufmann dedicated his entire life to studying Judaism. See Menahem Haran, "On the Border of Faith," 53.
1335 Kaufmann, *The Religion of Israel*, 447.
1336 Kaufmann, *The Religion of Israel*, 103.
1337 Kaufmann, *The Religion of Israel*, 447–448.

morals and ethics. Kaufmann credited Judaism with having a high universalistic character. He strenuously objected to the presuppositions of historians who degraded post-exilic Judaism. As Kaufmann put it:

> It is a widespread notion among historians of Israel that post-exilic Judaism is epigonous, that its creative impulse waned, that it became petrified. Judaism is alleged to have placed greater value on the observance of externals than on its ethico-religious content. Prophecy ceased, to be replaced by the casuistic study of the letter of the law. The universalism of the prophets – so it is said – gave way to a narrow, nationalistic exclusivism. This evaluation, however, is incorrect. Israelite religion continued fertile and creative throughout the period of the Second Temple, and in spite of appearances the direction of this creativeness was universalistic. Indeed, the Judaism of this age attained heights of universalism beyond anything achieved in the pre-exilic period.[1338]

Not only Wellhausen's theory was under the attack by Kaufmann, but also his presuppositions and ideologies were the subject of severe criticism. Kaufmann assailed what he regarded as the Christian dogma underlying Wellhausen's assessment of Judaism.[1339] As noted earlier, although Kaufmann did not reject the historical critical method, he nevertheless "recognized that biblical scholarship had in fact been presupposing certain Christian ideas, such as the priority of ethics and faith over ritual and community."[1340] In his defending the distinctive character of Judaism, Kaufmann regarded Wellhausen's perception of Judaism and law as representing a Christian theological preoccupation.[1341] Kaufmann

---

1338 Kaufmann, "The Biblical Age," 84.
1339 It has been argued that Kaufmann's position represented the secular national response against Christian scholarship. Haran, for example, points out that Kaufmann approached Israel's history from a secular point of view. See Menahem Haran, "On the Border of Faith," 53. In addition, Thomas Krapf contended that Kaufmann's contribution to the history of biblical religion was either neglected or ignored by the Christian scholarship. See Thomas M. Krapf, *Yehezkel Kaufmann: Ein Lebens- und Erkenntnisweg zur Theologie der Hebräischen Bibel*, 81. In this context, Benjamin Uffenheimer said that modern Jewish biblical research came into existence as a polemic response to protestant scholarship. See Benjamin Uffenheimer, "Some Reflections on Modern Jewish Biblical Research," 173. On this issue see further Hanna Liss, "Religionsgeschichte and its challenge to Jewish Bible Scholars in the Late 19th and Early 20th Century," in Ute E. Eisen and Erhard S. Gerstenberger, eds., *Hermann Gunkel Revisited: Literatur- und Religionsgeschichtliche Studien* (Berlin: Lit, 2010), 149–170.
1340 Ewald L. Greenstein, *Essays on Biblical Method and Translation* (Atlanta: Scholars Press, 1989), 25–26. See also Peter Slyomovics, "Kaufmann's Critique of Wellhausen," 87.
1341 In what appears to be a support of Kaufmann's hypothesis, Eliezer Schweid pointed out that Wellhausen approached the Bible from a Christian standpoint. He observes that Wellhausen did not appreciate that Israelite monotheism was neither philosophical nor a development out of primitive religion. See Eliezer Schweid, *A History of Modern Jewish Religious Philosophy*, 158.

therefore sought to show that Judaism was not only a religion of law and ritual but also recognized the prophetic doctrine of ethics.[1342] Moreover, Kaufmann rejected Wellhausen's judgment of Pharisaic Judaism. He contended, "Auch das pharisäische Judentum hat die Lehre vom Primat der Ethik vollständig anerkannt, wie aus dem bekannten Spruch Hillels (Sabb. 31a) hervorgeht".[1343] Against the portrayal by Wellhausen and Christian theology of Judaism as "church," Kaufmann asserted that Judaism was never a religious sect. In his words:

> In keinem Zeitpunkte ist das nachexilische Judentum bloß Sekte gewesen; es war immer Volk und empfand immer als Volk. Das Judentum hat aus seiner Geschichte nie eine samaritanische תולידה gemacht ... Erst die moderne christliche Theologie hat dem Judentum das ihm fremde Ideal der Priesterherrschaft zugeschoben und dieses Ideal in den Priesterkodex hineingedichtet. Daraus zog sie den Schluß, daß der Priesterkodex dem Geiste des nachexilischen Judentums entsprungen sei und kam somit in einem entscheidenden Punkte zu durchaus falschen Ergebnissen.[1344]

It requires little imagination to see that Wellhausen and Kaufmann's thoughts might have been shaped under certain prejudices. Still, it is true that both worked towards a historical presentation of the history of Israel. Nevertheless, the writings of Wellhausen and Kaufmann exhibit signs of the Jewish-Christian polemic.[1345] As we have seen, Wellhausen's attitude towards the law and rabbinic literature bore an anti-institutional bias. Seen from the Jewish perspective, "Wellhausen's theory... did not argue only against the unity of the Pentateuch and date its writing to a later time; it also questioned the story it tells about the history of the Jewish faith."[1346]

1342 Kaufmann wrote, "Auch das spätere Judentum hat diese Lehre ohne Einschränkung anerkannt. Sie war gleichsam mit den prophetischen Büchern zugleich kanonisiert. Namentlich in den Psalmen und in der Spruchliteratur wird oft hervorgehoben, daß nicht Opfer, sondern Rechttun und religiöse Gesinnung die wahre Frömmigkeit ausmachen." See Kaufmann, "Probleme der israelitisch-jüdischen Religionsgeschichte II," 40.
1343 Kaufmann, "Probleme der israelitisch-jüdischen Religionsgeschichte II," 40.
1344 Kaufmann, „Probleme der israelitisch-jüdischen Religionsgeschichte I," 31–32.
1345 Traces of this polemic can be followed back to Wellhausen's controversy with Abraham Geiger over the question of Pharisees and Sadducees. Another example for the Jewish-Christian polemic can be drawn from the differences between Wellhausen and the Jewish scholar Heinrich Graetz. R. E. Clements proposed that "the anti-Jewish polemic of the one can be compared with the anti-Christian polemic of the other." See R. E. Clements, "The Study of the Old Testament," in *Nineteenth Century Religious Thought in the West*, 132.
1346 Yaakov Shavit and Mordechai Eran, *The Hebrew Bible Reborn: From Holy Scripture to the Book of Books*, 101.

In addition, Wellhausen's view of Judaism as a degenerated, ritualistic and thus petrified religion of the law invited criticism. It is likely that Kaufmann in challenging Wellhausen's theory sought to uncover the ideological preconceptions underlying his thinking. Kaufmann assumed that Wellhausen was influenced by the German Protestant theology that shaped his view on Judaism.[1347] Also, Kaufmann never tired of reiterating that the modern interpretation of Israel's history has been dominated by Christian scholars. He contended that the negative attitude towards Israelite religion was inherent in the stereotypical Christian's idea of Judaism. Thus Kaufmann felt that scholars were not able to work with the idea that early Israelites had a monotheistic faith; "It is reflected in the scholarly axiom that the Israelite people was pagan, only the prophets and their circles transmitting the monotheistic idea."[1348]

6 Evaluation

In the preceding discussion I have pointed to a number of similarities and differences between Wellhausen and Kaufmann. We have seen that they began Israel's history with Moses as the formative period. Their views on religious development in ancient Israel indicate that they parted ways especially with regard to the origin of monotheism. According to Wellhausen, "Der Monotheismus war dem alten Israel unbekannt."[1349] Kaufmann, on the other hand asserted, "Our data compel us to assume that the monotheistic idea was not only born in Israel's initial period, but that already then it had effected a far-reaching revolution in the spirit of the people.'[1350] Another example that shows us the basic difference between Wellhausen and Kaufmann can be obtained from their understanding of the religion of the Jews in the Jewish colony of Yeb. Writing about the Jews living on Elephantine, Wellhausen described them as "a strange vestige of pre-legal Hebraism" and a "fossil remnant of not yet reformed Judaism in a distant

---

1347 Peter Skyomovics, "Yehezkel Kaufmann's Critique of Wellhausen," 87. For perception of Judaism in German Protestant thought, see Amy Newmann, "The Death of Judaism in German Protestant Thought from Luther to Hegel," *JAAR* 61, no. 3 (1993): 455–484. For more on this point see also Andres Gerdmar, *Roots of theological anti-Semitism: German biblical interpretation and the Jews, from Herder and Semler to Kittel and Bultmann* (Leiden: Brill, 2009).
1348 Kaufmann, *The Religion of Israel*, 403.
1349 Wellhausen, *Israelitische und jüdische Geschichte*, 29.
1350 Kaufmann, "The Bible and Mythological Polytheism," 197.

land."[1351] By contrast, Kaufmann affirmed that the Jewish religion on Elephantine was "not indicative of an earlier stage in the evolution of the religion of Israel. The Jews of Yeb were monotheists; their temple was a temple of Yahu."[1352]

With respect to their view on history and history writing, two points deserve mention. First, both Wellhausen and Kaufmann attempted to make sense out of the given text without referring to external data. Their respective histories lack any clear reference to archaeological findings. In other words they based their reconstruction on the internal evidence of the Hebrew Bible. Second, Wellhausen's and Kaufmann's interest in the history of Israel was indisputable. The titles of their respective works bear this out. Wellhausen started with analysis of sources and texts, as in his *Composition des Hexateuchs*. This was followed by an inquiry into the religious history of ancient Israel, which was the subject of *Prolegomena*. All of this was undertaken with the aim of reconstructing Israel's history as indicated in Wellhausen's historical synthesis, *Israelitische und jüdische Geschichte*. Kaufmann, too, though he took a different path, was interested in Israel's early history. The beginning for Kaufmann was a socio-historical investigation on the problem of Jewish exile and the origin of Judaism, which was the subject of *Golah veNechar*. This was followed by his comprehensive study on the history of Israelite religion, *Toledot*. Kaufmann then turned to constructing the early tradition of Israel in Canaan as shown in his commentaries on the books of Joshua and Judges.

Although Wellhausen's and Kaufmann's respective histories show some overlapping at points, the basis for each of them was different. Wellhausen, as might be expected, did not conceive of a particular revelation at the beginning of Israel. He considered the religion of the ancient Israelites to be a true representation of their lives, closely connected to the reality of their times. When they entered into the cultural land of Canaan they did not bring with them any abstract idea about God, but only Moses's instructions. Arguing from the opposite direction, Kaufmann held that monotheism was a creation of the genius Moses in the desert. Once Moses showed to his people how to walk in accordance with the laws of Yahweh, they never deviated from the right path. Kaufmann was convinced that Israel's history was indeed a history of a monotheistic people.

1351 Wellhausen, *Israelitische und jüdische Geschichte*, 176–178. See also Reinhard G. Kratz, "Temple and Torah: Reflections on the Legal Status of the Pentateuch between Elephantine and Qumran," in *The Pentateuch as Torah: New Models for Understanding its Promulgation and Acceptance* (ed. Gary N. Knoppers and Bernhard M. Levinson; Winona Lake: Eisenbrauns, 2007), 77–103 (82).
1352 Kaufmann, *History of the Religion of Israel, vol. IV: From the Babylonian Captivity to the End of Prophecy*, 530.

Based on criticism of the Pentateuch/Hexateuch sources, Wellhausen reconstructed not only the history of literary sources but also his history of ancient Israel and its religion. Wellhausen's outline of the history of ancient Israel defined
several main phases: early Israelite history in Canaan, the monarchic period and
the exile. According to Wellhausen, the first phase represented the time of the
old tradition. Monarchy and the time of the first three kings marked the beginning of Israel's political history. With the exile the history of ancient Israel
came to an end and the history of Judaism began.[1353]

Viewing Wellhausen's clear presentation of the different historical stages of
Israelite religion, several things can be observed in his system. Wellhausen
seems to have had little appreciation of pre-Yahwistic religion.[1354] Furthermore,
while Wellhausen's structure "totally ignores the Patriarchal narratives (figures
such as Abraham are projections into the past from much later times), it allows
that the Exodus and wilderness traditions may contain scraps of historical information."[1355] Wellhausen's stance towards the origin and function of the covenant
in biblical religion was a subject of sharp criticism. As Stephen Geller points out,
"In perhaps no other area has Wellhausen's theory been so decisively refuted by
later scholarship."[1356] On the other hand, it has been said that Wellhausen's "obsession with 'the original' prevented him from accepting that a secondary development such as the emergence of the Jewish law religion could also have provided the image of early Israel found in the Old Testament."[1357]

Kaufmann is known today as the Jewish Bible scholar who challenged Wellhausen's hypothesis on the history of Israelite religion.[1358] Though Kaufmann's
critique of Wellhausen offers many insights, his reconstruction of Israel's reli-

---

1353 For discussion see W. Baumgartner, "Wellhausen und der Heutige Stand der Alttestamen-
tlichen Wissenschaft," *Theologische Rundschau* 2 (1930): 287–307. Wellhausen was accused of
paying little attention to Israel's political history. For more on this issue, see Eduard Meyer, *Julius
Wellhausen und Meine Schrift "Die Entstehung des Judenthums": Eine Erwiderung* (Halle: Max
Niemeyer, 1897), 25, 26. See also Clements, *A Century of Old Testament Study*, 10. See further
Reinhard G. Kratz, "Die Entstehung des Judentums: Zur Kontroverse zwischen E. Meyer und J.
Wellhausen: Rudolf Smend Zum 65. Geburtstag." *ZThK* 95, 2 (1998): 167–184.
1354 Patrick D. Miller, "Wellhausen and the History of Israel's Religion," in *Julius Wellhausen
and his Prolegomena to the History of Israel*, 61–73.
1355 J.W. Rogerson, "Setting the Scene: A Brief Outline of Histories of Israel" in *Understanding
the History of Ancient Israel* (ed. H. G. Williamson; Oxford: Oxford University Press, 2007), 3–14
(8).
1356 Stephen Geller, "Wellhausen and Kaufmann," 44.
1357 Niels P. Lemche, *The Israelites in History and Tradition* (London: SPCK, 1998), 158.
1358 David Lieber pointed out that "in evaluating Kaufmann's thesis, one must begin by wel-
coming it as a long overdue corrective to the one-sided view so persuasively presented by Wellhausen." See David Lieber, "Yehezkel Kaufmann's Contribution to Biblical Scholarship." 258.

gion did not win many supporters and therefore remained known to only a narrow circle.[1359] It could be said that Kaufmann was a prisoner of the structured system of his interpretation. In my view there were at least, three reasons for the scholarly rejection of Kaufmann's hypothesis. First, Kaufmann came late to the study of the Hebrew Bible after historical criticism had gained a solid ground.[1360] Second, Kaufmann's characterization of Israelite religion as something that never occurred before in religious history is far from convincing. Moreover, it has been noted that Kaufmann, in his analysis of the origin of Israelite monotheism, embraced an uncompromising position. This appears, for example, in Kaufmann's postulate "that Israelite religion was an original creation of the people of Israel. It was absolutely different from anything the pagan world ever knew."[1361] He went further to claim that monotheism was never under the threat of pagan influence. As Kaufmann put it, "Israelite monotheism is particularly prominent: it operates in a world without gods."[1362] Here Kaufmann did

---

1359 Baruch Schwartz mentions three main reasons why Kaufmann's works did not find wider acceptance and support. First, he points out that Kaufmann's oeuvre was part of a comprehensive attempt to deal with Jewish national existence; thus, it was directed most naturally at a Jewish readership. In this sense, says Baruch Schwartz, Kaufmann's work was a function of time and place: the early twentieth century Jewish cultural milieu. The second reason, which in a way was an outgrowth of the first, relates to the language that Kaufmann chose to express his ideas. Kaufmann wrote virtually all his scholarly works in Hebrew; translations were partial and appeared late and were confined to English until recently. As for the third reason, Kaufmann dared to question the very fundamental assumptions of (mainly German) biblical scholars without distancing himself from their methods. Here Baruch Schwartz praises Kaufmann, maintaining that it would not be an exaggeration to claim that by attacking them on their own grounds, Kaufmann presented too formidable a challenge. Scholars found it simpler to ignore than to respond. On this see Baruch J. Schwartz, "The Pentateuch as Scripture and the Challenge of Biblical Criticism: Responses among Modern Jewish Thinkers and Scholars," 277.
1360 Menahem Haran drew attention to the fact that study of the Hebrew Bible was not the starting point of Kaufmann's research. See Menahem Haran, "On the Border of Faith." In addition, Eliezer Schweid noted that Kaufmann combined in his research the problem and the fate of Jewish people with the problem of Judaism. Kaufmann called for the problem of Jewish existence to be studied along with Judaism as one facet of Jewish history. See Eliezer Schweid, *A History of Modern Jewish Religious Philosophy*, 138–139.
1361 Kaufmann, *The Religion of Israel*, 2.
1362 Kaufmann, "The Bible and Mythological Polytheism," 196. Gottwald observed that Kaufmann "...came to the Hebrew Bible not so much to see what Israel's earliest religion was like but to show that it was monotheistic from the start just as it was monotheistic when it served to bond the Jewish people from the Exile onward." See Gottwald, *The Hebrew Bible in its Social World and in Ours*, 195. In addition, Zevit describes Kaufmann's explanation of monotheism as "an inexplicable almost static 'given' [that] is a mystifying, not a clarifying, element in his discussion." See Ziony Zevit, *The Religions of Ancient Israel*, 47.

not behave like an historian. It has further been noted that Kaufmann's views on the history of Israelite religion brought him close to a theological interpretation of the Hebrew Bible.[1363] Thus it was Kaufmann's obsession with the origin of biblical monotheism which led some scholars to assume that he was writing Old Testament theology.[1364]

The third reason that made Kaufmann's position untenable was related to his reconstruction of Israel's history. Kaufmann believed that the biblical story about Israel's origin and uniqueness was true.[1365] In his presentation of the history of ancient Israel from its beginning up to the monarchic period, Kaufmann followed the biblical account without questioning its content.[1366] In Kaufmann's view the patriarchs were historical figures. He treated the Exodus and wilderness tradition as a reliable description of the Israelite tribes before they entered into the land of Canaan. Kaufmann ascribed to the idea that the Israelites occupied Canaan by massive force of arms and that the stories of Joshua and Judges truly depicted the early Israelite tradition concerning conquest and settlement. As William Dever observed, Kaufmann, felt that "to write a history of Israel from early times, one need only paraphrase the Bible."[1367]

I find it appropriate to conclude the discussion with the following remark: While Kaufmann may have gone too far in his claims about the religious history

---

1363 See Thomas M. Krapf, *Yehezkel Kaufmann: Ein Lebens- und Erkenntnisweg zur Theologie der Hebräischen Bibel*, 94.
1364 Isac Leo Seeligmann pointed out the affinity between Kaufmann's interpretation of Israelite religion as it appeared in *Toledot* and Gerhard von Rad's *Theologie die prophetischen Überlieferung II*. On this see Isac Leo Seeligmann, "Yehezkel Kaufmann," 11–12. It has also been noted that Kaufmann's treatment of Israelite religion "has recourse to more conceptual presentations of Israelite religious phenomena and is at points highly constructive and normative in its historical reflections." See Werner E. Lemke, "Old Testament Theology," in *Anchor Bible Dictionary*, vol. 6 (ed. David Noel Freedman; New York: Doubleday, 1992), 449–473 (470). This view was strongly suggested by Benjamin Sommer, who emphasized that "Kaufmann's *Toledot* shares essential features with many works of biblical theology." See Benjamin Sommer, "Dialogical Biblical Theology: A Jewish Approach to Reading Scripture Theologically" in *Biblical Theology: Introducing the Conversation* (ed. Morgan Sommer Perdue; Nashville: Abingdon, 2009), 1–53 (45).
1365 Stephen Geller suggests that Kaufmann's greatest mistake was "to explain Israel's uniqueness. It seemed necessary to him to posit its spiritual isolation from the rest of mankind. This view does not, in general, correspond to that aspect of living complication and complexity that characterizes all human development; specifically, it does not do justice to Israel's real achievement." See Stephen Geller, "Wellhausen and Kaufmann," 48.
1366 Kaufmann, *Toledot* II.
1367 William G. Dever, *Who Were the Early Israelites and Where Did They Come From?* (Grand Rapids: Eerdmans, 2003), 129.

of ancient Israel and the origin of the monotheistic idea, it is also fair to say that Wellhausen outdid Kaufmann in his intense criticism of the Mosaic law and history of Judaism. To say that Wellhausen's thoughts presuppose certain Christian dogmas about Judaism is balanced by saying that Kaufmann followed the traditional Jewish exegesis of the Hebrew Bible.

The question then arises as to which of their theories, Wellhausen's or Kaufmann's, stands up better to criticism. Answering this question in a direct way could do an injustice to the great contributions of either or both scholars. It is true that the works of these two great men are to some extent a product of their times and it would be unreasonable to judge their work only from today's perspective. Nevertheless, we should clearly see that future scholarship needs to understand the foundation on which it is building or the ideas it is rejecting and must examine earlier, classical masterpieces to do so. I am convinced that instead of a complete denial of Wellhausen and Kaufmann's reconstruction,[1368] we should look for what can be learned from the works of these two gifted scholars. For some of the thoughts of Wellhausen and Kaufmann regarding the history of ancient Israel and its religion still surprise us.

1368 David Lieber, for example, mentioned that Kaufmann's Toledot "can be better understood if it is read as a running commentary on the latter's Prolegomena to the History of Israel." See David Lieber, "Yehezkel Kaufmann's Contribution to Biblical Scholarship," 255. Peter Slyomovics points out that both Wellhausen and Kaufmann were extremes. He says that the former saw the beginning of Israelite religion as paganistic religion with no hints of monotheism. The second refused to see any trace of paganism in Israel and claimed that Israelite religion was monotheistic all the time. See Peter Slyomovics, "Yehezkel Kaufmann's Critique of Wellhausen," 84 – 85. Furthermore, Stephen Geller suggests that Kaufmann "is a satellite of Wellhausen, on whom he is fatally dependent; [he] can shed no more light than his sun. The negative passion for undoing the work of Wellhausen deformed his own spirit and blinded him to new realities". See Stephen Geller, "Wellhausen and Kaufmann," 46. Recently, Jonathan Klawans rejected both Wellhausen and Kaufmann. He writes, "Attempts by Wellhausen or Kaufmann to trace [religious developments in the Hebrew Bible] fail on grounds of bias and method. We simply cannot date texts on the basis of any preconceived notion of how religious traditions do or should develop. Moreover, we cannot assume that all the differences between our sources can be explained by positing that they emerged in distinct historical periods. It must be recognized that too much of this business is circular." See Jonathan Klawans, *Purity, Sacrifice, and the Temple: Symbolism and Supersessionism in the Study of Ancient Judaism* (Oxford: Oxford University Press, 2006), 98 – 99.

Conclusion

This study has focused on the dissention between Julius Wellhausen and Yehez-kel Kaufmann. In order to get at the roots of their dispute, I first analyzed Well-hausen's main arguments concerning Israel's religious history and then scruti-nized Kaufmann's interpretation of Israelite religion and at some points his critique of Wellhausen, summing up the results of my examination with a com-parison between Wellhausen and Kaufmann in which I highlight points of sim-ilarities and differences.

As far as Wellhausen is concerned, I show that he built his historical recon-struction on results derived from literary criticism of pentateuchal sources. Well-hausen took a text critical approach to the literary sources on which he based his history of the Israelite religion. The first chapter examines Wellhausen's source and literary criticism, focusing on the critical results that he later used as a foun-dation for his historical synthesis of ancient Israel. The second chapter high-lights two points: Wellhausen's inquiry into the "law" and his portrayal of Isra-el's religious history. This chapter describes how Wellhausen placed the question of the Priestly Law at the centre of his historical inquiry, defending his assump-tion that it belonged to the period of the Second Temple. We may observed that Wellhausen made a distinction between the religion of early Israel, prophetic re-ligion and the religion of Judaism, proposing that the freshness and naturalness of early Israelite religion was denaturalized by introducing the law.

Chapter 3 of Part 1 in this study centres on Wellhausen's historical recon-struction of early Israel. It delineates the main features of pre-monarchic Israel. From my examination of Wellhausen's structure, I come to the conclusion that he disregarded much of biblical tradition, especially the legislative portions, as he maintained that they appeared later and could therefore not be used for histor-ical purposes. Wellhausen assumed that Israel's history was like others – and not a sacred one. The formative period of ancient Israel began with the formula "Je-hovah the god of Israel and Israel the people of Jehovah" first introduced by Moses. Moreover, Wellhausen asserted that the Mosaic Law was not the starting point of Israel's history, which implies that Wellhausen discarded the account of the law having been given at Sinai. As for the traditions of conquest and settle-ment, we have seen that Wellhausen rejected the biblical account of Joshua's conquest of Canaan. He argued that early and original tradition preserved in the Book of Judges revealed that it was only after the lapse of centuries that the Israelites were able to subjugate the Canaanites. Wellhausen made clear the point that only individual tribes were involved and the "all Israel" hypothesis reflected later redaction. A final conclusion in this chapter is related to Wellhausen's assertion that it was the Israelites' gradual fusion with the Canaanites that made Israel's history different from that of its neighbours, Edom, Moab and Ammon. That is to say Wellhausen appreciated the importance of the cultural intermingling between the ancient Israelites and the Canaanites.

With regard to Kaufmann, we have discussed how the point of departure was his study on the history of Jewish exile. Kaufmann was concerned in this undertaking with the idea that it was Judaism itself that preserved Jewish survival. He moved from pursuing Jewish history and Judaism to the foundation of that history in the Hebrew Bible. Kaufmann postulated that Judaism was what set the Jews apart from other nations. The origin of this idea is found in biblical religion. This religion, a monotheistic one, was a creation of the people of Israel from the beginning. Kaufmann, then, proposed that the history of ancient Israel was the history of the monotheistic idea. More revealing was Kaufmann's hypothesis that the Torah was the fountainhead of monotheistic faith.

Focusing on Kaufmann, Chapter 4 begins with an examination of his literary analysis of the Torah literature and its relationship to the prophets. Kaufmann's main concern was to prove that the Torah literature, with the Priestly Code at its core, contained ancient materials originating from before the age of classic prophecy. Kaufmann contended that the antiquity of the Priestly Code was evidenced by its predeuteronomic characteristics. The Torah was the earliest stage in the history of Israelite religion and therefore the monotheistic idea of the Torah predated the ethical monotheism of the prophets. Kaufmann's far-reaching conclusion was that the prophets received monotheism as part of the inheritance of popular religion. Building on this, Kaufmann deduced that the Torah was a historical source on which he could base his writing of the early history of Israel.

Having examined the relationship of the Torah and the prophets, Kaufmann proceeded to identify the distinguishing characteristics of Israelite religion. He employed a comparative and morphological approach by which he sought to isolate the religion of Israel from its environment. Chapter 5 explores Kaufmann's interpretation of the history of Israelite religion. It examines his thoughts on paganism, idolatry and the distinction between polytheism and monotheism. From my discussion on Kaufmann, it should be clear that he regarded the religion of Israel as distinctly different from other, paganistic religions. He worked with the idea of a supreme and transcendent God which was essential to an understanding of the essence of the religion of Israel. Unlike other religions of the times, Kaufmann believed that Yahweh the god of Israel was not a metadivine power, but rather a non-mythological god. Another conclusion in this chapter is related to Kaufmann's description of the popular religion as non-idolatrous. He defined Israelite idolatry as a fetish religion, the idolatry aspect here being merely a superficial phenomenon that did not penetrate into the culture of the people of Israel. Moreover, the evolution hypothesis, which envisages that Israelite religion moved gradually from polytheism to monotheism, was rejected by Kaufmann's as being historically impossible because they represented two different worldviews. The belief in mythological gods, which is the essence of polytheism, was absent from the religion of Israel. In support of his view on the origin of Israelite monotheism, Kaufmann put forward the idea that historical monotheism began with Moses. He believed that it was Moses's apostolic prophecy that brought about a monotheistic revolution in Israel.

As discussed in Chapters 4 and 5, Kaufmann connected the history of biblical literature with the history of Israelite religion, contending that the Torah reflected the early stage of the religion of Israel. In order to strengthen his hypothesis on Israelite monotheism, Kaufmann dealt with the history of ancient Israel in the monarchic period, and did not question the general outline of the biblical account. For the importance of Kaufmann's reconstruction of early Israelite tradition, I dedicated Chapter 6 to examining the main arguments of Kaufmann. In Kaufmann's view, the biblical story from Moses to Joshua was an actual historical description of early Israel. The patriarchs were historical figures. Exodus and the events associated with it were reliable accounts of the life of the Israelite tribes before their entry into the land of Canaan. In their march towards the Promised Land, the people of Israel constituted a nation. Thus Kaufmann assumed that the tribes of Israel invaded Canaan as one group; the conquest was a military undertaking carried out in destructive campaigns under the command of Joshua. From his analysis of conquest and settlement traditions, Kaufmann endeavoured to make two points. First, the land of Canaan was occupied by military force. Second, the Israelite religion remained intact and never became interwoven with the Canaanite religion. I conclude that Kaufmann's arguments were meant to show that there had been no fusion with the residents of Canaan, nor that the Israelites ever became syncretistic. According to Kaufmann, the speculation that there had been a Canaanite-Israelite god "Yahweh-Baal," was groundless.

To gain insight into the sources of Kaufmann's exegetical approach, I devoted Chapter 7 to examining this issue. It begins with a clarification of Kaufmann's attitude towards biblical criticism. We have observed that Kaufmann had great reservations concerning what he perceived to be Christian preconceptions brought to bear on biblical scholarship. Kaufmann claimed that scholars deliberately blurred the monumental facts of biblical literature by imposing onto it their preconceived philosophies. My conclusion is that Kaufmann sought to refine and correct the findings of the literary criticism that could be brought to match his system of interpretation. Another point made in this chapter is that

Kaufmann inherited the tradition of Jewish rationalist thought – a tradition that goes back to Maimonides. I also draw attention to the influence of Hermann Cohen's thinking on Kaufmann's perception of the idea of transcendent god. A final conclusion of this chapter concerns Kaufmann's nationalistic inclinations. His ideas on the unfolding of Jewish history and the origin of Judaism were shaped under the impact of the Jewish nationalistic movement of the mid-twentieth century. Kaufmann's definition of religion as an intuitive idea of the creative spirit of the people of Israel, which developed out of a national culture, indicates his interest in national matters.

The previous chapters have set forth and discussed many issues relevant to Wellhausen's and Kaufmann's respective histories. I have highlighted their main directions of thought and their arguments regarding the history of ancient Israel and its religion. Chapters 8 and 9 sum up the numerous strands of my work on Wellhausen and Kaufmann. My comparison of the views of these two scholars is set out in these chapters, as derived from their different understandings of religion, history, and the authority of biblical texts. As for the history of Israelite religion, I have shown that Wellhausen based his structure on the late dating of the Priestly Code. In Wellhausen's thinking, pre-exilic Israel was without a book and the written Torah did not exist from the very beginning, but was rather a product of Jewish tradition at the time of Second Temple. Monotheism first emerged with the centralization of the cult in Jerusalem, though, idolatry continued to subsist. The ethical monotheism of the prophets developed out of the historical conditions. Regarding the significance of Moses, however, Wellhausen wrote, "Es führt zu wunderlichen Konsequenzen, wenn man Moses als den Stifter des Monotheismus ansieht."[1368] Kaufmann took quite a different direction. He suggested that monotheism arose as an entirely new intuition in religious history, beginning with Moses. "It is only in the time of Moses that monotheism becomes the faith of an entire nation, of Israel."[1369] What strikes me immediately here is that Wellhausen, a trained theologian, held that monotheism was a product of Israel's history. By contrast, we note that Kaufmann, a trained philosopher and historian, asserted that monotheism started as a mysterious spark that needed no further explanation.

Another aspect of the comparison between Wellhausen and Kaufmann concerns history and history writing. Here we must not overlook as certain essential affinity between Wellhausen and Kaufmann. Both agreed that the Hebrew Bible was the master text on which to base writing the history of ancient Israel. They

---

1368 Wellhausen, *Israelitische und jüdische Geschichte*, 31.
1369 Kaufmann, "The Biblical Age," 14.

supported the inside paradigm, according to which Israel's history was to be constructed on the basis of its internal tradition, in this case, the literary tradition. However, Wellhausen and Kaufmann parted ways on the question of historical reconstruction. What was essential and fundamental to Kaufmann was dispensable and superfluous to Wellhausen. That is to say Wellhausen disregarded much of the Sinai tradition. The bringing down of the law and establishment of the tribes' unity through a covenant with Yahweh, was regarded by Wellhausen as unsubstantiated, and playing no part in Israel's subsequent history. Kaufmann, on the other hand, was inclined to regard the Covenant as a crucial event in Israel early history. While the covenant theology plays no essential part in Wellhausen's reconstruction of ancient Israel, Kaufmann considered it to be the credo of Judaism. Thus Kaufmann concluded, "The quarrel between Judaism, Christianity and Islam is a quarrel of covenants."[1370]

The gap that separated Wellhausen's and Kaufmann's thinking became wider with regard to their understanding of the role of Moses. While Moses was needed in Wellhausen's structure as a founder of a nation, he also asserted that Moses was not the introducer of an "enlightened conception of God". Contrary to Wellhausen's position, Kaufmann affirmed that Moses's message brought about a religious revolution. Wellhausen, however, maintained that the people of Israel were people just like any others. To his mind, the determining change in their history was due to their acceptance of civilization and absorption of Canaanite culture. Kaufmann, in contrast, represented the tribes of Israel as a uniquely distinct people. He believed that Yahweh's grace was known only to Israel. My conclusion up to this point is that Wellhausen was interested in a reconstruction of historical events and examined the sources with this purpose in mind. Kaufmann, on the other hand, seemed to have preferred a literal reading of the Hebrew Bible. It should come then as no surprise that Kaufmann accepted as fact what the Hebrew Bible recounted about Israel's history. I favour the idea that whereas the historical development of Israel's history was the primary issue for Wellhausen, Kaufmann was obsessed with the uniqueness of Israel's religion and its monotheistic faith.

To go into more depth on the differences between Wellhausen and Kaufmann, I dealt with their different attitudes towards the authority of the biblical text. Wellhausen believed that the text was a composite of its time. Employing the insights of tendency criticism, he sought to reconstruct the original and/or the natural account of the biblical text and the genuine tradition. Though Kaufmann recognized source-critical analysis, he found it unnecessary to apply much

---

1370 Kaufmann, *Golah ve-Nekhar* I, 322.

criticism to the text – because it did little to change the received biblical account which he considered to already be a reliable description of historical events. Thus, unlike Wellhausen who called for a screening of the tradition to remove "alluvial deposits," Kaufmann insisted that much has survived untouched. In Kaufmann's view, to write the history of Israel, it would be sufficient to flesh out the biblical story with leading motifs of the various strata of the biblical literature. As I see it, Wellhausen worked out a critical appraisal of the sources, while Kaufmann was much more willing to accept the authority of the biblical texts.

The chasm between Wellhausen and Kaufmann widens when their perception of the theocratic ideal in Israel's history is considered. Chapter 9 examines this issue closely. Wellhausen averred that theocracy did not exist in ancient Israel as a hierocratic institution, but rather as an idea. He held that the sacred institutions were not known in Israel earliest times, but developed after loss of political independence. Defending the origin of institutions in premonarchic Israel, Kaufmann contended that Wellhausen's postulate did not do justice to reality. According to Kaufmann, theocracy existed in Israel's history from the times of Moses as "prophetic theocracy". Hence, the political organization of the period of Judges was established under this prophetic theocracy. Moreover, Kaufmann rejected Wellhausen's premise that the Priestly Code portrayed the high priest as the hierocratic ideal. He observed that neither in pre-exilic literature nor in Judaism did such an ideal ever exist. More important was Kaufmann's view that the Priestly Code gave Moses the Prophet priority over Aaron the Priest.

In my discussion of Wellhausen and Kaufmann positions, I come to the conclusion that while Wellhausen conceived of theocracy as mainly the rule of priests, Kaufmann assigned to prophecy the greater part in constituting polity in ancient Israel. While Wellhausen assumed that the Priestly Code took the place of monarchy, Kaufmann maintained that the Priestly Code did not deviate from the state. Thus, Kaufmann deduces that David and his kingdom remained the ideal political institution. The hierocratic ideal appeared only later in the Hellenistic period. Moreover, Kaufmann argued that prophetic theocracy extended from Moses to Saul. With the emergence of a monarchy, this prophetic theocracy became part of an historical past. Another conclusion is that Wellhausen regarded Judaism as a new stage in the history of Israel. He distinguished between Israel as "folk" and Judaism as "sacred congregation." Unlike Wellhausen, Kaufmann asserted that Judaism was at no time a 'sect', and that throughout its history, it existed as 'folk'; "Judaism had never aspired to be the faith of a sect."[1371]

In my reading, Wellhausen found it difficult to believe that the religion of Israel was of moral character from its outset. He worked out a historical synthesis according to which the religion of Israel was developed gradually:

> Das Volk Israel hat sich nicht von Anfang an in einem inhaltlichen Gegensatz zu allen andern Völkern gewusst und sie als Heiden von sich abgewiesen. Es ist nicht mit einem Sprunge zur Zeit Abrahams oder zur Zeit Moses aus dem Heidentum ausgewandert, sondern hat sich langsam daraus emporgearbeitet.[1372]

Kaufmann's judgment of the Israelite religion, on the other hand, was guided by different underlying principles than that of Wellhausen. That is to say, Kaufmann exalted the *idea* of monotheism higher than *history:*

> This idea...first appeared as an insight, an original intuition...The new religious idea never received an abstract, systematic formulation in Israel. It expressed itself rather in symbols, the chief of which was the image of an omnipotent, supreme deity, holy, awful, and jealous, whose will was the highest law. Taking on popular forms, the new idea pervaded every aspect of Israelite creativity.[1373]

In his studies of ancient Israel and early Islam, Wellhausen was fascinated by the combination of religion and history. He therefore wrote, "Der Jahvismus und der Islam lehren, welchen gewaltigen Einfluß die Religion auf die Kultur ausüben kann."[1374] More revealing is Wellhausen's conclusion, "Die Stufen der Religion, wie die Stufen der Geschichte überhaupt, bleiben neben einander bestehen."[1375] This is certainly a thoughtful discerning of the correlation between religion and history. Wellhausen's presentation, however, is hindered by two flaws: an anti-institutional bias and an obsession with original forms of tradition.

Kaufmann, likewise, believed in the power of religion and its effect on modelling Israel's history and culture. He describes the pivotal role of religion in the history of Israel, maintaining, "Religion forged and strengthened the character of the people from earliest times. It struck ineradicable roots – the very basis of the nation's existence. By virtue of its religion, Israel became a solidly resistant en-

1371 Kaufmann, *Christianity and Judaism: Two Covenants*, 15.
1372 Wellhausen, *Grundrisse zum Alten Testament*, 80.
1373 Kaufmann, *The Religion of Israel*, 60.
1374 Kaufmann, *The Religion of Israel*, 370.
1375 Wellhausen, *Israelitische und jüdische Geschichte*, 371.

tity insured against absorption into the religions of the gentiles."[1376] Kaufmann's hypothesis, however, is beclouded by insistence on the peculiar character of an Israelite religion that did not deviate from the perfectly straight. He contended, "Monotheism in Israel was encapsulated in fixed religious forms which could not be altered."[1377] In my discussion of Kaufmann's thoughts, I have shown that his basic tenet was that Israel was ignorant of paganism, which was radically uprooted from the outset. In Kaufmann's eyes, the faith of Israel was purely monotheistic. He believed that the monotheistic mainstream of Israelite religion had no antecedents in paganism.[1378] Consistent with his stance, Kaufmann worked with a revolutionary and perseverant monotheistic essence. I would conclude with remarking that Kaufmann was excessively taken with the monotheistic idea.

1376 Kaufmann, *Christianity and Judaism: Two Covenants*, 183.
1377 Kaufmann, *Christianity and Judaism*, 181.
1378 Kaufmann, *The Religion of Israel*, 2.

Bibliography

Aharoni, Yohanan. *The Land of the Bible: A Historical Geography*. Translated from the Hebrew by A. F. Rainey. Philadelphia: Westminster Press, 1967.

Albertz, Rainer. *Geschichte und Theologie: Studien zur Exegese des Alten Testaments und zur Religionsgeschichte Israels*. Berlin: de Gruyter, 2003.

Albright, William. F. "Archaeology Confronts Biblical Criticism." *AmSc* VII (1938): 176–88.

—— "The Ancient Near East and the Religion of Israel." *JBL* 59 (1940): 85–112.

—— *The Biblical Period from Abraham to Ezra*. New York: Harper & Row Publishers, 1949.

—— *Yahweh and the Gods of Canaan: A Historical Analysis of Two Contrasting Faiths*. London: Athlone Press, 1968.

—— "Moses in Historical and Theological Perspective." In *Magnalia Dei: The Mighty Acts of God: Essays on the Bible and Archaeology in Memory of G. Ernest Wright*, eds. Frank Moore Cross et al., 120–31. Garden City: New York, 1976.

Alt, Albrecht. "Die Landnahme der Israeliten in Palästina." In *Kleine Schriften zur Geschichte des Volkes Israel* I, 89–125. München: Beck, 1953.

—— "Judas Gaue unter Josia." *PJB* 21 (1925): 100–17.

—— "Utopien." *ThLZ* 81(1965): 521–28.

Arkush, Allan. "Biblical Criticism and Cultural Zionism prior to the first World War." *Jewish History* 21 (2007): 121–58.

Baden, Joel S. *J, E, and the Redaction of the Pentateuch*. Tübingen: Mohr Siebeck, 2009.

Balentine, Samuel E. *The Torah's Vision of Worship*. Minneapolis: Fortress Press, 1999.

Bammel, Ernst. "Judentum, Christentum, und Heidentum: Julius Wellhausens Briefe an Theodor Mommsen 1881–1902." *ZKG* 80 (1969): 221–54.

Banks, Diane. *Writing the History of Israel*. New York, London: T & T Clark, 2006.

Baron, Salo W. *History and Jewish Historians: Essays and Addresses*. Philadelphia: Jewish Publication Society of America, 1964.

Barr, James. "The Meaning of 'Mythology' in Relation to the Old Testament." *VT* 9 (1959): 1–10.

Barstad, Hans M. "The History of Ancient Israel: What Directions Should We Take?" In *Understanding the History of Ancient Israel*, ed. Hugh G. M. Williamson, 25–48. Oxford: Oxford University Press, 2007.

Barton, John. "Wellhausen's Prolegomena to the History of Israel: Influences and Effects." In *Text and Experience: Towards a Cultural Exegesis of the Bible*, ed. D. Smith-Christopher, 316–29. Sheffield: Sheffield Academic Press, 1995.

—— *The Nature of Biblical Criticism*. Louisville: Westminster John Knox Press, 2007.

Bauer, Michael. "Julius Wellhausen." In *Klassiker der Theologie*, 2 vols, ed. Friedrich W. Graf, 123–40. München: Beck, 2005.

Baumgartner, Walter. "Wellhausen und der heutige Stand der alttestamentlichen Wissenschaft." *ThR* 2 (1930): 287–307.

Bechtoldt, Hans-Joachim. *Die jüdische Bibelkritik im 19. Jahrhundert*. Stuttgart: Kohlhammer, 1995.

Berlinerblau, Jacques. "The 'Popular Religion' Paradigm in Old Testament Research: A Sociological Critique." *JSOT* 60 (1993): 3–26.

Becker, Carl. H. "Julius Wellhausen." *Der Islam* 9 (1918): 95–99.

—— *Islamstudien: Vom Werden und Wesen der islamischen Welt*. Hildesheim: Olms, 1967.

Becker, Uwe. "Von der Staatsreligion zum Monotheismus. Ein Kapitel israelitisch-jüdischer Religionsgeschichte." *ZThK* 102 (2005): 1–16.
— "Julius Wellhausens Sicht des Judentums." In *Biblische Theologie und historisches Denken: Wissenschaftsgeschichtliche Studien: Aus Anlass der 50. Wiederkehr der Basler Promotion von Rudolf Smend*, eds. Martin Kessler and Martin Wallraff, 279–309. Basel: Schwabe, 2008.
— "Altisrael, Judentum und Pharisäismus bei Julius Wellhausen." In *Christentum und Judentum. Akten des Internationalen Kongresses der Schleiermacher-Gesellschaft in Halle, März 2009*, eds. Roderich Barth, Ulrich Barth and Claus-Dieter Osthövener, 561–73. Berlin: de Gruyter, 2012.
Bediako, Gillian M. *Primal Religion and the Bible: William Robertson Smith and his Heritage.* Sheffield: Sheffield Academic Press, 1997.
Ben-Chorin, Schalom. *Jüdischer Glaube: Strukturen einer Theologie des Judentums anhand des Maimonidischen Credo.* Tübingen: Mohr, 1975.
Berquist, Jon L. *Judaism in Persia's Shadow: A Social and Historical Approach.* Minneapolis: Fortress Press, 1995.
Black, John S., George W. Chrystal and William R. Smith, eds. *Lectures & Essays of William Robertson Smith.* London: Adam and Black, 1912.
Blau, Joseph L., ed. *Essays on Jewish Life and Thought: Presented in honor of Salo Wittmayer Baron.* New York: Columbia University Press, 1959.
Bleek, F., ed. *Einleitung in das Alte Testament.* Berlin: Reimer, 1893⁶.
Blenkinsopp, Joseph. *Prophecy and Canon: A Contribution to the Study of Jewish Origins.* Center for the Study of Judaism and Christianity in Antiquity 3. University of Notre Dame: Notre Dame, 1977.
— "An Assessment of the Alleged Pre-Exilic Date of the Priestly Material in the Pentateuch." *ZAW* 108 (1996): 495–518.
— "Pentateuch." In *The Cambridge Companion to Biblical Interpretation*, ed. John Barton, 181–97. Cambridge: Cambridge University Press, 1998.
— *Treasures Old and New: Essays in the Theology of the Pentateuch.* Grand Rapids: W.B. Eerdmans, 2004.
Boer, Roland T. "Book Review: Prolegomena to the History of Israel, with a reprint of the article "Israel" from the Encyclopaedia Britannica by Julius Wellhausen." *JBL* 124 (2005): 349–54.
Boschwitz, Friedemann. *Julius Wellhausen: Motive und Maßstäbe seiner Geschichtsschreibung.* 2nd ed. Darmstadt: Wissenschaftliche Buchgesellschaft, 1968.
Braulik, Georg and Ernst Haag. *Gott, der einzige: Zur Entstehung des Monotheismus in Israel.* Freiburg: Herder, 1985.
Brenner, Michael. *Jüdische Geschichte Lesen: Texte der jüdischen Geschichtsschreibung im 19. und 20. Jahrhundert.* München: C.H. Beck, 2003.
Breuer, Edward and Chanan Gafni. "Jewish Biblical Scholarship between Tradition and Innovation." In *The Hebrew Bible, Old Testament: The History of its Interpretation*, ed. Magne Sæbø, 262–302. Göttingen: Vandenhoeck & Ruprecht, 2013.
Breuer, Edward. *The Limits of Enlightenment: Jews, Germans, and the eighteenth-Century Study of Scripture.* Cambridge: Harvard University Press, 1996.
Bright, John. *A History of Israel.* Philadelphia: Westminster Press, 1981.
— *Early Israel in Recent History Writing: A Study in Method.* London: SCM Press, 1956.

Britt, Brian. *Rewriting Moses: the Narrative Eclipse of the Text*. London: T&T Clark International, 2004.

Buss, Martin J. "The Relevance of Hermann Gunkel's Broad Orientation." In *Hermann Gunkel Revisited: Literatur- und Religionsgeschichtliche Studien*, eds. Ute E. Eisen and Erhard S. Gerstenberger, 71–80. Berlin: Lit, 2010.

Cassuto, Umberto. *The Documentary Hypothesis and the Composition of the Pentateuch: Eight lectures*. Jerusalem: Magnes Press, 1961.

—— *Biblical and Canaanite Literatures*. Jerusalem: Magnes Press, 1972.

Cataldo, Jeremiah W. *A Theocratic Yehud? Issues of Government in a Persian Province*. New York: T&T Clark, 2009.

Clarke, Terrance A. "Complete v. Incomplete Conquest: A Re-examination of three Passages in Joshua." *TynBul* 61 (2010): 89–104.

Clements, Ronald E. *A Century of Old Testament Study*. Guildford, London: Lutterworth Press, 1976.

—— "The Study of the Old Testament." In *Nineteenth Century Religious Thought in the West*, eds. Ninian Smart et al., vol. 3, 109–41. Cambridge: Cambridge University Press, 1985.

Cohen, Hermann. "Julius Wellhausen: Ein Abschiedsgruß." *Neue Jüdische Monatshefte* 1918. (= Jüdische Schriften I , Zur jüdischen Zeitgeschichte, Berlin 1924, 463–68).

—— *Religion of Reason: Out of the Sources of Judaism*. Atlanta: Scholars Press, 1995.

Collins, John J. *The Bible after Babel: Historical Criticism in a Postmodern Age*. Grand Rapids: Eerdmans, 2005.

Conrad, Joachim. *Karl Heinrich Grafs Arbeit am Alten Testament. Studien zu einer wissenschaftlichen Biographie*. Berlin: de Gruyter, 2011.

Davies, Philip R. *In Search of "Ancient Israel"*. Sheffield: JSOT Press, 1992.

De Moor, Johannes C. *The Rise of Yahwism: The Roots of Israelite Monotheism*. Leuven: University Press, 1997^2.

Dever, William G. *Who Were the Early Israelites, and Where did they come from?* Grand Rapids: Eerdmans, 2003.

Donner, Herbert. *Geschichte des Volkes Israel und seiner Nachbarn in Grundzügen*. Göttingen: Vandenhoeck & Ruprecht, 1995^2.

Dörrfuß, Ernst M. *Mose in den Chronikbüchern. Garant theokratischer Zukunftserwartung*. Berlin: de Gruyter, 1994.

Dozeman, Thomas B. "Geography and Ideology in the Wilderness Journey from Kadesh through the Transjordan." In *Abschied vom Jahwisten: Die Komposition des Hexateuch in der jüngsten Diskussion*, ed. Jan C. Gertz et al., 173–89. Berlin: de Gruyter, 2002.

Dumm, D. R. "Review of Kaufmann's the Religion of Israel." *CBQ* 23 (1961): 68–69.

Edgar, John. "The Present Position of Old Testament Criticism." In *The People and the Book: Essays on the Old Testament*, ed. Arthur S. Peake, 183–219. Oxford: Clarendon Press, 1925.

Eisen, Ute E., and Erhard S. Gerstenberger. *Hermann Gunkel Revisited: Literatur- und Religionsgeschichtliche Studien*. Berlin: Lit, 2010.

Eisenstadt, Shmuel N. *The Origins and Diversity of Axial Age Civilizations*. Albany: State University of New York Press, 1986.

Eissfeldt, Otto. "Die Eroberung Palästinas durch Altisrael." *WO* 2 (1955): 158–71.

—— "Wellhausen, Julius," *RGG*, 3d ed., 6 (1962): 1594–95.

Ewald, Heinrich. *Geschichte des Volkes Israel bis Christus*. Göttingen: Dieterich, 1843–1859.

Faur, José. "The Biblical Idea of Idolatry." *JQR* 69 (1978): 1–15.

Fishbane, Michael A. and Paul R. Flohr. *Texts and Responses: Studies Presented to Nahum N. Glatzer on the Occasion of his Seventieth Birthday by his Students.* Leiden: Brill, 1975.

Freedman, David Noel. "Review: The Religion of Israel, from Its Beginnings to the Babylonian Exile by Yehezkel Kaufmann." *JBL* 81 (1962): 185–90.

Frei, Hans W. *The Eclipse of Biblical Narrative: A Study in Eighteenth and Nineteenth Century Hermeneutics.* New Haven: Yale University Press, 1974.

Frerichs, Ernest S. "The Jewish School of Biblical Studies." In *Judaic Perspectives on Ancient Israel*, ed. Jacob Neusner et al., 1–6. Philadelphia: Fortress Press, 1987.

Galling, Kurt. "Geschichte Israels: Ein kritischer Bericht." *ThR* 2 (1930): 94–128.

Geller, Stephen. "Wellhausen and Kaufmann." *Midstream* 31, 10 (1985): 39–48.

Gerdmar, Andres. *Roots of Theological anti-Semitism: German Biblical Interpretation and the Jews, from Herder and Semler to Kittel and Bultmann.* Leiden: Brill, 2009.

Gevirtz, Stanley. "Review of The Religion of Israel: From its Beginnings to the Babylonian Exile." *JNES* 21 (1962): 158–60.

Ginsberg, H. L. "Yehezkel Kaufmann, 1889–1963." *Reconstructionist* 29 (1963): 27–29.

Glatzer, Nahum N. "The Beginnings of Modern Jewish Studies." In *Studies in Nineteenth-Nentury Jewish Intellectual History*, ed. Alexander Altmann, 27–45. Cambridge: Harvard University Press, 1964.

Gnuse, Robert Karl. *No Other Gods: Emergent Monotheism in Israel.* Sheffield: Sheffield Academic Press, 1997.

—— "The Emergence of Monotheism in Ancient Israel: A Survey of Recent Scholarship." *Religion* 29 (1999): 315–36.

Gooch, George Peabody. *History and Historians in the Nineteenth Century.* London: Longmans, Green, 1954².

Gooder, Paula. *The Pentateuch: A Story of Beginnings.* Edinburgh: T&T Clark, 2005.

Gottwald, Norman K. *The Hebrew Bible in its Social World and in Ours.* Atlanta: Scholars Press, 1993.

Grabbe, Lester L. *Can a 'History of Israel' Be Written?* Sheffield: Sheffield Academic Press, 1997.

Green, Emanuel. "Kaufmann, Yeḥezkel (1889–1963)." In *Encyclopaedia Judaica*, ed. Michael Berenbaum and Fred Skolnik, 2nd ed., vol. 12, 33–35. Detroit: Macmillan Reference USA, 2007.

—— *Universalism and Nationalism as Reflected in the Writings of Yehezkel Kaufmann with Special Emphasis on the Biblical Period.* Ph.D. diss., New York University, 1968.

Greenberg, Moshe. "A New Approach to the History of the Israelite Priesthood." *JAOS* 70 (1950): 41–47.

—— *The Hab/piru.* New Haven: American Oriental Society, 1955.

—— *Studies in the Bible and Jewish Thought.* Philadelphia: Jewish Publication Society, 1995.

Greenstein, Edward L. *Essays on Biblical Method and Translation.* Atlanta: Scholars Press, 1989.

Gressmann, Hugo. "Die Aufgabe der Alttestamentlichen Forschung." *ZAW* 42 (1924): 1–33.

Gruenwald, Ithamar. "God the "stone/rock": Myth, Idolatry, and Cultic Fetishism in Ancient Israel." *JR* 76, 3 (1996): 428–49.

Hahn, Herbert F. *The Old Testament in Modern Research.* London: SCM Press, 1956.

—— "Wellhausen's Interpretation of Israel's Religious History: A Reappraisal of his Ruling Ideas." In *Essays on Jewish Life and Thought. Presented in Honor of Salo Wittmayer Baron*, eds. Joseph L. Blau et al., 299–308. New York: Columbia University Press, 1959.

Hakohen, Ran. *Reclaiming the Hebrew Bible: German-Jewish Reception of Biblical Criticism.* Berlin: de Gruyter, 2010.

Halbertal, Moshe, Avisha Margalit and Naomi Goldblum. *Idolatry.* Cambridge: Harvard University Press, 1992.

Halpern, Baruch. "'Brisker Pipes than Poetry': The Development of Israelite Monotheism." In *Judaic perspectives on Ancient Israel*, 77–107.

—— *The First Historians: The Hebrew Bible and History.* San Francisco: Harper & Row, 1988.

Hammann, Konrad. *Hermann Gunkel: eine Biographie.* Tübingen: Mohr Siebeck, 2014.

Handy, Lowell K. "The Reconstruction of Biblical History and Jewish-Christian Relations." *SJOT* 5, 1 (1991): 1–22.

Haran, Menahem. *Yehezkel Kaufmann Jubilee Volume: Studies in Bible and Jewish Religion; Dedicated to Yehezkel Kaufmann on the Occasion of his seventieth Birthday.* Jerusalem: Magnes Press, 1960.

—— "On the Border of Faith." (In Hebrew) *Moznaim* 24 (1966): 53–55.

—— *Biblical Research in Hebrew: A Discussion of its Character and Trends.* Jerusalem: Magnes Press, Hebrew University, 1970.

—— "From Early to Classical Prophecy: Continuity and Change." *VT* 27 (1977): 385–97.

—— "Behind the Scenes of History: Determining the Date of the Priestly Source." *JBL* 100 (1981): 321–33.

—— "Midrashic and Literal Exegesis and the Critical Method in Biblical Research." In *Studies in Bible*, ed. Sara Japhet, 19–48. Jerusalem: The Magnes Press, 1986.

—— *Temples and Temple-Service in Ancient Israel: An Inquiry into the Character of Cult Phenomena and the Historical Setting of the Priestly School.* Oxford: Clarendon Press, 1978.

Harrelson, Walter. "Review of Kaufmann's The Religion of Israel." *Int* XVI (1962): 457–60.

Harrison, R. K. *Introduction to the Old Testament.* London: The Tyndale Press, 1969.

Hartman, David. *Maimonides: Torah and Philosophic Quest.* Philadelphia: Jewish Publication Society of America, 1976.

Hayes, John H. "Wellhausen as a Historian of Israel." In *Julius Wellhausen and His Prolegomena to the History of Israel*, 37–60.

—— *Dictionary of Biblical Interpretation.* 2 vols. Nashville: Abingdon Press, 1999.

—— "Kaufmann, Yehezkel (1889–1963)." In *Dictionary of Biblical Interpretation*, 2 vols. Nashville: Abingdon Press, 1999, 16–17.

—— "Historiographical Approaches: Survey and Principles." In *Method Matters: Essays on the Interpretation of the Hebrew Bible in Honor of David L. Petersen*, ed. Joel M. LeMon et al., 195–212. Resources for Biblical study 56. Atlanta: Society of Biblical Literature, 2009.

Hayes, John H., and J. Maxwell Miller. *Israelite and Judaean History.* Philadelphia: Westminster Press, 1977.

Hess, Richard S., Gerald A. Klingbeil, and Paul J. Ray. *Critical Issues in Early Israelite History.* Winona Lake: Eisenbrauns, 2008.

Hillers, Delbert R. "Analyzing the Abominable: Our Understanding of Canaanite Religion." *JQR* 75, 3 (1985): 253–69.

Hoffmann, Christhard. *Juden und Judentum im Werk deutscher Althistoriker des 19. und 20. Jahrhunderts.* Leiden: Brill, 1988.

Hoffmann, David. *Die wichtigsten Instanzen gegen die Graf-Wellhausensche Hypothese.* Berlin, 1914.

Hoffmann, Horst. *Julius Wellhausen: Die Frage des absoluten Maßstabes seiner Geschichtsschreibung*. Marburg: University Dissertation, 1967.

Homan, Michael M. "How Moses Gained and lost the Reputation of Being the Torah's Author: Higher criticism prior to Julius Wellhausen." In *Sacred History, Sacred Literature: Essays on Ancient Israel, the Bible, and Religion in Honor of R.E. Friedman on his sixtieth birthday*, ed. Shawna Dolansky, 111–31. Winona Lake: Eisenbrauns, 2008.

Howard, Thomas A. *Religion and the Rise of Historicism: W.M.L. de Wette, Jacob Burckhardt, and the Theological Origins of Nineteenth-Century Historical Consciousness*. Cambridge: Cambridge University Press, 2000.

Hübener, Wolfgang "Die verlorene Unschuld der Theokratie," In *Religionstheorie und politische Theologie, Bd. 3:Theokratie*, ed. Jacob Taubes, 29–64. München: Fink, 1987.

Hurvitz, Avi. *A linguistic Study of the Relationship between the Priestly Source and the Book of Ezekiel: A new Approach to an Old Problem*. Paris: Gabalda, 1982.

Hyatt, J. Philip. "Yehezkel Kaufmann's View of the Religion of Israel." *JBR* 29 (1961): 52–57.

Jeffers, Adrian. "Ideal Versus Real History in the Book of Joshua." *JETS* 12 (1969): 183–87.

Jepsen, Alfred. "Wellhausen in Greifswald: Ein Beitrag zur Biographie Julius Wellhausens." In *Der Herr ist Gott: Aufsätze zur Wissenschaft vom Alten Testament*, 254–70. Berlin: Evangelische Verlagsanstalt, 1978.

Jindo, Job Y. "Revisiting Kaufmann: Fundamental Problems in Modern Biblical Scholarship: From Yehezkel Kaufmann's Criticism of Wellhausen." *JISMOR* 3 (2007): 41–77.

—— "Recontextualizing Kaufmann: His Empirical Conception of the Bible and its Significance in Jewish Intellectual History." *JJTP* 19/2 (2011): 95–129.

Kaiser, Walter C. *A History of Israel: From the Bronze Age through the Jewish Wars*. Nashville: Broadman & Holman, 1998.

Kaufmann, Yehezkel. "Probleme der israelitisch-jüdischen Religionsgeschichte I." *ZAW* 48 (1930): 23–43.

—— "Probleme der israelitisch-jüdischen Religionsgeschichte II." *ZAW* 51 (1933): 35–47.

—— *Toledot Ha-'Emunah Ha-Yisre'elit Mi-Yeme Ḳedem 'ad Sof Bayit Sheni* (4 vols., Tel Aviv: Bialik Institute-Devir, 1937–1956).

—— "Israelite Religion." (In Hebrew) In *Encyclopaedia Biblica*. vol. 2, ed. Eleazar L. Sukenik, 747–50. Jerusalem, 1954.

—— "The Bible and Mythological Polytheism." *JBL* 70 (1951): 179–97.

—— *The Biblical Account of the Conquest of Palestine*. Translated from the Hebrew by A. Dagut. Jerusalem: Magnes Press, Hebrew University, 1953.

—— "Der Kalender und das Alter des Priesterkodex." *VT* 4 (1954): 307–13.

—— "The Biblical Age." In *Great Ages and Ideas of the Jewish People*, ed. Leo W. Schwarz, 3–92. New York: Random House, 1956.

—— *The Book of Joshua* (Hebrew). *With an Introduction to Joshua and Juges (1–3)*. Jerusalem: Kiryat Sepher, 1959.

—— *The Religion of Israel: An Abridgment Translation of the first 7 Volumes of Kaufmann's Toledot Ha-'Emunah Ha-Yissre'elit Mi-Yeme ḳedem 'ad Sof Bayit Sheni*. Chicago: University of Chicago press, 1960.

—— "Traditions Concerning Early Israelite History in Canaan." *Scripta Hierosolymitana* 8 (1961): 303–34.

—— *Commentary on the Book of Judges* (Hebrew). Jerusalem: Ḳiryat Sefer, 1962.

—— *From the Secret of the Biblical World* (In Hebrew). Tel Aviv: Devir, 1966.

—— *The Babylonian Captivity and Deutero-Isaiah.* Translated by C.W. Efroymson. New York: Union of American Hebrew Congregations, 1970.
—— *History of the Religion of Israel, Volume IV: From the Babylonian Captivity to the End of Prophecy.* Jerusalem: Hebrew University, 1977.
—— *Christianity and Judaism: Two Covenants.* Jerusalem: Magnes Press, Hebrew University, 1988.
Kautzsch, E. Rec. "Wellhausen, J., 'Geschichte Israels." *ThLZ* 2 (1879): 25–30.
Keel, Othmar. *Monotheismus im Alten Israel und seiner Umwelt.* BiBe 14: Fribourg, 1980.
Kegel, Martin. *Los von Wellhausen! Ein Beitrag zur Neuorientierung in der alttestamentlichen Wissenschaft.* Gütersloh: Bertelsmann, 1923.
Kippenberg, Hans G. *Die Entdeckung der Religionsgeschichte: Religionswissenschaft und Moderne.* München: Beck, 1997.
Klatt, Werner. *Hermann Gunkel: Zu seiner Theologie der Religionsgeschichte und zur Entstehung der formgeschichtlichen Methode.* Göttingen: Vandenhoeck & Ruprecht, 1969.
Klawans, Jonathan. *Purity, Sacrifice, and the Temple: Symbolism and Supersessionism in the Study of Ancient Judaism.* Oxford: Oxford University Press, 2006.
Knauf, Ernst Axel. *Data and Debates: Essays in the History and Culture of Israel and its Neighbors in Antiquity=Daten und Debatten: Aufsätze zur Kulturgeschichte des antiken Israel und seiner Nachbarn.* Münster: Ugarit-Verlag, 2013.
—— "From History to Interpretation." In *The Fabric of History: Text, Artifact and Israel's Past,* ed. Diana V. Edelman, 26–64. Sheffield: JSOT Press, 1991.
Knight, Douglas A. *Rediscovering the Traditions of Israel: The Development of the Traditio-Historical Research of the Old Testament, with Special Consideration of Scandinavian Contributions.* Missoula: University of Montana, 1973.
—— ed. *Julius Wellhausen and his Prolegomena to the History of Israel.* Chico: Scholars Press, 1983.
—— "Wellhausen and the Interpretation of Israel's Literature." In *Julius Wellhausen and His Prolegomena to the History of Israel,* 21–36.
Knohl, Israel. "The Priestly Torah versus the Holiness School: Sabbath and the Festivals." *HUCA* 58 (1987): 65–117.
—— *Biblical Beliefs: Limits of the Scriptural Revolution* (In Hebrew). Jerusalem: Magnes Press, 2007.
Kraeling, Emil G. H. *The Old Testament since the Reformation.* London: Lutterworth Press, 1955.
Krapf, Thomas M. *Yehezkel Kaufmann: Ein Lebens- und Erkenntnisweg zur Theologie der Hebräischen Bibel.* Berlin: Institut Kirche und Judentum, 1990.
—— *Die Priesterschrift und die vorexilische Zeit: Yehezkel Kaufmanns vernachlässigter Beitrag zur Geschichte der biblischen Religion.* OBO 119: Freiburg, 1992.
—— "Jüdische Identität und Neuhebräisch: Anmerkung zu Yehezkel Kaufmanns Verhältnis zur Wissenschaft des Judentums." *Judaica* 49 (1993): 69–80.
—— "Biblischer Monotheismus und vorexilischer JHWH-Glaube. Anmerkungen zur neueren Monotheismusdiskussion im Lichte von Yehezkel Kaufmanns Polytheismus-Monotheismus-Begriff." *BTZ* 11 (1994): 42–64.
—— "Some Observations on Yehezkel Kaufmann's Attitude to Wissenschaft des Judentums." In *Proceedings of the Eleventh World Congress of Jewish Studies,* ed. David Assaf, vol. 2, 69–76. Jerusalem: World Union of Jewish Studies, 1994.

Kratz, Reinhard G. "Die Entstehung des Judentums: Zur Kontroverse zwischen E. Meyer und J. Wellhausen: Rudolf Smend Zum 65. Geburtstag." *ZThK* 95 (1998): 167–84.
—— *The Composition of the Narrative Books of the Old Testament*. London: T&T Clark, 2005. Translated by John Bowden from the German *Die Komposition der erzählenden Bücher des Alten Testaments*. Göttingen: Vandenhoeck & Ruprecht, 2000.
—— "Temple and Torah: Reflections on the Legal Status of the Pentateuch between Elephantine and Qumran." In *The Pentateuch as Torah: New Models for Understanding its Promulgation and Acceptance*, eds. Gary N. Knoppers and Bernhard M. Levinson, 77–103. Winona Lake: Eisenbrauns, 2007.
—— "Wellhausen, Julius (1844–1918)." *TRE* 35 (2003): 527–36.
—— *Das Judentum im Zeitalter des Zweiten Tempels*. Tübingen: Mohr Siebeck, 2004, 2013².
—— "Eyes and Spectacles: Wellhausen's Method of Higher Criticism." *JTS* 60 (2009): 381–402.
—— "The Pentateuch in Current Research: Consensus and Debate." In *The Pentateuch: International Perspectives on Current Research*, eds. Thomas B. Dozeman, Konrad Schmid and Baruch J. Schwartz, 31–61. Tübingen: Mohr Siebeck, 2011.
—— *Historisches und biblisches Israel: Drei Überblicke zum Alten Testament*. Tübingen: Mohr Siebeck, 2013.
Kraus, Hans-Joachim. *Geschichte der historisch-kritischen Erforschung des Alten Testaments*. Neukirchen-Vluyn: Neukirchener Verlag, 1982³.
Kusche, Ulrich. *Die unterlegene Religion: Das Judentum im Urteil deutscher Alttestamentler: Zur Kritik theologischer Geschichtsschreibung*. Berlin: Institut Kirche und Judentum, 1991.
Lang, Bernhard. *Der einzige Gott: Die Geburt des biblischen Monotheismus*. München: Kösel, 1981.
—— *Monotheism and the Prophetic Minority: An Essay in Biblical History and Sociology*. Sheffield: Almond Press, 1983.
Lemche, Niels P. *The Israelites in History and Tradition*. London: SPCK, 1998.
—— *The Old Testament between Theology and History: A Critical Survey*. Louisville: Westminster John Knox Press, 2008.
Lemke, Werner E. "Old Testament Theology." In *The Anchor Bible Dictionary*, ed. David Noel Freedman, vol. 6, 449–473. New York: Doubleday, 1992.
Levenson, Jon D. "The Theologies of Commandment in Biblical Israel." *HTR* 73 (1980): 17–33.
—— "Yehezkel Kaufmann and Mythology." *Conservative Judaism* 36 (1982): 36–43.
—— *Sinai and Zion: An Entry into the Jewish Bible*. Minneapolis: Winston Press, 1985.
—— "The Hebrew Bible, the Old Testament, and Historical Criticism." In *The Future of Biblical Studies: The Hebrew Scriptures*, ed. R. E. Friedman, 19–59. Atlanta: Scholars Press, 1987.
—— "Why Jews are Not Interested in Biblical Theology." In *Judaic Perspectives on Ancient Israel*, 281–307.
Lieber, David. "Yehezkel Kaufmann's New Synthesis." *Reconstructionist* 27 (1961): 25–28.
—— "Yehezkel Kaufmann's Contribution to Biblical Scholarship." *Journal of Jewish Education* 34 (1964): 254–61.
Liebeschütz, Hans. *Das Judentum im deutschen Geschichtsbild von Hegel bis Max Weber*. Tübingen: Mohr (Siebeck), 1967.
—— *Von Georg Simmel zu Franz Rosenzweig. Studien zum Jüdischen Denken im deutschen Kulturbereich*. Tübingen: Mohr, 1970.

Liss, Hanna. "Religionsgeschichte and its challenge to Jewish Bible Scholars in the Late 19th and Early 20th Century." In *Hermann Gunkel Revisited: Literatur- und Religionsgeschichtliche Studien*, eds. *Eisen, Ute E., and Erhard S. Gerstenberger*, 149–170. Berlin: Lit, 2010.

Lohfink, Norbert. "Zur Geschichte der Diskussion über den Monotheismus im Alten Israel." In *Gott, der einzige: Zur Entstehung des Monotheismus in Israel*, eds. Braulik, Georg and Ernst Haag, 9–25. Freiburg: Herder, 1985.

Long, V. P. *Israel's Past in Present Research: Essays on Ancient Israelite Historiography*. Winona Lake: Eisenbrauns, 1999.

Loretz, Oswald. *Habiru-Hebräer: Eine sozio-linguistische Studie über die Herkunft des Gentiliziums 'ibrî vom Appellativum ḫabiru*. Berlin: de Gruyter, 1984.

Luz, Ehud. "Jewish Nationalism in the Thought of Yehezkel Kaufmann." In *Binah: Studies in Jewish History, Thought, and Culture*, ed. Joseph Dan, 177–90. New York: Praeger, 1989.

MacDonald, Nathan. *Deuteronomy and the Meaning of "Monotheism"*. Tübingen: Mohr Siebeck, 2003.

Machinist, Peter. "The Road Not Taken. Wellhausen and Assyriology." In *Homeland and Exile: Biblical and Ancient Near Eastern Studies in Honour of Bustenay Oded*, ed. Alan R. Millard et al., 469–531. Leiden: Brill, 2009.

Maimonides, Moses. *The Guide of the Perplexed, Volume 1*. Translated by Leo Strauss. Chicago: University of Chicago Press, 1963.

Marti, Karl, ed. *Studien zur semitischen Philologie und Religionsgeschichte: Julius Wellhausen zum 70. Geburtstag am 17. Mai 1914 gewidmet von Freunden und Schülern*. Giessen: Töpelmann, 1914.

Mazar, Benjamin. *Judges*. London: Allen, 1971.

McKane, William. "Prophet and Institution." *ZAW* 94 (1982): 251–66.

McKeating, Henry. "Book Reviews: Idiosyncratic Jewish History." *ExpTim* 89 (1978): 150.

McKenzie, John L. "Hebrew Attitude Towards Mythological Polytheism." *CBQ* 14 (1952): 323–35.

—— "Book Review: The Biblical Account of the Conquest of Palestine." *CBQ* 17 (1955): 95–97.

Mendenhall, George E. "The Hebrew Conquest of Palestine," *BA* 25, no. 3 (1962): 65–87.

—— *The Tenth Generation: The Origins of the Biblical Tradition*. Baltimore: Johns Hopkins University Press, 1973.

Meyer, Eduard. *Die Entstehung des Judenthums: Eine historische Untersuchung*. Halle: Niemeyer, 1896.

—— *Julius Wellhausen und meine Schrift "Die Entstehung des Judenthums": Eine Erwiderung*. Halle: M. Niemeyer, 1897.

Meyer, Michael A. *Ideas of Jewish History*. Detroit: Wayne State University Press, 1999.

Milgrom, Jacob. "Priestly Terminology and the Political and Social Structure of Pre-Monarchic Israel." *JQR* 69 (1978): 65–81.

—— "The Antiquity of the Priestly Source: A Reply to Joseph Blenkinsopp." *ZAW* 111 (1999): 10–22.

Miller, J. Maxwell. *The Old Testament and the Historian*. Philadelphia: Fortress Press, 1983.

—— "Is it Possible to Write a History of Israel without Relying on the Hebrew Bible? In *The Fabric of History: Text, Artifact and Israel's Past*, ed. Philip R. Davies, 93–102. Sheffield: JSOT Press, 1991.

Miller, Patrick D. "Wellhausen and the History of Israel's Religion." In *Julius Wellhausen and his Prolegomena to the History of Israel*, 61–73.

—— *Israelite Religion and Biblical Theology: Collected Essays.* Sheffield: Sheffield Academic Press, 2000.

Moeller, Bernd. *Theologie in Göttingen: Eine Vorlesungsreihe.* Göttingen: Vandenhoeck & Ruprecht, 1987.

Momigliano, Arnaldo. "Religious History without Frontiers: J. Wellhausen, U. Wilamowitz, and E. Schwartz." *History and Theory* 21, 4 (1982): 49–64.

Moore, Megan B. *Philosophy and Practice in Writing a History of Ancient Israel.* New York: T&T Clark, 2006.

Morrow, Jeffrey L. "The Politics of Biblical Interpretation: A 'Criticism of Criticism'." *New Blackfriars* (2010): 528–45.

Müller, Hans-Peter. "Monotheismus und Polytheismus: II Altes Testament," *RGG*⁴ vol. 5 (2008): 1459–62.

Newmann, Amy. "The Death of Judaism in German Protestant Thought from Luther to Hegel." *JAAR* 61 (1993): 455–84.

Nicholson, Ernest W. *The Pentateuch in the Twentieth Century: The Legacy of Julius Wellhausen.* Oxford: Clarendon Press, 1998.

Noth, Martin."Studien zu den historisch-geographischen Dokumenten des Josuabuches." *ZDPV* 58 (1935): 185–255.

—— *Das Buch Josua.* Tübingen: Mohr, 1938.

—— *Überlieferungsgeschichte des Pentateuchs.* Stuttgart: Kohlhammer, 1948.

—— *Geschichte Israels.* Göttingen: Vandenhoeck & Ruprecht, 1950. (English translation *The History of Israel*, Rev. ed. New York: Harper & Row, 1960).

O'Dea, Janet Koffler. "Israel With and Without Religion: An Appreciation of Kaufmann's Golah Ve-Nekhar." *Judaism* (Winter 1976): 85–97.

O'Neill, John. C. *The Bible's Authority: A Portrait Gallery of Thinkers from Lessing to Bultmann.* Edinburgh: T&T Clark, 1991.

Oeming, Manfred. *Der eine Gott und die Götter: Polytheismus und Monotheismus im antiken Israel.* Zürich: TVZ, 2003.

Olyan, Saul M. and Robert C. Culley. *"A Wise and Discerning Mind": Essays in Honor of Burke O. Long*, eds. Olyan, Saul M. and Robert C. Culley. Providence: Brown Judaic Studies, 2000.

Oron, Michal and Amos Goldreich, eds. *Masuot: mehkarim be-sifrut ha-Kabalah uve-mahshevet Yisrael mukdashim le-zikhro shel Prof. Efrayim Gotlib.* Jerusalem: Bialik Institute, 1994.

Osswald, Eva. *Das Bild des Mose in der kritischen alttestamentlichen Wissenschaft seit Julius Wellhausen.* Berlin: Evangelische Verlagsanstalt, 1962.

Peake, Arthur S. *The People and the Book: Essays on the Old Testament.* Oxford: Clarendon Press, 1925.

Pedersen, Johannes. "Die Auffassung vom Alten Testament." *ZAW* 49 (1931): 161–81.

Peri, Chiara. "The Construction of Biblical Monotheism: An Unfinished Task." *SJOT* 19 (2005): 135–42.

Perlitt, Lothar. *Vatke und Wellhausen. Geschichtsphilosophische Voraussetzungen und historiographische Motive für die Darstellung der Religion und Geschichte Israels durch Wilhelm Vatke und Julius Wellhausen.* Berlin: Töpelmann, 1965.

—— *Allein mit dem Wort: Theologische Studien: Lothar Perlitt zum 65. Geburtstag*, ed. Hermann Spieckermann. Göttingen: Vandenhoeck & Ruprecht, 1995.

Pfoh, Emanuel. *The Emergence of Israel in Ancient Palestine: Historical and Anthropological Perspectives.* London: Equinox, 2009.

Polish, David. *Give Us a King: Legal Religious Sources of Jewish Sovereignty.* Hoboken: KTAV, 1989.

Polzin, Robert. *Biblical Structuralism: Method and Subjectivity in the Study of Ancient Texts.* Philadelphia: Fortress Press, 1977.

Provan, Iain W., V. Philips Long, and Tremper Longman. *A Biblical History of Israel.* Louisville: Westminster John Knox Press, 2003.

Pury, Albert de. *Israel Constructs its History: Deuteronomistic Historiography in Recent Research.* London: Continuum International Publishing, 2000.

Rendtorff, Rolf "The Paragidm is changing: Hopes – and Fears," *Biblical Interpretation* 1 (1993): 34 –53.

Reventlow, Henning Graf. *Epochen der Bibelauslegung*, vol. 4. München: Beck, 2001. (English translation *History of Biblical Interpretation.* Atlanta: Society of Biblical Literature, 2010).

Roberts, Jimmy Jack McBee. "The Decline of the Wellhausen Reconstruction of Israelite Religion." *ResQ* 9 (1966): 229 –40.

Rofé, Alexander. "Clan Sagas as a Source in Settlement Traditions." In *"A Wise and Discerning Mind": Essays in honor of Burke O. Long*, eds. Saul M. Olyan and Robert C. Culley, 191– 203. Providence: Brown Judaic Studies, 2000.

—— *Introduction to the Literature of the Hebrew Bible.* Jerusalem: Simor, 2009.

Rogerson, John W. "Geschichte und Altes Testament im 19. Jahrhundert." *BN* 22 (1983): 126 – 38.

—— *W.M.L. de Wette, Founder of Modern Biblical Criticism: An Intellectual Biography.* Sheffield: Sheffield Academic Press, 1992.

—— "Setting the Scene: A Brief Outline of Histories of Israel." In *Understanding the History of Ancient Israel*, ed. Hugh G. M. Williamson, 3 –14. Oxford: Oxford University Press, 2007.

Römer, Thomas. "Higher Criticism: The Historical and Literary-critical Approach – with Special Reference to the Pentateuch." In *Hebrew Bible, Old Testament: The History of its Interpretation* III/1 , 393 – 423.

Rosenzweig, Franz. *Der Mensch und sein Werk: gesammelte Schriften*, Bd 1: *Briefe und Tagebücher* (ed. Rachel Rosenzweig and Edith Rosenzweig-Scheinmann; The Hague: Nijhoff, 1979).

Rotenstreich, Nathan. "Jewish Thought." In *Nineteenth Century Religious Thought in the West III*, ed. Ninian Smart, 76 – 82. Cambridge: Cambridge University Press, 1985.

Rowley, Harold H. "Living Issues in Biblical Scholarship: The Antiquity of Israelite Monotheism." *ExpTim* 61 (1950): 333 – 38.

Rudolph, Kurt. "Wellhausen as an Arabist." In *Julius Wellhausen and His Prolegomena to the History of Israel*, 111– 55.

Saebø, Magne and Peter Machinist. *Hebrew Bible, Old Testament: The History of its Interpretation.* Göttingen: Vandenhoeck & Ruprecht, 2013.

Sarna, Nahum. "From Wellhausen to Kaufmann." *Midstream* 7 (1961): 64 – 74.

Sasson, Jack M. "On Choosing Models for Recreating Israelite Pre-Monarchic History." *JSOT* 21 (1981): 3 – 24.

Schäfer, Peter, ed. *Geschichte, Tradition, Reflexion: Festschrift für Martin Hengel zum 70. Geburtstag, I: Judentum.* Tübingen: Mohr, 1996.

Schmid, Herbert. *Mose: Überlieferung und Geschichte.* Berlin: Töpelmann, 1968.

Schmid, Konrad "Zurück zu Wellhausen?" *ThR* 69 (2004): 314–28.

Schmidt, Ludwig. "Königtum: II Altes Testament." *TRE* 19 (1990): 327–33.

Schniedewind, William M. *How the Bible Became a Book: The Textualization of Ancient Israel.* Cambridge: Cambridge University Press, 2004.

Scholtz, Gunter. "The Phenomenon of 'Historicism' as a Backcloth of Biblical Scholarship." In *Hebrew Bible, Old Testament: The History of its Interpretation* III/I, 64–89.

Schorsch, Ismar. "The Last Jewish Generalist." *AJS Review* 18 (1993): 39–50.

Schultz, Hans J. *Tendenzen der Theologie im 20. Jahrhundert: Eine Geschichte in Porträts.* Stuttgart: Kreuz-Verlag, 1966.

Schreiner, Stefan. "Kaufmann, Yehezkel," *RGG*⁴ vol. 4 (2008): 906–907.

Schwartz, Baruch J. "The Pentateuch as Scripture and the Challenge of Biblical Criticism: Responses among Modern Jewish Thinkers and Scholars." In *Jewish Concepts of Scripture,* ed. Benjamin Sommer, 203–29. New York: New York University Press, 2012.

Schwartz, Eduard. *Gesammelte Schriften 1: Vergangene Gegenwærtigkeiten, Exoterica, Inter arma et post cladem, Dis manibus.* Berlin: Gruyter, 1938.

Schwartz, Leo W. *Great Ages and Ideas of the Jewish People.* New York: Random House, 1956.

Schweid, Eliezer. "Biblical Critic or Philosophical Exegete? The Influence of Hermann Cohen's The Religion of Reason on Yehezkel Kaufmann's History of Israelite Religion (Hebrew)." In *Masuot: Mehkarim be-sifrut ha-Kabalah uve-mahashevet Yisrael mukdashim le-zikhro shel Prof. Efrayim Gottlieb,* 414–28.

—— *A History of Modern Jewish Religious Philosophy.* 5 vols. [In Hebrew]. Tel Aviv: Am Oved, 2001–2006.

Seeligmann, Isac Leo. "Yehezkel Kaufmann." In *Yehezkel Kaufmann Jubilee Volume: Studies in Bible and Jewish Religion,* ed. Menahem Haran, IX – XII. Jerusalem: Magnes Press, 1960.

—— *Gesammelte Studien zur Hebräischen Bibel.* Tübingen: Mohr Siebeck, 2004.

Seidensticker, Tilman. "Julius Wellhausen und das 'arabische Heidentum'." In *Biblische Theologie und historisches Denken. Wissenschaftsgeschichtliche Studien: aus Anlass der 50. Wiederkehr der Basler Promotion von Rudolf Smend,* 303–13.

Shahar, David. "The Historical-Cultural Heritage and its Educational Significance in Yehezkel Kaufmann's Outlook." (In Hebrew) מעוף ומעשה 5 (1999): 135–56.

Shaviṭ, Yaacov and Mordechai Eran. *The Hebrew Bible Reborn: From Holy Scripture to the Book of Books: A History of Biblical Culture and the Battles over the Bible in Modern Judaism.* Berlin: de Gruyter, 2007.

Shmueli, Efraim. "The Jerusalem School of Jewish History (A Critical Evaluation)." *PAAJR* 53 (1986): 147–78.

Silberstein, Laurence J. *History and Ideology: The Writings of Y. Kaufmann.* Unpublished Ph.D. diss., Brandeis University, 1971.

—— "Religion, Ethnicity, and Jewish History: The Contribution of Yehezkel Kaufmann." *JAAR* 42 (1974): 516–31.

—— "Exile and Alienation: Yehezkel Kaufmann on the Jewish Nation." In *Texts and Responses: Studies Presented to Nahum N. Glatzer on the Occasion of his 70. Birthday by his Students,* ed. Michael A. Fishbane, 239–56. Leiden: Brill, 1975.

—— "Historical Sociology and Ideology: A Prolegomena to Yehezkel Kaufmann's Golah v'Nekhar." In *Essays in Modern Jewish History: A Tribute to Ben Halpern,* eds. Phyllis Albert and Frances Malino, 173–95. Rutherford: Fairleigh Dickinson University Press, 1982.

—— "Kaufmann, Yehezkel." In *Encyclopedia of Religion,* ed. Lindsay Jones, 5108–9. Detroit: Macmillan Reference USA, 2005.

Simpson, C. A. "Reviews," *JTS* VI (1955): 257–58.

Ska, Jean Louis. "The 'History of Israel': Its Emergence as an Independent Discipline," In *Hebrew Bible, Old Testament: The History of its Interpretation III/I,* ed. Magne Sæbø, 307–345.

Skolnik, Fred and Michael Berenbaum. *Encyclopaedia Judaica.* Detroit: Macmillan Reference USA, 2007.

Slyomovics, Peter. *Yitzhak Julius Guttmann and Yehezkel Kaufmann: The Relationship of Thought and Research* (In Hebrew). Jerusalem: The Hebrew University, 1980.

—— "Yehezkel Kaufmann's Critique of Wellhausen: A Philosophical-Historical Perspective." (In Hebrew) *Zion* 49 (1984): 61–92.

Smart, Ninian. *Nineteenth Century Religious Thought in the West, Volume III.* Cambridge: Cambridge University Press, 1985.

Smend, Rudolf (sen). "Über die Genesis des Judentums." *ZAW* 2 (1882): 94–151.

Smend, Rudolf. *Wilhelm Martin Leberecht de Wettes Arbeit am Alten und am Neuen Testament.* Basel: Helbing & Lichtenhahn, 1958.

—— *Das Mosebild von Heinrich Ewald bis Martin Noth.* Tübingen: Mohr (Siebeck), 1959.

—— *Die Mitte des Alten Testaments.* Zürich: EVZ-Verlag, 1970.

—— "Wellhausen und das Judentum." *ZThK* 79 (1982): 249–82.

—— "Wellhausen in Göttingen." In *Theologie in Göttingen: Eine Vorlesungsreihe,* ed. Bernd Moeller, 306–24. Göttingen: Vandenhoeck & Ruprecht, 1987.

Smend, Rudolf. "Das uneroberte Land," In *Zur ältesten Geschichte Israels, Gesammelte Studien,* Bd. 2, 217–228. München: Kaiser, 1987.

—— "Wellhausen und die Kirche." In *Wissenschaft und Kirche. Festschrift für Eduard Lohse,* eds. Kurt Aland and Siegfried Meurer, 225–31. Bielefeld: Luther-Verlag, 1989.

—— *Deutsche Alttestamentler in drei Jahrhunderten.* Göttingen: Vandenhoeck & Ruprecht, 1989.

—— *Epochen der Bibelkritik: Gesammelte Studien 3.* München: Kaiser, 1991.

—— "William Robertson Smith and Julius Wellhausen." In *William Robertson Smith: Essays in Reassessment,* ed. William Johnstone, 226–42. Sheffield: Sheffield Academic Press, 1995.

—— "Israelitische und jüdische Geschichte: Zur Entstehung von Julius Wellhausens Buch." In *Geschichte, Tradition, Reflexion: Festschrift für Martin Hengel zum 70. Geburtstag,* ed. Peter Schäfer, 35–42. Tübingen: Mohr, 1996.

—— "Julius Wellhausen (1844–1918)." In *Dictionary of Biblical Interpretation,* vol. 2, ed. John H. Hayes, 629–31. Nashville: Abingdon Press, 1999.

—— *Julius Wellhausen: Ein Bahnbrecher in drei Disziplinen.* München: Carl Friedrich von Siemens Stiftung, 2006.

—— *From Astruc to Zimmerli: Old Testament Scholarship in three Centuries.* Tübingen: Mohr Siebeck, 2007.

—— "The Work of Abraham Kuenen and Julius Wellhausen." In *Hebrew Bible, Old Testament: The History of its Interpretation III/I: From Modernism to Post-Modernism (the Nineteenth and Twentieth Centuries)*, ed. Magne Sæbø, 424–453. Göttingen: Vandenhoeck & Ruprecht, 2013.

—— *Briefe: Julius Wellhausen.* Tübingen: Mohr Siebeck, 2013.

Smith, Mark S. *The Origins of Biblical Monotheism: Israel's Polytheistic Background and the Ugaritic Texts.* New York: Oxford University Press, 2001.

Smith, W. Taylor. "Review of Wellhausen's Israelitische und jüdische Geschichte." *The Biblical World* 5, 3 (1895): 231–35.

Soggin, Jan Alberto. *Introduction to the Old Testament: From its Origins to the Closing of the Alexandrian Canon.* Translated by John Bowden. Philadelphia: Westminster Press, 1976.

—— *An Introduction to the History of Israel and Judah.* London: SCM Press, 1993.

Sommer, Benjamin D. "Dialogical Biblical Theology: A Jewish Approach to Reading Scripture Theologically." In *Biblical Theology: Introducing the Conversation*, ed. Morgan S. Perdue, 1–53. Nashville: Abingdon, 2009.

—— "Biblical Theology: Judaism." *Encyclopaedia of the Bible and its Reception* 3 (2011): 1138–50.

—— *Jewish Concepts of Scripture: A Comparative Introduction.* New York: New York University Press, 2012.

Sperling, S. D. "Israel's Religion in the Ancient Near East." In *Jewish Spirituality from the Bible through the Middle Ages*, ed. Arthur Green, 5–31. New York: Crossroad, 1986.

—— *Students of the Covenant: A History of Jewish Biblical Scholarship in North America.* Atlanta: Scholars Press, 1992.

—— "Monotheism and Ancient Israelite Religion." In *A Companion to the Ancient Near East*, ed Daniel C. Snell, 408–20. Malden: Blackwell, 2005.

Spieckermann, Hermann. "Exegetischer Individualismus: Julius Wellhausen (1844–1918)." In *Profile des neuzeitlichen Protestantismus*, ed. Friedrich W. Graf, 231–50. Gütersloh: Gütersloher Verlagshaus Mohn, 1993.

—— "YHWH Bless You and Keep You: The Relation of History of Israelite Religion and Old Testament Theology Reconsidered." *SJOT* 23 (2009): 165–82.

—— "From Biblical Exegesis to Reception History." *HeBAI* 1 (2012): 1–24.

Staubli, Thomas. *Wer knackt den Code? Meilensteine der Bibelforschung.* Düsseldorf: Patmos-Verlag, 2009.

—— "Yehezkel Kaufmann: Die Berner Jahre eines Genies." In *Wie über Wolken: Jüdische Lebens- und Denkwelten in Stadt und Region Bern, 1200–2000*, eds. René Bloch and Jacques Picard, 241–252. Zürich: Chronos, 2014.

Stocking, George W. *Victorian Anthropology.* New York: The Free Press, 1987.

Surburg, Raymond F. "Wellhausen Evaluated after a Century of Influence." *Concordia Theological Quarterly* 43 (1979): 78–95.

Talmon, Shemaryahu. "Yehezkel Kaufmann's Approach to Biblical Research." *Conservative Judaism* 25 (1971): 20–28.

Thompson, James Westfall. *A History of Historical Writing, vol. 2: The Eighteenth and Nineteenth Centuries.* New York: Macmillan, 1942.

Thompson, Robert. J. *Moses and the Law in a Century of Criticism since Graf.* Leiden: Brill, 1970.

Thompson, Thomas L. "Text, Context and Referent in Israelite Historiography." In *The Fabric of History: Text, Artifact and Israel's Past*, ed. Diana V. Edelman, 65–92. Sheffield: JSOT Press, 1991.

—— *Early History of the Israelite People: From the Written and Archaeological Sources.* Leiden: Brill, 1992.

—— "Historiography in the Pentateuch: Twenty Five Years after Historicity?" *SJOT* 13 (1999): 258–83.

—— "Lester Grabbe and Historiography: An Apologia." *SJOT* 14 (2000): 140–61.

Trüper, Henning, "Wie es uneigentlich gewesen: Zum Gebrauch der Fußnote bei Julius Wellhausen (1844–1918)." *Zeitschrift für Germanistik* 23 (2013): 329–42.

Turner, Joseph. "The Notion of Jewish Ethnicity in Yehezkel Kaufmann's Golah Venekhar." *Modern Judaism* 28 (2008): 257–82.

Uffenheimer, Benjamin. "Some Features of Modern Jewish Bible Research." *Immanuel* 1 (1972): 3–14.

—— "Yehezkel Kaufmann: Historian and Philosopher of Biblical Monotheism." *Immanuel* 3 (1973): 9–21.

—— "Jecheskel Kaufmann – der Bibelwissenschaftler der jüdischen Renaissance." *Immanuel* 4 (1975): 159–67.

—— "Biblical Theology and Monotheistic Myth." *Immanuel* 14 (1982): 7–25.

—— "Myth and Reality in Ancient Israel." In *The Origins and Diversity of Axial Age Civilizations*, ed. Shmuel N. Eisenstadt, 135–68. Albany: State University of New York Press, 1986.

—— *Creative Biblical Exegesis: Christian and Jewish Hermeneutics through the Centuries.* Sheffield: JSOT Press, 1988.

—— *Early Prophecy in Israel.* Jerusalem: Magnes Press, Hebrew University, 1999.

Ulrich, Eugene, ed. *Priests, Prophets, and Scribes: Essays on the Formation and Heritage of Second Temple Judaism in Honour of Joseph Blenkinsopp.* Sheffield: JSOT Press, 1992.

Urbach, Efraim. "Neue Wege der Bibelwissenschaft." *MGWJ* 82 (1938): 1–22.

—— *Collected Writings in Jewish Studies*, eds. Robert Brody and Moshe D. Herr. Jerusalem: Hebrew University Magnes Press, 1999.

Van Seters, John. *Abraham in History and Tradition.* New Haven: Yale University Press, 1975.

—— *Der Jahwist als Historiker.* Zürich: Theologischer Verlag, 1987.

—— *The Life of Moses: The Yahwist as Historian in Exodus-Numbers.* Louisville: John Knox Press, 1994.

—— "An Ironic Circle: Wellhausen and the Rise of Redaction Criticism." *ZAW* 115 (2003): 487–500.

Vaux, Roland de. *The Early History of Israel. Vol. 2: To the Period of the Judges.* Translated by David Smith. London: Darton, Longman & Todd, 1978.

—— "The Hebrew Patriarchs and History." In *Israel's Past in Present Research: Essays on Ancient Israelite Historiography*, ed. V. Philips Long, 470–479. Winona Lake: Eisenbrauns, 1999.

Vink, J. G. "The Date and Origin of the Priestly Code in the Old Testament." in *The Priestly Code and Seven Other Studies.* Brill: Leiden, 1969.

Watts, James. W., ed. *Persia and Torah: The Theory of Imperial Authorization of the Pentateuch.* Atlanta: Society of Biblical Literature, 2001.

Waubke, Hans-Günther. *Die Pharisäer in der protestantischen Bibelwissenschaft des 19. Jahrhunderts.* Tübingen: Mohr Siebeck, 1998.

Weidmann, Helmut. *Die Patriarchen und ihre Religion im Licht der Forschung seit Julius Wellhausen.* Göttingen: Vandenhoeck & Ruprecht, 1968.

Weidner, Daniel. "Geschichte gegen den Strich bürsten: Julius Wellhausen und die jüdische 'Gegengeschichte'." *ZRGG* 54 (2002): 32–61.

Weinfeld, Moshe. "Cult Centralization in Israel in the Light of a Neo-Babylonian Analogy." *JNES* 23 (1964): 202–12.

—— "The Period of the Conquest and of the Judges as Seen by the Earlier and the Later Sources." *VT* 17 (1967): 93–113.

—— *Deuteronomy and the Deuteronomic school.* Oxford: Clarendon Press, 1972.

—— *Getting at the Roots of Wellhausen's Understanding of the Law of Israel, on the 100th Anniversary of the Prolegomena.* Jerusalem: The Institut for Advanced Studies, The Hebrew University, 1979.

—— "Julius Wellhausen's Understanding of the Law of Ancient Israel and its Fallacies." In *Shnaton: An Annual for Biblical and Ancient Near Eastern Studies 4,* 62–93. Jerusalem: Magnes Press, 1980.

—— "The Pattern of the Israelite Settlement in Canaan." In *Congress Volume: International Organization for the Study of the Old Testament,* ed. J. A. Emerton, 270–83. Leiden: Brill, 1988.

—— *The Place of the Law in the Religion of Ancient Israel.* Leiden: Brill, 2004.

Weippert, Manfred. *Die Landnahme der israelitischen Stämme in der neueren wissenschaftlichen Diskussion: Ein kritischer Bericht.* Göttingen: Vandenhoeck & Ruprecht, 1967.

—— "Geschichte Israels am Scheideweg," *ThR* 58 (1993): 71–103.

—— *Jahwe und die anderen Götter: Studien zur Religionsgeschichte des antiken Israel in ihrem syrisch-palästinischen Kontext.* Tübingen: Mohr Siebeck, 1997.

Wellhausen, Julius. *Der Text der Bücher Samuelis.* Göttingen: Vandenhoeck & Ruprecht, 1871.

—— *Die Pharisäer und die Sadducäer: Eine Untersuchung zur inneren jüdischen Geschichte.* First published Greifswald: Bamberg, 1874; 1924[2]; 1967[3]. English translation *The Pharisees and the Sadducees. An Examination of Internal Jewish History.* Macon: Mercer University Press, 2001.

—— *Geschichte Israels I,* 1878; 2nd ed. 1883 *Prolegomena zur Geschichte Israels;* 3rd ed. 1899, reprinted 1927, 1972, 1981, 2001. ET (of 2nd ed.) *Prolegomena to the History of Israel.* Edinburgh, 1885, reprinted 1957 (= *Prolegomena to the History of Israel: With a Reprint of the Article "Israel" from the Encyclopaedia Britannica.* Atlanta: Scholars Press, 1994).

—— "Israel." In *Prolegomena to the History of Israel,* 429–542. First appeared in *Encyclopaedia Britannica,* 9th ed. (1881): 396–431.

—— *Muhammed in Medina: Das ist Vakidi's Kitab al-Maghazi, in verkürzter deutscher Wiedergabe.* Berlin: G. Reimer, 1882.

—— "Die Israelitisch-Jüdische Religion." In *Die Kultur der Gegenwart: Ihre Entwicklung und Ihre Ziele,* ed. Paul Hinneberg, 1–40. Berlin: Teubner, 1906.

—— "Moses." *Encyclopaedia Britannica* 16 (1883): 860–61.

—— "Muhammedanism." *Encyclopaedia Britannica* 16 (1883): 545–65.

—— *Skizzen und Vorarbeiten. 1: Abriß der Geschichte Israels und Juda's. 2: Lieder der Hudhailiten, arabisch und deutsch.* Berlin: Reimer, 1884.

—— "Pentateuch and Joshua." *Encyclopaedia Britannica* 18 (New York: Hall, 9th ed., 1885), 505–14.

—— *Israelitische und jüdische Geschichte: Mit einem Nachwort von Rudolf Smend.* Berlin: de Gruyter, 2004[10].

—— *Reste arabischen Heidentums*. Berlin: Reimer, 1897.

—— "Zur apokalyptischen Literatur." In *Skizzen und Vorarbeiten VI*, 215–49. Berlin: Reimer, 1899.

—— *Die Composition des Hexateuchs und der historischen Bücher des Alten Testaments*. Berlin: W. de Gruyter, 1899[2]; 1899[3]; 1963.

—— *Das arabische Reich und sein Sturz*. Berlin: Reimer, 1902.

—— *Grundrisse zum Alten Testament*. München: Kaiser, 1965.

Wette, Wilhelm M. L. de. *Beiträge zur Einleitung in das Alte Testament, Erster und zweiter Band*. First published Halle, 1806/1807; new reprint edition Hildsheim: Olms, 1971.

Wiedebach, Hartwig. *The National Element in Hermann Cohen's Philosophy and Religion*. Leiden: Brill, 2012.

Wiese, Christian. *Challenging Colonial Discourse: Jewish Studies and Protestant Theology in Wilhelmine Germany*. Leiden: Brill, 2005.

Williamson, Hugh G. M. *Understanding the History of Ancient Israel*. Oxford: Oxford University Press, 2007.

Wright, G. E. "Review: The Biblical Account of the Conquest of Palestine." *JBL* 75 (1956): 154–55.

—— *Biblical Archaeology*. Philadelphia: Westminster Press, 1957.

Zeitlin, Irving M. *Ancient Judaism: Biblical Criticism from Max Weber to the Present*. Cambridge: Polity Press, 1991.

Zenger, Erich. "Priesterschrift." *TRE* 27 (1997): 435–46.

Zevit, Ziony. "Converging Lines of Evidence Bearing on the Date of P." *ZAW* 94 (1982): 481–511.

—— *The Religions of Ancient Israel: A Synthesis of Parallactic Approaches*. London; New York: Continuum, 2001.

Zimmerli, Walther. *The Law and the Prophets: A study of the Meaning of the Old Testament*. Oxford: Basil Blackwell, 1965.

Subject index

Index of names